Dams, Power, and the Politics of Ethiopia's Renaissance

OXFORD STUDIES IN AFRICAN POLITICS AND INTERNATIONAL RELATIONS

General Editors
Nic Cheeseman, Peace Medie, and Ricardo Soares de Oliveira

Oxford Studies in African Politics and International Relations is a series for scholars and students working on African politics and International Relations and related disciplines. Volumes concentrate on contemporary developments in African political science, political economy, and International Relations, such as electoral politics, democratization, decentralization, gender and political representation, the political impact of natural resources, the dynamics and consequences of conflict, comparative political thought, and the nature of the continent's engagement with the East and West. Comparative and mixed methods work is particularly encouraged. Case studies are welcomed but should demonstrate the broader theoretical and empirical implications of the study and its wider relevance to contemporary debates. The focus of the series is on sub-Saharan Africa, although proposals that explain how the region engages with North Africa and other parts of the world are of interest.

Dams, Power, and the Politics of Ethiopia's Renaissance

TOM LAVERS

with

FANA GEBRESENBET
BIRUK TERREFE
EMANUELE FANTINI
EDEGILIGN HAILU WOLDEGEBRAEL
AND
LUCA PUDDU

OXFORD
UNIVERSITY PRESS

OXFORD
UNIVERSITY PRESS

Great Clarendon Street, Oxford, OX2 6DP,
United Kingdom

Oxford University Press is a department of the University of Oxford.
It furthers the University's objective of excellence in research, scholarship,
and education by publishing worldwide. Oxford is a registered trade mark of
Oxford University Press in the UK and in certain other countries

Published in the United States of America by Oxford University Press
198 Madison Avenue, New York, NY 10016, United States of America

British Library Cataloguing in Publication Data

Data available

Library of Congress Control Number: 2024937957

ISBN 9780192871213

DOI: 10.1093/oso/9780192871213.001.0001

Printed and bound in the UK by
Clays Ltd, Elcograf S.p.A.

Acknowledgements

This book happened somewhat by accident. It was the product of a number of chance encounters and events over several years rather than the result of a clear plan. Shortly after I joined Manchester in 2016, in an effort to project collegiality and learn about my new department, I went along to an internal workshop about research on dams. Two hours later I emerged, surprised to find myself as the lead for the politics stream in a research proposal for a major interdisciplinary project on dams that combined social scientists with engineers and climate modellers. I did not expect the project to get funded (as most don't), but I had severely underestimated David Hulme's gift for securing grants. Six months later the project was approved and the 'Future Design and Assessment of Water-Energy-Food-Environment Mega Systems', or FutureDAMS, was born.

At that stage in 2016, Ethiopia and the Nile were not to be part of FutureDAMS. However, events conspired to make another case study unviable, and fortuitously the Nile Basin was added in its place. Given the well-known sensitivities regarding the Nile and the Grand Ethiopian Renaissance Dam (GERD) in particular, I did not expect research on the politics of Ethiopian dam building to get very far, but I nonetheless agreed to give it a try in the hope that I might be able to contribute a short paper to the project. Yet, 2018 and 2019 proved to be an opportune moment to conduct fieldwork in Ethiopia. During what ultimately transpired as an all-too-brief moment of political opening, many respondents turned out to be keen to talk and share their views on Ethiopia's dams and the major changes seen in the previous decades under the Ethiopian Peoples' Revolutionary Democratic Front (EPRDF) Government. What started with very modest ambitions quickly snowballed and, confronted with a mass of empirical material and with numerous fascinating lines of enquiry, a short paper morphed into a good-sized book.

Through this escalation of ambition, I was fortunate to be able to bring in collaborators and co-authors who made great contributions to the project and the final book. The book is based largely on fieldwork conceived and conducted by Tom Lavers, Fana Gebresenbet, and Biruk Terrefe, with valuable research assistance at points by Abera Tadesse. Furthermore, the book provided the opportunity for Emanuele Fantini, Edegilign Hailu Woldegebrael, and Luca Puddu to bring together their longstanding research interests in the work of Salini in Ethiopia's water projects. The result of this collaboration is an authored book, rather than an edited volume, with important contributions from each of those involved, albeit spread unevenly throughout the book. The majority of the final version was written by Tom Lavers. The main exception here is Chapter 5, which was researched and written by Emanuele Fantini, Edegilign Hailu Woldegebrael, and

Luca Puddu, with minor written and empirical contributions from Tom Lavers. Chapters 3, 4, and 9, meanwhile, draw heavily on fieldwork and written contributions to earlier drafts by Fana Gebresenbet and Biruk Terrefe, and Chapter 8 by Fana Gebresenbet. The remaining chapters were sole-authored by Tom Lavers.

The study of Ethiopia's dams also drew on support from a wide range of colleagues involved in the FutureDAMS consortium to whom I am indebted. Most notably, David Hulme originally entrusted the politics research stream to me, and was a consistent source of support, enthusiasm, and constructive critique as the project developed. Barnaby Dye was a fantastic addition to the FutureDAMS team with his encyclopaedic knowledge of dams and relentless energy. Barnaby helped conceptualize the politics stream of research, participated in the preparatory phase of the Ethiopian study, and ably took the lead in comparative research in Ghana. Dale Whittington was a source of useful advice and recommendations on the Nile Basin and Ethiopian dam building, while Mohammed Basheer was enormously helpful and showed great patience in educating a social scientist on the basics of dam engineering. Sarah Vaughan and Mesfin Gebremichael also made a valuable contribution to the Ethiopian project, contributing a fascinating study of resettlement at the GERD site that was eventually published elsewhere. Furthermore, the research could not have taken place without FutureDAMS' programme manager, Adam Randon. Finally, we gratefully acknowledge the support of UK Research and Innovation Economic and Social Research Council [ES/P011373/1] as part of the Global Challenges Research Fund through the 'Future Design and Assessment of Water-Energy-Food-Environment Mega Systems' (FutureDAMS) research project. Moreover, a substantial portion of the book writing was carried out while I was on a Leverhulme Research Fellowship. Again, the support of the Leverhulme Foundation is gratefully acknowledged.

In addition to our own fieldwork, I would like to thank Christopher Sneddon and John Waterbury who were both kind enough to share material from their own past research. Furthermore, many people generously donated their time to reading and commenting on draft papers and chapters, and, in doing so, helped to strengthen the material. In particular, Bill Adams and David Hulme read the entire manuscript, while Pritish Behuria, Ana Elisa Cascão, Barnaby Dye, Sam Hickey, Nick Jepson, John Waterbury, and Dale Whittington all provided comments on parts of the manuscript, as did anonymous reviewers for Oxford University Press and the FutureDAMS working paper series. Meanwhile, I am grateful to both Adam Swallow and Dominic Byatt for their enthusiasm about the book project, assistance in guiding it through the review process, and patience with several delays.

Finally, as always, I am most grateful of all to Arthur, Alice, and Shea for their unwavering support.

Tom Lavers

Contents

List of Figures

List of Tables

List of Abbreviations

ADF	African Development Fund
ADLI	Agricultural Development-Led Industrialization
AfDB	African Development Bank
AGOA	African Growth and Opportunities Act
ANDM	Amhara National Democratic Movement
ASMAE	Historical Archives of the Italian Ministry of Foreign Affairs
AVA	Awash Valley Authority
BADEA	Arab Bank for Economic Development in Africa
bcm	billion cubic metres
BPLM	Benishangul People's Liberation Movement
CEO	chief executive officer
CDB	China Development Bank
CDC	UK's Commonwealth Development Corporation, subsequently renamed British International Investment
CFA	Cooperative Framework Agreement
CGGC	China Gezhouba Group Company
CRGE	Climate-Resilient Green Economy
DBE	Development Bank of Ethiopia
DfID	Department for International Development, since subsumed into the UK's Foreign, Commonwealth, and Development Office
EAPP	Eastern African Power Pool
EC	Ethiopian calendar
ECWC	Ethiopian Construction Works Corporation
EEA	Ethiopian Electricity Agency, subsequently renamed the Ethiopian Energy Authority
EELPA	Ethiopian Electric Light and Power Authority
EEP	Ethiopian Electric Power
EEPCo	Ethiopian Electric Power Company
EEU	Ethiopian Electric Utility
EFFORT	Endowment Fund for the Rehabilitation of Tigray
EIC	Ethiopian Investment Commission
ELF	Eritrean Liberation Front
ENDF	Ethiopian National Defence Force
ENREP	Ethiopia National Rural Electrification Project
ENTRO	Eastern Nile Technical Regional Office
EPA	Environmental Protection Authority
EPC	engineering, procurement, and construction
EPLF	Eritrean People's Liberation Front

EPRDF	Ethiopian Peoples' Revolutionary Democratic Front
EPRP	Ethiopian People's Revolutionary Party
ESIA	Environmental and Social Impact Assessment
EWWCE	Ethiopian Water Works Construction Enterprise
FAI	Fondo Aiuti Italiano (Italian Aid Fund)
FAN	Finchaa-Amarti-Neshe
FAO	Food and Agriculture Organization
GDP	gross domestic product
GERD	Grand Ethiopian Renaissance Dam
GIS	Geographic Information System
GRMF	Geothermal Risk Mitigation Facility
GTP	Growth and Transformation Plans 1 (2010–2015) and 2 (2016–2020)
GWh	gigawatt-hours
HAUBR	Historical Archives of Unicredit, Banco di Roma Fund
HIPC	highly indebted poor countries
HVA	Handelsvereeniging Amsterdam
ICIPU	Istituto di Credito per le Imprese di Pubblica Utilità (Credit Institute for Public Utility Companies)
ICS	interconnected system
IDFC	International Development Finance Corporation
IFC	International Finance Corporation
IFI	international finance institution
IMF	International Monetary Fund
Impresit	Imprese Italiane all'Estero
IPDC	Industrial Parks Development Corporation
IPoE	International Panel of Experts
IPP	independent power producer
JICA	Japanese International Cooperation Association
JMP	joint multipurpose project
kV	kilovolt
kWh	kilowatt-hours
LRMC	long-run marginal cost
MetEC	Metals and Engineering Corporation
MIDROC	Mohammed International Development Research and Organization Companies
MoFA	Ministry of Federal Affairs
MoWIE	Ministry of Water, Irrigation, and Energy
MSE	micro and small enterprises
MTF	multi-tier framework
MW	megawatts
NaMA	National Movement of Amhara
NBI	Nile Basin Initiative
NEP	National Electrification Programme
NGO	non-governmental organization
NISRG	National Independent Scientific Research Group

OFC	Oromo Federalist Congress
OLA	Oromo Liberation Army
OLF	Oromo Liberation Front
ONLF	Ogaden National Liberation Front
OPDO	Oromiya People's Democratic Organization
PASDEP	Plan for Accelerated and Sustained Development to End Poverty
PPA	power purchase agreement
PPP	public–private partnership
PSMP	Power Sector Masterplan
REGREP	Renewable Energy Guarantee Programme
SAIDE	Societa Agricoltura Industriale nel Etiopia
SCS	self-contained system
SDPRP	Sustainable Development and Poverty Reduction Programme
SEPDM	Southern Ethiopian People's Democratic Movement
SNNPR	Southern Nations, Nationalities, and Peoples Region
SPLA	Sudan People's Liberation Army
SPLA-N	Sudan People's Liberation Army-North
TDF	Tigray Defence Force
TPLF	Tigrayan People's Liberation Front
TPSC	Tendaho Plantation Share Company
UAE	United Arab Emirates
UEAP	Universal Electrification Access Programme
UK	United Kingdom
US	United States
USAID	United States Agency for International Development
USBR	United States Bureau of Reclamation
USSR	Union of Soviet Socialist Republics
WWDSE	Water Works Design and Supervision Enterprise

List of Authors

Emanuele Fantini is a Senior Lecturer in water politics and communication at IHE Delft Institute for Water Education (The Netherlands), with 20 years of experience in international development cooperation, working both long-term and consultancy positions in Ethiopia. Emanuele is currently involved in crossover projects with researchers, journalists, photographers, and artists on the role of media and culture in water conflicts in the Nile Basin. Committed to engagement outside academia, he hosts several podcasts, including 'The Sources of the Nile', and is the editor of the IHE Delft Water Governance blog, FLOWs.

Fana Gebresenbet is the Director of the Institute for Peace and Security Studies and Associate Professor of Peacebuilding and Development at IPSS Addis Ababa University. He received his PhD in Global and Area Studies with special emphasis on peace and security in Africa from Leipzig University and Addis Ababa University in 2016. Fana's current research includes the politics of development, political economy, security, and peacebuilding in Ethiopia and the Horn of Africa. He has published numerous journal articles and book chapters, and co-edited two books, *Lands of the Future* (Berghahn, 2021) and *Youth on the Move* (Hurst, 2021).

Edegilign Hailu Woldegebrael is a Postdoctoral Research Fellow in Migration, Urbanization, and Conflict at the Institute for Peace and Security Studies, Addis Ababa University. His research interests include governance and development, the politics and governance of urban informality and conflict, and the political economy of hydropower dams in Ethiopia. His publications include articles in *L'Espace Politique* and *Annales d'Éthiopie*, among others.

Tom Lavers is a Reader in Politics and Development at the University of Manchester's Global Development Institute. He has been researching the politics and political economy of land, industrial policy, infrastructure, and social protection in Ethiopia since 2005. His publications include the 2023 monograph *Ethiopia's 'Developmental State': Political Order and Distributive Crisis* published by Cambridge University Press, as well as articles in *Development and Change*, the *Journal of Agrarian Change*, and *World Development*, among others.

Luca Puddu is an Assistant Professor of African History at the Department of Political Science and International Relations, University of Palermo. He researches the political and economic history of the Horn of Africa region in the twentieth century, with particular reference to the entanglement between international aid, foreign investments, and state building. His works have been published in the *Journal of African History*, the *Journal of Eastern African Studies*, and *Africa: Journal of the International African Institute*, among others.

Biruk Terrefe is a Departmental Lecturer in African Politics in the University of Oxford's Department of Politics and International Relations. He has been researching the politics of infrastructure and urbanization in Ethiopia since 2016. His doctoral work focused on the politics of infrastructural statecraft in the Ethiopian Peoples' Revolutionary Democratic Front's last years. His recent publications include articles on urban megaprojects in Addis Ababa and the discourses of infrastructure development in the *Journal of Eastern African Studies* and *Critical African Studies*, respectively.

Advance praise for Dams, Power, and the Politics of Ethiopia's Renaissance

This book offers a fascinating analysis of the internal contradictions and the external entanglements of Ethiopia's dam program in the last two decades. Combining analytical depth and simple language, the book addresses the academic community, as well as policy and media circles interested in understanding Ethiopia's politically ambitious but technically and economically problematic hydropower projects.

Dr Rawia Tawfik, Associate Professor, Faculty of Economics and Political Science, Cairo University

This is a superb book that has a massive amount to offer anyone concerned with Ethiopia in particular and African development more generally, while also being thoroughly relevant to big issues in current global environmental politics.

Professor Christopher Clapham, Emeritus Professor, University of Cambridge

Tom Lavers and his coauthors have produced a remarkable and fascinating book, rich in historical detail, theoretical flair, and pragmatic lessons that should draw rapt attention from anyone in the public sphere concerned with dams and development.

Professor Christopher S. Sneddon, Professor of Geography and Environmental Studies, Dartmouth College

Providing unique detail and multi-layered perspectives on dam building in Ethiopia, this book's significance goes far beyond the Nile Basin and is instructive for students of energy transitions across the developing world. The complexities of political and electric power are interwoven throughout the book and convincingly argued to be inseparable.

Dr Harry Verhoeven, Senior Research Scholar, School of International and Public Affairs, Columbia University

1
Dams, Power, and State-Led Development
Situating Ethiopia's Dams Boom

Tom Lavers

> Ethiopia is now beginning to walk but will one day be running. Fifteen to twenty years from now it could contemplate doing what Turkey is doing in the Euphrates [by unilaterally building a dam on the Blue Nile] ... we build our economy and promote growth so that some day we can forgo international finance of big projects.
>
> Meles Zenawi, 2 April 1996[1]

Fifteen years to the day after making this statement, on 2 April 2011, Meles Zenawi laid the foundation stone for what would become the Grand Ethiopian Renaissance Dam (GERD), domestically funded and, at 5,150 megawatts (MW) of installed capacity and 74 billion cubic metres of water storage, one of the largest dams in the world. As Turkey had unilaterally built a series of dams upstream on the transboundary Euphrates,[2] Ethiopia was to do the same in the face of opposition from downstream Egypt and Sudan on the Blue Nile (see Figure 1.1). Beyond the remarkable coincidence of timing, this quote illustrates a key point that is central to this book. Namely, rather than a spur-of-the-moment idea in response to the arrival of the Arab Spring in Egypt, as has sometimes been suggested (Fabricius 2013; Johnson 2018), the decision to build the GERD was the culmination of very long-term processes. Ethiopian governments at least as far back as that of Emperor Haile Selassie (1930–1974) had ambitions of damming the Blue Nile. Past regimes made significant progress in studying the river basin and identifying potential dam sites. Yet this ambition remained unfulfilled due to Egyptian opposition to upstream development, internal political divisions, and economic weakness in Ethiopia, and Ethiopia's limited strategic importance to the global powers that might support such a project. More directly, the GERD was the culmination of a 20-year project under Meles Zenawi, and the Ethiopian Peoples' Revolutionary Democratic Front (EPRDF) Government that he led, to transform the Ethiopian

[1] Based on notes provided by John Waterbury.
[2] See Çarkoglu and Eder (2010) and Kibaroglu and Scheumann (2011).

Dams, Power, and the Politics of Ethiopia's Renaissance. Tom Lavers et al., Oxford University Press. © Tom Lavers (2024).
DOI: 10.1093/oso/9780192871213.003.0001

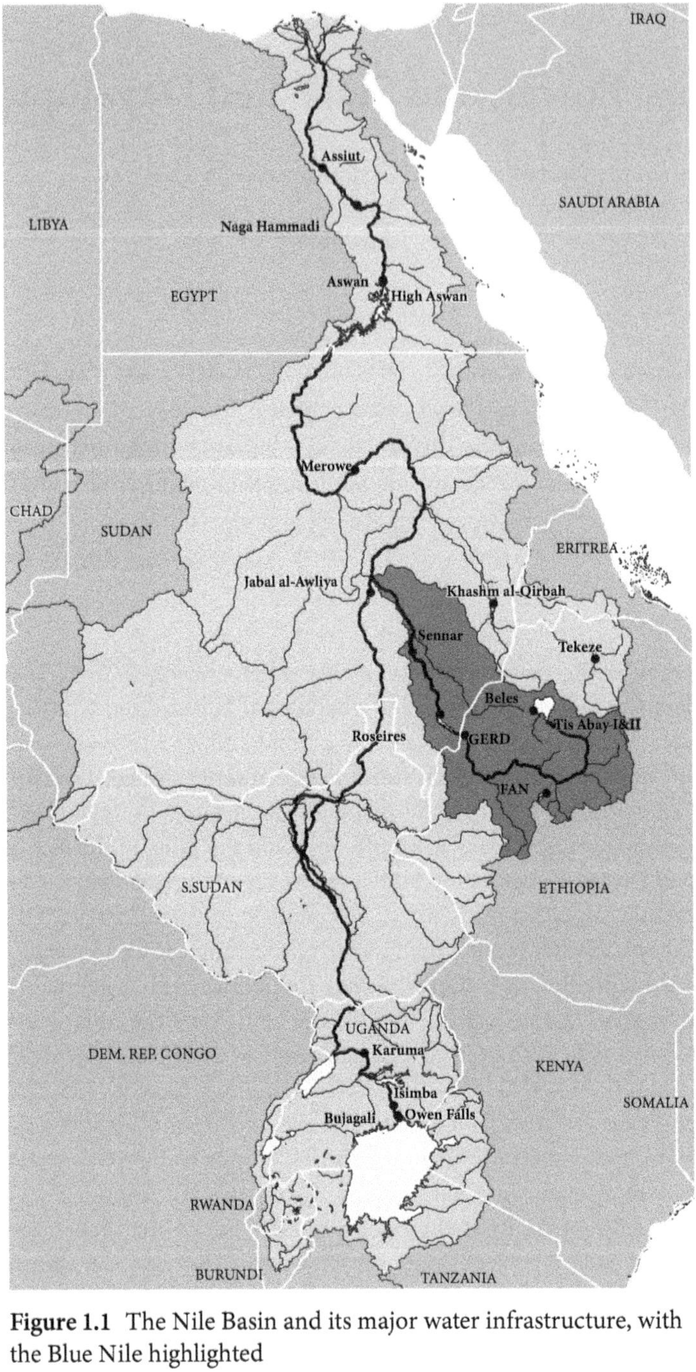

Figure 1.1 The Nile Basin and its major water infrastructure, with the Blue Nile highlighted

Data source: Author based on Lehner and Grill (2013).

economy, and in doing so address the political and economic weaknesses that had prevented past attempts at building a Blue Nile dam. The pursuit of hydroelectric power was interwoven with the dynamics of political power.

This book argues that the Ethiopian dam-building programme, of which the GERD is merely the largest and most controversial project, is symbolic of the successes and limitations of the EPRDF's attempts to build a 'developmental state' and to transform the Ethiopian economy and society.[3] Throughout its time in office (1991–2019), the EPRDF governed in a context of political vulnerability. The EPRDF was established by leaders from a minority-ethnic group that enjoyed little elite or popular support outside their home region of Tigray. Moreover, a series of political crises in the early 2000s further underscored the threat to the ruling elite posed by popular unrest and ethnic divisions. The result was that the EPRDF leadership pursued a project of economic transformation that aimed at broad-based distribution of access to land, agricultural livelihoods, and industrial employment as a means of binding the masses to the regime and thereby maintaining political order (Lavers 2023). For the EPRDF, economic growth and the structural transformation of the economy were synonymous with the Front's political survival.

In pursuit of this project of national development, the EPRDF actively resisted the dominant global trend towards free markets and rolling back the state. Instead, given the imperative of rapid development, the government envisaged a strategy—distinctly out of favour at the time—in which the state would take a central role in agricultural development, industrial policy, and required infrastructural investments. The result was that in the 15 years since Meles made the statement with which this chapter began, Ethiopia had indeed begun to 'run', entering the most rapid and sustained period of economic growth in the country's history that made it one of the fastest-growing economies in the world. This economic growth, moreover, translated into rapid improvement in virtually every available social indicator from poverty reduction to education to health outcomes.

A key driver of this economic progress was massive state infrastructure investment (Moller 2017). In particular, the government sought to build a series of ever-larger and more complex dams that were primarily focused on providing low-cost electricity as a subsidy to nascent industrial production, a form of mass service delivery, and a source of exports and foreign exchange earnings. This hydropower investment was, furthermore, strategically framed as a means of crafting a sustainable 'green economy' that would bypass the carbon-intensive growth of the early industrializers.[4] The result was a massive dam-building programme which

[3] In this book, the term 'developmental state' refers to the development model and ideology espoused in the later years of the EPRDF Government. It is not intended to classify Ethiopia as a developmental state along East Asian lines.

[4] Hydropower was, of course, initially an important part of the energy mix in many of these countries, before fossil fuels became dominant.

required strategic use of concessional lending, domestic resource mobilization, and, latterly, higher-risk commercial finance. The EPRDF began with a cascade of hydropower projects in the Gibe-Omo Basin in southern Ethiopia. In doing so, these projects addressed many of the weaknesses that had prevented the realization of Ethiopian ambitions on the Blue Nile under previous regimes. First, as Meles emphasized in the quote above, the economic growth achieved during the 2000s greatly enhanced the resources available for state investment and, therefore, the government's room for manoeuvre in financing infrastructure projects. Second, the experience of overseeing the construction of successively larger dams strengthened state capacity in the planning and delivery of complex infrastructure projects and, just as importantly, built up a trusted relationship between political leaders and Salini Impregilo, a civil engineering firm that carried out the Gibe-Omo projects and went on to build the GERD.[5] Third, throughout this period, the EPRDF sought to forge internal political cohesion as the basis of a foreign policy focused on securing close relations with the US and China—the world's dominant powers—and building a coalition of upstream countries to change the balance of power on the Nile. Moreover, the government came to frame its development project in nationalist terms, mobilizing the Ethiopian population to deliver an *Ethiopian Renaissance*. The result was that by 2011, Ethiopia had independent access to the finance, technical capacity, and political power required to launch construction of the GERD despite ongoing Egyptian opposition.

From one perspective, therefore, the EPRDF's project of state-led development was a major success, delivering rapid socioeconomic development, massively expanding economic infrastructure, and providing the political and economic power required to tackle the longstanding national ambition of building a Blue Nile dam. While the dams boom exemplifies the successes of this period, however, it also symbolizes many of the failings of the EPRDF era. Many of the dam projects, of which the GERD is merely the largest, and other major infrastructure projects, such as the Djibouti railway, have been subject to lengthy delays and major cost overruns, creating a growing debt burden, as well as proving an inefficient way of addressing the country's infrastructure needs. Indeed, the urgency with which politicians pressed for ever-larger infrastructure projects to meet their growing developmental ambitions served to undermine the fiscal sustainability of the entire state-led development model.

A key tension within this dam-building programme—and infrastructural development more broadly—concerned the mismatch between the urgency with which the political elite pursued infrastructure development and the availability and influence of technical expertise within state agencies to shape decision making. The political imperative of rapid development led the government to launch a bewildering array of ever-larger and more ambitious projects to deliver on

[5] Salini has subsequently been re-named WeBuild.

leaders' developmental ambitions. In doing so, however, planning became a politically driven process, bypassing the limited technical capacity that existed in key state agencies. This politically driven over-ambition contributed to the inefficient design of many projects which are ill suited to meeting Ethiopia's energy needs and lengthy delays as projects have pushed the country's financial and implementation capacities beyond their limit. These problems relate not just to electricity generation but also to the equal challenge of bringing the electricity generated to industrial and household users. A political focus on headline-grabbing generation projects was not matched by equivalent investment in transmission and distribution infrastructure. The result is that investors in Ethiopia's new industrial parks have struggled to secure reliable electricity supplies, as do the minority of households with grid connections, while more than half of the Ethiopian population remains without any connection (MoWIE 2019). The public promise of the GERD is that massively enhanced electricity generation capacity will soon translate into mass access for the Ethiopian population. The reality, however, is that grid expansion and connections are likely to lag behind generation capacity for many years to come.

These challenges have multiplied in the wake of the political and economic crisis that engulfed Ethiopia from the mid-2010s. Lengthy delays and inefficiency meant that many of the EPRDF's infrastructure projects failed to deliver promised economic growth, employment generation, and export earnings. Partly as a consequence, mass anti-government protests and factional divisions within the EPRDF eventually forced a political transition that brought Prime Minister Abiy Ahmed to power in 2018 (Lavers 2023). These factional divisions within the EPRDF ultimately led to the outbreak of civil war in 2020 at the enormous cost of human lives, finance, and the destruction of infrastructure. The conflict, moreover, unravelled the carefully constructed internal political cohesion and international relations that supported Ethiopia's development project. Ultimately, the irony is that while Ethiopia's 'developmental state' was explicitly framed as an alternative to the 'neoliberalism' of the World Bank and International Monetary Fund (IMF) (Zenawi 2006a, 2006b, 2012), the excesses of this state-led infrastructure boom subsequently exposed Ethiopia to a level of debt that has provided external actors with an opening to push for liberalization and the dismantling of the state-led development model. Meanwhile, the new government, and the country as a whole, is labouring under the financial burden of completing the final set of megaprojects launched under the EPRDF, including the GERD.

This book examines how domestic Ethiopian politics combined with international relations to shape Ethiopia's dam-building programme and the role of electricity within Ethiopia's project of state-led development. In tackling these issues, this book addresses a notable gap in the existing literature. The construction of the GERD has, of course, attracted considerable attention already. However, the almost exclusive focus of research to date has been on the design of the dam and its implications for water sharing within the Nile Basin, whether from an international relations or engineering perspective (e.g. Jeuland and Whittington 2014; Whittington et al. 2014; Cascão and Nicol 2016a; Tawfik 2016a, 2016b; Yihdego et al. 2017; Abtew and Dessu 2018). While a number of previous studies have examined the intersection of domestic and international dynamics in shaping Nile hydropolitics, these were largely written before Ethiopia launched its massive dam-building programme and thereby focus on explaining dam development elsewhere in the Nile Basin, notably Egypt, Sudan, and Uganda, and, to the extent that Ethiopia is addressed, they seek to explain the absence of dam building in the country (Waterbury 1979, 2002; Collins 1990; Verhoeven 2015; Gore 2017). There is therefore a great need to update these analyses in light of Ethiopia's dam building and its disruption of Nile hydropolitics.

Domestic politics has not been entirely absent from analysis of Ethiopian dam building. Many studies have highlighted how historic political marginalization has been a key factor shaping displacement and the destruction of livelihoods as a result of dams, particularly in the Gibe-Omo Basin (Turton 2011; Abbink 2012; Kefale and Gebresenbet 2014; Stevenson 2018; Woldegebrael 2018; Gabbert et al. 2021). A number of studies, moreover, examine the political dynamics shaping the planning and construction of individual projects (Fantini and Puddu 2016; Fantini et al. 2018; Woldegebrael 2018), analyse Ethiopian dam building as part of the EPRDF's state-building project (Verhoeven 2013, 2021), or examine the nationalist framing of the GERD (Menga 2017). This book goes further, however, building on these valuable existing contributions to analyse how international and domestic politics combined to shape the spatial dynamics of Ethiopia's dam-building programme, the design of Ethiopia's dams, and the role of water and energy infrastructure in the EPRDF's development project.

Furthermore, there is also an important gap in the literature regarding the vital political economy dynamics shaping the Ethiopian electricity sector. The vast majority of existing work consists of technical analyses of the Ethiopian electricity system and the potential of different energy sources to meet projected demand (Block and Strzepek 2012; Asress et al. 2013; Demissie and Solomon 2016; Mondal et al. 2017). From a social science perspective, contributions are limited to Cuesta-Fernández's (2015) analysis of the challenges of realizing Ethiopia's targets for electricity exports, while Chiyemura (2019) provides a detailed discussion of new windfarms. This book builds on and extends this work, analysing the electricity sector and renewable energy generation within the political economy of state-led development in Ethiopia.

The story of Ethiopia's dam-building programme and the development project of which it was a key part is both fascinating and noteworthy in its own right. However, Ethiopia's dams boom also constitutes a case study of central importance to a number of major contemporary debates concerning the political economy of development, with important consequences for development trajectories and development theory. The following sections examine three of these debates in turn and situate the present book within these literatures, namely: state-led development and electricity sector governance; the twenty-first-century resurgence in dam building; and renewable energy transitions.

State-Led Development and the Electricity Sector

The appropriate role for the state and market in development has been subject to extensive, and often heated, debate over many decades, while actual state practice has been deeply influenced by shifting global ideas (Blyth 2002). Nowhere is this more relevant than in the role of the state in the electricity sector and infrastructure investment. The EPRDF's post-millennium attempt to build a 'developmental state' has helped to reinvigorate this debate, raising questions as to whether the Ethiopian experience offers a model for other late-developing countries.

Following World War II, the state was widely seen as the main actor responsible for promoting economic catch-up with the advanced economies. In particular, the state was expected to play key roles in agricultural and industrial development and in providing public goods, including infrastructure. Indeed, the need for state infrastructure investment was central to the 'big push' approach to development (Rosenstein-Rodan 1943; Rostow 1960). While early electric grids were based on private investment, from the 1920s electricity came to be seen as a natural monopoly and a public good, justifying state control from generation to distribution. State monopolies were created in most countries, with large-scale state investment in electricity seen as a key element of industrial policy and economic modernization (Hirschman 1967; Gratwick and Eberhard 2008). Examples include Brazil (Tendler 1968), South Korea (Amsden 1992), and China (Zhang and Heller 2007), where state agencies and corporations made major investments in electricity generation, often explicitly as a means of supporting industrialization. During the Cold War, many developing countries were able to secure external finance for large-scale investments from the United States, the Soviet Union, and their allies as these global powers sought to build alliances.

The debt crises of the early 1980s, brought about in part by the poor performance of many debt-financed infrastructure investments, heralded a sea change in the role of the state as a development actor. Increasingly, the state was seen not as the solution to developmental failings but as the cause of them (Krueger 1990; Williamson 1990). As part of the Washington Consensus, structural adjustment exchanged debt relief from the international finance institutions (IFIs) for liberalization and privatization aiming to roll back the state, stimulate markets, and 'get the prices right'. A common focus was the liberalization of financial sectors, removing one of the central tools that states had previously used to mobilize resources for infrastructure investment. Likewise, in the electricity sector, early experiments with privatization and competition in the UK, US, and Chile were promoted as model reforms that would lead to greater efficiency and remove political influence from the sector (Gratwick and Eberhard 2008; Lee and Usman 2018). During the 1990s, these reforms crystallized into what became known as the 'Standard Model', entailing the commercialization and corporatization of state utilities, followed by vertical unbundling—the creation of separate entities responsible for generation, transmission, and distribution—and horizontal unbundling—whereby multiple firms, including the private sector, would compete in the generation and distribution of electricity. This Standard Model was actively promoted globally by the World Bank and a handful of allied consultancy firms (World Bank 1993; Gratwick and Eberhard 2008).

Despite active promotion of the Standard Model, however, very few countries globally and none in Africa implemented the full package of reforms. Most countries did not go further than corporatizing state electric authorities, introducing independent regulators and allowing private firms to generate and sell electricity as independent power producers (IPPs) (Victor and Heller 2007; Lee and Usman 2018; Gore et al. 2019). Reforms advanced furthest in countries where the World Bank was most influential and where regimes faced little in the way of civil society opposition, such as Uganda (Gore 2017; Gore et al. 2019). A common result has been 'hybrid markets' in which IPPs sell to state-owned grids based on long-term take or pay power purchase agreements (PPAs) alongside state-owned generation (Gratwick and Eberhard 2008). Indeed, recent years have seen some acknowledgement from the World Bank that the reforms it promoted for the last 25 years were rarely fully implemented and, in the words of one World Bank paper, that the Standard Model is 'neither necessary nor sufficient' for an effective electricity sector (Lee and Usman 2018, p. ii).

The challenge to the minimal role of the state in mainstream policy prescriptions has been gradual. Rapid development in the 'developmental states' of South Korea and Taiwan, and subsequently China, highlighted the valuable role played by the state (Wade 1990; Amsden 1992; Mkandawire 2001; Ang 2016). The initial response from multilateral development agencies in the 1990s acknowledged the need for good governance reforms to enable states to provide the regulatory frameworks to enable market development, while promoting a greater state role in social service delivery in pursuit of poverty reduction. Subsequently, however, the commodity boom provided financial leeway and policy space for some commodity exporters (Jepson 2020), while the Global Financial Crisis of 2008 reinforced doubts about market-based development and renewed attention to the role of the state. The result has been resurgent interest in state industrial policy and state investment in the infrastructure required to integrate national economies into the global economy (Esteban et al. 2013; Lin Yifu 2013; Schindler and Kanai 2021).

As in the post-World War II era, this post-2000 infrastructural turn has been shaped by global powers providing financial and technical support. This time,

China has played a key role, first as part of its 'Going Out' strategy from the late 1990s and subsequently in response to the 2008 Financial Crisis (Bräutigam 2009; Mohan and Tan-Mullins 2019). China's Belt and Road Initiative has fuelled a massive expansion of infrastructure projects in an attempt to build 'Sino-centric global production and trade networks' connecting China to natural resources, markets, and offshoring locations for labour-intensive manufacturing (Lampton et al. 2020; Liu et al. 2020; Schindler and Kanai 2021). Chinese support has included financing—often state-backed lending from the China ExIm Bank and China Development Bank (CDB)—and construction—with contracting to Chinese firms sometimes a lending requirement (Mohan and Tan-Mullins 2019).

Massive Chinese investments have also spurred a more modest response from the US government through the International Development Finance Corporation (IDFC) and PowerAfrica. In the context of increasingly fractious relations between the US and China, this infrastructural competition has been framed by some as a New Cold War with the two global powers vying for supremacy (Schindler and Kanai 2021; Schindler et al. 2022). Moreover, multilateral organizations, which had previously reduced support for infrastructure investment, have also changed tack with increased lending (Nugent 2018). This re-engagement of Western donors has not, however, entailed a return to the state lending of the past. Instead, the favoured modality of the World Bank and US Government is public–private partnerships (PPPs) in which private firms—usually transnational companies—finance, construct, and operate infrastructure in return for guaranteed income flows, backed where necessary by risk guarantees by multilaterals. The aim is to leverage private finance to plug the financing gap for infrastructure projects while drawing on private sector expertise, avoiding the problems of state investment of the past (World Bank 2014). The outcome has been the creation of infrastructure as an asset class for investment, with states and their multilateral backers seeking to de-risk infrastructural investments for private firms (Gabor 2021).

The result is that the early twenty-first century has seen new opportunities for late-developing states to play key roles in the development of their economies, albeit in a quite different global political economic context to that faced by earlier industrializers. This discussion, in turn, raises related questions about the circumstances under which states take advantage of the windows of opportunity provided by these shifting global trends and successfully pursue economic development, infrastructure investment, and structural transformation. A recurrent finding in the political science literature is that governments undertake the challenging reforms required to mobilize resources and pursue economic transformation when leaders face severe existential threats to their political survival (Migdal 1988; Doner et al. 2005; Doner 2009; Vu 2010; Whitfield et al. 2015; Lavers 2023). Under such circumstances, elites are forced to act collectively, promoting a shared vision of economic transformation, enabling long-run investments in developmental progress and limiting opportunities for potential opposition that might veto reforms.[6] An additional requirement, moreover, is that state technocrats are sufficiently politically empowered and possess the necessary capabilities to design appropriate strategies to deliver on these developmental ambitions (Johnson 1982; Kohli 2004). For the most part, discussions of state capacity have focused on the features of states required to carry out effective industrial policy, often highlighting the importance of Weberian characteristics—meritocracy, an esprit de corps, and autonomy from private interests—as well as embeddedness with private sector actors in order to be able to understand and respond to the challenges they face (Evans 1995). While some analyses emphasize the (very) long-run origins of state capacity (Kohli 2004; Rueschemeyer 2005), other work concludes that where elites perceive particularly severe threats, they can invest in a rapid expansion of state capacities that can be put to developmental uses (Skocpol 1979; Doner et al. 2005; Slater 2010; Vu 2010). Although rarely a subject of detailed analysis, a plausible hypothesis, therefore, is that existential crises that force leaders to pursue development and the expansion of state capacity are also likely to enable development of the electricity sector and the large-scale construction of hydropower as part of this developmental project.

Ethiopia is a vital case for these debates about state-led development. In important respects, Ethiopia diverged from the global trends in development thinking described above, with the EPRDF actively resisting donor pressure to liberalize the economy in the 1990s, including in key sectors such as electricity. As global ideas began to shift during the 2000s and Ethiopia's state-led development project delivered impressive economic growth, the country came to be recognized as a notable exception to the global norm of liberalization and a test case for those advocating greater state intervention in the economy. Moreover, Meles Zenawi became increasingly assertive in questioning 'neo-liberal' orthodoxy and proclaiming Ethiopia's 'developmental state' as a model for other African countries to follow (Zenawi 2006a, 2006b, 2012). Massive debt-financed state infrastructure investments were a key driver of economic growth in this period, while the provision of cheap electricity was seen by the EPRDF Government as a vital form of industrial policy and key to delivering on its ultimate objective of the structural transformation of the economy. This book provides the first detailed analysis of the political economy of the electricity sector under the EPRDF, situating the sector within the government's state-led development model. Moreover, the book comes at an important moment at which the subsequent Prosperity Party Government—once again somewhat against current global trends—is contemplating far-reaching reform of the state-dominated electricity sector and a move towards the Standard

[6] For Doner et al. (2005, p. 331), as in this book, ruling elites are considered to be 'the political leaders atop the incumbent regime'.

Model. The book examines the drivers of these reforms and the challenges in implementing them.

Hydropolitics and the Dam Resurgence

The literature on the politics of dams exhibits similarities with that on infrastructure, but with certain specificities related to the politics of water.[7] Rapid population growth, urbanization, and the need for renewable energy—discussed in the following section—have only increased demand for water infrastructure. Meanwhile, Ethiopia's emergence as one of the world's most prolific dam builders makes it a vitally important case study for examining the contemporary dam resurgence.

A consistent theme of this vast literature is that dam construction is not just a technical but an inherently political concern. Politicians have long prioritized dams as symbols of nationalism and modernity, and humanity's technological triumph over the vagaries of nature, as much as for the electricity and water storage that they provide (McCully 1996; Miescher 2014; Swyngedouw 2015; Verhoeven 2015). Indeed,

> A hydroelectric project is fine political capital ... The hydro complex has drama and style, and there is an air of extravagance in its hugeness and grace which is awesome in a country trying to mobilize scarce resources for development. Though hydro supplies a basic necessity, it creates the aura of a country which no longer has to scrimp and save, but can spend with largesse. (Tendler 1968, pp. 250–251)

Moreover, it is not just politicians that drive dam construction but also the powerful hydraulic bureaucracies, or 'hydrocracies', assembled to carry out water infrastructure projects. Karl Wittfogel (1957) first emphasized the links between water infrastructure and state formation. Indeed, the first era of large dam construction from the 1930s resulted in the creation of powerful hydrocracies, often with a narrow, techno-scientific worldview focused on taming rivers and overcoming nature (Molle et al. 2009).[8] Dam construction and river basin planning are among the main examples of what James Scott (1998, p. 4) called 'high modernism', whereby dams are presented as a key means of transforming backward and irrational peoples through the 'uncritical, unskeptical' belief in the transformative power of science and engineering. Prominent early examples include the US Bureau of Reclamation that re-plumbed the western United States (Worster 1985; Reisner 1993) and the Hydrological Planning Agency in the Soviet Union

[7] This section draws on an earlier, more detailed review article by Lavers and Dye (2019).

[8] The industry-standard definition of a large dam is one that measures 15 metres or more from foundation to crest.

(McCully 1996). These hydrocracies undertook the 'hydraulic mission', namely the effort to ensure that every drop of water flowing in rivers across national territory is put to human use before reaching the sea (Molle et al. 2009, p. 332; Wester et al. 2009, p. 75). The result was that water infrastructure often became 'an end in itself, rather than a means to an end' (Molle et al. 2009, p. 328). Moreover, these modernist and nationalist narratives are often reinforced by more materialist concerns, with dam projects constituting a means of distributing rents to politicians, construction companies, urban water and electricity users, and large irrigation farmers (Reisner 1993). The result has been described as an 'iron triangle' between state agencies, politicians, and interest groups that drives project construction (McCool 1994).

By the second half of the twentieth century, most potential sites in the US had been dammed, while environmental groups opposing dam construction had become increasingly influential (Khagram 2018). In a pattern that would repeat in other major dam-building countries, from the Soviet Union to Norway, China, and Brazil, the Bureau of Reclamation sought to sustain itself by exporting its services (Sneddon 2015). The wave of independence of former colonies after World War II and competition between global powers during the Cold War therefore led to a second wave of dam construction as modernizing leaders sought the legitimizing power of large dams, drawing on financial and technical support from competing sides in the Cold War (Mitchell 2002; Swyngedouw 2007, 2015; Miescher 2014; Sneddon 2015). The World Bank, established in the aftermath of World War II, soon became the leading agency supporting dam construction in developing countries (Salman 2009; Khagram 2018).

The resulting dams often failed to live up to expectations and resulted in negative environmental and social impacts. Engineers and economists in the grip of a 'planning fallacy' were 'systematically and predictably too optimistic about the time, costs, and benefits of a decision' (Ansar et al. 2014, p. 44; Hirschman 1967; Flyvbjerg et al. 2009). Moreover, this fallacy was often complemented by deception—deliberately underestimating costs and overstating benefits to secure project approval (Reisner 1993; McCully 1996). The result is that the mean cost overrun for dams is 96 per cent and the average time delay is 44 per cent, figures that, if accurately estimated in advance, would often destroy a dam's economic case (Ansar et al. 2014, pp. 48–49). Moreover, the focus of politicians and engineers on the hydraulic mission routinely leads planners to ignore or understate the social and environmental impacts of dams (Adams 1992; McCully 1996; Scudder 2019). Common environmental impacts include reduced water quality and increased evaporation, blocking sediment flows leading to loss of soil fertility, erosion, and salinization, delayed floods, and reduced peak floods, as well as the destruction of habitats and blocking of migratory routes for fish (McCully 1996; Everard 2013). Meanwhile, a wealth of research has repeatedly highlighted the long-term, negative impacts on those displaced and those living downstream, whose livelihoods and communities are disrupted (McCully 1996; Scudder 2005, 2012). Dams therefore have important distributive impacts. The main beneficiaries tend to be the industrial and domestic users of electricity, often in faraway urban centres, and large landholders who benefit from irrigation, while those negatively affected are invariably the most politically marginalized, with differential impacts by gender, class, and ethnicity (McCully 1996; Tsikata 2006; Schulz and Adams 2019).

Influential national and transnational anti-dam movements formed in response to dams' negative environmental and social impacts (Khagram 2018; Atkins 2020). These movements have been most influential in democracies and/or through what has been described as a 'boomerang strategy', whereby local resistance connects to transnational social movements to exert pressure on governments, international construction firms, and financiers (Keck and Sikkink 1998). Perhaps the most significant example is the campaign that forced the World Bank to withdraw from India's Sardar Sarovar dam (Roy 1999; Khagram 2018). The Bank also subsequently co-sponsored the World Commission on Dams whose report in 2000 acknowledged the many problems with dams and sought to promote a participatory approach to dam design and construction to address their social and environmental failings (World Commission on Dams 2000; Schulz and Adams 2019).

The 1980s and 1990s saw a sharp reduction in dam construction, often attributed to growing social and environmental awareness (Khagram 2018). Yet these negative impacts have done little to impede a third major wave of dam construction since 2000 with an estimated 3,700 major dams planned or under construction, particularly in developing countries (Zarfl et al. 2015). This new phase of dam construction has been shaped by the return to state-led development and infrastructure investment, often accompanied by familiar forms of high modernism (Dye 2016, 2018). Moreover, the dam resurgence has been spurred by new sources of finance and technical expertise, particularly from emerging economies, with Chinese firms emerging as the leading dam builders globally, linked to the 'Going Out' strategy and Belt and Road Initiative (Bräutigam 2009; McDonald et al. 2009; Mohan 2013; Siciliano and Urban 2017; Brautigam and Hwang 2019; Mohan and Tan-Mullins 2019).[9] These emerging economies contested the conclusions of the World Commission on Dams and have been less swayed by transnational social movements (Schulz and Adams 2019). China's dominance of global dam building has led the World Bank to re-engage also. However, reflecting the move towards private investment in infrastructure more broadly, World Bank support has focused on forging PPPs to invest in hydropower (World Bank 2009a). To date, however, this has been far from successful. With the exception of Rwanda (Dye 2019) and Uganda (Gore 2017), investors have considered low-income

[9] Also Brazil (Dye and Alencastro 2020) and India (Dye 2021).

countries to be too high risk, instead targeting middle-income countries (Plummer Braeckman and Markkanen 2021).

The experience of late-developing countries with hydropower mirrors that of industrial policy. Early dam builders assembled high levels of technological expertise within hydrocracies and private firms as they carried out their hydraulic missions. In contrast, most developing countries have instead relied on international expertise to plan and build dams, with advances in the technological frontier for civil and particularly electro-mechanical works making it very difficult for domestic firms to enter the sector. The development of a domestic dam industry has only been achieved in relatively rare cases, such as Brazil and China, where latecomers deliberately pursued industrial policies to promote learning and build capacity (Tendler 1968; Bosshard 2009). The result is that late-developing governments rely on a small pool of international firms for the civil engineering—including Chinese firms Sinohydro and China Gezhouba Group Company (CGGC), Brazilian Odebrecht, and Italian Salini—and electro-mechanical engineering—primarily Alsthom, General Electric, Siemens, and Voith—to build dams. Rather than engineering powerhouses, late-developing hydrocracies are instead primarily contracting agencies that channel significant revenues but do not necessarily develop great technological expertise. In turn, this raises important questions about the power and influence of hydrocracies in decision making on dams amidst the latest dam resurgence.

Beyond national-level decision making and the interaction with foreign expertise and finance, the politics of dams and water raises a host of other questions concerning spatial scales. Water flows across political jurisdictions both within and between countries, forcing political analysis beyond the confines of the nation-state (Warner and Zawahri 2012). At the sub-national level, dams, and associated irrigation schemes and industry, have frequently been used to extend the territorial reach of the state into peripheral areas, and in doing so they have re-ordered local society and enhanced state power, often to the detriment of the most politically marginal (Wittfogel 1957; Mann 1986; Scott 1998; Swyngedouw 2015). Furthermore, dams on transnational rivers are inevitably shaped by and highlight relations between riparian countries. International law regarding transboundary water remains at a formative stage. As late as the 1950s there were no 'widely accepted principles of international law governing the uses and sharing of international rivers' (Salman 2009, p. 10). Subsequently, debates have contrasted the territorial sovereignty of a country to utilize the water that flows within its borders with the need to avoid causing significant harm to other riparians. Eventually, the 1966 Helsinki Rules that prioritize 'reasonable and equitable utilization' have come to be regarded as 'customary international law' (Salman 2009, p. 56). However, the reality is that, in the absence of universally accepted international water law, water disputes are largely determined by political power and diplomacy rather than legal adjudication (Zeitoun and Warner 2006).

Hydro-hegemony is a prominent theory developed to analyse these power relations between riparian countries which are neither collaborative nor escalate into water wars. From this perspective, stability is achieved once a hegemonic riparian establishes control over the river basin by persuading 'subordinate actors to accept not just the hegemon's authority, but to adopt and internalize its values and norms' (Zeitoun and Warner 2006, p. 438). The power relations between riparians, meanwhile, are contingent upon physical factors (e.g. dependence on and use of the river) but also overt and covert use of material power, whether economic or military power, bargaining power, or discursive power (Cascão and Zeitoun 2010; Kibaroglu 2017). Alliances between riparians and regional and international powerbrokers are vital sources of influence within river basins, providing or denying access not just to finance and expertise to construct water infrastructure but also the broader economic, diplomatic, and military resources used to establish dominance (Zeitoun and Warner 2006; Warner and Zawahri 2012).

Analysis of the Ethiopian case therefore provides a vital entry point for engaging with the large literature on dams and questioning key facets of the ongoing third wave of dam building. For example, will this latest dam resurgence fall prey to the same high modernist and technocratic supremacy as earlier waves? And will the shifting global political economy and ideas about state-led development that motivate this dam resurgence consolidate or upend existing power relations that underpin hydro-hegemony in river basins? Despite being one of the main protagonists in recent dam resurgence, Ethiopia's dam-building programme remains under-researched and poorly understood. The Ethiopian Government's state-led development model led it to navigate the shifting global trends described above in pursuit of a major dam-building programme. Yet, Ethiopia's ambitions to build a major dam on the Blue Nile confronted the dominant power in that river basin—Egypt. The EPRDF's dam programme drew initially on support from the World Bank and one of the first Chinese-built dams in Africa. However, the Ethiopian Government also sought to develop its financial independence and, unusually, technological expertise to carry out dam projects independently by building state capacities and forging exceptionally close relations with Salini Impregilo. The series of ever-larger dams built in Ethiopia since 1991 culminated in the decision to launch construction of the GERD in 2011, a dam which is set to weaken Egyptian dominance of the Nile. This dam-building programme has, predictably, resulted in a pattern of marginalization of displaced populations, justified by a common narrative of modernization and progress. Moreover, Ethiopia's dam-building programme has fundamentally re-shaped Ethiopia also. While hydropower was initially conceived as a means to an end—primarily the generation of cheap electricity for industry—Ethiopian dams, and the GERD in particular, came to take on a life of their own. The EPRDF promoted the GERD as a symbol of an Ethiopian Renaissance, returning to the historical glories of the past when Ethiopia was regarded as among the leading ancient civilizations. Indeed, the symbolism of the

GERD has outlived the party and leadership that launched it, and has become a rare unifying symbol of Ethiopian nationalism at a time when political divisions threaten the existence of the country itself. Ethiopia is as important a case as any for understanding the political drivers and ramifications of the new wave of dam building.

Climate Change and Energy Transitions

The third wave of dam building is taking place within the context of growing calls for a transition to renewable energy as a means of addressing climate change.[10] While the primary focus of these debates concerns the need to eliminate fossil fuels, hydropower has a hotly contested place within this proposed energy transition. As such, the EPRDF's effort to frame dam building as a central pillar of its 'green developmental state' highlights important issues concerning the ability of late-developing countries to power the structural transformation of their economies using renewable energy.

With the lowest electrification rates in the world, there is an urgent need to expand the supply of and access to electricity in African countries.[11] Yet, the main fossil energy sources that powered earlier industrializers are incompatible with environmental constraints. Realizing the goal of limiting global warming to 2°C above pre-industrial levels is simply infeasible within the current trajectory of capitalist growth in the advanced economies, much less a world in which all countries attain an equivalent standard of living through economic growth of a comparable carbon intensity (Newell 2021). There is therefore an urgent need for a transition to renewable energy sources such as solar, wind, and geothermal, and, in all likelihood, limits to growth-centred development models.[12]

Although prominent in the energy plans for many countries, the role for hydropower in this energy transition is contested. While many argue that hydropower *is* a sustainable energy source and an essential means of addressing the climate crisis (World Bank 2009a; Siciliano and Urban 2017; Atkins 2020; Hochstetler 2020), the reality is more complex. Not only do dams have well-documented negative impacts on the environment and those living in the vicinity of dams, but dams can also be a major source of greenhouse gas emissions. The carbon footprint of dams includes the emissions produced when making the vast quantities of cement and steel used in construction, but also, and

[10] This section was greatly aided by an excellent, unpublished review by Matt Tyce (2021).

[11] According to the World Development Indicators, access to electricity in sub-Saharan Africa was just 48 per cent in 2020, despite a rapid increase in the previous two decades.

[12] Calls for de-growth present a fundamental challenge to the prevailing capitalist system (Hickel and Kallis 2020). Yet, de-growth can hardly be considered a plausible answer for developing economies, which have made the least contribution to climate change and which desperately need further economic development to raise living standards (Jackson 2011; Cosme et al. 2017; Chiengkul 2018).

more significantly, the emissions produced by reservoirs throughout their lifetime (Fearnside 2002, 2003). Studies have found that methane emissions are particularly high in shallow, tropical reservoirs with the result that some dams actually produce more greenhouse gas emissions than an equivalent fossil fuel plant (Giles 2006; Gunkel 2009; Kuriakose et al. 2022). The green credentials of hydropower cannot therefore be assumed.

Initial research examining the factors shaping the energy mix and the potential for energy transitions showed how socio-technical systems comprising fossil fuel technology, infrastructure, and supporting institutions underpin path dependence (Unruh 2000, 2002; Geels 2002; Verbong and Geels 2007). However, a growing body of research focuses specifically on the political economy of energy transitions, recognizing the distributive implications of energy transitions and the potential for resistance from those benefitting from the status quo (Baker et al. 2014; Geels 2014; Moe 2015; Scoones et al. 2015; Newell and Phillips 2016; Power et al. 2016, Hochstetler 2020; Newell 2021). From this perspective, energy transitions require not just innovation and technological change but a transformation of the political economies on which the prevailing energy system is based (Mitchell 2013; Malm 2016; Newell 2021).

To date, most research on the political economy of energy transitions has focused on advanced and middle-income economies—by far the largest source of emissions—and their specific challenges in transforming existing systems of energy generation and grid infrastructure, and the political economic interests that underpin these (Unruh 2002; Moe 2015; Newell 2021). Far less studied, however, is the distinct challenge facing late-developing countries, where electricity generation and access remain relatively limited. In these countries, governments must massively expand electricity generation and work towards universal access, doing so through emerging and sometimes somewhat unproven renewable technology (Kelsey and Zysman 2013). This is to be achieved, moreover, in a context in which the norm of the Standard Model limits the state to providing incentives for private sector investment. While the challenge facing late-developing countries is formidable, low-income countries do have the potential to learn from the environmental mistakes of advanced economies (Goldemberg 1998). Moreover, where countries with limited existing generation capacity do not face powerful, entrenched fossil fuel interests, the political economy barriers to renewable energy transitions may be more modest compared to many advanced and middle-income countries (Kelsey and Zysman 2013; Hochstetler 2020; Ohlendorf et al. 2022; Pedersen and Andersen 2023).

The political economy shaping the energy mix and possible energy transitions is multi-faceted and multi-scalar, encompassing not just actors directly involved in generation but also industrial, commercial, and domestic consumers of electricity, manufacturers involved in new industries and their workers, those affected by the siting of generation plants, and politicians and the general public debating climate change (Hochstetler 2020; Newell 2021). A key element here concerns the trade-off between those industries—capitalists, workers, and allied politicians and bureaucrats—that stand to lose out from change and new industries that stand to benefit. State industrial policy has the potential to tip the balance, creating new growth industries and political constituencies among capitalists and workers in renewable energy (Kelsey and Zysman 2013; Schmitz et al. 2015; Hochstetler 2020; Newell 2021). However, just as with the development of a domestic hydropower industry, discussed above, late-developing countries face the industrial policy challenge of establishing a competitive domestic industry in renewables and catching up with leading global producers (Pegels 2014; Schmitz et al. 2015; Chen and Lees 2016; Hochstetler 2020). To date, most countries have struggled in this regard, with research and development and manufacturing instead dominated by firms from a few advanced economies and, increasingly, China (Chen and Lees 2016; Behuria 2020; Hochstetler 2020).

Sustainability is a prime example of the free rider problem, in which everyone has an interest in preventing large-scale climate change but also minimizing their individual costs in achieving it. For many reasons, therefore, the state has a vitally important role to play in realizing the public good of clean and sustainable energy production (Pegels 2014). Yet, government policy never solely responds to necessity but is rather the outcome of a complex calculation based on the time horizon of the ruling party, its strategy for maintaining political power, and its assessment of the balance of power in society. The reality is that in most cases, states have been unwilling to confront the difficult choices inherent to promoting energy transitions and have been limited to relatively modest action to pursue 'green growth' that maintains capitalist development, while switching to somewhat less carbon-intensive forms of production (World Bank 2012a; Death 2016; Rowell 2017). In many cases, this amounts to little more than 'greenwashing' in which existing carbon-intensive practices are wrapped in a narrative of environmental sustainability.

To a considerable degree, the ability of late-developing states working within the Standard Model to promote energy transitions will be dependent on the availability of finance to fund new generation. Indeed, the efforts of international organizations to promote renewable energy have heavily focused on market-based solutions to the climate crisis in line with the trend towards the liberalization of the financial and electricity sectors. A number of climate finance schemes, such as the Clean Development Mechanism of the Kyoto Protocol and the United States' PowerAfrica programme, support private investment in renewables. In doing so, these schemes seek to de-risk renewable energy investments for international firms, while constraining the space for industrial policy to support domestic firms (Gabor 2021; Newell 2021).

Ethiopia's effort to navigate this complex political economy in pursuing a 'green developmental state' is therefore an important, and thus far neglected, case in the comparative analysis of energy transitions. Ethiopia's limited electricity generation capacity has long relied almost exclusively on hydropower, with the state taking a central role in constructing a series of ever bigger dams to expand generation capacity. On several occasions, this has meant forgoing options to invest in fossil fuel-powered plants, which would have offered cheaper and quicker short-term solutions to Ethiopia's energy problems. Moreover, recent efforts to diversify the energy mix have focused on the expansion of non-hydro renewable energy. The focus on hydropower enabled the Ethiopian Government to frame its green economy strategy as a central feature of its 'developmental state' model. Furthermore, based on this stated commitment to sustainability, Meles Zenawi took a leading role in global climate negotiations representing Africa, arguing for greater financial support for African countries that had done little to create the growing climate crisis but are likely to suffer some of its most severe consequences. The majority of the literature on energy transitions to date has focused on advanced and middle-income economies. The Ethiopian case, meanwhile, raises important and distinct questions regarding the challenges facing late-developing countries seeking to catch up with more advanced economies through the development of renewable energy. Notably, these include, first, whether it is possible to pursue state-led development and structural transformation based on renewable energy and, second, what political processes might lead late-developing countries to pursue low-carbon energy trajectories.

Conceptualizing the Multi-Scalar Politics of Dam Building

The focus of this book is to examine how a late-developing country, such as Ethiopia, navigates these shifting trends and power relations in the pursuit of state-led development in which infrastructure investment and hydro-electricity generation and access are prioritized. The brief review above serves to highlight three consistent themes within each of the literatures on state-led development, dams, and energy transitions. In turn, each of these themes forms a key part of the analytical framework that guides this book. First, government decisions are the product of the power relations within the political elite, between political leaders and the bureaucracy, and between state and societal forces. Second, these relations are shaped both by the material interests of the actors involved and dominant ideologies, and the ways in which these are discursively framed and communicated. Third, although national governments are a particularly important locus of decision making, state-led development, dam building, and energy transitions are inherently multi-scalar challenges that require integration of different levels of analysis from the global to the micro.

The framework places elite politics at the centre of the analysis. The starting assumption is that for governments to pursue the construction of major infrastructure projects, including both dams and electricity infrastructure more broadly, three key factors are required: the commitment of political elites; access to the technical capacity to design and implement projects; and access to necessary financial resources. First, drawing on existing work on state-led development (Waldner 1999; Doner et al. 2005; Slater 2010; Khan 2018), political elite cohesion is a vitally important factor that extends politicians' time horizons and centralizes the political power required to mobilize financial resources, invest in increased state capacity, undertake long-term investments, and counter potential international and domestic opposition to new projects.[13] All major infrastructure projects involve significant financial costs and negatively impact on certain groups, while potential benefits can take many years to realize. This is particularly the case for dams, with large upfront construction costs, long timeframes for planning and construction, and long payback periods. Ruling elite cohesion, meanwhile, is the product of power relations between elite factions and their assessment of the threats to their rule posed by societal divisions along class or ethnic lines (Doner et al. 2005; Slater 2010). Moreover, shared ideologies can provide the basis for elite cohesion as well as the justification for ambitious developmental projects.

Second, political leaders committed to major infrastructure projects must have access to the technical capacity required to plan, design, and realize construction. The relationships between political leaders, state technocrats, and private contractors are essential to the decisions regarding electricity planning priorities, the preferred energy mix, and the siting, design, and construction of particular projects. Late-developing countries face a choice. On the one hand, they can invest in domestic technical capacity in state agencies and private firms, as was the case with many early industrializers and some emerging economies. Certainly, there are benefits to doing so in terms of reducing costs, job creation, and the potential to transfer accumulated expertise to other sectors. On the other hand, there are also important risks. Infrastructure projects, and particularly dams, are complex and developing the required engineering, hydraulic, and organizational expertise is difficult and slow. A strategy focused on building domestic capacity therefore risks reduced efficiency and delayed project completion. In most cases, late-developing countries instead rely on leading international contractors, which are likely to be centrally focused on financial returns and potentially influenced by international relations. In either case, effective decision making depends on a delicate balance of relations between politicians, technocrats, and private firms (Evans 1995; Kohli 2004; Dasandi and Esteve 2017). On the one hand, politicians must politically

[13] Elite cohesion in this sense is a situation in which the most powerful political elites are in broad agreement about key priorities and strategies, and commit to their realization, whether based on shared material interests and/or shared ideological commitments.

empower proficient technocrats, with political interference in technical decisions likely to be detrimental (Johnson 1982). On the other hand, however, a common feature in the history of dams is overly empowered hydrocracies pursuing projects as 'an end in itself, rather than a means to an end' (Molle et al. 2009, p. 328; Reisner 1993; Scott 1998). Effective planning therefore requires that politicians support the technocracy and prioritize technical expertise in decision making, while maintaining control of strategic vision and oversight of the sector.

Finally, realization of major infrastructure projects requires access to finance. Political leaders can secure project finance from a wide variety of sources. First is domestic revenues, which are dependent both on economic growth and, vitally, the political bargains between political leaders, business, and society regarding taxation (Mann 1986; Tilly 1992; Bräutigam et al. 2008). The reality confronting many late-developing countries, however, is that the tax base is limited and infrastructural investments are often intended to kick-start economic growth and cannot rely on vibrant economic activity and rising tax income. As such, leaders of late-developing countries are forced to turn to international sources to enable their infrastructural ambitions. Of particular importance is of course the availability of concessional lending. While appealing in terms of the low cost of borrowing, however, negotiating access to aid is dependent on donors' strategic interests (Whitfield 2009). Increasingly, Western donors favour a growing role for the private sector in infrastructure development, supporting the de-risking of private investments rather than financing projects directly.

The decision-making process regarding dams, electricity infrastructure, and the energy mix is therefore conceptualized as one in which national governments seek to secure the cohesion, capacity, and finance required to deliver on their plans. However, to do so they must navigate intersecting political economy dynamics across additional scales of analysis beyond the national level, seeking compatible outcomes domestically and internationally (Putnam 1988; Waterbury 2002; Warner and Zawahri 2012). In the context of late development, governments are invariably dependent to some degree on external support for both the technical expertise and financial resources required for major infrastructure investments. Moreover, in developing countries, where state-building and territorial control remain incomplete (Mamdani 1996; Herbst 2000; Boone 2003), evolving relations between national and sub-national elites also shape the spatial design of infrastructural plans and their distributive impacts. Decision making about electricity infrastructure and, in particular, those related to hydropower projects are therefore the product not just of national politics but also government's ability to find alignment between domestic bargains and dynamics at each of the global, river basin, regional, sub-national, and local levels.

Beyond the national level and its focus on elite politics, and technical and financial capacity, the second level of analysis in the framework concerns the major global powers, and the multilateral agencies on which they exert strong influence. Global actors have been the main source of finance for major infrastructure projects, as well as providing cutting-edge technical expertise in terms of planning, civil, and electro-mechanical works (Collins 1990; Reisner 1993; Sneddon 2015; Brautigam and Hwang 2019). As such, alignments between national governments and these global powers have vitally important implications for governments' ability to mobilize required resources. Over the time period covered in this book, the global balance of power has shifted from the European colonial powers, to Cold War rivalries, to US post-Cold War hegemony, to the subsequent emergence of China as a potential rival to the US. In turn, this shifting global political economy provides opportunities and constraints to national governments due to the changing availability of finance and technical expertise, and the ways in which access to these is embedded in changing norms related to the role of the state and market in development, the energy mix, and dam construction.

The third level of analysis concerns the river basin and how this is embedded within regional political economies and related patterns of trade and security. While global power politics dominated international relations theory during the Cold War, in many instances global powers actually sought to expand their power and influence by taking sides in existing rivalries in what Buzan and Wæver (2009) call 'regional security complexes'. These complexes are geographic clusters within which security issues facing the relevant parties are interdependent and marked by 'durable patterns of amity and enmity' (Buzan and Wæver 2009, p. 45). The importance of these regional complexes has grown in the post-Cold War era with the decline of great power engagement (Katzenstein 2005; Buzan and Wæver 2009). Meanwhile, dams on transboundary rivers inevitably raise sensitive political and legal issues related to the allocation of water both within and between these regional clusters. As such, river basin politics and riparians' ability to utilize a river's waters are shaped not just by the economic, military, and discursive power relations between riparians (Cascão and Zeitoun 2010; Kibaroglu 2017) but also by the ways in which these riparians are embedded within regional power politics.

National governments seeking to build dams also confront complex subnational domestic political dynamics. Dams and other electricity generation projects necessarily create both winners and losers with spatially differentiated impacts by displacing some existing land users, changing water flows, and disrupting livelihoods, while providing new economic and political opportunities for other groups. The fourth level of analysis, therefore, examines the role of subnational political elites. These sub-national elites are analysed with respect to the agrarian class relations and communal hierarchies that shape the potential for subnational actors to negotiate with or to resist state modernization plans (Hechter and Brustein 1980; Boone 2003) and the ways in which these are embedded in particular histories of state-building. In particular, where hierarchical communal and class structures concentrate power over people and resources, sub-national actors are well placed to contest national interventions (Boone 2003). National governments must therefore either bargain with relevant sub-national elites to secure agreement for new projects, or have sufficient power to be able to suppress and disregard these sub-national interests.

The fifth and final level of analysis concerns the local vicinity of electricity projects and the individuals and households whose homes, livelihoods, and cultural attachments are directly affected by siting decisions. The ability of local populations to contest projects or to receive an improved distribution of the costs and benefits of the project depends on their ability to mobilize politically. As such, the salience of local-level resistance is dependent on the broader political system and the space for popular mobilization, and the specific ways in which the locality is embedded within sub-national politics. In contexts in which political mobilization is constrained, resistance may depend on forging links with transnational social movements that are often better placed to exert pressure on those providing financial and technical support for the project (Keck and Sikkink 1998).

This analytical framework offers conceptual novelty in two main ways. The first is to integrate insights regarding the politics of electricity and infrastructure from three literatures, which, despite important links between them, are usually considered separately, namely those on state-led development, dams, and energy transitions. Second, the book integrates insights from comparative politics and international relations to show how multi-scalar processes combined to shape access to the finance and technical capacity the Ethiopian Government required to invest in electricity infrastructure and realize a series of large dam projects; the spatial distribution of these dams across Ethiopia's river basins; the relative influence of technical expertise and political factors in planning and decision making; the impact of dam building on people living in the vicinity and downstream of new projects; and the distribution and use of the hydroelectric power produced.

Methodology

This framework is applied to the Ethiopian case using a process-tracing methodology (George and Bennett 2004; Collier 2011; Bennett and Checkel 2014), which is used to reconstruct the decision-making process on the electricity sector and dams in Ethiopia and the Nile Basin. Process tracing entails the theoretically guided analysis of a sequence of events, with empirical evidence used to assess the explanatory power of competing theoretical propositions. To do so, the analysis employs a range of data generation techniques to triangulate between data sources.

The central focus of analysis in the book is the boom in dam construction undertaken in Ethiopia since the 1990s and the role these hydropower dams play in the electricity sector in the country and beyond. As such, the majority of the analysis focuses on the Ethiopian EPRDF era (1991–2019), although the book also examines the early stages of the subsequent Prosperity Party Government and apparently significant changes within the electricity sector. To conduct this analysis, the book situates contemporary events within an analysis of historical political dynamics, particularly from the early twentieth century when the first Ethiopian dams and electricity generation capacity were installed. Furthermore, the politics of the Nile River is situated within a longer history of Ethiopia's relations with Egypt and other Nile riparians going back many centuries. The end point of the analysis lies in mid-2023, when the final draft of the manuscript was put together. Naturally, given the fast-changing and unpredictable nature of politics in Ethiopia and across the Nile Basin, there is the risk that important changes may have already occurred by the time the book is actually published.

A major data source for the book is more than 100 key informant interviews conducted between June 2018 and March 2020 by all of the authors of the book. These interview respondents include past and present Ethiopian politicians and technocrats in the Ministry of Water and Ethiopian Electric Power, and representatives of the state-owned enterprises involved in infrastructure development. Respondents also include a wide range of Ethiopian and foreign consultants, engineers, and diplomats involved in the planning, negotiation, construction, and operation of Ethiopia's dams and electricity infrastructure. Unfortunately, fieldwork was limited to Ethiopia and, as such, Egyptian and Sudanese perspectives on Ethiopia's dams are based on public statements by state officials and the extensive existing literature. Given the extreme political sensitivities concerning Ethiopia's dams and electricity, all interview respondents have been anonymized to protect their identities.

These interview data are complemented with archival research by Tom Lavers focusing particularly on the numerous dam feasibility studies and river basin studies commissioned as part of the planning process for Ethiopia's dam building over the last century, in the Ministry of Water's library in Addis Ababa, the IMF library in Washington, DC, and the British Library in Boston Spa. Luca Puddu also conducted research in the archives of the Banco di Roma and the Italian Ministry of Foreign Affairs. Finally, these qualitative data were triangulated where appropriate with official data and statistics.

Structure of the Book

The book begins the analysis in Chapter 2 by examining the emergence of Ethiopia's dam-building ambitions across two regimes—the Imperial regime of Haile Selassie, first as regent, then emperor (1916–1974), and the military-Marxist Derg (1974–1991). Despite the initiatives of British and Italian colonialists, the

United States, and the Ethiopian Government itself, a combination of international, river basin, and domestic politics prevented the development of a major dam on the Blue Nile in Ethiopia. Instead, the two regimes' dam building focused on Ethiopia's least advantageous river basins in eastern Ethiopia that were less politically charged—domestically and internationally. Nevertheless, this early dam-building programme established a pattern that has continued through to the present whereby dam building has served the dual purpose of extending the territorial reach of the state and pursuing the economic modernization of the periphery, often at the expense of those living in affected areas.

Chapters 3 and 4 focus on the key political dynamics shaping the EPRDF's developmental ambitions, its efforts to build technocratic capacity to plan and construct large-scale water and electricity infrastructure, and its changing approach to financing these investments. Chapter 3 focuses on the period covering the EPRDF's entry into office in 1991 up to the late 2000s. The new government's initial approach was to commit to state control of key sections of the economy in the face of donor pressure for liberalization and privatization, despite the government's perilous economic position. While the political leadership had high hopes for the electricity sector at this time, its initial plans were constrained by the availability of finance to relatively small dams that avoided the political tensions associated with the Nile. However, a key shift occurred in the early 2000s with a series of political crises that allowed Meles Zenawi to consolidate power, resulting in renewed attempts to build technocratic capacity and to engage strategically with donors willing to finance key infrastructural projects of the 'developmental state'.

Chapter 4 examines a distinct phase beginning from the late 2000s as the government's developmental and infrastructural ambitions further expanded. At this point, the government's strategy for financing its vast infrastructural investments became increasingly risky in embracing commercial loans, while the government also made increased efforts to build technical capacity within Ethiopia. Moreover, the state's longstanding focus on hydropower as a means of meeting the country's electricity needs came to be wrapped within a narrative of the construction of a 'green developmental state', in line with growing global concern about the threat of climate change. Overall, the result was a highly centralized and politically driven decision-making process that bypassed technical expertise in the electricity sector, with politicians pursuing successively larger and more ambitious hydropower projects and accumulating vast debts in the process.

Chapter 5 focuses on the key role played by Salini Impregilo in Ethiopian dam building. While efforts to build technocratic capacity within the Ethiopian state faltered, the government came to rely on Salini—a firm with a longstanding presence in Ethiopia—to carry out its key hydropower projects. The chapter examines three Salini projects: the Legadadi dam (1967–1971) constructed under Haile Selassie; the Tana-Beles project (1986–1992) carried out under the Derg; and Gilgel Gibe cascade (1990s–present) under the EPRDF. The chapter shows that a key factor underpinning Ethiopia's dam-building programme was the emergence of Salini, not only as a capable contractor but also as a trusted partner that remained committed to high-profile and controversial projects such as Gilgel Gibe III and the GERD.

Chapter 6 situates Ethiopia's growing developmental ambitions and dam building within the context of the country's shifting international relations. Given the EPRDF's initially weak position, politically and economically, its early dams, like those of previous regimes, avoided the contentious Blue Nile River, instead focusing primarily on the Gibe-Omo. However, the Nile remained part of the government's long-term ambitions, and Ethiopia initiated efforts to renegotiate the division of the Nile waters and to tackle a collaborative project on the Blue Nile. The ultimate failure of these efforts in the late 2000s after many years of negotiation led the government to change tack. By this point, Ethiopia was no longer in such a weak position politically or economically and the government made the decision to pursue its Blue Nile ambitions unilaterally.

Chapter 7 focuses on the GERD, asking why the government settled on this particular design, which bears little resemblance to previous proposals for the river. While the GERD occupies a site long identified for a Blue Nile dam, the GERD is far larger than any other previous proposal in the basin and occupies the furthest downstream site within Ethiopian territory, unlike past proposals that had prioritized water storage in the Ethiopian highlands. However, technocratic river basin planning has never aligned with actual power relations and patterns of political authority within the basin. The result is that the GERD's design, like that of other dams built in the Nile Basin, is the product not only of technical inputs but also of domestic political priorities and the adversarial nature of basin politics.

For the government, dams were a key part of a political and economic strategy that sought to subsidize industrialization through the provision of low-cost electricity, secure popular acquiescence through electricity access, and generate vital foreign exchange earnings. However, Chapter 8 argues that major increases in generation have, thus far, not translated into the successful realization of these political economic outcomes. The prioritization of generation over transmission and distribution, coordination challenges amidst growing political fragmentation, and the difficulty of negotiating access to external markets have all blunted the ability of Ethiopia's dams to deliver, while a majority of Ethiopians and many industrial users continue to lack reliable access to electricity.

Chapter 9 focuses on the important political changes in 2018–2023 and their implications for Ethiopia's dam building and electricity sector. Mass protests and elite fragmentation led to regime change from within the EPRDF in 2018, with Abiy Ahmed of the Oromo branch of the ruling party displacing the once dominant Tigrayan People's Liberation Front (TPLF). The resulting political upheaval coincided with a growing debt crisis to produce a fundamental change in the 'developmental state' model pursued under the EPRDF and its approach to the electricity sector. In particular, the government, amidst strong donor pressure, agreed to the liberalization of the electricity sector and the promotion of private sector investment in generation. This, in turn, has necessitated a shift in future plans for Ethiopia's energy mix. Donors have been selective in providing guarantees for investors, promoting renewable energy projects but refusing to do so for further hydropower investments. Consequently, the GERD and Koysha are the final two megaprojects in the EPRDF's dams boom, creeping slowly towards completion amidst financial challenges and tense international negotiations regarding the GERD's eventual operation.

Finally, Chapter 10 concludes by reflecting on the implications of Ethiopia's dams boom for recent debates about dam resurgence, state-led development, and renewable energy transitions. Despite the many economic and social achievements of the EPRDF Government, the book's analysis of Ethiopia's dam building highlights significant limitations of its state-led infrastructure model. While the centralization of political power was a vital means of overcoming past political, financial, and technical barriers to dam building, it also often meant the marginalization of technical expertise in decision making that undermined planning processes. Moreover, the vast ambitions of the political elite resulted in state indebtedness and reconciliation with the World Bank and other pro-market institutions, leading to a turn away from the state-led model of the past.

2

Modernization, State-Building, and the Hydraulic Mission in Imperial and Revolutionary Ethiopia

Tom Lavers

Ethiopia has frequently been proclaimed the 'Water Tower of Africa'.[1] This phrase is in part a recognition that Ethiopia is somewhat unusual in being the upstream country on every major river within its borders. However, the phrase also harbours resentment at Ethiopia's inability to capitalize on these abundant water resources, despite the provision of water to all Ethiopia's neighbours. Ever since the construction of the original Aba Samuel dam in 1912 to power the palace of Emperor Menelik II in Addis Ababa, dams have been seen as key tools for Ethiopia's modernization and development, while electricity has been equated with hydropower. For Ethiopia's rulers, the attraction of dams lies both in their symbolic value as manifestations of Ethiopia's modernization and in their potential economic contribution through electrification, irrigation, and industrialization.

This chapter considers Ethiopia's dam-building ambitions across two regimes—the Imperial regime of Haile Selassie, first as regent and then emperor (1916–1974), and the military-Marxist Derg regime under Mengistu Hailemariam (1974–1991). It was in this period that Ethiopia launched its hydraulic mission, namely 'the strong conviction that the state should develop hydraulic infrastructure to capture as much water as possible for human uses' (Wester et al. 2009, p. 75). The chapter examines why the two regimes' common ambition of building dams to expand the reach of the state and transform the economy led to a pattern of dam construction dominated by Ethiopia's least advantageous river basins. In contrast, river basins with the most hydroelectric potential—the Blue Nile and the Omo—remained relatively untapped until after the fall of the Derg. Despite much writing on the broader Nile Basin, there has been relatively little attention to Ethiopia's dam building in this period (but see Waterbury 2002;

[1] A phrase used by Emperor Haile Selassie (Selassie 2011, p. 576) and, according to some, originally attributed to him (Carr 2017).

Dams, Power, and the Politics of Ethiopia's Renaissance. Tom Lavers et al., Oxford University Press. © Tom Lavers (2024).
DOI: 10.1093/oso/9780192871213.003.0002

Arsano 2007a) and no attempt to explain the spatial variation of dam construction within Ethiopia. This chapter addresses this gap.

The argument developed is that the spatial variation in Ethiopia's historical dam building can be understood as the interplay between technical expertise and the feasibility of different engineering solutions, on the one hand, and the intersection of political processes across five levels of analysis from the global to the local, on the other. Although Haile Selassie's government and the Derg were inspired by sharply divergent ideologies, they shared a common desire to modernize Ethiopia, with water infrastructure playing a central symbolic and material role. Yet, both regimes faced similar technological challenges, and international and domestic political economy constraints that limited dam building to comparatively low potential sites and, particularly, prevented exploitation of the river with the greatest hydropower potential—the Blue Nile.

As a late-developing country, Ethiopian dam building necessitated external financial and technological support. However, Ethiopia's access to international support was constrained by its positioning within regional security dynamics within the Horn of Africa and its links to the Middle East. A consistent theme throughout the twentieth century was that Ethiopia was seen by the major global powers of the day as a lower geo-strategic priority than its Nile riparian, Egypt. The result was that the UK, the US, and the Union of Soviet Socialist Republics (USSR) prioritized Egyptian use of the Nile waters and ultimately withheld the financial and technical support that would have been required for Ethiopia to develop a major Nile dam. Ethiopia's dam building therefore focused on other, less advantageous river basins that faced lesser transboundary political barriers. Sub-national politics also played an important role in shaping the pattern of dam and irrigation development. Internal political divisions undermined an early attempt to build a dam on the Blue Nile, while both Haile Selassie and the Derg tended to avoid large-scale infrastructure development that would cause major disruption to social structure in the highland core. Instead, a persistent feature of the hydraulic mission has been an intertwined process by which the state extended its territorial reach through infrastructure development and economic modernization that further marginalized those living in the periphery.

While Ethiopia's ambitions on the Blue Nile went unfulfilled in this period, downstream riparians Egypt and Sudan were more successful in leveraging their important positions on the Red Sea and in Middle East politics to secure the international finance and expertise required for their own hydraulic missions. However, their decision making was also shaped by the wave of independence following World War II. In a pattern that has continued thereafter across the basin, both Egypt and Sudan built dams that focused on maximizing control over the Nile waters *within their own borders*. In doing so, both countries turned their backs on basin-wide, cooperative approaches to managing the Nile waters.

The chapter begins with an overview of Ethiopia's river basins, their potential for hydroelectricity and irrigation, and how this physical geography maps onto the history of Ethiopian state formation. The story of Ethiopian dam building, meanwhile, begins with the unrealized ambitions of British colonialists to build a dam on the Blue Nile. The failure to secure support for a dam on the Blue Nile led the Ethiopian Imperial Government to turn first to the modernization of the Awash Basin, before another stalled attempt to dam the Blue Nile with US support during the Cold War. Finally, the chapter discusses the post-revolutionary dam-building efforts. Despite major international and domestic political realignments, the Derg was no better placed to tackle the hydraulic development of the major river basins than the emperor.

Water, State-Building, and Modernization in Imperial Ethiopia

Ethiopia's topography comprises a highland plateau in the centre of the country, which is bifurcated by the Rift Valley (see Figure 2.1). The major rivers flow from these highlands—where the vast majority of the rain falls and where most of the Ethiopian population resides—to the lowland periphery in the west, south, and east. Rainfall is far greater in the west of the country, with the result that those rivers with catchment areas in the west—the Blue Nile, or *Abay* as it is known in Ethiopia, Baro-Akobo, and Omo—contain the vast majority of Ethiopia's waters (see Table 2.1). Various Nile tributaries flow from the western highlands towards the Sudanese border, of which the main ones are the Blue Nile itself, the Tekeze (which becomes the Atbara in Sudan), and the Baro-Akobo (Sobat), a tributary of the White Nile. The Omo-Gibe River flows from Jimma in the southwestern highlands southwards into Lake Turkana on the border with Kenya; and the Wabe Shabele flows from Bale and Haraghe in central and eastern Ethiopia into Somalia. The Awash is the only major internal river, since it disappears through evaporation and seepage in Afar region before crossing the border and has consequently been described as 'the most Ethiopian' of rivers because 'it does not carry Ethiopian soil outside the country' (Zewde 2008a, p. 120).[2]

The flow of these rivers is highly seasonal, dictated by the rainy seasons in the highlands, which in most of the country comprise a short rainy season in March to April (*belg*) and a main rainy season in June to September (*meher*), with relatively little rainfall outside these periods. There is a widespread perception that these rains are becoming increasingly unreliable, with *belg* rains, in particular, frequently failing altogether or arriving late and merging with the *meher* rains.

Over the past century, the idea that these rivers constitute a vital resource for national development, and that the only way of realizing this potential is through

[2] The Awash is nonetheless believed to re-charge important groundwater sources in Djibouti.

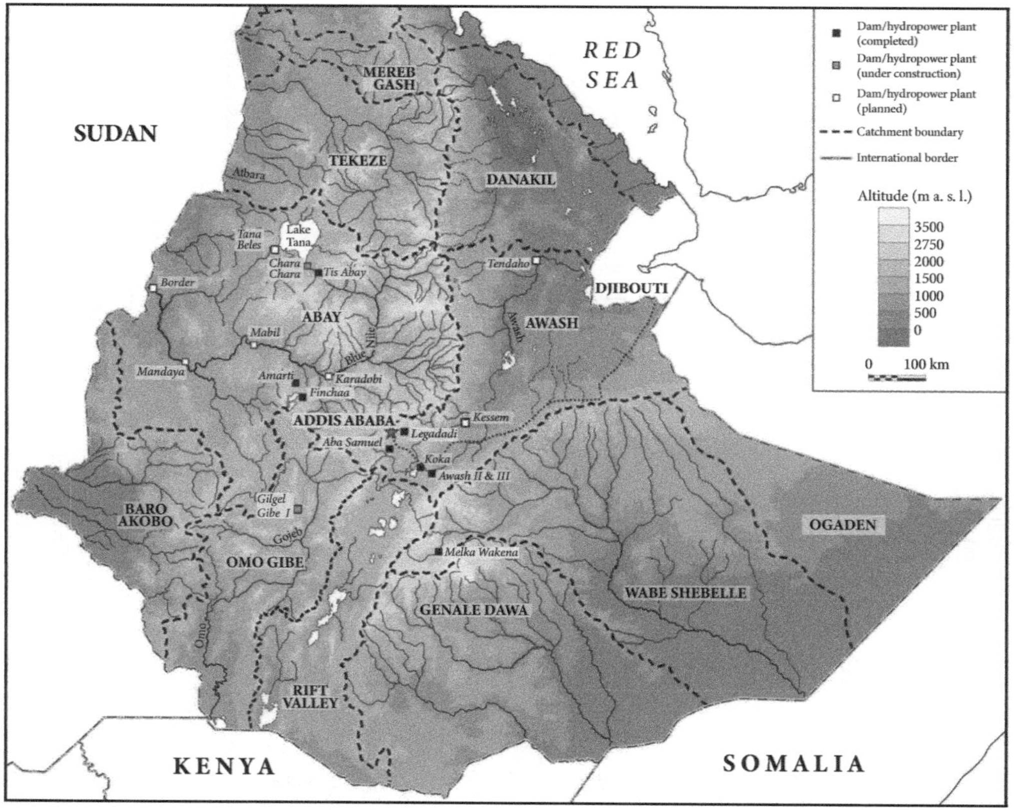

Figure 2.1 Ethiopia's river basins and dams pursued before 1991

Source: Author and Manchester Cartographic Unit.

Table 2.1 Ethiopia's river basins

Basin	Catchment area		Annual discharge	
	km^2	%	Billion m^3	%
Blue Nile	199,812	18	54	43
Baro-Akobo	74,102	7	23	19
Omo-Gibe	78,200	7	17	15
Tekeze	90,000	8	8	6
Genale-Dawa	171,050	15	6	5
Rift Valley Lakes	52,740	5	6	5
Awash	112,700	10	5	4
Wabe Shebele	200,214	18	3	3
Danakil	74,002	7	1	1
Mereb	5,900	1	1	0
Ogaden	77,100	7	0	0

Data source: Abtew and Dessu (2018, p. 40)

dams and the control of the waters, has become deeply engrained. This potential, however, varies between river basins. In terms of hydropower, the Blue Nile and Omo Rivers are the most important, with large rivers descending through the sort of steep, narrow gorges that attract the attention of dam engineers. While the Tekeze also has very suitable topography, its more limited water flow means that hydropower potential is more modest (Blackmore and Whittington 2008). There is considerable potential for irrigation along the various Blue Nile tributaries flowing into its source, Lake Tana, and the main river. However, along the Blue Nile's main course steep gorges provide few options for irrigation. The Omo floodplains after the river has descended the escarpment into the lowlands, on the other hand, have attracted considerable interest in terms of irrigation potential. Hydroelectric potential is quite limited in the Awash Basin. The headwaters of the Awash where rivers descend into the Rift Valley provide the required head for hydropower, yet here water flow is limited.[3] In contrast, the water flow is larger in the relatively flat Rift Valley which does not provide sufficient head. However, the Awash is perhaps the most suited to irrigation development (Halcrow 1989). Given the seasonality and annual variability of water flow in all these river basins, year-round irrigation and hydropower production require dams to regulate water flows. Historically, these rivers have also played a key role in maintaining downstream soil fertility through flooding and the deposit of sediment both in Ethiopia and beyond. However, from the perspective of dam engineers, heavy sedimentation presents a

[3] The head, along with the water flow, is one of the key factors shaping the energy production potential of a dam. Head is the difference in water elevation between the reservoir level and the turbines and therefore dependent on the height of the dam and the drop in altitude of the existing watercourse.

major challenge, threatening rapid reduction in water storage and hydroelectric generation capacity.

The rivers with by far the greatest international significance are those that feed into the Nile. In total it is estimated that Ethiopia provides 86 per cent of the waters of the Nile as measured at Aswan in Egypt, with the Blue Nile the most important with 59 per cent, followed by the Baro-Akobo with 14 per cent and Tekeze 13 per cent (Ethiopian Technical Experts 1996, p. 67). The Equatorial Lakes region combined only contributes 14 per cent of the Nile waters due to the vast water losses through evaporation in the Sudd.

The physical geography of Ethiopia's rivers closely maps onto the country's political and human geography, and the particular pattern of state-building that shaped the country (Donham 2002). The Ethiopian state originates in the north of contemporary Ethiopia—principally Tigray, Eritrea, Wollo, Begemder, and Gojjam provinces (see Figure 2.2)—several thousand years ago. Over the centuries, the territory administered by Ethiopian polities ebbed and flowed, while the centre of power gradually shifted to the south, with the expansion of the Orthodox Church and the Amharic language central to the state-building project. Land grants to the nobility were the basis of state power, with the emperor ruling through a landed nobility granted the power to extract tax and tribute from peasants accessing land through *rist*, a descent-based tenure system (Hoben 1973; Rahmato 1984).

However, it was not until the period of the European Scramble for Africa at the end of the nineteenth century that the Ethiopian state became increasingly centralized under Emperor Menelik II, enabling a rapid expansion into the southern highlands and lowland periphery, stopping only when it encountered European colonialists in Sudan, Kenya, and Somalia, and creating something like Ethiopia's contemporary borders. Southern highlands were gradually pacified and incorporated through land grants to military leaders as reward for service, while provincial boundaries were drawn so as to administer (loosely speaking) lowland peripheries from an administrative centre in the highlands, ignoring the boundaries between ethnic groups, which were divided between provinces. Practically, the Ethiopian state's main intervention into many lowland areas continued to be periodic raids for slaves and ivory. Meanwhile, the highland political elite discriminated against lowland populations based on their supposed inferiority in race, culture, language, and livelihoods (Young 1999; Garretson 2002; James 2002a; Lavers 2016). This gave rise to a loose distinction between a highland core in the north, a highland periphery in the southern highlands, and a lowland periphery in the west, south, and east (Markakis 2011). There were also clear differences in population density, between densely populated highlands where a landed elite extracted an agrarian surplus from the peasantry, to sparsely populated lowland peripheries in the west, south, and east where the population practised various forms of pastoralism and shifting cultivation (Figure 2.3).

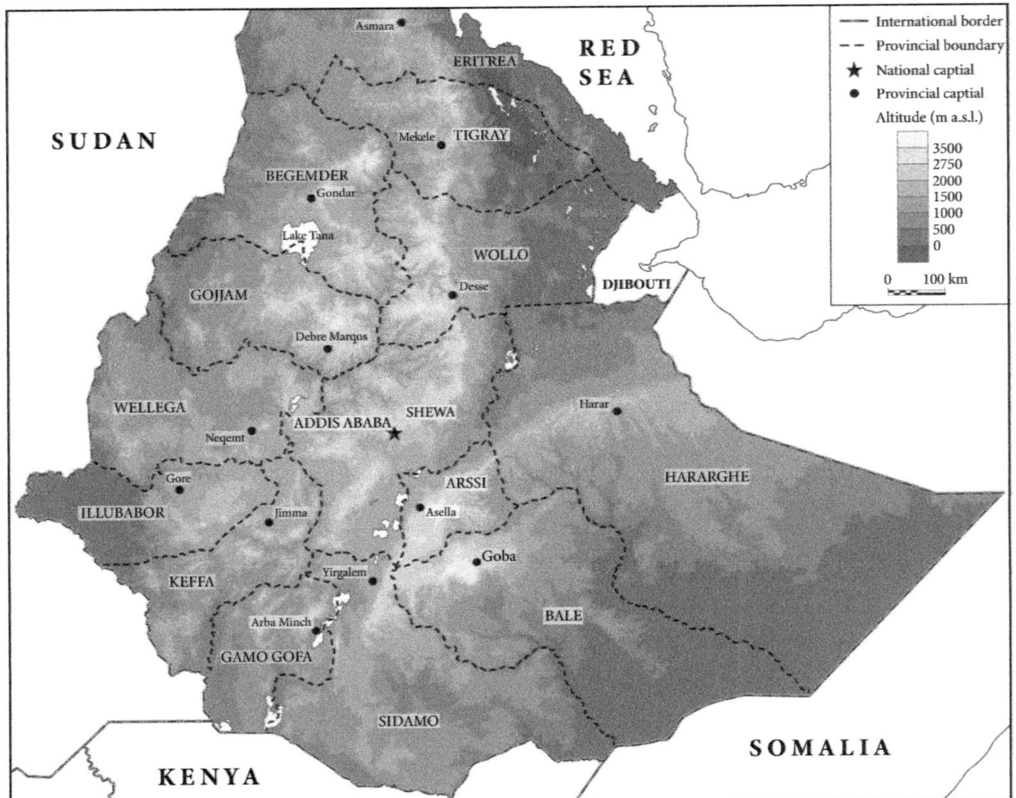

Figure 2.2 Ethiopia's topography and provinces (approximately 1963–1987)

Source: Author and Manchester Cartographic Unit.

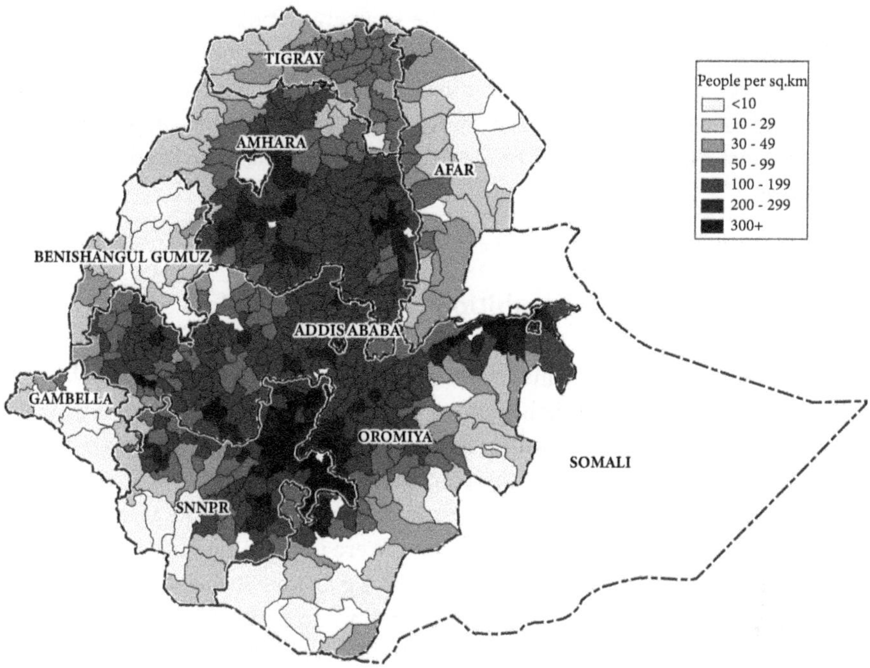

Figure 2.3 Population density by *wereda*
Data source: CSA (2008a).
Note: No data are available for Somali region.

The threat of European colonialism and the growing recognition that Ethiopia had fallen behind the most advanced economic powers prompted Menelik and then Haile Selassie to pursue projects to modernize Ethiopia through political reform, state-building, and economic development. However, as with any mediated state, dependent on a landed elite, the Imperial regime faced the inherent challenge that modernization risked undermining its own political power (Skocpol 1979; Waldner 1999). Following the brief Italian occupation (1936–1941), Haile Selassie created a state bureaucracy, largely by co-opting the landed elite into positions as ministers and civil servants. At this time, there was also a push to modernize the economy by attracting foreign investment in large-scale agriculture and some industry. However, the emperor's unwillingness to pursue land reform, which would directly threaten the political and economic basis of the landed elite and the Imperial state, meant directing agricultural investment to the lowland periphery, where the land use of pastoralists and shifting cultivators could more easily be ignored (Ashami 1985).

As a result of both hydrology—with the main dam sites located in the gorges descending from the highlands—and politics—with the need to avoid disrupting the existing political order in the highlands—the main focus of dam building for hydropower and irrigation was on the sparsely populated lowland periphery. The result is that populations that were only incorporated into Ethiopia relatively recently at the end of the nineteenth century, and who have tended to be marginalized and stigmatized by Ethiopia's state-building project, tend to be those most directly affected by dams, reservoirs, and associated plantation agriculture.

Colonial Ambitions on the Blue Nile

The first attempts to build dams in Ethiopia were largely undertaken by British colonialists in the early twentieth century. British engineers were focused on controlling the entirety of the Nile waters for the benefit of irrigated cotton agriculture in Egypt and Sudan, ignoring Ethiopian sovereignty or interests. In response, Ethiopia under Haile Selassie began to explore options to build its own Blue Nile dam with US support. However, these efforts were undermined by internal rivalries and, just when a negotiated agreement with Egypt and Sudan seemed possible, the Italian invasion in 1936. Ultimately the failure to secure alignment between political dynamics at global, river basin, national, and sub-national levels meant that these dam ambitions went unfulfilled before World War II.

The Nile is Egypt's only renewable source of freshwater.[4] Although the Nile's exact hydrology was unknown until relatively recently, Egypt and Ethiopia have long been aware that Ethiopia is the main source of the Nile waters on which Egypt is so dependent. Moreover, as Erlich (2002) lays out, Egypt and Ethiopia have been connected since the fourth century AD by the ties between the Ethiopian Orthodox Church and the Egyptian Coptic Church of Alexandria. The Coptic Church provided the first Egyptian *abun*—the head of the Ethiopian Church—in 333 AD and continued to do so until the 1950s, with the result that Ethiopia became reliant on the Egyptian Coptic Church for its Christian state-building project (Erlich 2002). Consequently, the Nile and Church links became intertwined in relations between the two countries. It was widely believed in Egypt that Ethiopia had the ability to divert the Nile, and periodic droughts leading to reduced flow of the Nile were often attributed to Ethiopian interference (Collins 1990; Erlich 2002). Indeed, this was a myth that the Ethiopians and the Egyptian Copts were happy to propagate as a means of increasing their leverage with Egypt's Islamic leaders (McCann 1981). For Egyptians, the Nile was considered a gift, albeit dependence on the Nile waters created a set of 'anxieties and myths that, in themselves, went to the core of the Egyptian soul' (Erlich 2002, p. 4). In contrast, for Ethiopia the river offered

[4] Aquifers under the western desert are estimated to contain about 600 years of the Nile's flow, but this deposit is the result of rainfall thousands of years ago that cannot be recharged and is therefore non-renewable (Sims 2015, pp. 40–41).

little potential for irrigation and presented a major barrier to transportation and communication. Instead, for the Ethiopians the Nile was mainly of strategic use as 'their best card in their desire to retain their most important connection with the Middle East' (Erlich 2002, p. 8).

From the nineteenth century there were various attempts by Egypt and Britain, on Egypt's behalf, to control the Blue Nile for irrigated cotton production in Egypt. Under Muhammed Ali (1805–1849), Egypt began to limit its historical dependence on the Nile floods by constructing a network of dams, barrages, and canals, enabling the introduction of cotton as a cash crop. Yet, Egypt's dependence on the Nile led to an expansion of its desire to control the river's flow. In 1820–1821 Muhammed Ali's army conquered much of Sudan and later founded Khartoum, bringing most of the White Nile Valley under Egyptian rule (Erlich 2002). Ismail, Muhammed Ali's grandson, went further, occupying much of contemporary Eritrea and Harar in what is now eastern Ethiopia. Ismail's pretentions to control the whole of the Nile Valley up to Lake Tana ended, however, when the Egyptians were defeated by Ethiopia in Eritrea in 1875–1876, a defeat that precipitated Egyptian colonization by the British (Erlich 2002; Verhoeven 2015).

Three European colonial powers—the British, Italians, and French—all harboured ambitions regarding Ethiopia at the end of the nineteenth and early twentieth century. Ethiopia was of particular geo-strategic importance once the Suez Canal opened in 1869 as a result of its Red Sea coastline and ports in Eritrea, in addition to providing the source of the Nile and potential influence over the river's flow. Italy failed in its first attempt to conquer Ethiopia as a result of military defeat by Menelik's army at the Battle of Adwa in 1896. Ethiopia agreed to cede Eritrea to Italy, but Italy retained its interest in Ethiopia, which was key to linking its colonies in Eritrea and Somalia. Meanwhile, the French occupied what is now Djibouti and focused its attention on the railway concession from Djibouti to Addis Ababa built from 1897 to 1917. For the British, the main concern was to ensure that the French were kept out of the Nile headwaters. Following the British occupation of Egypt in 1882 to secure control of the Suez Canal, the British authorities launched a series of studies of the Nile Valley with the aim of developing Egypt's cotton industry. Indeed, protecting and enhancing the Nile's flow to Egypt was a major driver of British colonialism in East Africa, leading to the occupation of the Sudan in 1898–1899 (Collins 1990; Verhoeven 2015). The British also established a trading post in Gambella in Ethiopia, attempting to use the White Nile as a trading route (Collins 1990; Zewde 2008b).

Having built the first Aswan Dam in Egypt in support of cotton agriculture in 1902, the British colonial authorities turned their attention to enhancing the flow of the Nile through water projects upstream. The initial focus was on the White Nile, with proposals to increase storage at Lake Albert in Uganda and reduce evaporation in Sudan's Sudd with the Jonglei Canal (Collins 1990). However, attention soon turned to Ethiopia's Blue Nile. The British dispatched an envoy to Ethiopia, and Menelik II signed a 1902 treaty regarding the border between Ethiopia and Sudan. Article III of the treaty, however, has resulted in longstanding controversy. While the English version states Menelik's agreement not to interfere with the flow of the Nile without British consent, the Amharic version apparently differs, stating merely that the Nile waters could not be 'completely stopped' (Abtew and Dessu 2018, p. 16; McCann 1981; Zewde 1991; Erlich 2002).

Menelik consented to initial studies conducted by British engineers for the colonial-era Egyptian Irrigation Service. A study by Dupuis (1904) focused on exploiting Lake Tana as a natural reservoir in the cool Ethiopian highlands, thereby minimizing evaporation, and maximizing and regulating the flow to Egypt and Sudan. There was no consideration of irrigation or hydropower potential in Ethiopia. Meanwhile, the study doubted the viability of dams along the Blue Nile gorge itself because of the heavy sedimentation that would quickly render the dams useless (Garstin 1904). The study also seems to have been the first to propose digging a tunnel that would release water from Lake Tana into another Nile tributary, in this case the Rahad, albeit this was dismissed as prohibitively expensive and with little benefit (Dupuis 1904, p. 24). Ultimately, however, Menelik's incapacitation after a stroke in 1906 and the internal struggle over succession prevented Ethiopian negotiation over the project (Collins 1990; Zewde 1991; Erlich 2002). Instead, the British, French, and Italians signed a 1906 agreement that divided Ethiopia into spheres of influence with western Ethiopia, including Lake Tana and the Blue Nile, recognized by the Europeans as a sphere of British influence.

The importance of enhancing the flow and reliability of the Nile grew in the early twentieth century with booming demand for cotton, leading to a series of agreements that completely disregarded Ethiopian sovereignty and interests, despite Ethiopia's 1923 admission into the League of Nations. The 1925 agreement between Britain and Mussolini's Italy acknowledged Ethiopia as an Italian sphere of influence in exchange for Italian support for Britain to build the Lake Tana Dam (Zewde 1991; Erlich 2002, p. 82). Meanwhile, the Egyptian declaration of independence in 1922 under British oversight meant growing contestation between Egypt and colonial Sudan over the Nile waters. The British built the Sennar Dam in 1926 to supply water for Sudan's Gezira irrigation scheme (Collins 1990; Verhoeven 2015). However, colonial Sudan's water use was hotly contested by Egypt, whose economy remained dominated by unprocessed cotton, despite modest industrialization efforts (Waterbury 1983). The result was the 1929 Egyptian-Sudanese Water Agreement that ignored Ethiopia and other upstream riparians and heavily favoured Egypt in its division of the Nile waters (Collins 1990).

Further missions by Egyptian and Sudanese colonial representatives in 1916 and 1920–1921 visited Lake Tana, with a view to regulating 'the Nile in the joint interests of Egypt and the Sudan' (Grabham and Black 1925, p. xi). The study took detailed measurements that for the first time highlighted the importance of the

Blue Nile in the total Nile flow (Erlich 2002). These studies again proposed constructing a barrage at the mouth of Lake Tana to regulate the flow of the Blue Nile (Grabham and Black 1925).[5] Meanwhile, the British offered Ethiopia rental fees for water rights and territory in exchange for a deal on the dam (McCann 1981). Ethiopian leaders were—rightly—concerned about European ambitions on Ethiopia, as well as the prospect that a dam that raised the height of the lake to maximize storage would flood important Orthodox monasteries located on islands in the Lake (Grabham and Black 1925; McCann 1981). Ras Tafari Mekonnen, then regent and heir to Empress Zewditu (1916–1930), also feared that the British scheme would strengthen the position of the powerful leaders of Begemder and Gojjam provinces—contenders for the throne. The Ethiopian response was to engage with the British but to delay and play for time (McCann 1981). Grabham and Black (1925, p. 31) also raised the possibility of diverting water from Lake Tana through a tunnel into the Dinder or Beles Rivers, rather than the Rahad, but like Dupuis discounted this as being too expensive and of little benefit.

In the face of growing European encroachment, Ras Tafari sought to seize the initiative. As a late-developing country, Ethiopia required external finance and expertise to tackle a dam and approached the US Government in 1927 to request assistance to develop the Nile to the benefit of Ethiopia, while tying the key provinces of Gojjam and Begemdir to Addis Ababa through infrastructural development. The result was a 1931 study produced by JG White Engineering Corporation. As with the British-sponsored studies, the proposal centred on a barrage at Lake Tana. While the British investigations appear to have taken little interest in the possibility of using the dam to benefit Ethiopian development, the JG White study did so, proposing a dam that would maintain Lake Tana at its maximum annual height, to avoid flooding important Orthodox monasteries, as well as developing small hydropower projects downstream at the Tis Isat Falls. Yet Ethiopia remained in the midst of the extended succession struggle that followed Menelik's death. While Ras Tafari was keen to pursue the project, it was resisted by Ras Gugsa of Begemdir and Ras Hailu of Gojjam—the powerful governors of the two provinces in which Lake Tana sat (McCann 1981; Collins 1990; Zewde 1991). The regent lacked the power to impose his plans for a dam and the project stalled.

It was not until the military defeat of Ras Gugsa in 1930, shortly followed by the death of Empress Zewditu, that Ras Tafari was crowned Emperor Haile Selassie (Zewde 1991). Having removed an influential competitor and centralized power, Haile Selassie was now free to pursue the Lake Tana scheme and follow-up studies were conducted by JG White in 1931–1934. However, by this time the Great

[5] While the early proposals all focused on Lake Tana, other options were periodically considered. Major Cheesman speculated on two potential dam sites on the Blue Nile itself (Cheesman 1936, pp. 295, 360–361). The first was probably the Karadobi site and another near the Sudanese border just upstream from the site of the Grand Ethiopian Renaissance Dam (USBR 1964, p. 9).

Depression had contributed to falling cotton prices, while the 1929 Egypt–Sudan water agreement had guaranteed Sudan a share of the Nile waters, removing the British Empire's sense of urgency for upstream storage and regulation (McCann 1981). Britain opted to delay discussion of the dam and failed to attend a planned conference in 1935. The invasion of Ethiopia by Mussolini's Italy in October 1935 meant that Ethiopian and colonial ambitions to dam the Blue Nile remained unfulfilled.

Modernization and State-Building in the Awash Valley

As discussed below, securing alignment between international and domestic politics for a Blue Nile dam was no easier after Haile Selassie returned to the throne following the Italians' expulsion in 1941. However, Haile Selassie's attempts to modernize the Ethiopian state and economy necessitated investment in electricity generation and agricultural development. The result was that Imperial Ethiopia switched its priorities from the politically charged Blue Nile to the more straightforward challenge of developing the internal Awash River. The government sought foreign support to produce hydropower and expand irrigated agriculture along the Addis–Djibouti railway that runs through much of the river basin as part of an intertwined project of state-building and economic modernization.

Over the following three decades, Haile Selassie pursued a series of reforms to modernize the country and strengthen its independent status, expanding the bureaucracy and promoting economic development. In terms of foreign policy, the emperor sought to develop relations with a wide range of key countries, albeit the main focus was an alliance with the US as counterweight to the British colonial presence all around Ethiopia (Clapham 1988; Patman 2009). From the US perspective, Ethiopia was seen as a key anchor state in the Cold War rivalry with the USSR (Verhoeven and Woldemariam 2022). Links with the US were consolidated by providing access to the strategic Kagnew communications base in Eritrea and by sending Ethiopian troops to fight in the Korean War. Ethiopia also became the first African member of the World Bank and first recipient of support on the continent in an era in which the World Bank was the main financer of infrastructure, including dams. While Ethiopia allied to the west, the USSR came to support rival regimes in Egypt (following Nasser's rise to power) and Somalia, particularly after Siad Barré seized power in 1969 (Patman 2009).

While the Blue Nile had dominated plans before the war and would become a major focus for Haile Selassie afterwards, it was the Awash Basin that was the main focus of Ethiopia's dam building in this period. The Awash offered advantages over other river basins, many of these related to technical feasibility. While other river basins, such as the Baro and Omo, offer much greater potential for hydropower production, they are located further away from the economic centre and the main centres of demand for electricity—Addis Ababa and the string of towns located at the stations on the Djibouti railway (Figure 2.4). Developing sites further afield would require more challenging engineering and much greater investment in transmission lines (Waterbury 2002). Yet Ethiopia's demand for electricity in the 1950s and 1960s was itself modest and could be met by a series of small hydroelectric plants on the nearby Awash. Moreover, the Awash is perhaps the most favourable basin to the development of irrigated agriculture (FAO 1965), providing the possibility of agricultural commercialization and reliable transport on the Ethio-Djibouti railway—either to the main domestic market in Addis or for export. Multipurpose dams could regulate the water flow, providing year-round water for large-scale irrigated agriculture.

Development of the Awash was also favoured by political factors. As the only river internal to Ethiopia, it avoided the transboundary challenges and objections from riparians that would dominate negotiation regarding the Nile and prevent Ethiopia's access to international finance and technical expertise. Moreover, though the Upper and Middle Awash Valley are situated relatively close to Addis Ababa, in this early post-war period, much of this lowland area was avoided by highlanders as a result of malaria and the presence of supposedly 'backward' pastoralists (Kloos 1982). For the most part, the Awash Valley lacked the powerful sub-national elites that had earlier resisted a dam at Lake Tana. The result was that Imperial efforts focused on developing this 'near periphery' where the valley offered great potential for an intertwined project of state-building and economic modernization.

The potential for irrigated agriculture and hydropower in the Awash Basin was initially explored during the Italian occupation. Societa Agricoltura Industriale nel Etiopia (SAIDE) constructed a 1,600-hectare (ha) sugar plantation, with unrealized plans for a sugar factory to follow (Zewde 2008a). Furthermore, the Italians made plans for and began construction of a small hydropower dam at Koka (Last 1958). The Imperial Government's transformation of the river basin sought to mobilize foreign investment and support. The first step in this direction was the Wenji-Shoa sugar factory and 5,000-ha plantation as a joint venture with Dutch firm HVA (Handelsvereeniging Amsterdam) in 1954 (Zewde 2008a). Following an Ethiopian Government request, the US Bureau of Reclamation (USBR) was then commissioned to carry out a study of the topography and hydrology of the Awash, particularly focused on the construction of a larger Koka Dam. At the time, the Bureau was just beginning its international strategy and, in doing so, was deeply embedded in Cold War politics and the advancement of US interests around the globe (Sneddon 2015). The close relations between the Imperial Government and the US, and the Americans' Cold War strategy in the Horn, were key to securing technical support from the Bureau.

In 1957 construction of the first dam on the Awash began. The 43-MW Koka Dam was completed in 1960 and placed under the recently created (1956)

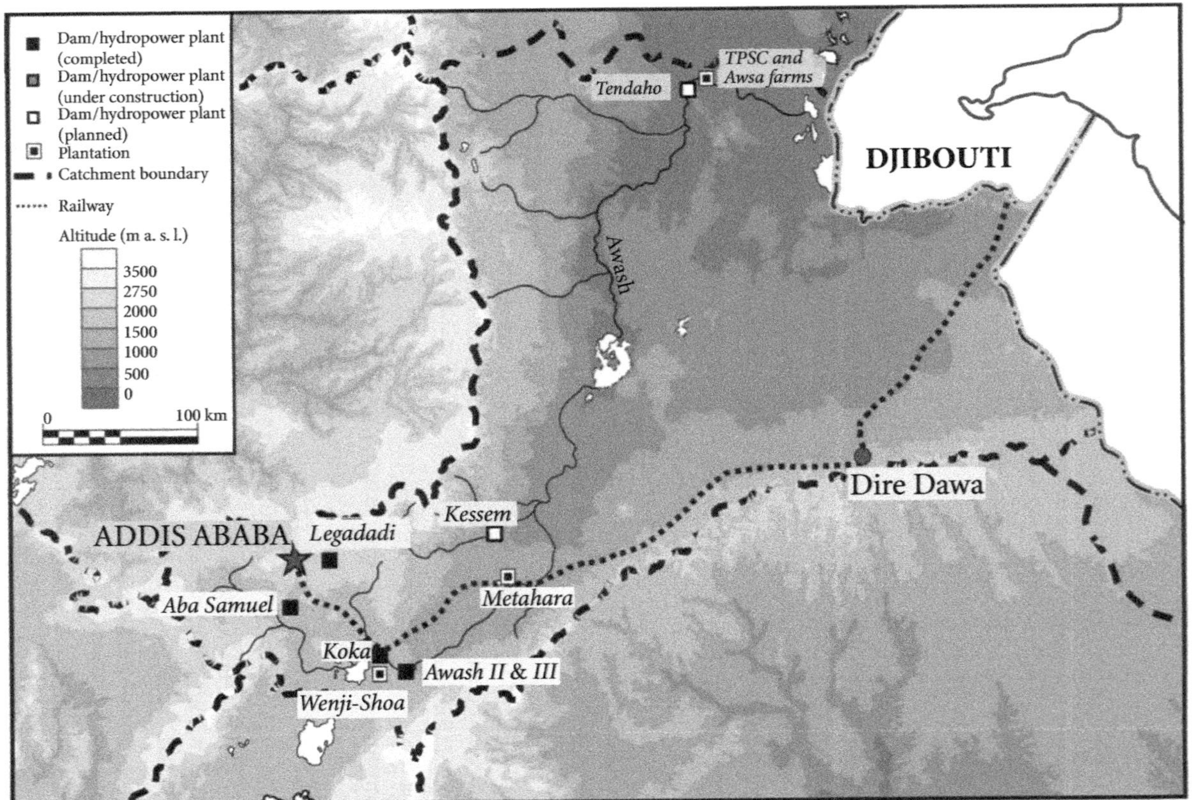

Figure 2.4 Dams and main agricultural projects in the Awash Basin

Source: Author and Manchester Cartographic Unit.

state-owned Ethiopia Electric Light and Power Authority (EELPA). Rather than US support, however, it was Italian reparations for the occupation of Ethiopia that were used to finance dam construction, built by Italian firm Imprese Italiane all'Estero (Last 1958; see Chapter 5). Although small by later standards, the Koka Dam was at the time considered a major dam and doubled the country's existing generation capacity. Moreover, Emperor Haile Selassie's opening speech was an opportunity to emphasize the significance of Koka as a first step in developing the country's water resources:

> It is the duty and privilege of this generation and of posterity to conserve and develop these precious [water] resources. To fail to do so will be to fail in our God-given responsibility... This project is but the first step in a similar programme We have in mind for the other water courses of Our Empire, such as the Nile with its volume and potentialities so vastly greater, as well as the Baro the Sobat, the Akobo and the Webi Shebeli. (Haile Selassie 1958)

Koka was always intended as the regulator dam for a cascade of hydropower projects, with the World Bank-funded 32-MW Awash II (1966) and Awash III dams (1974) following afterwards. The planned fourth dam in the cascade, however, was never realized. As well as producing electricity for Addis Ababa and Dire Dawa—for a long time Ethiopia's second largest city—the regulation provided by the dams enabled further irrigated agricultural concessions downstream (Last 1958; Nicol 2000). Also built in this period was the Legadadi Dam (1964–1970) on the Akaki River, part of the Awash Basin, to provide water for Addis Ababa. While only a small water storage dam, it is, nonetheless, noteworthy as the first dam in Ethiopia to be built by Salini Costruttori[6] and designed by Studio Pietrangeli, a team that would come to fundamentally shape Ethiopia's dam building in subsequent decades (see Chapter 5).

During the 1960s, plans to develop commercial agriculture in the basin expanded. British company Mitchell Cotts, inspired by Sudan's Gezira scheme and backed by the British authorities, approached the government to establish cotton production in the Awash (Ashami 1985; Fantini and Puddu 2016). The resulting Tendaho Plantation Share Company (TPSC) was another joint venture with the government that was granted 18,000 ha in the lower Awash which began operations in 1961 (Ashami 1985). The Imperial Government, with support from the United Nations' Food and Agriculture Organization (FAO), subsequently created the Awash Valley Authority (AVA) in 1962, modelled on the United States' Tennessee Valley Authority, tasked with developing irrigation and commercial agriculture. The government claimed all lands not covered by *rist* tenure as state

[6] Salini Costruttori took over Impregilo in 2012 to form Salini Impregilo. The firm re-branded itself in 2020 as WeBuild.

domain under the control of the AVA, which granted concessions to a series of smaller projects along the river (Ashami 1985; Nicol 2000). Meanwhile, a 1965 study of the basin by the FAO proposed dams at Kessem and Tendaho to make available an additional 163,000 ha of irrigated land (FAO 1965, p. 15). Although the dams would be multipurpose, the small hydroelectric element was a secondary concern to irrigation. These plans were not realized during the Imperial era; however, commercial agriculture did expand with the opening of HVA's Metahara 4,500-ha plantation and sugar factory downstream in 1970 alongside a number of other smaller commercial farms (Kloos 1982).

As noted above, the development of the Awash Basin was intertwined with a state-building project to integrate what had previously been a peripheral area. Supposedly 'backward' and 'uncivilized' pastoralists—Oromo in the Upper Awash Valley and Afar in the Middle and Lower Awash—who lacked centralized political authorities were easily pushed off the land targeted by the government and investors (Harbeson 1978; Ashami 1985; Zewde 2008a; Behnke and Kerven 2013; Lavers 2016).[7] The exception here is the Awsa Sultanate in the Lower Awash. For several centuries farmers had practised irrigated agriculture in Awsa, sustaining a centralized authority. While Awsa was militarily defeated by Menelik in 1895, no Ethiopian administrative presence was established and the Sultanate remained largely beyond state control (Harbeson 1978; Ashami 1985; Nicol 2000). Indeed, the Sultanate resisted the AVA, retaining control of access to land and water in its territory. As such, having received Imperial approval, Mitchell Cotts had to negotiate directly with the Sultan to secure land for the Tendaho development (Ashami 1985), and the government established administrative and police posts nearby as part of the project agreement (Fantini and Puddu 2016). Moreover, an agreement was made for Awsa farmers to supply cotton to the Tendaho project, resulting in a major expansion of Awsa capitalist agriculture, enhancing the economic power of the Awsa elite, and limiting potential for further AVA land grants to outside investors (Ashami 1985).

Overall, these attempts at economic modernization and state-building were 'an unmitigated disaster' for local pastoralists (Markakis 2011, p. 139; Behnke and Kerven 2013). State intervention in the form of dams and reservoirs, the conversion of 52,370 ha of prime land into plantations (Kloos 1982, p. 28), and the creation of the Awash National Park restricted the access of the Afar and Jille, Kereyu, and Arsi Oromo pastoralists to key water and land resources. These developments have been linked to the catastrophic effects of the 1972–1973 famine amongst pastoralist populations, leading to the deaths of 100,000–200,000 people or 25–30 per cent of the Afar population (Kloos 1982; Ashami 1985; Markakis 2011; Behnke and Kerven 2013). Nonetheless, the government continued to

[7] Puddu (2012) similarly notes how a World Bank-funded agricultural project was used by the Ethiopian Government to extend the state's territorial reach and strengthen its claims along the Sudanese border.

frame pastoralism itself as inherently unsustainable, necessitating modernization through the expansion of settled agriculture (Rettberg 2010). The first settlement schemes in Afar were launched under the Imperial Government by the AVA just before the 1974 revolution (Harbeson 1978; Ashami 1985) and were then expanded by the Derg (Kassa 1997; Markakis 2011).

The focus on the transformation of the Awash Basin in the post-war years was therefore the result of both technical feasibility and an alignment of political interests across multiple scales of analysis. The US, World Bank, and Italy were all willing to provide finance and expertise to build dams in this internal river basin as means of consolidating alliances with a key ally. Meanwhile, this phase of dam building was enabled by and contributed to the centralization of power during Haile Selassie's modernization drive, and the political marginalization of the largely pastoralist population of the Awash Valley.

Imperial Ethiopia's Ambitions on the Nile

Haile Selassie had ambitions to use the Awash Basin as a stepping-stone to the development of other river basins and, in particular, the Nile. For Haile Selassie, the Nile was of key significance, both for the development of the country, and as a symbol of modernization and the legitimacy of his rule (Sneddon 2015):

> It is of paramount importance to Ethiopia, and a problem of the first order, that the waters of the Nile be made to serve the life and needs both of our beloved people now living and those who will follow us in centuries to come. However generously Ethiopia may be prepared to share this tremendous God-given wealth of hers with friendly neighbouring countries for the lives and welfare of their people, it is Ethiopia's primary and sacred duty to develop her water resources in the interest of her own rapidly expanding population and economy. (Haile Selassie 1957, cited in Erlich 2002, p. 134)

However, the alignment of technical feasibility and multi-scalar political dynamics in the Awash was not replicated elsewhere. Following the war, efforts at comprehensive basin-wide management of the Nile collapsed, leading to a series of uncoordinated national projects in Egypt and Sudan focused on meeting domestic objectives, often at the cost of basin-wide benefits. Meanwhile, Ethiopia was constrained by its inability to mobilize international support for dam building in the Nile Basin. While the Ethiopian emperor was unable to realize his ambitions before his demise in 1974, he nonetheless advanced plans for the development of the Blue Nile that would prove influential decades later.

Following World War II and in the dying days of British influence in Egypt, the Egyptian Ministry of Public Works published its famous study by Hurst, Black, and Simaika (1946) on *The Future Conservation of the Nile*. This study introduced the concept of 'Century Storage'—essentially the water storage capacity required to maintain average water flow, even in the most exceptional drought years. The proposals focused on massively increasing storage in the upstream Albert and Victoria Lakes in Uganda, and Lake Tana in Ethiopia, where evaporation would be modest, and construction of an enlarged Jonglei Canal to transport the White Nile through the Sudd without major evaporation losses. The study noted the possibility of a hydroelectric plant at Tis Isat, just downstream from the proposed Tana regulator dam, as a means of appealing to the Ethiopian Government (Hurst et al. 1946, p. 98). However, hydroelectricity was not studied in any detail and the objective remained to 'control the Nile in the interests of irrigation in Egypt and the Sudan, and also to provide flood protection for Egypt' (Hurst et al. 1946, p. 1).

In a pattern that would frequently repeat on the Nile, supposedly optimal engineering proposals for management of the entire basin foundered on the political reality of divergent national interests, however. In 1952 the revolutionary command council, led by General Nasser, seized power in Egypt and secured agreement for British withdrawal. With Britain insisting that Sudan should remain independent of Egypt, the new Egyptian Government was forced to accept the impossibility of establishing political control over the entire Nile Basin, a major blow to Century Storage (Erlich 1994). Egypt, and colonial-era Sudan and Uganda, did agree to build the Owen Falls Dam in Uganda, which opened in 1954 under the permanent watch of an Egyptian engineer. However, having built Owen Falls, Uganda would gain little from the subsequent projects required to deliver Century Storage, while facing the political challenge of large-scale land loss (Collins 1990). With Ethiopia unwilling to discuss a Lake Tana Dam, the Century Storage plan was effectively dead by the mid-1950s.

Instead, the new Egyptian Government focused on securing water supply internally through construction of the High Aswan Dam (Waterbury 1979; Collins 1990; Erlich 2002).[8] A large dam at Aswan had been proposed decades before but was given little consideration by colonial-era engineers intent on finding an optimal technical solution for the management of the whole Nile Basin (Collins 1990). From the perspective of basin-wide water management, the Aswan Dam is simply 'the wrong dam in the wrong place' (Collins 1999, p. 3). Instead of storing water in the comparatively cool Ethiopian and Ugandan highlands to minimize evaporation, Aswan stores vast amounts of water in a flat, hot desert, resulting in massive losses through evaporation, estimated at 12–16 billion cubic metres (bcm) annually or approximately one-sixth of the river's flow, and, to a much lesser degree, through seepage of less than 1 per cent (Hussein 2018, pp. 5–60).[9] Yet for a revolutionary government seeking to build its legitimacy and confronting

[8] For more detailed accounts of Egyptian and Sudanese dam building, see Waterbury (1979) and Collins (1990).

[9] The 1959 agreement allows for a slightly lower amount of 10 bcm evaporation loss (United Arab Republic and Sudan 1959).

the fragmentation of political authority in the Nile Basin, Aswan fit the bill. The government promoted Aswan as a key nationalist symbol, with the dam providing Egypt with over-year storage capacity within Egypt's borders (Mitchell 2002; Hanna and Allouche 2018). As such, it was an attempt to 'free Egypt from being the hostage of upstream riparian states by providing for century storage within the boundaries of Egypt', addressing what was increasingly regarded as a key national security issue (Collins 1990, p. 239).

The massive dam located in southern Egypt flooded extensive areas of northern Sudan and therefore required Sudanese support. Negotiations with Sudan revisited the 1929 agreement and eventually produced the 1959 Nile Waters Agreement that allocated 55.5 bcm of the annual flow of the Nile to Egypt and 18.5 bcm to Sudan, once again ignoring the water rights of all other Nile riparians (United Arab Republic and Sudan 1959). While heavily favouring Egypt, the 1959 agreement increased Sudan's water allocation and secured Egyptian support for Sudan's Roseires Dam, which was built in 1965. Following the failure to negotiate the Lake Tana Dam with Ethiopia, Roseires was, like Aswan, an attempt at a national solution to the failure of basin-wide planning. Roseires enabled Sudan to expand irrigation and utilize some of the increased water allocation secured in the 1959 agreement (Collins 1990, p. 251). While the US and British Governments and the World Bank had all initially explored the possibility of financing Aswan, the 1956 Suez Crisis led the British and American governments to withdraw.[10] Consequently, Nasser turned to the USSR, with construction beginning in 1960 and completed by 1970 (Waterbury 1979).

Far from solving Egypt's water problems, the Aswan Dam has enabled ever-growing demand for water in the country through efforts to expand agriculture and settlements into the desert. After 1952, Nasser's government undertook land reform that promised to end 'feudalism' and dominance of the powerful land-holding elite in the Egyptian economy and politics. However, the reforms stopped short of a far-reaching reorganization of agricultural production. The government established a land ceiling and redistributed 12 per cent of the land, destroying the base of the richest 2,000 landlords, but left the middle farmers and the existing system of production intact, impeding modernization of agriculture and irrigation systems (Bush 2007). Nasser's government did attempt industrial deepening through import substitution, leading to increased employment and improved welfare. However, the government failed to discipline firms to deliver productivity improvements, eventually resulting in economic crisis amidst the high costs of subsidies (Waterbury 1983). In the absence of agricultural and industrial transformation, the consistent official narrative from this time onwards has been that

[10] The World Bank underwent a learning process with respect to international waters in its early years, in parallel to the development of international water law. At this time, there were no established procedures. World Bank support depended on agreement between Egypt and Sudan, but not upstream riparians (Salman 2009, p. 25).

population growth and land shortages along the Nile necessitate 'greening the deserts'. In this way, the Egyptian Government sought to avoid what would be politically complex reforms to existing agriculture or disciplining industrial firms (Waterbury 1983; Mitchell 1995; Sims 2015; Hanna and Allouche 2018). The result has been a series of large-scale irrigation schemes, based on diverted Nile waters from Aswan, most of which have been spectacular failures (Sims 2015). Nasser announced the New Valley scheme in 1958 that aimed to irrigate 3 million feddans and resettle some 4 million people. However, less than 120,000 feddans were ever realized and only 57,000 people resettled (Sims 2015, p. 50). The Tahrir Province Scheme, announced in 1954, was more successful, irrigating more or less the intended 600,000 feddans but only after many years of investment and operation (Sims 2015).

The 1959 agreement provoked a fallout between Egypt and Ethiopia. Ethiopia responded in a diplomatic note verbale that rejected Egypt's unilateral actions, signalling that this did not foreclose Ethiopia's future right to use the Nile waters. Furthermore, the Ethiopian Orthodox Church finally separated from the Coptic Church in Alexandria in 1959, ending a connection that had lasted 1,600 years. The 1959 agreement required Egypt and Sudan to negotiate jointly with upstream countries, as and when they made demands for a share of the Nile waters. However, both countries' stance on the Nile hardened subsequently, insisting on the protection of their 'historic rights' to the Nile and rejecting any reduction in their 1959 allocations (Waterbury 2002). To this end, Egypt has blocked access to international finance for any upstream projects and provoked internal instability in Ethiopia in particular (Erlich 2002). Notably, Egypt helped to form and train the Eritrean Liberation Front (ELF) in 1959 to pursue an 'Arab' revolution, while also promoting Somali territorial claims in Ethiopia (Erlich 1994; Woldemariam 2018).

Ethiopia's relations with Sudan also deteriorated, not only due to the Nile but also because of the border between the two countries that was never adequately demarcated in agreements between Ethiopia and Britain. Following Sudanese independence in 1956, contestation particularly focused on the fertile Al-Fashaga triangle that attracted an influx of Ethiopian settlers connected to cotton and sesame production in the 1960s (Puddu 2017). Meanwhile, Sudanese support to the ELF in Eritrea was reciprocated by Ethiopian support for the Anyanya movement that was fighting the government in the growing civil war in Sudan (Erlich 1994). Tensions grew to the brink of war between Ethiopia and Sudan in 1967.

Meanwhile, the Imperial Government responded to the 1959 agreement and construction of Aswan by requesting that the USBR follow up its work on the Awash River with another, more substantial study of the Blue Nile. For the US Government, the project was intended to threaten Egypt, which had turned to the USSR for assistance with the High Aswan Dam, through its dependence on the Nile. This threat, however, did not translate into full-blooded support for Ethiopia or a willingness to provide the resources to construct a major dam on the Nile. Rather, the intention was to use the study to force Egypt back into the US camp in the Cold War (Sneddon 2015). As Sneddon shows, however, the Bureau of Reclamation team was certainly full-blooded in its re-imagining of the Blue Nile Basin. In line with the Bureau's approach to the development of the western US (Reisner 1993), the Bureau envisaged

> an incredible array of projects that, if built, would have radically transformed the Blue Nile into a modern basin ... [providing] nearly complete control over the flows of the river and its tributaries. (Sneddon 2015, p. 90)

In total, the study proposed some 30 irrigation, hydropower, and multipurpose projects that would provide 433,754 ha of irrigated land and 8,660 MW of installed capacity (USBR 1964, p. vii).

Like with the pre-war proposals, a regulator dam at Lake Tana was among the USBR projects. However, the aim of maximizing the use of the river for Ethiopian development meant that the Bureau expanded its scope to cover projects for irrigation and hydropower development across the entire river basin. The study took up the idea floated earlier by Dupuis and Grabham and Black of digging a tunnel to drain some of the water from Lake Tana into another Nile tributary, in this case the Beles River. While earlier studies found no rationale for the considerable expense involved, the USBR envisaged a major hydropower project and large-scale irrigation schemes on the Beles, projects that would subsequently be tackled by both the Derg and the Ethiopian Peoples' Revolutionary Democratic Front (EPRDF) (see below and Chapters 4 and 5). However, the centrepiece of the USBR study was a cascade of four hydropower dams on the Blue Nile itself (Table 2.2).[11] By far the largest dam was to be Karadobi, upstream in the cool highlands, which would regulate the flow for downstream dams. As such, and as is standard practice with dam cascades, the expectation was that construction would begin with Karadobi and then move on to successive downstream dams. Combined, these four Nile dams would have 73 bcm of water storage capacity and 5,570 MW of installed generation capacity, which could produce 25,149 GWh of firm energy per year. Notably, with respect to subsequent projects, each of the proposed dams was designed to have a plant factor based on firm energy generation[12] over a six-year time period of around 50 per cent (USBR 1964, p. 157). As such, the designs suggest a balance between baseload and peaking power.

The proposed dams across the basin would prove enormously influential during the Derg and, particularly, EPRDF eras. Indeed, this includes the Border Dam

[11] In this sense the proposals build on a study conducted during the Italian occupation (1936–1941) by Pontecorvo that rejected the idea of using Lake Tana as a reservoir and instead proposed a cascade of three dams on the Blue Nile (Pontecorvo 1938, cited in USBR 1964, p. 11).

[12] Firm energy refers to the guaranteed energy generation regardless of the inter-annual variability of river flow. The plant load factor (or capacity factor) is the actual energy generation of a plant over a year divided by its maximum potential energy generation. A high plant factor indicates that a power plant is operating continuously at near full capacity providing baseload energy, while a low plant factor

Table 2.2 Hydropower projects proposed on the Blue Nile by the Bureau of Reclamation

Dam	Installed capacity (MW)	Firm energy (GWh/year)	Plant factor (per cent)	Water storage (billion cubic metres)
Karadobi	1,350	5,835	49	32.5
Mabil	1,200	5,314	51	13.6
Mandaya	1,620	7,800	55	15.9
Border	1,400	6,200	51	11.1

Data source: USBR (1964)

site, identified by the USBR study, which was eventually selected for the Grand Ethiopian Renaissance Dam (GERD). However, other than the dam's location, the design of the GERD and Border Dam bear no resemblance to each other. The Border Dam proposal was for a relatively small dam, roughly one-seventh the water storage capacity of the GERD and dependent on upstream regulation of the water flow to enable year-round energy generation (see Chapter 7).

Despite its ambitions, the Bureau's study acknowledged that this vast array of proposed projects was beyond the capacity or requirements of Ethiopia in the foreseeable future. The study proposed several small projects to be developed before 2000, of which the multipurpose project at Finchaa on a tributary of the Blue Nile was to be the first. The USBR study envisaged Finchaa as the first and largest in a complex of three dams on adjacent rivers—Finchaa, Amarti, and Neshi—that together would provide hydroelectric power and water regulation for a large-scale plantation (USBR 1964). The dams on the Blue Nile itself were not expected to be feasible before 2000, depending on the growth of the economy and electricity demand.

Yet US political and financial support did not follow. According to a US National Security Council member, the study was considered 'the best hold this country [the US] could possibly have on Nasser for bargaining purposes' rather than the starting point of a major programme of investment (Sneddon 2015, pp. 89–90). Moreover, by the late 1960s, advances in satellite communications meant the declining importance to the US of the Kagnew base and with it the US's strategic interests in Ethiopia (Patman 2009). While the US 'was lukewarm concerning the strategic importance of Ethiopia to broader American geopolitical goals', Egypt remained the main US priority (Sneddon 2015, p. 97).

indicates that the plant operates at full capacity for only short periods, usually coinciding with peak demand.

It was only after extensive lobbying by Haile Selassie that the US Government and World Bank finance was eventually provided to fund Italian firm Impresit's construction of the Finchaa Dam in 1969–1972, adding 84 MW to Ethiopia's installed capacity and extending the grid centred on Addis. By this stage the World Bank's 1965 Operational Memorandum required all transboundary water projects to consider the impact on other riparians. In particular, World Bank staff had to state that either the transboundary issues raised were covered by arrangements between countries; that the affected riparians had stated no objection; or that the project had no impact on the riparians and their consent was therefore immaterial (Salman 2009, p. 100). Despite Egypt's apparent protest against Finchaa (Waterbury 2002, p. 121), the World Bank's assessment was that 'the volume of water stored and released, when compared with the flow of the Blue Nile where the Finchaa enters its stream, would be insignificant' (IBRD 1969, p. 5). The World Bank's willingness to bypass Egyptian and Sudanese opposition was limited to Finchaa and would not apply to dams on the Blue Nile itself where the impacts could not be so lightly dismissed.

It should be noted that while the political reforms undertaken since World War II had considerably strengthened the position of the emperor and the bureaucracy at the expense of the landed nobility, limits to Imperial authority remained at this time. While the USBR survey team's work was facilitated in several riverine provinces by personal connections between the emperor and provincial governors, they faced challenges in Gojjam, where the survey team felt the local population 'had not accepted the government of Ethiopia' (Sneddon 2015, p. 91).[13] The result was that the team was accompanied at all times by four armed guards for their protection. Compensation procedures for the Finchaa Dam were also shaped by the land tenure system and prevailing agrarian structure. While the project required the resettlement of approximately 3,115 people, it was only the landholding elite that received compensation for their losses, not the tenants who actually worked their land (Müller-Mahn and Gebreyes 2019, p. 6).

The USBR study also had a lasting impact on technical capacity within Ethiopia. Although USBR engineers led the work, the massive study was seen as a means of building local capacity (Sneddon 2015). The study led to the creation in 1956 of the Water Resources Department in the Ministry of Public Works and Communications, originally staffed by just one engineer and 50 technicians (Abate 1994; Arsano 2007a; Haile 2018, p. 93). The USBR study 'helped train an entire generation of Ethiopian hydrologists' (Waterbury 2002, p. 116), and though the Water Resources Department was disbanded on completion of the study in 1964, the staff involved in the project provided the core of the National Water Resources Commission created in 1971.

[13] Indeed, proposed tax reforms at this time that sought to bypass the landed elite and strengthen Imperial control over producers failed in Gojjam as a result of mass protests and rebellions (Tareke 1991).

The only other development in the Blue Nile Basin at this time was the first Tis Abay hydroelectric plant, completed by Italian and Yugoslav contractors in 1964 with the remaining Italian war reparations at a site identified by the American study in 1931 (Last 1958). Throughout this period Haile Selassie maintained multiple prongs to his foreign policy strategy, expanding relations with the USSR and Soviet bloc countries, primarily with a view to coaxing greater support from the US (Patman 2009; Fantini and Puddu 2016). It is possible that Yugoslav involvement was the result of this strategy. The project relied on a weir to divert part of the Blue Nile shortly after leaving Lake Tana, and was rated at 7.7 MW, with potential for future expansion to 11.4 MW (JICA 1977). Tis Abay provided electricity for a self-contained grid centred on Bahir Dar, including a new textile factory. As a run of the river dam, Tis Abay did not create a reservoir and the project had no real impact on downstream flows. With no regulation of Lake Tana, the flow of the river and consequently electricity generation varied considerably through the year.

Unlike on the Awash, Haile Selassie never secured the necessary constellation of political forces to pursue major projects on the Nile. International support—so important for both finance and technical expertise—from the US Government was tentative, using detailed and far-reaching studies to apply pressure to Egypt, but not going so far as to damage a country of great strategic importance. The Finchaa and Tis Abay projects did reduce Ethiopian electricity dependence on the drought-prone Awash Basin. Yet by the end of Haile Selassie's reign in 1974, 55 per cent of Ethiopian hydropower continued to be generated by a cascade of relatively small dams on the Awash.

Revolutionary Ethiopia and Cold War Realignments

The late 1960s and early 1970s brought major changes to national politics in Egypt, Ethiopia, and Sudan, as well as a complete re-alignment of Cold War allegiances in the region. Yet, these changes did nothing to improve alignment of political interests regarding a negotiated settlement over the Nile or Ethiopia's prospects of unilaterally building a Nile dam. Although undermined by external and internal military threats, the Derg Government was able to mobilize limited external support towards dam construction outside the Blue Nile Basin.

In Ethiopia, the powerful landed elite resisted far-reaching political and economic reforms, resulting in stagnation and growing political instability (Clapham 1988). Ultimately, a 'creeping coup' deposed Haile Selassie following months of protests and strikes in 1974. Ethiopia was initially ruled by the Derg, a committee of junior military officials, though Mengistu Hailemariam emerged as the unchallenged leader as he gradually eliminated competitors. In 1975, the new government launched rural and urban land reforms that eradicated the economic base of the nobility (Clapham 1988). Internationally, Mengistu aggressively pursued the support of the USSR and other socialist countries in the early years following the revolution (Clapham 1988; Tekle 1989; Patman 2009). The USSR, which had been providing military aid to Siad Barré's regime in Somalia, initially sought to reconcile fractious relations between Somalia and Ethiopia (Farer 1979; Patman 2009). However, the Ethio-Somali War (1977–1978), in which Somalia sought to claim territory occupied by ethnic Somali within Ethiopia, forced the Soviets to make a choice. In 1977, Mengistu's emergence to supremacy led the USSR to switch sides, as a result of the greater strategic importance of Ethiopia's Red Sea coastline and the greater prospects of the Ethiopian revolution (Patman 2009). Soviet and Cuban military support was vital to reversing initial Somali gains (Clapham 1988; Tekle 1989; Erlich 1994). While the US did not initially break ties with the new Ethiopian Government, the turn to the USSR in 1977 led to the expulsion of US officials and an end to US military support (Patman 2009).

Downstream on the Nile, Egypt and Sudan trod the reverse path by switching from Soviet to Western alliances, while also shifting security relations within the Middle East. Following Nasser's death in 1970, and Egypt's defeat in the 1967 and 1973 conflicts with Israel, President Sadat moved Egypt away from pan-Arabism, leading to reconciliation with the US through the Camp David agreement in 1978 and Israeli peace agreement in 1979. After 1979, Egypt abandoned Nasser's state-subsidized import substitution, instead adopting a strategy of promoting foreign investment and export-led growth while cutting back on the state's distributive commitments (Sallam 2022). As a result, Sadat opened up to investment from Saudi Arabia and other Gulf countries—previously dismissed as Western puppets under Nasser—while also cultivating the Muslim Brotherhood as a counterbalance to the political left that resisted liberalization (Waterbury 1983; Sallam 2022). Meanwhile, a leftist military coup in 1969 led by Ja'afar Nimeiri in Sudan aimed initially at revolutionary state-building and the promotion of national development. Following a split with the communists in 1971, however, the Nimeiri regime reached out to the West, Sadat, and the Gulf as sources of investment (De Waal 2015; Verhoeven 2015).

These realignments did not greatly increase the resources available for Ethiopian infrastructure investment. Ethiopia developed close relations with several Soviet bloc countries, sending significant numbers of Ethiopian officials for education and training (Tekle 1989). Ethiopia also developed close relations with North Korea—to some degree independently of the USSR—with Mengistu making regular visits to Pyongyang (Clapham 1988; Tekle 1989). Much like the US support to Imperial Ethiopia, however, the Soviet assessment of the strategic importance of Ethiopia seems to have been ambiguous while the Soviets grew frustrated at slow pace of the Ethiopian revolution (Patman 2009). The result was that the USSR provided just 22 per cent of Ethiopia's aid between 1983 and 1986, to Mengistu's considerable disappointment (Patman 2009, p. 275; Fantini and Puddu

2016). Indeed, Soviet alignment failed to translate into the kind of support that had been extended to Egypt in constructing the High Aswan Dam. While socialist countries supported the construction of several medium-sized dams outside the Nile Basin, as discussed below, significant international support for the development of the Blue Nile was not forthcoming. Meanwhile, Ethiopia did not entirely terminate its relations with the West. Trade relations were maintained with many countries in the capitalist camp, and both the European Economic Community and the Italian Government continued to provide aid in the 1980s (Tekle 1989).

From the moment it took power, the Derg faced internal insurrections, the majority of which were socialist and ethno-nationalist, favouring greater autonomy or secession for Ethiopia's ethnic groups in contrast to the Derg's 'Ethiopia First' nationalism (Clapham 1988).[14] As such, the military threat to the regime did not disappear with the end of the Ethio-Somali War in 1978, but rather intensified as the Derg switched its focus to insurrections in Eritrea, Tigray, Oromiya, and elsewhere. The result was that much of Ethiopia's internal resources and external support were directed to military expenditure rather than infrastructure development. Likewise, political instability meant that the new regime was unable to consolidate the Imperial regime's initial efforts to build technocratic capacity through the Water Resources Commission and the AVA (Waterbury 2002; Arsano 2007b). The Awash was subsequently incorporated into the Ethiopian Valleys Development Studies Authority, but instability and regular purges of staff meant that Ethiopia did not develop the capacity to lead major water projects itself.

In the meantime, Egypt and Sudan both continued to increase their utilization of the Nile waters fuelled by Gulf finance, threatening to exceed the allocations made under the 1959 agreement. Under Sadat, Egypt maintained its push to green the desert and thereby ease population pressure in the Nile Valley, albeit now through foreign private investment rather than state projects (Sims 2015). After the return of the Sinai to Egypt in 1980, this included a plan to settle 5 million people in the peninsula based on the pumping of Nile waters. Unsurprisingly, the project was even less successful than the New Valley project (Sims 2015). Likewise, grandiose plans to build new towns and cities in the desert were poorly thought out and failed to meet high expectations (Sims 2015). Meanwhile, the key to Sudan's economic plans was irrigated agriculture, using Nile waters, with capital-intensive foreign investments intended to make the country the breadbasket of Africa and the Middle East through a massive expansion of irrigated agriculture (Verhoeven 2015).

Egypt and Sudan's growing water use amidst the constraints of the Nile's annual flow and the 1959 allocations led to the revival of the Jonglei Canal as a means of reducing water losses through evaporation and thereby increasing the Nile's

[14] One exception here was the Ethiopian People's Revolutionary Party (EPRP) that fought against the Derg, prioritizing class-based revolution over ethno-nationalist organization.

flow in northern Sudan and Egypt (Collins 1990, p. 271; Verhoeven 2015). The 1972 peace agreement that ended Sudan's 17-year civil war paved the way for the beginning of construction in 1978 (Collins 1990, p. 308). However, excavation was slow and difficult, while the canal sparked a mutiny of the Sudan People's Liberation Army (SPLA) and the resumption of the civil war in 1984, putting an end to construction shortly before its expected completion in March 1985 (Collins 1990; Verhoeven 2015).

Bilateral relations between Ethiopia and its downstream Nile riparians, meanwhile, became ever more hostile. Mengistu issued periodic threats to reduce the flow of the Nile in response to Egyptian plans to expand irrigation (Swain 1997; Erlich 2002). Meanwhile, President Sadat's response was that if 'Ethiopia takes any action to block our right to the Nile water, there will be no alternative for us but to use force' (cited in Swain 1997, p. 687). Sadat's assassination in 1981 that brought Hosni Mubarak to power in Egypt did little to improve interactions. Ethiopian relations with Sudan were similarly problematic, with Ethiopia providing a base for the SPLA in its fight against the Sudanese government, while Sudan provided support to the Eritrean People's Liberation Front (EPLF), Oromo Liberation Front (OLF), Tigrayan People's Liberation Front (TPLF), and Benishangul People's Liberation Movement (BPLM) in their fight against the Derg (Tekle 1989; RVI 2023). Clearly there was no possibility of a negotiated agreement with downstream riparians over a Blue Nile dam, something that would be required to access World Bank funds, for example. Indeed, dam planning on the Blue Nile did not progress significantly in this period, with the water development masterplan of 1990 merely replicating the USBR's plans (WAPCOS 1990).

Despite Ethiopia's Soviet alliance, several water projects in this period were funded by the West as it sought to recover influence in Ethiopia (Patman 2009). The Derg renewed efforts to regulate Lake Tana through a dam at the Chara-Chara cataracts, requesting a Japanese study of a weir to regulate the river, enabling the expansion of the existing hydropower plant at Tis Abay and construction of a second plant nearby (JICA 1977). Construction of the weir eventually began in 1984, but was incomplete by the time the Derg was removed from power (McCartney et al. 2009). The Chara-Chara weir was also a key part of the Tana-Beles scheme launched under the Derg and contracted to Salini Costruttori with Italian Government funding (see Chapter 5). This project aimed to realize proposals dating back to the early twentieth century to divert water from Lake Tana into the Beles River to enable hydropower generation and large-scale irrigation. Tana-Beles was framed as a response to the 1984/5 famine (Arsano 2007a; Haile 2018, p. 99), though the scheme actually became a means of forcibly resettling Tigrayan peasants and potential supporters of the TPLF from their home areas to undermine the Front. Moreover, and as with most other water projects in Ethiopia, the Tana-Beles scheme was used to strengthen state control over the area while marginalizing Gumuz-practising mobile livelihoods (Fantini et al. 2018; Fedeler

2021). Unsurprisingly, Egypt and Sudan raised strong objections to Tana-Beles (Fedeler 2021, p. 110), which would enable large-scale irrigation in the Beles Valley, extracting water and reducing the flow downstream. Despite the ambitious plans, the diversion tunnel from Lake Tana was not realized at this time and construction focused solely on infrastructure and irrigation works. Moreover, the project was abandoned as the civil war frontline advanced towards the project area shortly before Mengistu lost power (Fedeler 2021).

The Derg did build the Amarti Dam, the second of the USBR-proposed Finchaa-Amarti-Neshe complex, with European Economic Community funding (EEC 1985). Completed in 1987, the dam provides additional water storage to raise the capacity of the Finchaa plant from 84 MW to 100 MW (Müller-Mahn and Gebreyes 2019) and to irrigate a 6,000-ha state farm. Meanwhile, a Soviet study was also conducted of the Baro-Akobo Basin, a tributary of the White Nile, that identified several potential dam sites, but located far from the main demand for electricity, there was no move to develop the projects (Waterbury 2002, p. 125). The only dam built on the Baro-Akobo was the relatively small Alwero Dam, built by the state-owned Ethiopian Water Works Construction Enterprise for irrigation but unused until decades later.

While the Derg failed to realize its ambitions in the Nile Basin (Arsano 2007a, p. 174; Swain 1997), like the Imperial regime, it was more successful in tackling other river basins. The 153-MW Melka Wakena Dam in the Wabe Shebele Basin was completed in 1988, increasing national generation capacity by 70 per cent. The dam was constructed in the Bale highlands in the headwaters of the river with the support of the USSR and Czechoslovakia (Clapham 1988; Cheryachukin and Sitnin 2000; Patman 2009). The dam had significant impact downstream on farmers in Ethiopia's Somali region (Hagmann 2007) and was also viewed with hostility by Somalia (Carr 2017). However, following military victory in the Ethio-Somali War, Somalia had little ability to resist and irritating Siad Barré probably was not a major concern to Mengistu. Completion of Melka Wakena significantly reduced Ethiopia's dependence on the Awash Basin for power. While further plans for the Awash were advanced through feasibility studies of Tendaho and Kessem Dams, and a Basin Masterplan in 1989 (Halcrow 1989), the focus on the basin had shifted from electricity—for which little potential remained—to irrigation. As part of its land reforms, the Derg nationalized commercial plantations including sugar factories at Wenji-Shoa and Metehara in 1975, and redistributed the lands held by the Sultan of Awsa when he was forced into exile (Markakis 2011). However, little progress was made on the large-scale expansion of irrigated agriculture.

Ethiopia's hydroelectric ambitions also shifted for the first time to the Omo Basin, one of the largest rivers by discharge and second only to the Blue Nile in hydropower potential. The initial site selected was upstream, in the highlands near Jimma and close to the existing grid. A North Korean company started developing a dam at what would become the site of Gilgel Gibe I (see Chapter 5) and North

Korea provided several engineers to plan a 250,000-ha state farm in the Omo Valley (Clapham 1988, p. 235). However, neither scheme had advanced far by the time the Derg was defeated by the EPLF and TPLF, leading to abandonment of the projects.

Despite the vast hydropower potential of the Blue Nile, Baro-Akobo, and Omo Basins, by the fall of the Derg in 1991, Ethiopia's electricity generation capacity remained very low, with 70 per cent dependence on the much more limited Awash and Wabe Shebele Basins (see Table 2.3). Likewise with irrigated agriculture, considerable potential remained unrealized and many past projects fell out of production due to the inept management of state farms (Clapham 1988).

The reality is that the Derg was in no position to tackle major projects on the Blue Nile or elsewhere, and no better placed than Haile Selassie in terms of the financial or technocratic capacity to tackle Ethiopia's hydraulic mission. The government's attention and financial resources throughout were focused on military confrontation—consolidating power following the revolution, repelling the Somali invasion, and then fighting a losing battle against growing insurrections in Eritrea and Tigray. Moreover, the Derg remained dependent on access to foreign expertise to realize its projects. Meanwhile, international support was faltering, with the USSR and socialist allies providing support, but never in a way that threatened the region's main geo-strategic prize—Egypt.

Conclusion

This chapter examines Haile Selassie and the Derg's efforts to launch Ethiopia's hydraulic mission and the resulting spatial distribution of Ethiopia's dam-building programme in this period. The analysis shows that technical inputs into dam

Table 2.3 Hydropower generation capacity in Ethiopia in 1991

Basin	Dam	Installed capacity (MW)	Percentage of hydropower capacity
Blue Nile	Tis Abay	7.7	29
	Finchaa	100	
Awash	Koka	46	30
	Awash II	32	
	Awash III	32	
Wabe Shebele	Melka Wakena	153	41
Total		370.7	100

Data source: Author's calculations.

planning and decision making were filtered through political dynamics at multiple intersecting scales of analysis and, in particular, the attempts of national governments to balance the competing pressures of international and domestic politics.

The technical feasibility of dam projects was undoubtedly a factor shaping decision making on dams, particularly by favouring sites in river basins close to the main load centre in Addis Ababa. However, political dynamics from the global to local levels played a vital role in shaping the spatial distribution of Ethiopia's dams. Notably, the shifting global context from the colonial era to the Cold War was a major factor given Ethiopia's dependence, as a late-developing country, on international finance and technical expertise to develop water infrastructure. These international alignments intersected with river basin politics and regional security and, in particular, growing competition between Egypt and Ethiopia over the Nile waters. Throughout this period, Egypt was considered of greater strategic importance to the key powers of the day, from Britain in the early twentieth nineteenth century to the US and USSR during the Cold War. As such, Egypt was either able to block upstream developments or the major powers refrained from taking action that would damage Egypt. In contrast, international support—shifting from the US in the Imperial era to socialist countries after the revolution—was more forthcoming for dam projects in other river basins, first the Awash and then the Wabe Shebele, or minor Nile projects that would have an insignificant impact on Egypt. The result was that by the time the EPRDF Government came to power in 1991, Ethiopian electricity generation capacity was tiny for a country of Ethiopia's size and largely dependent on two river basins that offered among the lowest hydropower potential in the country. Meanwhile, the vast hydropower potential of the western half of the country remained largely untapped.

The EPRDF's subsequent dam-building programme far surpassed that of the emperor or the Derg and in doing so has fundamentally altered the spatial pattern of Ethiopian dam building. However, in certain other respects these early attempts to tackle the hydraulic mission helped to establish particular continuities that shape dam development to the present. First, as a result of the physical and political geography of Ethiopia, dam development has entailed an intertwined project of state-building to consolidate the territorial gains secured under Menelik at the end of the nineteenth century and economic modernization through dams and agricultural investments. While justified in terms of the modernization of the economy and national development, benefits of this dam building have accrued to the centre, while the costs of dam and agricultural development are disproportionately borne by politically marginal populations in the periphery.

Second, early attempts to negotiate a dam on the Blue Nile consolidated the antagonistic positions taken by Ethiopia and Egypt. For Egypt, its red lines in negotiation have been its existing water infrastructure and its historic rights to use the Nile waters, while Ethiopia insisted that past unilateral Egyptian projects did not foreclose its future use of the Nile's waters. While Ethiopia remained politically divided, economically weak, and of limited geo-strategic importance before 1991, Egypt was able to maintain what has been described as a position of 'hydro-hegemony' (Cascão 2008). Ethiopia's weakness began to change, however, when the EPRDF came to power in 1991.

3
Political Vulnerability and the Origins of the EPRDF's Dams Boom

Tom Lavers, Fana Gebresenbet, and Biruk Terrefe

During the Ethiopian Peoples' Revolutionary Democratic Front's (EPRDF's) time in office from 1991 to 2019, the installed generation capacity supplying Ethiopia's grid increased more than 10-fold, almost all of it from hydropower. Indeed, under the EPRDF, Ethiopia built the largest hydroelectric generation capacity on the African continent, even prior to the completion of the Grand Ethiopian Renaissance Dam (GERD). Moreover, this investment in hydropower and other economic infrastructure was among the main factors driving economic growth in the country, in a period in which Ethiopia was one of the fastest-growing economies globally (Moller 2017). The contrast with past regimes, whose dam-building ambitions were severely constrained by internal political divisions, fiscal and technical capacity constraints, and the geo-strategic interests of global powers, is stark. This chapter begins to provide an explanation for the EPRDF's achievements where other regimes had previously failed. The analysis here focuses on the government's development strategy and the role of electricity within it, and the spatial distribution of the government's dam-building strategy during the EPRDF's first two decades in office from 1991 to 2010. Drawing on the framework outlined in Chapter 1, the discussion focuses on the intersection between elite politics, technocratic capacity, and finance, and the ways in which these critical factors were shaped by intersecting political dynamics from the global to the local.

The chapter shows that the motivation for the EPRDF's dams boom can be located in the government's broader approach to development. For the new government, rapid, broad-based development was considered essential to addressing the political vulnerability facing the regime, with industrialization and the mass creation of manufacturing jobs key to its political survival (Lavers 2023). The government's ambitions regarding the electricity sector largely stem from this goal of structural transformation. Moreover, given its central importance to the EPRDF's economic project, the government considered the retention of electricity and a handful of key economic sectors under state control to be a necessity. The result was that the EPRDF's economic and infrastructural ambitions were in conflict with the Western donors on whom Ethiopia depended and the dominant economic ideas of the time that favoured liberalization and privatization.

Dams, Power, and the Politics of Ethiopia's Renaissance. Tom Lavers et al., Oxford University Press. © Tom Lavers, Fana Gebresenbet, and Biruk Terrefe (2024). DOI: 10.1093/oso/9780192871213.003.0003

The EPRDF's focus on investment in hydropower as part of delivering economic transformation was a consistent theme throughout its time in office. However, the resulting boom in dam construction proceeded in distinct phases, shaped by political dynamics within the ruling elite, the availability of finance domestically and internationally, and the technocratic and administrative capacity of the state to deliver on politicians' developmental ambitions. The chapter begins by focusing on the political challenges facing the EPRDF when it took office both domestically and in terms of donor relations. The analysis then examines why the government's efforts focused almost exclusively on hydropower and not other available energy sources. The government's focus on state investment in hydropower meant that, much like past regimes, its ambitions remained severely constrained during the 1990s and largely dependent on external support. Consequently, dam building followed the availability of donor funds to river basins other than the contentious Blue Nile Basin. The final section, however, argues that a series of political crises in the early 2000s marked a defining shift. The result was the centralization of power around the prime minister, Meles Zenawi, and renewed commitment to a project of state-led development. As this strategy began to deliver economic results, the government's ambitions steadily expanded, with the government strategically engaging with donors and mobilizing greater domestic resources to finance a series of increasingly ambitious hydropower projects.

The EPRDF in Power: Political Vulnerability and Developmental Ambitions

The Tigrayan People's Liberation Front (TPLF) originated in the student movement in Haile Selassie I University in the 1970s (Berhe 2008, 2020). Although sharing certain socialist ideas with the Derg, the TPLF, like many other groups, differed when it came to the 'national question', with the TPLF favouring ethnonationalist mobilization as a precursor to class consciousness while the Derg considered ethnicity to be a mere distraction (Zeleke 2019). From the mid-1970s the TPLF and other liberation groups established rural insurrections to challenge the Derg, ultimately fighting the Ethiopian military to a standstill and leading to the regime's collapse in 1991 (Young 1997; Tareke 2009).[1] The TPLF's approach to the conflict combined an ethno-nationalist message with a Maoist strategy, securing the support of the Tigrayan peasantry through the distribution of land and social services, and launching surprise raids on the Derg forces while avoiding direct confrontation (Young 1997; Berhe 2008). In the late 1980s as the TPLF shifted from an ethno-regional insurgency to a movement with ambitions on national government, it formed the EPRDF, a coalition of ethnic parties to

[1] Notably, of course, this included the Eritrean People's Liberation Front (EPLF).

represent Ethiopia's main ethnic groups. However, these hastily formed parties lacked the discipline and cohesion forged through struggle that was the hallmark of the TPLF. While formally all four EPRDF parties carried equal weight within the coalition, the TPLF exerted disproportionate influence, particularly early on.

The EPRDF came to power in 1991 as the dominant partner in a transitional government and governed alone after several opposition parties withdrew from the 1995 national elections, which the EPRDF won resoundingly. Despite its military and electoral dominance, the ruling coalition was in an extremely vulnerable position, however. Outside Tigray, EPRDF parties had had little time to win popular support and were viewed with apprehension, and in some cases open hostility, by the rural and urban masses and elite actors across the country. The EPRDF leadership's concerns about the lack of a popular base were exacerbated by rapid population growth, which was leading to growing land shortages in rural areas and, so the Front feared, would result in urban migration, widespread unemployment, and social unrest (Office of the Prime Minister 1993; TGE 1994a). Moreover, growing ethno-nationalism—not least the result of political mobilization by the TPLF and other ethno-nationalists—posed a distinct threat to a regime that was widely perceived to be dominated by the Tigrayan ethnic minority, whatever the claims of coalition between EPRDF parties.

The EPRDF sought to address these threats and consolidate its hold on power through a dual-pronged strategy (Lavers 2023). On the one hand, the EPRDF established a federal system that fundamentally re-shaped the Ethiopian state. Scrapping previous administrative provinces, new regions (*kilil*)—based on ethno-linguistic criteria—were created to provide for self-administration of Ethiopia's 'nations, nationalities, and peoples' (see Figure 3.1). Inspired by the Leninist-Stalinist approach to the national question, the EPRDF intended this ethno-linguistic federalism to put to an end what they viewed as the Amhara-dominated central government's historical exploitation of the rest of the country.[2] New regional governments would enable ethnic groups to administer their own resources in their own interests, promoting cultural activities and requiring local languages—rather than Amharic—as the medium of local administration and primary education. The result was a constitution that devolved many powers such as land administration to regional states, although electricity and water remained the preserve of the federal government.[3] Each of the new regional states was administered by an EPRDF party or affiliate.

On the other hand, the government set rapid and broad-based development of the economy and, in particular, industrialization and structural transformation as its top economic priority (TGE 1994a). Expanding economic opportunities distributed through party-state structures would bind the masses to the ruling

[2] Lenin and Stalin's approach to the national question (see Martin 2001) was a key theme of debates in the Ethiopian student movement and inspired the EPRDF's federal system (Clapham 2002; Zeleke 2019).

[3] The federal constitution placed land under state ownership. However, within these constitutional constraints regions were given responsibility for land administration (see Lavers 2023).

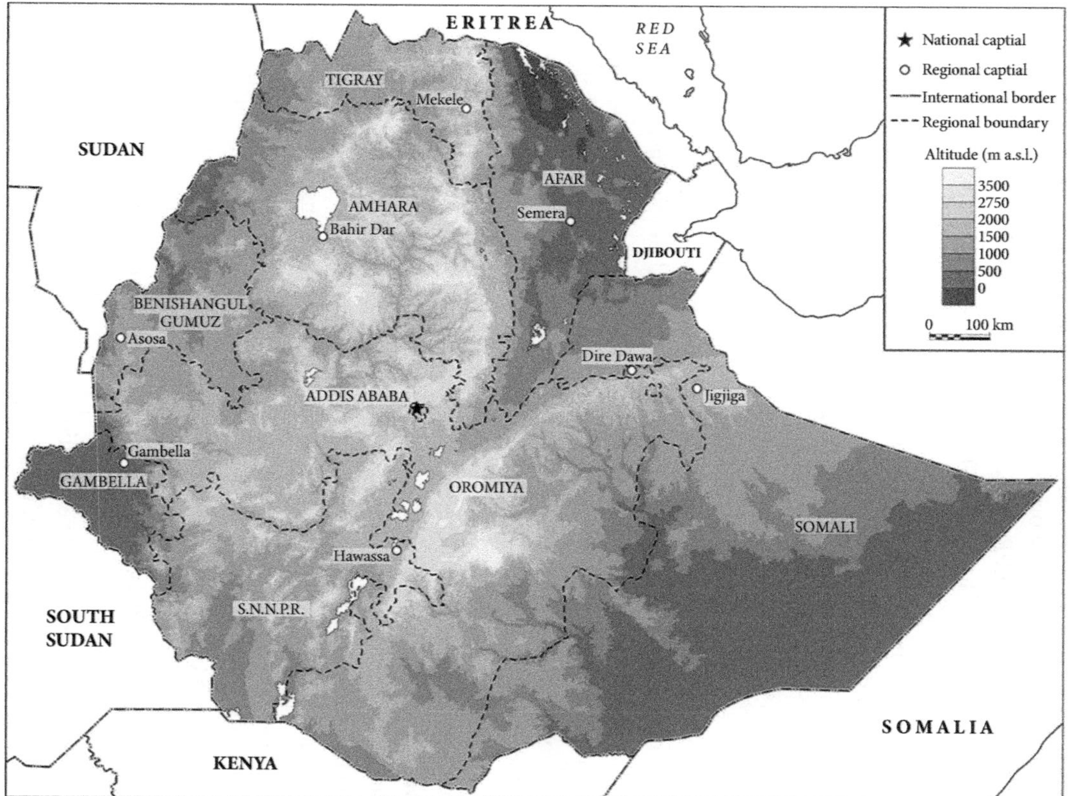

Figure 3.1 Ethiopia's topography and post-1994 ethnic federal regions

Note: Since 2019, Southern Nations, Nationalities, and Peoples Region (SNNPR) has separated into four new regions as these have successively voted for statehood.

Source: Author and Manchester Cartographic Unit.

coalition and thereby consolidate its political position (Lavers 2023). In the short term, the EPRDF focused on consolidating its control of the smallholder majority through the distribution of state-owned land and agricultural inputs. In the medium to long term, however, mass industrial employment creation was seen as the only solution to Ethiopia's rapidly growing population and the inability of the agricultural sector to absorb this expanding labour surplus (MoPED 1993; TGE 1994a). While governments worldwide routinely state their desire to promote industrialization, for the EPRDF structural transformation was, from very early on, identified as essential to the coalition's political survival rather than mere rhetoric.

The government's initial development strategy identified Agricultural Development-Led Industrialization (ADLI) as the means of linking these goals. ADLI focused initially on raising the agricultural productivity of smallholder farmers—through increased use of improved seeds, fertilizer, and irrigation—as a means of creating an agrarian surplus, which could then be used to subsidize industrial investment and establish production linkages between the expanding smallholder agricultural sector and nascent rural-based industry (TGE 1994a). In spite of the new federal division of powers, this national development strategy necessitated the centralization of decision-making power over land and agricultural and industrial policy within the federal government. The result was that newly created regions were largely limited in practice to implementing centrally defined plans.

The government considered the expansion of electricity generation and access as vital to the structural transformation of the economy (TGE 1994b). Indeed, electricity was considered a question of 'life and death' according to one TPLF Central Committee member at the time.[4] In the early 1990s, total installed capacity supplying the grid was just 370 MW, while a mere 4 per cent of the population, almost exclusively urban, was connected to the grid (World Bank 1996). Post-conflict economic recovery in the early 1990s meant that demand rapidly outpaced this limited supply, while periodic droughts disrupted generation from existing hydroelectric projects (World Bank 2006a). A major programme of investment in electricity generation, transmission, and distribution was required.

However, when the EPRDF came to power in 1991, 'the fiscal situation inherited from the Derg was disastrous' as a result of the perilous state of the economy, low tax collection, and massive military expenditure during the civil war (Mascagni 2016, p. 30). To finance reconstruction and stabilization of the economy, the government had little option but to turn to Western donors and multilateral agencies. In line with the Washington Consensus of the time, any support from these donors came with the condition to liberalize the economy and privatize state enterprises, which directly contradicted the formative ideas within the new government

[4] In Amharic, *heywetem, tefatem*. Interview EG46, former TPLF Central Committee member, Addis Ababa, 7 August 2019.

about state-led development. Moreover, the US and other governments remained sceptical about the new government and its socialist past. The EPRDF sought to downplay its socialist history (Berhe 2008), while fighting to preserve autonomy in decision making, resisting pressure to privatize key sectors such as land, finance, electricity, and telecommunications (Borchgrevink 2008; Furtado and Smith 2009; Feyissa 2011). The result was that the government agreed three modest stabilization and structural adjustment packages during the 1990s, providing much-needed financial support. However, the government limited the scope of these agreements and delayed implementation. As Meles Zenawi, president from 1991 to 1994 and then prime minister from 1995, later reflected,

> While I cannot say that we had an alternative to the neo-liberal reforms that the IMF [International Monetary Fund] and World Bank wanted us to introduce, we have never been comfortable with it from the very beginning. Our initial reaction was in effect to conduct a rear-guard battle of delaying and preventing the introduction of reforms that would reduce the state to the proverbial night watchman without presenting an adequately articulated alternative. (Zenawi 2006a)

The government did agree to a limited number of privatizations to placate donors. In practice, however, many of these firms were sold to politically connected companies including: the TPLF-owned Endowment Fund for the Rehabilitation of Tigray (EFFORT) and to a lesser degree similar conglomerates controlled by other EPRDF parties, and the MIDROC conglomerate owned by Sheik Al-Amoudi, an Ethio-Saudi businessman and EPRDF supporter (Vaughan and Gebremichael 2011; Weis 2015).[5] As one former TPLF Central Committee member recalled,

> We withdrew from small factories, such as textile, leather, state farms, which were not attractive and were operating at a loss. This helped us to appear that we are in sync with the World Bank and IMF structural adjustment and helped appease them.[6]

This delicate balance was upset in 1998/9, however, when the IMF pushed for further reforms, including opening the financial sector to foreign investment. Reforms in 1994 had enabled the Ethiopian private sector to invest in banking, but the EPRDF refused to go further, even at the cost of IMF withdrawal (Wade 2001; Stiglitz 2003; Manyazewal 2019). This episode undoubtedly constrained government finances in the short run, but vitally ensured that the financial sector

[5] Party endowments were established with resources and material left over at the end of the civil war. See Vaughan and Gebremichael (2011). MIDROC was originally an abbreviation of Mohammed International Development Research and Organization Companies.

[6] Interview EG46, former TPLF Central Committee member, Addis Ababa, 7 August 2019.

remained largely under state control and signalled to donors that the government would not cross certain red lines.

The Political Origins of Ethiopia's State Hydropower Dominance

This general pattern was exemplified by the electricity sector. The EPRDF inherited an integrated state electric utility, the Ethiopian Electric Light and Power Authority (EELPA), from the Imperial regime and the Derg. The TPLF's socialist ideology remained a prominent influence on the EPRDF's approach to the electricity sector in the early years of its administration. One former TPLF Central Committee member recalls that the key reference point within the EPRDF remained Lenin's famous statement:[7]

> Communism is Soviet power plus the electrification of the whole country... Only when the country has been electrified, and industry, agriculture and transport have been placed on the technical basis of modern large-scale industry, only then shall we be fully victorious. (Lenin 1920)

TPLF/EPRDF party documents from the civil war onwards repeatedly stated that electricity and other key economic sectors should remain 'under state control' in the interests of creating a self-reliant economy free of 'imperialist' influence (TPLF 1983, p. 11; EPRDF 1993). Shortly after taking power, EPRDF documents reasserted that 'imperialism and the comprador class' were 'enemies' of the Front, while the national bourgeoisie was an untrustworthy 'vacillating force' (EPRDF 1993). As such, the EPRDF retained all electricity generation, transmission, and distribution under state control within EELPA, while foreign investors 'should never be allowed to involve at any scale in basic services such as telephone, electricity, train transport, etc' (EPRDF 1993).[8]

Despite foreign aid providing the majority of the electricity sector budget in the early 1990s (World Bank 1996, p. 22), the EPRDF remained committed to state control of the electricity sector in the face of pressure from the World Bank and other agencies. In the mid-1990s World Bank support for the electricity sector, including the Gilgel Gibe I Dam, discussed below, was made conditional on electricity sector reform (World Bank 1996, 1997). But the government refused to move away from state ownership. As one senior and longstanding official in the sector outlined,

[7] Interview EG46, former TPLF Central Committee member, Addis Ababa, 7 August 2019.
[8] Paulos Milkias (2003) claims Prime Minister Meles planned to privatize EELPA in the 1990s but this move was vetoed by the TPLF leadership. This claim is completely at odds with all other evidence from the time and we have been unable to find any evidence in support of it.

> There was concern about the direction of reform—the World Bank was pushing for privatization and deeper reform ... Our government was ardent and unyielding on privatization, but incremental privatization on generation was accepted. They told the Bank, 'this is the extent we can go and if that is not enough then we don't want your money'.[9]

As such, EELPA was corporatized in 1997 and re-named the Ethiopian Electric Power Company (EEPCo) overseen by an independent regulator, the Ethiopian Electricity Agency (EEA). Subsequently, the 2002 investment proclamation permitted private investors to generate electricity and sell to EEPCo for the first time (FDRE 2002) and the government committed to introduce cost reflective tariffs. In reality, however, the changes were aesthetic. EEA lacked the capacity to regulate the larger and more powerful EEPCo. Meanwhile, the government maintained a deliberate policy of setting low tariffs for industrial and mass users (see Chapter 8), which meant that EEPCo—tasked with making massive investments in generation and transmission—could not possibly operate as a corporatized state enterprise, while low tariffs discouraged any private investment.

Hydropower dominance in Ethiopia's energy mix is closely linked to this state dominance of the electricity sector. The planning and construction of dams under previous regimes meant that hydropower had gradually become embedded within the state bureaucracy and the limited existing knowledge and expertise. As such, water was seen both within the state and general population as *the* potential source of energy, and dams were key to national development as the means of realizing this potential. As one long-term official in the sector emphasized,

> Water has been the message since childhood. It is what you are told in school—that the country's key resource is the water. It comes from that mentality.[10]

This longstanding dominance of hydropower was further reinforced under the EPRDF. The EPRDF's leadership planned to remain in office over the long term, and although hydropower requires major upfront investment and takes a long time to come online, it tends to be a relatively cheap source of power in the long term thanks to low operational costs. According to one former minister and an architect of Ethiopia's development strategy,

> From the very beginning it was clear always that power depends on hydropower. The difficulty is that we are looking to industrialize, the service sector and urban areas are expanding demand. We have to meet those demands. We were looking

[9] Interview EG6, senior official in the energy sector, Addis Ababa, 3 October 2019.

[10] Interview EG2, former senior Ministry of Water, Irrigation, and Energy official, Addis Ababa, 3 September 2019, 13 February 2020.

> forward over a long period to industrialization and rural electrification. It is the only way.[11]

Consequently, the EPRDF Government recurrently chose to invest in hydropower, rather than alternatives which might have provided economically and politically easier short-term solutions. For example, in the mid-1990s the World Bank pushed for investment in thermal generation, which could be more quickly brought online to address looming shortages (World Bank 1996). The government resisted, however, due to concerns about dependence on fossil fuel imports, even at the risk of increased power shortages in the short run. While the initial costs of thermal generation are relatively low, operational costs—particularly the purchase of fuel—remain high throughout the lifetime of the plant and, in a country lacking domestic resources, subject to fluctuations in international prices.

While Ethiopia certainly possesses vast hydropower potential, estimated at some 45,000 MW, the country also has very significant undeveloped potential in renewable energy sources, including geothermal, solar, and wind (see Table 3.1). Indeed, Ethiopia's Rift Valley has among the greatest potential for geothermal energy of any country in the world.[12] The main challenges facing geothermal development, however, were the high upfront costs required to explore and develop wells, and the lack of domestic expertise. Early geothermal exploration in Ethiopia started in 1969, but little progress was made (Teklemariam and Beyene 2005). The first geothermal pilot project was established in 1998, producing 7 MW at Aluto Langano under an engineering, procurement, and construction (EPC) contract, with EEPCo retaining ownership in line with the government's

Table 3.1 Estimated potential of energy sources in Ethiopia

Source	Estimated potential
Hydropower	45,000 MW
Geothermal	10,000 MW
Wind	5,000 MW
Solar	5.2 kWh/m^2/day

Data source: Mengistu et al. (2015), based on figures from the Ministry of Water, Irrigation, and Energy.

[11] Interview EG44, former senior minister and one of the architects of Ethiopia's development plans, Addis Ababa, 1 November 2019.

[12] Interview EP16, investor in geothermal energy, Addis Ababa, 19 August 2019.

general approach to electricity generation.[13] However, it was quickly recognized that further development would necessitate foreign investment to bring required technical expertise that was unavailable internally. As such, geothermal presented a direct challenge to the government's state-controlled electricity sector and its longstanding concerns about private sector involvement. Plans were side-lined in favour of hydropower.

Ethiopia also has considerable potential in solar and wind power. Areas with high wind speeds suitable for windfarms are found primarily on the eastern ridge of the northern highlands and in parts of the southeast in Somali region, while areas with the highest solar irradiation are found primarily in the north and east of the country, although solar has potential across the country (Parsons Brinckerhoff 2014). At least as early as 1996, the World Bank was promoting solar energy, particularly as an off-grid solution for rural areas (World Bank 1996, p. viii). However, in the 1990s both wind and solar were still relatively new and unproven technologies in which Ethiopia had no expertise, as well as being expensive. As such, they were a poor fit for the EPRDF's state-led model for the electricity sector. Furthermore, as the World Bank acknowledged, there was 'an almost complete lack of analysis' of the feasibility of renewable energy in Ethiopia (World Bank 1996, p. viii).

The government's almost exclusive commitment to hydropower, therefore, is rooted in the distribution of power within the ruling elite and its long-term outlook that aligned with the low long-run costs of hydropower. The government's aim was to make long-term, economically sustainable investments in electricity generation that avoided adding dependence on limited foreign exchange reserves. This decision to focus on hydropower led to a boom in dam building that is key to the subsequent successes and limitations of the EPRDF's economic project, its claims to have promoted ethnic self-determination, and its international relations. While hydroelectric power was undoubtedly the main driver of the dam-building programme, the government also consistently sought to link dam construction to the promotion of large-scale irrigation in lowland areas, providing a supplemental rationale for focusing on dams (MoPED 1993; TGE 1994a).[14] Finally, it is worth noting that at this early stage, the government's justification for focusing on hydropower was entirely related to the availability of resources, cost, and the commitment to state investment. At this point, there was no reference in available documents to any environmental benefits of hydropower over other energy sources.

[13] An EPC is a turnkey construction contract, with the commissioning utility retaining ownership and responsible for operation once completed.

[14] Also interview EG45 with Newai Gebre-Ab, advisor to the prime minister, Addis Ababa, 1 October 2018; and EG46, former TPLF Central Committee member and member of the EELPA board, Addis Ababa, 7 August 2019.

Dam Ambitions amidst Capacity Constraints

Ethiopia certainly had greater experience and expertise in hydropower compared to other renewable energy sources. However, this is not to say that the Ethiopian state possessed great technical capacity in hydrology or hydroelectric power. Indeed, the EPRDF Government soon identified a lack of capacity as a major barrier to its ambitions and one that would need to be quickly addressed. Past analyses of Ethiopia's unfulfilled ambitions to develop the Nile waters frequently identified the lack of technical capacity as among the major barriers. The political upheaval and regular purging of officials under the Derg meant that initial investments in training as part of the United States Bureau of Reclamation (USBR) study in the 1960s had not resulted in a strong cadre of expertise in water and hydropower (Waterbury 2002). Moreover, overlapping, unclear, and frequently changing remits of relevant agencies undermined government efforts (Abate 1994, p. 62). The result, according to John Waterbury, was that 'Ethiopia seems perpetually at the very beginning of a Nile learning curve' (Waterbury 2002, p. 71). A comparable situation pertained within EELPA itself, with a World Bank study concluding that

> EELPA does not appear to have the technical or administrative capacity required for a major expansion of its activities. (World Bank 1996, p. vii)

These specific challenges within the water and electricity sectors were further compounded by problems within the civil service in general. After taking power in 1991, the EPRDF confronted a bureaucracy that was largely resistant to the Tigrayan-dominated movement that had seized power through force. An inimical relationship between the EPRDF and the bureaucracy was established based on the dominant view within the party leadership that the latter was the hotbed of 'bureaucratic capitalism' whereby public office was a route to self-enrichment (EPRDF 1990). The antagonistic nature of initial relations was noted by Vaughan and Tronvoll (2003, p. 94) who recall that during the transitional government of the early 1990s,

> many EPRDF officials openly expressed the view that the 'moribund' civil service was 'the next enemy we have to fight now that we have overcome the Dergue'.

The TPLF/EPRDF had always been a vanguard party, responsible for mobilizing and raising the consciousness of the masses under a framework of revolutionary democracy and democratic centralism (EPRDF 1993, 2010a). According to democratic centralism, debate and discussion is encouraged within party structures, but once the vanguard comes to a decision on the way forward, this decision is considered binding on all. The result was that the EPRDF vanguard saw its role as controlling and pressurizing the bureaucracy to adhere to the Front's directives (De Waal 2015). According to one TPLF official cited by Weis (2015),

> Through policies, supervision, monitoring and through pressure, so somehow the bureaucracy will split into those who will really cope up with the system, and those who will not cope up. And that is a long process.

To dominate the civil service, many EPRDF fighters were trained as civil servants through the Civil Service College and placed in key positions, including leading many state enterprises (Vaughan and Tronvoll 2003). Furthermore, the system of *gimgema* which the TPLF had used as a means of ensuring accountability and discipline during the civil war was extended to the civil service as a whole (Berhe 2020). *Gimgema* is a process of critique and self-critique undertaken by individuals in front of their superiors and subordinates. While it may have some potential as a rudimentary system of performance evaluation, it is widely viewed as a mechanism of political discipline, 'a basis on which to attack, often even humiliate, those who promoted alternative viewpoints' (Vaughan 2011, p. 628). As such, it has been widely resented by the civil service. Nonetheless, the party gradually fused with the bureaucracy, providing the political leadership with greater control over the administrative apparatus.

The study, planning, financing, construction, and operation of dams also required an expansion of technical and administrative expertise. To this end, in the mid-1990s the government sent a select group of government officials, including engineers and economists, to study for master's degrees in the UK.[15] Many of these officials subsequently returned to leadership positions in the hydropower sector. Among the priorities were the Ministry of Water,[16] including its Hydropower Study Department that is responsible for commissioning river basin studies and project feasibility studies to prepare candidate projects. These various studies were, by and large, contracted to leading global firms with established expertise. However, in 1998 the government also created the Water Works Design and Supervision Enterprise (WWDSE) to provide domestic capacity to study irrigation schemes and small storage dams.

[15] Interview EG46, Addis Ababa, 7 August 2019 and EG13, former head of planning EEPCo, Addis Ababa, 19 February 2020.

[16] At this point, the energy brief was housed within the Ministry of Mines and Energy, with a distinct Ministry of Water.

According to the formal division of powers, candidate projects identified by the Ministry of Water would then be passed to EEPCo, which had responsibility for planning electricity generation to meet estimated future demand through the periodic Power Sector Masterplans (PSMPs). For the most part, these Masterplans were also contracted out to foreign consultants, though EEPCo did attempt plan updates itself.[17] Once projects were selected, contractors for project design and construction should be selected through competitive tenders, according to national laws. EEPCo retained responsibility for overseeing construction on an EPC basis and, on completion, taking over operation of the hydropower project. Effectively, then, EEPCo's role was to recruit and oversee firms to carry out the projects, and then to operate the completed dams. As one senior official admitted,

> everything is outsourced ... There is expertise as supervisors, but we don't have expertise as contractors or in engineering.[18]

The main Ethiopian agency with civil engineering capacity, the Ethiopian Water Works Construction Enterprise (EWWCE), was created during the Imperial regime. However, by the 1990s its largest venture was the relatively small Alwero Dam in Gambella built under the Derg.[19] Under the EPRDF, EWWCE was tasked with building several water storage dams, such as the Angereb Dam that provides water for Gondar, completed in 1997, and Midmar that provides water for Adwa, completed in 1996.[20] In addition, Sur Construction, established as part of the TPLF-owned EFFORT conglomerate in 1992, developed into a leading domestic firm in the construction of roads, airports, and large buildings, and was also brought in as a sub-contractor on several dam projects (Vaughan and Gebremichael 2011). While the government therefore sought to support domestic firms to develop expertise in the long term, the reality was that in the short to medium term domestic capacity in the study and design of dams through to the civil and electro-mechanical engineering works remained severely limited. Delivering on the government's ambitions for large-scale hydropower development would inevitably require the involvement of foreign firms.

Soon after taking office, the new government commissioned river basin masterplans for all the major river basins, and these were completed in the late 1990s (Richard Woodroofe and Associates 1996; MoWR 1998, 1999). This included plans for dams on the main Nile. Yet, the government's resources—in terms of

[17] Interview EG8, senior official in the electricity sector, Addis Ababa, 3 October 2019 and 11 February 2020.
[18] Interviews EG8, senior official in the electricity sector, Addis Ababa, 3 October 2019 and 11 February 2020; and EP17, consultant in the electricity sector, Addis Ababa, 4 June 2019.
[19] Interview EG5, ECWC official, Addis Ababa, 11 February 2020.
[20] Interview EG5, ECWC official, Addis Ababa, 11 February 2020.

finance and technical expertise—did not match these ambitions. Ethiopia lacked the ability to carry out or finance projects without significant external support, which would not be forthcoming for a Nile dam. While the ambition was undoubtedly to move towards autonomy in dam building, this could only be a long-term goal. For the time being, the government's ambitions on the Nile were limited to negotiating with Egypt and Sudan in an attempt to secure a collaborative agreement (see Chapter 6).

Instead, the government developed a series of comparatively small projects that would go some way to addressing the looming shortage of electricity generation capacity and expand irrigation, while focusing on economic growth that would ultimately give the government greater independence. As Meles underscored,

> We do not have billions and billions of dollars stacked somewhere in the banks—that's why we're poor. What we have in abundance is labour. You do not build big hydro-powered dams with labour only—you need money, you need resources. So what we have tried to do is focus on agriculture—promote agricultural growth as a means of kick-starting the process of industrialization [i.e. ADLI] ... As we accumulate resources, then we can have large scale irrigation projects and hydro-powered dams. How fast we can go in this regard will depend on whether we accumulate adequate resources of our own or whether our resources are adequately augmented from outside. (Meles, cited in BBC News 2005)

As such, the EPRDF Government's first steps were significant, albeit relatively modest compared to later dam building. One important initiative was the plan to build thousands of micro-dams across highland Ethiopia, including the broader Nile Basin, to provide irrigation for smallholder farmers (Waterbury and Whittington 1998). These dams could be built without international finance and largely through contributions of labour from the farmers themselves. In addition, the government pursued an initial set of hydroelectric projects, several of which restarted projects initiated by the Derg but abandoned after the change in government. These included expanding hydroelectric generation at Tis Abay on the Blue Nile and restarting Gilgel Gibe I, as well as a new venture that would signal Ethiopia's ambitions on the Nile: Tekeze. These projects, unlike their successors, were located in areas of relatively high population density, near to population centres with unmet demand for electricity or on the existing electric grid. Given the political importance of securing a political base amongst the smallholder majority, the EPRDF Government has long sought to minimize displacement of smallholders. However, given the size of the projects, the total number of people affected was relatively small.

Tis Abay was selected as it did not require construction of a major dam and could therefore add to installed capacity in a much shorter timespan than other projects (Coyne and Bellier et al. 1996). The project finally realized a century's worth of plans to regulate the flow of water from Lake Tana with construction of the Chara-Chara weir. However, without adding storage capacity, the projects did little to affect the flow to downstream riparians. The weir was subsequently expanded to regulate the waters for a second Tis Abay plant with 73-MW capacity, completed in 2001 (McCartney et al. 2009) (see Figure 3.2). The most visible impact of the project was to divert water away from the Tis Issat (Blue Nile) Falls, an important tourist attraction that was reduced to a trickle during plant operation. Moreover, the regulation of Lake Tana negatively impacted the Negede Woito, a marginalized minority group who mainly eke out a livelihood by making and operating canoes made of papyrus, and selling papyrus trunks to urban dwellers. The drying up of the lake shores led to an influx of recession farmers, compromising the livelihoods of the Negede Woito (Gebre et al. 2008).

On a larger scale, the government restarted construction of the 184-MW Gilgel Gibe I Dam, which was completely redesigned and construction started from scratch. For a project of this size, the government had no option but to seek foreign finance and technical expertise. Funding was eventually secured from the World Bank, European Investment Bank, and Nordic Development Fund as part of a reform package for the electricity sector, which required Ethiopia to corporatize EEPCo. Compared to subsequent projects on the Omo, Gilgel Gibe I was relatively uncontroversial. Located on the Gilgel Gibe tributary near Jimma (see Figure 3.3), the dam is relatively small and has a modest impact on the main river downstream. As a result, the Kenyan Government's statement of 'no objection', required for World Bank support on a transboundary river, was forthcoming without issue (World Bank 1997, p. 12). Under World Bank procurement rules, the works were divided into multiple competitively tendered lots, resulting in the involvement of 12 international firms including the Italian firms Enel Power, Trevi, and Salini, the Spanish firm Necso, and German company Zueblin (EELPA 1997a; Tunnelbuilder 2008). Most significantly, Salini undertook much of the civil engineering work, the first of what would be many hydropower projects under the EPRDF (see Chapter 5). The reservoir required the resettlement of some 2,000 households, apparently in line with World Bank procedures (World Bank 1997, p. 11). The dam was finally completed in 2004.

Rather than the beginning of a new partnership in dam building, however, Gilgel Gibe I signalled an end to the World Bank's direct financing for Ethiopian

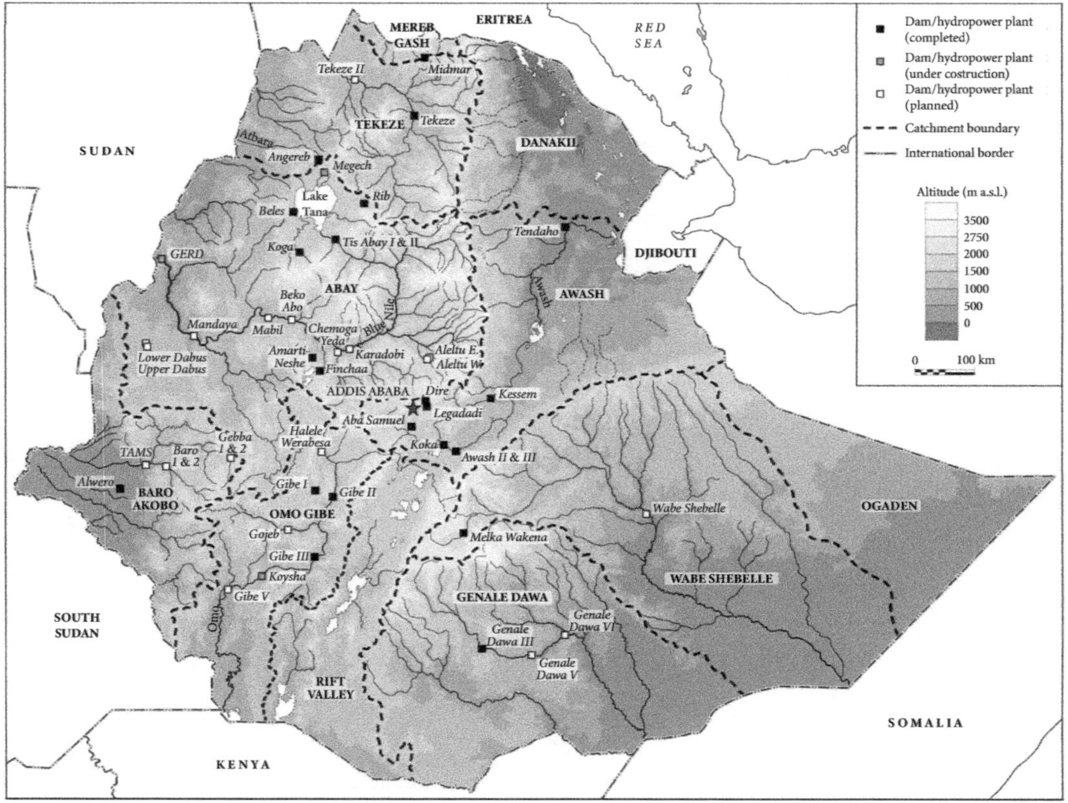

Figure 3.2 Ethiopia's dams and hydropower projects

Source: Author and Manchester Cartographic Unit.

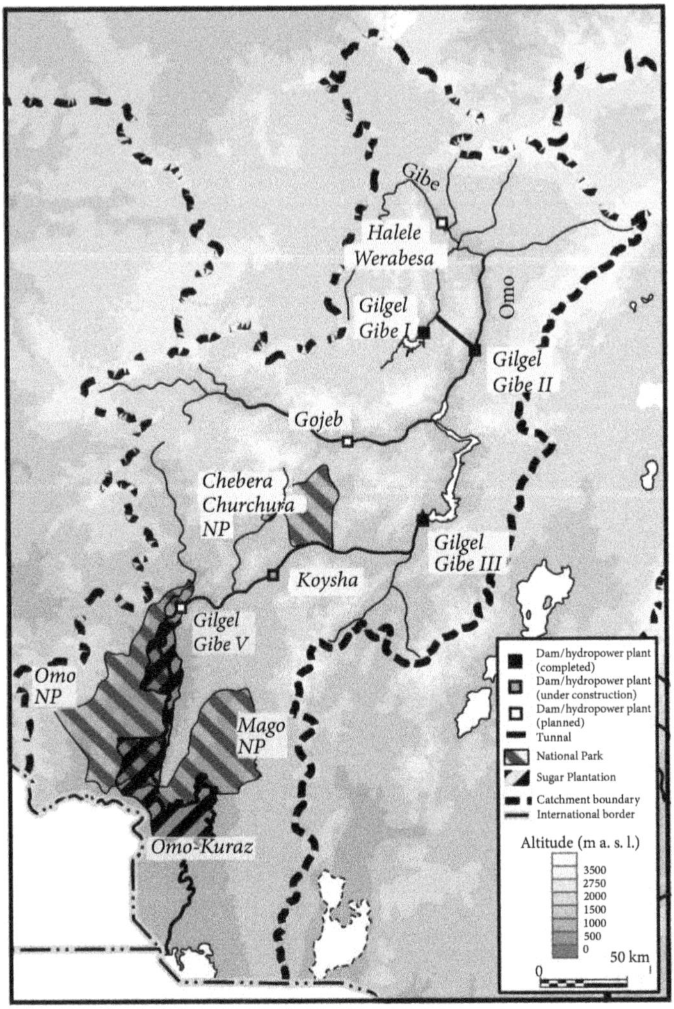

Figure 3.3 Major projects in the Omo Basin
Source: Author and Manchester Cartographic Unit.

dams, in line with the Bank's reduction in support for dam projects globally.[21] As an economic advisor to Meles noted,

> The World Bank told us, 'this is the last time that we will assist you. From now on it will have to be based on private sector investment'. Well, we were not impressed.

[21] However, the World Bank did play a key role in the Nile Basin Initiative that sought a collaborative approach to dam building on the Blue Nile (see Chapter 6).

> We didn't expect foreign investment in hydropower. It is too much of a long-term investment. We concluded we have to do it ourselves, we can do a small 100 MW project on our own. But as you go along, the ambition develops ...[22]

Indeed, even at this early stage the government did make efforts to mobilize domestic resources for power projects and other infrastructure investments. According to a former TPLF Central Committee member,

> We knew very well that we will not get assistance from the donors for dams, especially in the Nile Basin. Thus, there was a unanimous agreement on financing dams by ourselves. This led to a serious storage of foreign currency outside the sight of IMF. This was not accounted in official reserves, and not seen by IMF experts. We managed to save 600 million USD this way.[23]

These efforts were derailed, however, by the Eritrean War that began in 1998. The flashpoint for the outbreak of war was a border dispute. However, the conflict has deeper roots related to Ethiopia's attempts to industrialize through import substitution, which excluded Eritrea from the Ethiopian market, and contestation over the creation of an Eritrean currency (Negash and Tronvoll 2000). The conflict constituted a major drain on Ethiopian financial resources with the result that this secret store of foreign exchange was instead used for military expenditure.[24] The result was that by the time the Eritrean conflict ground to a halt in 2000, the government's finances remained in a perilous state, placing a serious constraint on its developmental ambitions.

The third project pursued at this time, the 300-MW Tekeze hydropower project, also had far-reaching significance. Built by a Chinese firm on the Tigray–Amhara border, Tekeze was particularly significant within the Nile hydropolitics as a unilateral and apparently self-financed major dam on a Nile tributary (see Chapter 6).[25] The decision to build Tekeze was taken in the mid-1990s based on a series of studies undertaken even before the Tekeze River Basin masterplan was produced. Studies of the Tekeze Basin in the 1980s had concluded that it offered the least potential of any of the river basins in western Ethiopia, while the

[22] Interview EG45, Newai Gebre-Ab, former advisor to the prime minister, Addis Ababa, 1 October 2018.

[23] Interview EG46, former TPLF Central Committee member and member of the EELPA board, Addis Ababa, 7 August 2019.

[24] Interview EG46, former TPLF Central Committee member and member of the EELPA board, Addis Ababa, 7 August 2019.

[25] There remains some doubt about the financing of Tekeze. Brautigam and Hwang (2019) were unable to locate a loan agreement and therefore conclude that it was likely fully funded by the Ethiopian Government, as have others (Waterbury and Whittington 1998). Yet Foster et al. (2009, pp. 116–117) report data, apparently confirmed by official Chinese sources, that the Chinese Exim Bank committed $50 million of the $224 million construction costs.

project was technically challenging and, following Eritrean secession, there was no major existing demand for electricity in the area (Waterbury 2002, p. 109). Some respondents even claimed that consultants had previously rejected a dam at the site.[26] Consequently, many have concluded that Tekeze was chosen over other more favourable sites in other river basins in order to provide power for Mekele, the capital of Tigray, and as a means of stimulating economic development in the TPLF's home region (Waterbury 2002). The construction contract was competitively tendered with Chinese firms Sinohydro and China Gezhouba Group Company (CGGC) selected ahead of competitors such as Salini (Brautigam and Tang 2012). As such, this suggests that in the 1990s Salini was merely one of many potential contractors, not at that time the trusted and favoured contractor it was to become later on. The Tekeze reservoir required displacement of 1,549 households, largely in Amhara, as well as disruption for many more who were cut off from previous livelihoods and transport routes by the reservoir (Gizachew 2017, p. 68).

The EPRDF Government therefore came into power viewing the rapid development of the country as a political imperative for the consolidation of its rule, with the expansion of electricity generation expected to play a central role in structural transformation. The reality, however, was that initial progress was modest. Economic growth throughout the 1990s was highly erratic with some recovery from the conflict, but several years of negative growth as a result of drought. Moreover, the outbreak of war with Eritrea diverted the leadership's attention from the economy and led to growing political divisions. Nonetheless, these initial projects, which would not be completed for several years, were a sign of growing ambitions and a shift from the Awash and Wabe Shebele, which still provided the majority of Ethiopia's electricity in the early 1990s to the Omo and the broader Nile Basin. In themselves, Tis Abay and Tekeze had little downstream impact on Sudan and Egypt. However, they demonstrated future ambitions and were a useful signal to Egypt—as it unilaterally initiated the Toshka irrigation project around the same time—that Ethiopia could also unilaterally pursue projects on the Nile (Waterbury 2002; Cascão 2009). Moreover, Tekeze introduced an unknown quantity into Nile Basin dynamics: Egypt had been very effective at blocking multilateral and Western finance for upstream dams. As China emerged as a major player in dam finance and construction in Africa, it was far from clear whether Egypt would have also sufficient influence to block Chinese involvement on the Nile (Cascão 2009).

[26] Interview EG9, senior engineer in the energy sector, Addis Ababa, 23 July 2019 and 17 September 2019.

Armageddons and the Emergence of the 'Developmental State'

The government's focus on economic growth and industrialization as the basis of its political survival was reinforced by political upheaval in the early 2000s. A major split in the TPLF in 2001 is widely acknowledged as a key juncture in the trajectory of the EPRDF and Ethiopian politics more broadly, and this had important implications for the government's approach to the electricity sector also. The split was sparked by a power struggle between then Prime Minister Meles Zenawi and the TPLF leadership in Mekele, and a debate over the handling of the Eritrean War (1998–2000) (Milkias 2003; Tadesse and Young 2003). In retrospect, the split and the victory of Meles' faction led to a shift away from the previous system of collective leadership in the TPLF towards increased centralization of power under the prime minister. In doing so, this split also entailed the removal of many among the left wing of the party, with Meles' EPRDF formally embracing capitalist development thereafter (Milkias 2003; Tadesse and Young 2003; Simon 2011; Lefort 2012). As one TPLF Central Committee member remarked,

> One group saw the other as lenient, subservient, capitalist, while the other had views of the counterpart as die hard, socialist, and leftist.[27]

This political crisis within the TPLF was soon followed by further upheaval: a wave of anti-government protests in Addis Ababa in 2001 that began in Addis Ababa University but soon spread across the city; and a major food crisis in 2002/3. Combined, these crises highlighted the limited progress with the government's development strategy and the risk that growing rural land shortages and urban unemployment presented to the ruling coalition (Lavers 2023). The outcome of these crises was Meles Zenawi's consolidation of power and increased coherence amongst the political elite around the goal of creating an East Asian-style 'developmental state' to deliver rapid development as a necessity to avert the looming 'Armageddons' that threatened the EPRDF and the country.[28] This developmental commitment was further reinforced by the 2005 elections. Initially confident of success, the EPRDF was surprised by the coherence of opposition coalitions and the mass support they secured in urban areas, Amhara and Oromiya in particular (Arriola 2008; Tronvoll 2009). According to official results, opposition parties secured almost all urban seats and about one-third of the total parliamentary seats,

[27] Interview EG46, former TPLF Central Committee member and member of the EELPA board, Addis Ababa, 7 August 2019.

[28] 'Armageddons' was a term coined by Meles, according to EG48, Deputy Prime Minister Addisu Legesse, Addis Ababa, 7 October 2014, and Bereket Simon (2011).

while opposition leaders organized large-scale demonstrations in May and June, claiming overall victory.

The government's response to the electoral crisis was, on the one hand, to close space for political opposition, arresting opposition leaders and renewing EPRDF party mobilization efforts (Tronvoll 2011). On the other hand, however, the ruling elite doubled down on rapid development and service delivery as a means of securing popular compliance (Lavers 2023). Subsequently, rapid development was seen by the EPRDF not just as desirable but as a necessity to avert the existential threat of poverty and unemployment, effectively the 'securitization of development' (Gebresenbet 2014).

A series of strategic documents published at this time laid out the basis of what became known as Ethiopia's 'developmental state' model, drawing explicitly on the experiences of South Korea and Taiwan (MoI 2002a, 2002b; MoFED 2003). The government outlined increasingly ambitious plans for structural transformation based on massive state investment in infrastructure, promotion of agricultural and industrial production, and expansion of social services. The central focus of this developmental push was an updated, more detailed version of the ADLI strategy that was first outlined in the 1990s (MoFED 2003). ADLI retained its focus on raising the agricultural productivity of smallholder farmers through provision of improved agricultural inputs. However, the government also outlined a concerted strategy to attract foreign and domestic agricultural investors, where these offered increased productivity and export potential (MoFED 2005). Many capital-intensive agricultural investments would focus on the lowlands and required dams to provide irrigation. Moreover, the EPRDF issued its first explicit industrial strategy, which focused primarily on agro-industries based in rural areas to exploit linkages with the agricultural sector, particularly textiles and apparel, leather and leather products, sugar, and floriculture (MoI 2002a). This rural focus was supplemented by the cement industry, seen as a vital input for the construction industry in general (Oqubay 2015) and dam construction in particular.

In turn, this centralization of power further eroded regional autonomy. The EPRDF had always pulled back from full implementation of the federal system it had created due to its concerns about devolving political power to ethno-regional administrations, and the potential for political fragmentation and ethno-nationalism (Vaughan 2003; Fiseha 2006; Lavers 2018). Since the late 1990s, the EPRDF came to embrace Ethiopian national symbols, most notably in its attempt to frame the goal of the 'developmental state' as an *Ethiopian Renaissance.* This nationalist turn sought to cast the EPRDF as reviving the glories of past Ethiopian civilizations from a millennium earlier, and stood in sharp contrast to previous efforts to promote ethno-nationalism as a means of addressing the inequalities inherent to Ethiopia's Imperial history (Orlowska 2013).

The industrial strategy sought to draw lessons from the East Asian industrial experience, building up domestic firms through secure access to the domestic market and joint ventures with foreign investors, but providing industrial policy incentives and penalties to incentivize productivity improvements, enabling firms to move into export markets (Brautigam et al. 2016; Chang and Hauge 2019). As such, the 'developmental state' was to play a key role in disciplining and directing the private sector and, where necessary, intervening directly in the economy (EPRDF 2006; Zenawi 2006a, 2012). The EPRDF divided the private sector between 'productive' investors who could be partners in the 'developmental state' project and 'parasitic' rent seekers that should be suppressed (EPRDF 2010a, p. 7). In practice, the EPRDF often turned to politically connected firms and state corporations to intervene in priority sectors, including EFFORT and other party endowments, MIDROC, and a range of diaspora firms encouraged to invest in Ethiopia.

A key pillar of the development strategy was a major expansion of infrastructure. Rural electrification was seen as vital to the realization of the agriculture-focused development strategy (MoFED 2003). Moreover, reliable access to electricity was a pre-requisite for rural-based industrialization, and cheap electricity a key means of subsidizing industrial investors (MoI 2002a). As such, despite the EPRDF's formal embrace of capitalism, the government still considered state control of the electricity sector to be a red line. For the government, private investment in electricity would likely lead to 'rent seeking', whereas state ownership enabled the government to keep electricity tariffs low as an important subsidy to industry, as well as a means of reaching out to the masses.[29] Low tariffs, in contrast, meant that private investments in generation were unviable. Meles subsequently outlined this reasoning in a 2012 discussion:

> if the private sector were to engage in the generation of electricity ... what will be the cost? Their discount rate is steep. They have to have their profits and who is going to pay for that? It's the manufacturing factory. So, which one do I want to support more? The private sector that generates electricity or the private sector that uses electricity? For me, supporting the private sector that uses electricity is more important for transformation, than allowing the private sector to generate electricity.[30]

According to a senior official, there was one early attempt to work with an independent power producer (IPP) in Ethiopia on the Gojeb Dam in the Gibe-Omo Basin. Advanced negotiations were held with MIDROC, the company owned by

[29] The Universal Electrification Access Programme (UEAP), launched in 2005, is discussed in Chapter 8.

[30] Comments made at the World Economic Forum (2012). Quote is taken from 43 minutes onwards.

Ethio-Saudi billionaire Sheik Mohammed Al-Amoudi who had close ties to the EPRDF. Yet the deal collapsed precisely because of the government's low electricity tariffs:

> there was a mismatch, a misunderstanding. EEPCo wanted to buy electricity cheaply, but MIDROC wanted to make returns quickly by selling at a high price ... they couldn't agree on the PPA [power purchase agreement]. So Gojeb was cancelled.[31]

The result was that the private sector and its 'rent-seeking' tendencies remained excluded from electricity generation, with opportunities limited to EPC contracts for state-planned and operated projects. Meanwhile, the government's growing ambitions for electricity generation would have to be met by the financial and technical resources that could be mobilized by the state.

Building Capacity for Ethiopian Developmentalism

The TPLF split in 2001 and Meles Zenawi's subsequent consolidation of power heralded a step change in government ambitions and, with it, the government's strategy for financing its infrastructural plans and building the state's capacity to deliver. This strategy involved mobilizing all available external funding in support of the development strategy, while maximizing domestic resource mobilization to address the gaps.

Part of the government's approach is laid out in the 2002 Foreign Policy and Strategy (MoI 2002b), authored by Meles, which examines how the government should engage strategically with foreign donors and international partners in the pursuit of its development ambitions. This approach entailed actively identifying areas of shared commitment in which donors would be willing to finance government priorities, while reserving available state resources for government priorities not shared by donors, thereby enhancing government resources and policy autonomy (Furtado and Smith 2009).

During the 2000s, Ethiopia assumed greater geo-strategic importance for many Western donors. Ethiopia had been prioritized by the US and some other donors as an ally in the Horn of Africa from the 1990s based on US anti-terrorism policy, given the rise of radical Islam in Sudan and Somalia (Feyissa 2011). This relationship with the US and the flow of resources to Ethiopia was only strengthened in the wake of the 11 September 2001 attacks and the US's 'War on Terror', with the result that Ethiopia came to be seen as a trusted ally and a key source of political stability in the Horn of Africa. The EPRDF was able to leverage this geo-strategic

[31] Interview EG9, senior EEP official, Addis Ababa, 23 July 2019 and 17 September 2019.

importance into increased economic and diplomatic support. Nevertheless, in this period, Western donors had also embraced the Millennium Development Goals and the anti-poverty agenda, leading to a primary focus on basic social services and anti-poverty programmes (Mkandawire 2010). As such, Western aid provided funding for a major expansion of education, healthcare, and social protection, but relatively little for other government priorities such as infrastructure and industrial development.

An important exception was the 420-MW Gilgel Gibe II hydropower plant, which was built with finance from the Italian Government and the European Investment Bank. As discussed in Chapter 5, Studio Pietrangeli's proposal of the idea for Gibe II and Salini's ability to broker finance from the Italian Government enabled the emergence of Salini as the go-to contractor for Ethiopia's dam building. The Gibe II project itself was relatively uncontroversial since it did not involve additional water storage, merely taking advantage of the outflow from Gibe I to produce additional energy downstream. Critics of the project instead focused on the tunnel linking the two hydropower projects, raising concerns about the danger of seismic activity and financing arrangements for the project.

Given the limited interest of Western donors in infrastructure at the time, an important development in this period was the emergence of China as a major source of finance and technical expertise for infrastructure projects in Africa and globally (Bräutigam 2009; Brautigam and Hwang 2019). The Ethiopian Government, and Meles in particular, actively sought Chinese support for Ethiopian development from the late 1990s (Cheru 2016). During the 2000s this strategy began to bear fruit with a growing portfolio of loans, particularly focused on upgrading the mobile phone and road networks (Foster et al. 2009). In terms of dams, China's Exim Bank provided a $116 million loan for the Neshe Dam, the final part of the Finchaa-Amarti-Neshe complex commenced under Haile Selassie, in 2007, as well as $270 million in 2009 for Genale Dawa III (GDPC 2022), both of which were contracted to the CGGC. Meanwhile, Chinese firms and finance would also go on to build a series of dams elsewhere in the Nile Basin, notably in Sudan and Uganda (see Chapter 6).

In addition to external support, during the 2000s, the Ethiopian Government was able to draw on gradually expanding domestic resources to finance its plans. Ethiopia was one of the countries that qualified for debt relief under the highly indebted poor countries (HIPC) initiative in the mid-2000s and this provided some fiscal space (Manyazewal 2019). The government also undertook a series of tax reforms aimed at increasing revenue mobilization after 2001, albeit these initially delivered few positive results as a result of low compliance (Mascagni 2016). More importantly, the EPRDF's experiment with state-led development delivered a period of rapid economic growth that averaged more than 10 per cent per year in

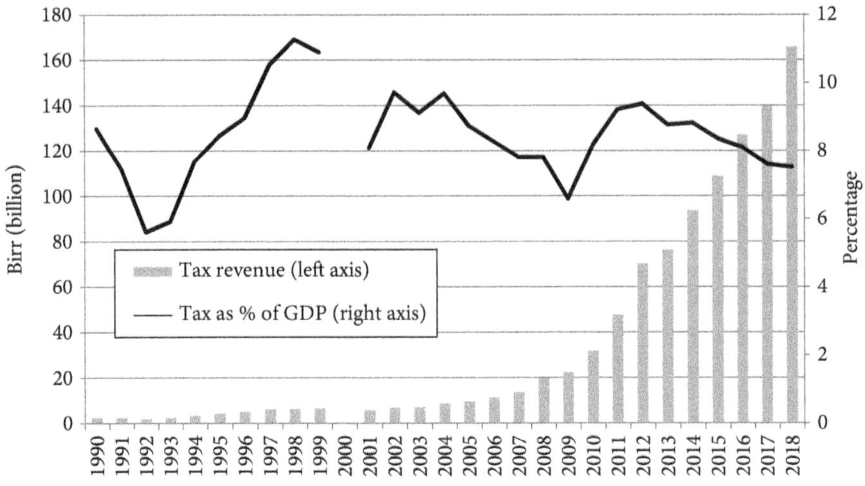

Figure 3.4 Tax revenues and rates
Data source: World Development Indicators.

the 15 years from 2004, greatly expanding tax revenues, even though tax as a proportion of gross domestic product (GDP) changed little (see Figure 3.4). Indeed, this economic success and the growing financial support provided by China led to a distinct change in approach in Ethiopia's donor relations. Rather than attempting to placate Western donors with superficial liberalization as in the 1990s, Meles Zenawi became increasingly strident in his criticism of 'neo-liberalism' and advocacy for a 'developmental state' as the solution to the economic challenges facing not just Ethiopia but Africa in general (Zenawi 2006b, 2006a, 2012).

The renewed focus on rapid development also led to a series of civil service reforms in the early 2000s to build state capacity to deliver on the government's increasingly ambitions plans.[32] These included an expansion of staffing from federal to regional and *wereda* (district) levels and a focus on developing strategic planning and service delivery, along with a range of new initiatives inspired by New Public Management (World Bank 2017). In particular, the institutionalization of five-year plans resulted in national development targets being cascaded down through ministries and state agencies as performance targets for directors and managers. Achievement of these targets was, as ever, assessed through *gimgema*. While these reforms are credited with incremental improvements in state capacity, the government also deliberately kept civil service wages low through below-inflation pay increments to keep budgets under control.[33] The result has been that civil service salaries declined compared to those in the private

[32] Interview EG14, former minister, Addis Ababa, 1 November 2018.
[33] Interview EG48, Addisu Legesse, former deputy prime minister, Addis Ababa, 7 October 2015; World Bank (2017).

sector and the aid industry, resulting in a continual drain of many of the most capable officials from state agencies.

With respect to the electricity sector, national development plans are expected to take the demand projections in the periodic PSMPs to set generation targets for EEPCo, with key officials from the CEO down, made accountable for the achievement of these targets.[34] In 2000–3, EEPCo commissioned Acres International to produce a new masterplan, which formed the basis of targets in the Sustainable Development and Poverty Reduction Programme (SDPRP) of 2002–5 (MoFED 2002). In retrospect, that initial strategy was relatively modest in its ambitions and the SDPRP target for 2005 was met with the completion of the Gilgel Gibe I Dam (184 MW) (see Figure 3.5). As a former Ethiopian Electric Power (EEP) official noted, the masterplan

> planned not so big an economic growth forecast. The government acted in a different mode then.[35]

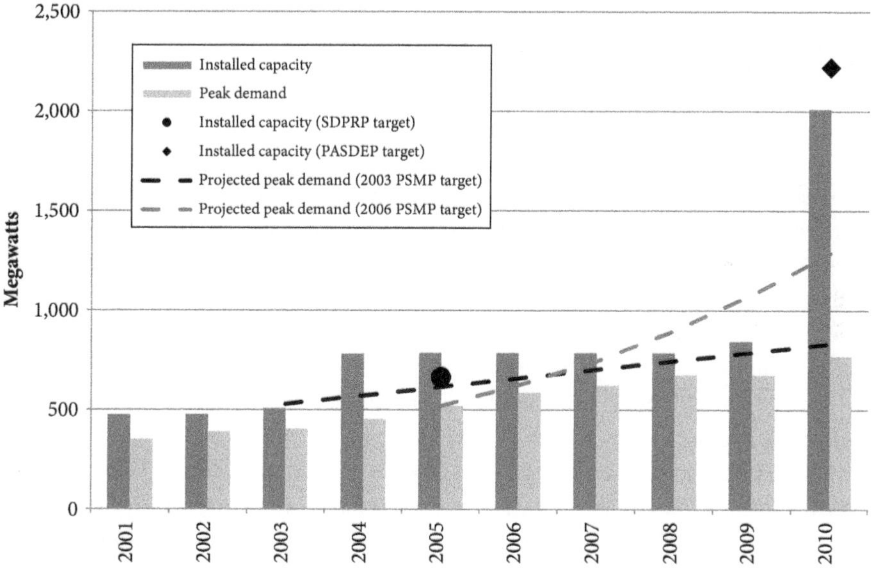

Figure 3.5 Installed capacity and targets during SDPRP and PASDEP, 2001–2010

Note: The 2003 PSMP did not set annual targets for peak demand, rather setting a target for 2012. The line on the graph is derived by pro-rating the increases between 2003 and 2012.
Data source: Acres International (2003), EEPCo (2006), MoFED (2002, 2005), USAID (2019).

[34] Interview EG8, senior electricity sector official, Addis Ababa, 3 October 2019 and 11 February 2020.

[35] Interview EG13, EEP former senior official in the energy sector, Addis Ababa, 19 February 2020.

By the time of the next development plan, the Plan for Accelerated and Sustained Development to End Poverty (PASDEP) (2005–10), government ambitions had risen significantly, however. In part, this was based on the economic successes already achieved. As an economic advisor to the prime minister recalled,

> we had planned for 7 per cent per year growth and unexpectedly found growth of 10 per cent one year [2004]. This demonstrated to us that double-digit growth is possible and that it should be maintained.[36]

This belief in the possibility of rapid growth was reinforced by the political dynamics at the time, notably the Armageddons of the early 2000s and the perceived need for rapid growth and mass electrification to consolidate EPRDF rule. PASDEP targets consequently required a near tripling of installed capacity over five years (MoFED 2005), a target which was well beyond the demand projections in the 2006 update to the masterplan, conducted by EEPCo itself (EEPCo 2006). As such, this constituted a first sign of a gap between the ambitions of the political elite and the technical input from EEPCo and its consultants. While no doubt challenging, EEPCo nonetheless came close to achieving this target through the completion of the long-conceived Tekeze Dam (300 MW) in 2009 and the Gilgel Gibe II hydroelectric project (420 MW) in 2010.

Conclusion

This chapter has located the origins of Ethiopia's dams boom in the political vulnerability and ideological commitments of the EPRDF. On taking power, the EPRDF identified ethnic federalism and structural transformation of the economy as the means of consolidating its power and addressing the vulnerabilities that it faced. Electricity was considered a key pillar of its agro-industrial strategy, while state ownership and state investment in hydropower was considered the only means by which Ethiopia could deliver increased generation and subsidized electricity access.

The EPRDF's initial ability to deliver on these ambitions was severely constrained due to tension with the international finance institutions, on whom the EPRDF depended for financial support, over the role of the state in development, the conflict with Eritrea, and internal political divisions. The 2001 party split and subsequent Armageddons, however, led to a centralization of political power and increasingly ambitious and concerted efforts to promote development as a means of consolidating EPRDF rule. The result was that Ethiopia became more assertive in mobilizing resources from foreign donors, including an increasingly

[36] Interview EG45, Newai Gebre-Ab, senior advisor to the prime minister, Addis Ababa, 1 October 2018.

expansive Chinese involvement in Africa, and domestic revenues to invest in a series of increasingly large hydroelectric projects. Indeed, by the late 2000s there were signs that the political imperative of rapid development had led politicians to bypass technical input into decision making, with EEPCo's performance targets for installed capacity comfortably exceeding those in demand projections.

Growing ambitions for hydroelectric power also had implications for the spatial distribution of new projects. While the new government had long-term ambitions on the Nile, the main priority in the 2000s was the Gibe-Omo, the basin with the second greatest potential for hydropower after the Blue Nile. The Gibe-Omo offered greater potential to secure external finance and expertise for dam construction than a controversial project on the Blue Nile. Moreover, it was through the development of the Gibe-Omo cascade that the government developed trust in the capacity and commitment of Salini, as well as growing belief amongst the political leadership in the government's ability to finance increasingly large-scale projects. This experience would be key to the subsequent decision to pursue a dam on the Blue Nile.

4
Powering the 'Developmental State'

Tom Lavers, Biruk Terrefe, and Fana Gebresenbet

Chapter 3 showed that the Ethiopian Peoples' Revolutionary Democratic Front's (EPRDF's) pursuit of rapid development can be traced to the ruling coalition's origins and its political vulnerability, with structural transformation seen within the leadership as the means of consolidating the ruling party's political position. Despite rapid economic growth and progress in socioeconomic indicators in the second half of the 2000s, this nonetheless fell well short of the EPRDF's ambitions. Ethiopia showed no sign of developing a manufacturing sector that might provide a significant source of employment for Ethiopia's rapidly growing and urbanizing population. Indeed, the government's experience with industrial policy throughout the 2000s had been decidedly mixed, with some successes in developing cement and floriculture industries but very little progress on key priorities such as textiles and apparel, and leather products (Oqubay 2015; Brautigam et al. 2016; Whitfield and Staritz 2021). By 2010, industrial employment remained stagnant at just 8 per cent of the labour force, and growing unemployment and landlessness constituted an increasingly acute political crisis (Lavers 2023).

The EPRDF's response was to double down on the goal of industrialization, and the two five-year Growth and Transformation Plans (GTP1 2010–2015, GTP2 2016–2020) were its response to this challenge. It was in this period that Ethiopia consolidated what the government described as its 'developmental state' strategy, which entailed a further massive upsurge in government ambitions with the goal of maintaining rapid economic growth rates, achieving middle-income economy status, and finally achieving the structural transformation of the economy and creation of mass industrial employment. To do so required state mobilization of ever-greater financial resources from both domestic revenues and external borrowing to fund the government's vast infrastructural plans. It was at this time that the Ethiopian Government finally secured the required combination of elite political cohesion, financial resources, and, through the engagement of Salini (discussed in Chapter 5), sufficient technical capacity to move from developing Ethiopia's less internationally problematic river basins to tackling a major Blue Nile dam. While the government continued to rely heavily on foreign expertise to deliver these projects, it also made renewed efforts to leverage state investment in dams to build domestic capacity, in doing so confronting the industrial policy challenge of building a domestic hydropower industry.

Dams, Power, and the Politics of Ethiopia's Renaissance. Tom Lavers et al., Oxford University Press. © Tom Lavers, Biruk Terrefe, and Fana Gebresenbet (2024). DOI: 10.1093/oso/9780192871213.003.0004

This chapter examines this upsurge in ambition and its implications for decision making in the electricity sector and the spatial distribution of Ethiopia's dams boom. In doing so, the analysis highlights a central contradiction in the EPRDF's 'developmental state' project. This is that, unlike the East Asian states that the government modelled itself upon, Ethiopia struggled to build and empower the technical and bureaucratic expertise required to deliver on the political elite's developmental ambitions. The result in the electricity sector was that political pressure for ever-more rapid progress combined with reliance on foreign contractors to politicize decision making while bypassing technical input. While the centralization of political power and the political elite's pressure for rapid progress was undoubtedly a major factor that drove Ethiopia's expansion of electricity generation capacity through construction of several large and politically challenging dams, the result was a series of increasingly risky and inefficient projects.

The chapter begins by discussing how new development strategies in 2010 and 2015 were tasked with further accelerating national development. The chapter then turns to the political efforts to expand the financial and technical capacity to deliver on the government's ambitions plans for the electricity sector, initially focusing on the Gibe-Omo cascade. Around the end of the 2000s, the government also began to frame its longstanding commitment to hydropower in terms of the creation of a 'green developmental state' compatible with sustainability goals, unlike the carbon-intensive growth of early industrializers. Finally, the chapter examines the political dynamics shaping the 'developmental state' following the death of its visionary, Meles Zenawi, in 2012.

Growth and Transformation

The government's ambitions were fuelled by successes in economic growth rates and other socioeconomic indicators during the 2000s, as well as the slow rate of industrial expansion and the concern that economic growth was not translating into increased employment (Lavers 2023). GTP1 (2010–2015) renewed the government's commitment to industrial development and key priority sectors such as textiles and apparel, leather and leather products, and agro-processing. Furthermore, within the agricultural sector, the plan outlined a new emphasis on commercialization with production of high-value agricultural products linked to agro-processing and export markets. The government actively promoted foreign and domestic investment in labour-intensive floriculture and horticulture in densely populated smallholder areas near to major airports, as well as large-scale mechanized plantations in lowland areas (Lavers 2012a, 2012b; Gebresenbet 2016; Melese 2017). This included a massive expansion of the state-owned sugar industry with expansion of existing plantations and vast new plantations and factories, primarily in lowland areas in the Southern Nations, Nationalities, and

Peoples Region (SNNPR), Oromiya, and Afar (Lavers 2012a; Gebresenbet and Kamski 2019). Much of the irrigated agriculture was dependent on the water provided by upstream dam development.

Once again, the political imperative of rapid development translated into expectations of ever-greater need for electricity. Industrial expansion and the planned construction of a 2,395-kilometre electric railway network linking Djibouti to Addis Ababa, Mekele, Weldiya, and Konso would require greatly increased generation capacity. Although initially focused on domestic energy requirements, ambitions also quickly grew beyond Ethiopia. The possibility of Ethiopia exploiting its hydropower potential to export to neighbouring countries had been identified since the 1960s (USBR 1964; WAPCOS 1990). Under the EPRDF these ambitions expanded, with electricity exports increasingly seen as a means of compensating for slower-than-expected growth in industrial exports, thereby addressing the country's increasingly acute foreign exchange shortages (see Chapter 8). One of the main architects of the national development strategies underscored the ceaseless pressure felt by the leadership to expand generation capacity in anticipation of ever-rising demand:

> we started with smaller ones [dams] that were ready and in the meantime we made others ready. Demand was growing all the time. We completed one project but [by then] the demand had grown. The only way was to overwhelm the problem—to see if that is feasible. Why not a dam of 1,000 MW that gives us the capacity to overwhelm the problem? Then if there is surplus we can discuss with other countries about exporting electricity ... The thinking grew but emanated from industrialization and the acceleration of domestic demand.[1]

The necessity of rapidly developing ever-bigger projects was also emphasized to a key contractor involved in several projects during this period:

> The idea was growth linked to electricity, energy. I don't know where they [the government] got the figure from but they always talked about 17 per cent annual growth of demand of energy and they wanted to anticipate that growth.[2]

The combined result of growing developmental ambitions, the perceived need to 'overwhelm' growing domestic demand, and the desire to become a major exporter is that around the mid- to late 2000s the political leadership subverted any technical input into electricity planning. Despite embracing the idea of a 'developmental state', the EPRDF approach to policymaking differs markedly

[1] Interview EG44, former senior minister and one of the architects of Ethiopia's development plans, Addis Ababa, 1 November 2019.

[2] Interview EP12, private contractor in the energy sector, by phone, 20 November 2019, 16 February 2020.

from the picture of a politically empowered technocracy that is often attributed such importance in the developmental successes in East Asia (Johnson 1982; Amsden 1992; Evans 1995). Meles' own writing highlighted the importance of state autonomy, alongside developmental vision, as key components of a 'developmental state' (Zenawi 2012). Yet the need for autonomy to protect against political capture was just one aspect of successful East Asian bureaucracies. Key EPRDF and government documents (EPRDF 2006, 2010b) are relatively silent on other aspects such as the importance of meritocracy and political empowerment of the bureaucracy (Lefort 2013; Chang and Hauge 2019; Gebresenbet and Kamski 2019). Instead, the EPRDF, from its inception and throughout its time in office, cast itself as a vanguard party responsible for mobilizing the masses under a framework of revolutionary democracy and democratic centralism (EPRDF 1993, 2010a). During the GTP period, the EPRDF further sought to ensure the political loyalty and ideological commitment of the bureaucracy by requiring party membership of many new recruits and organizing civil servants into '1-to-5 networks'.[3] These networks required one leader to instruct five followers, making up a 'change army' used to pursue political education and monitor performance through training sessions and distribution of pamphlets and other party propaganda (Vaughan and Tronvoll 2003; Fourie 2012; Weis 2015; World Bank 2017). As such, rather than empowering the bureaucracy to formulate strategies based on technical expertise, the EPRDF political vanguard identified political priorities and targets and instructed a subdued civil service towards implementation, while enforcing upward accountability to political leaders.[4]

The result of this political control over the bureaucracy was the imposition of ever-more fanciful plans and overly ambitious targets by politicians, with limited technical input into decision making. The targets set during GTP1 represented a major step-change in ambition. The target for electricity generation capacity required a five-fold increase to 10,000 megawatts (MW) by 2015 and bore no resemblance to the projections of the 2006 masterplan or any other plausible assessment of medium-term domestic demand or export potential (see Figure 4.1). Instead, the electricity target was based on the supposed need to meet the projected demand resulting from equally overly ambitious targets for economic growth of 11.4 per cent per annum and industrial growth of 20 per cent per annum, as well as the first phase of railway construction envisaged in GTP1 (MoFED 2010). One former minister described the general approach to target setting in GTP1:

> Obviously, the targets were very high. Prime Minister Meles used to say 'it's back-breaking', heavy investments. If we put all our efforts in, we will approach our targets, even if we don't reach them. We will have created a foundation that we can

[3] These structures were introduced across Ethiopian society and were subsequently brought to the civil service. See Lavers (2023).

[4] For similar dynamics in the sugar sector, see Gebresenbet and Kamski (2019).

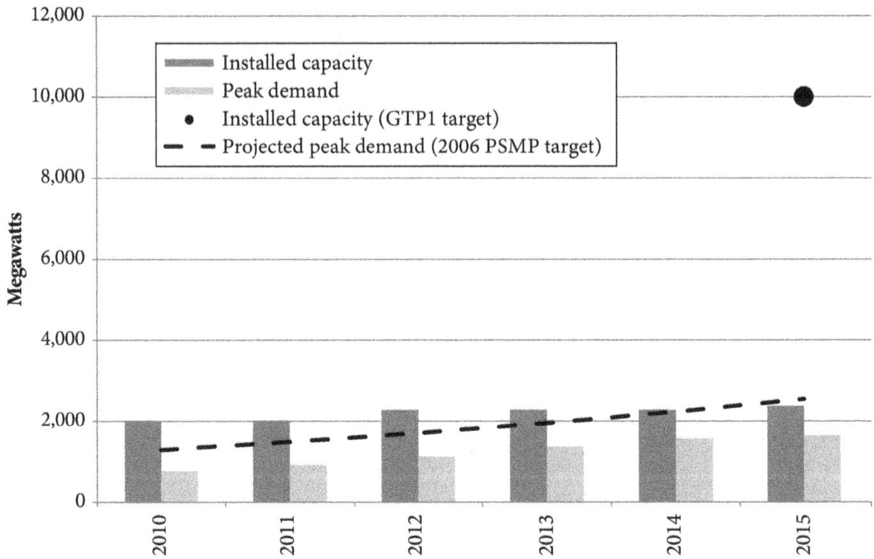

Figure 4.1 Installed capacity and targets during GTP1, 2010–2015
Data source: EEPCo (2006), MoFED (2010), and USAID (2019).

> subsequently make a big jump. Lowering the targets to our capacity would require less motivation. Pushing ourselves, that is the philosophy. (Cited in Terrefe 2022, p. 260)

One important result of this politically driven planning process was that, while GTP1 set targets for installed capacity, there are no targets at all for energy generation. The installed generation capacity of a power plant, often measured in MW, is the maximum amount of electricity that can be generated at any one point in time. In contrast, energy generation capacity is the amount of electricity produced over a given period of time, often measured in gigawatt-hours (GWh). Installed capacity is important to be able to generate sufficient electricity to meet peak demand at the point of the day or time of the year when demand for electricity is at its maximum. Energy generation capacity, in contrast, is the key factor when it comes to being able to meet the total demand for electricity year-round. Energy generation capacity is particularly important with respect to hydropower since a major constraint on generation is the availability of water, which, whether from the flow of a river or the store in a reservoir, is ultimately dependent on rainfall. A single-minded focus on raising installed capacity risks producing inefficient dams that can produce large amounts of electricity for a short period but which are ultimately constrained by the limits of water availability. Respondents were clear that installed capacity and not energy was the main priority for politicians throughout the EPRDF period. Indeed, GTP1 neglected energy generation entirely, only providing targets for installed capacity (MoFED 2010). This dominant focus on installed capacity constitutes a severe limitation to the planning process, which placed little emphasis on the ability of the system to generate sufficient energy year-round to meet demand. One long-time Ministry of Water, Irrigation, and Energy (MoWIE) official made the point clearly:

> The non-energy experts [politicians] got hooked on installed capacity ... The energy targets played a minor role, they didn't receive so much attention. The focus was on installing as much peaking capacity as possible ... This policymaking was conceived at the highest levels, it was not even in the ministry, it was the prime minister, deputy prime minister, and their advisors. But most of them were not energy specialists.[5]

This focus on hugely ambitious targets for installed capacity impacted not just on the planning processes in the electricity sector but also the specific design of individual dams, as discussed in Chapter 7.

Delivering the Plan: Finance and Domestic Capacity

In an attempt to make progress towards these 'back-breaking' targets, GTP1 entailed another push to expand the financial and technical capacity available to the government. In this period, the government undertook a significant change in the financing arrangements to deliver this infrastructure expansion. Mekonnen Manyazewal, a key figure in economic planning and one of the main architects of the GTPs, outlined this new approach in which project fundraising proceeded in parallel with construction:[6]

> The strategy is to include priority projects even if there is no apparent budgetary source allocated for these projects. Resource mobilizations are set in motion as the implementation of the plan proceeds. This was the experience during GTP-I for key infrastructure projects including railway projects now completed and those under construction. One instrument used when bids are issued for the construction of the projects is a requirement for prospective contractors to come up with a financing package with acceptable terms and conditions. This gives potential contractors a signal not to expect financing from the government. This strategy ensures that priority projects are not left out due to shortage of finance. (Manyazewal 2019, p. 178)

[5] Interview EG2, former senior official in the energy sector, Addis Ababa, 3 September 2019, 13 February 2020.

[6] Mekonnen had been state minister of the economy since the 1990s, and subsequently served as minister of industry (2010–2013) and national planning commissioner (2013–2018).

The result was that the major dam projects in this period—including Gilgel Gibe III and the Grand Ethiopian Renaissance Dam (GERD)—were launched without finance in place, with the government and contractors exploring multiple sources to secure funds (see Chapter 5 for Gibe III).

In many instances the government continued to draw on concessional financing for infrastructure projects. This included the World Bank, which, though no longer funding dam construction, nonetheless financed numerous electricity sector projects, including the Ethiopia–Sudan transmission lines to enable electricity export (IEG 2014). Chinese finance also became increasingly important, funding numerous infrastructure projects, including the electro-mechanical works in Gilgel Gibe III and others in the electricity sector, as discussed below. A major change in this period, however, was the government's decision to turn to non-concessional, commercial lending to meet the financing gap in its infrastructure plans. This included a $1 billion 10-year Eurobond issue in 2014 to finance eight industrial parks and a loan from Crédit Suisse to finance the Ethio-Djibouti railway (Manyazewal 2019, pp. 187–188). Although precise details are unavailable, commercial lending was also a key part of the finance for major dam projects launched in the GTP era, including Gilgel Gibe III (see Chapter 5) and the GERD. The result was a major shift in the composition of public debt. In 2007/8, debt to private creditors was just 10 per cent of the total, but this had ballooned to 27 per cent by 2016/17 (Manyazewal 2019, pp. 184–185).

Increased commercial borrowing was complemented by growing domestic revenue mobilization. Tax revenue increased significantly due to booming economic growth, rather than a significant increase in tax rates (see Figure 3.2 and Mascagni 2016). Moreover, the GERD's announcement saw the EPRDF launch a range of new initiatives to raise funds for the construction of this massive project. Originally estimated at a cost of $5 billion, the Renaissance label was applied to the GERD as a symbol of the economic transformation that the EPRDF sought to bring about and as an important nationalist framing that sought to mobilize people from every part of the country to contribute money to the project (Menga 2017). The result was a range of initiatives coordinated by the new Office of National Council for the Coordination of Public Participation on the Construction of the Grand Renaissance Dam.

Particularly prominent was the creation of GERD bonds, in denominations of 50 to 1 million *birr* issued by the Commercial Bank of Ethiopia. These bonds were actively promoted within Ethiopia and among the large Ethiopian diaspora through embassies around the world.[7] In addition, all state employees were required to contribute one month of their salaries to the GERD fund, with

[7] The government's success in raising $5.8 million in the United States in 2011–2014 was undermined when it was fined $6.5 million by the United States' Securities and Exchange Commission for failing to comply with regulations (US Securities and Exchange Commission 2016).

contributions automatically deducted from salaries. Moreover, the wide range of fundraising initiatives included a GERD lottery for both Ethiopians and the diaspora, a GERD music album, the 'I Will Run for Abay' fun run, and the Renaissance Cup that toured the country, promoting competition for fundraising between ethnic regions (Ethiopian Herald 2015, 2016a, 2016b; Ethiopian News Agency 2018; Teshome 2018).

The state also used its influence to mobilize a range of non-state actors, including religious leaders from the Orthodox Church and the Ethiopian Supreme Council for Islamic Affairs, to encourage people to contribute (Haile 2018, pp. 112–113). Moreover, particular milestones in the construction were actively used to mobilize public contributions, including the diversion of the Blue Nile to enable construction of the dam itself on 'Derg Downfall Day'—the anniversary of the victory of the EPRDF over the Derg—and the invocation of Ethiopian sovereignty throughout the protracted negotiations with Egypt, Sudan, and various mediators over the operation of the dam (see Chapters 7 and 9).

Field research in rural villages across Afar, Oromiya, and Tigray in early 2018 revealed how local government officials, development teams and 1-to-5 networks,[8] funeral associations (*iddir*), and text messages sent by the state telecoms company had all been repeatedly used to promote the GERD and to encourage people to contribute even small amounts of money by buying bonds as groups through their 1-to-5 networks or individually, depending on their capacity.[9] Local government officials were set financial targets for fundraising from their communities, with their fundraising performance assessed through *gimgema*.[10] In some instances this fundraising effort certainly went beyond voluntary contributions, with respondents in Oromiya noting that they were required to make contributions of 50–100 *birr* per household while paying their land tax.[11] These fundraising efforts appealed to nationalist sentiments in line with the Renaissance narrative, but state officials also cultivated high expectations that the GERD would quickly translate into direct material benefits. For the vast majority in rural areas who lacked access to electricity, the government cultivated the expectation that the completion of the GERD would quickly lead to their villages and households being connected to the grid. One focus group participant in Oromiya summed up the general expectation that when the GERD is finished 'all citizens will get electric light in their house'.[12]

[8] In theory, the entire Ethiopian population was organized into male, female, and youth 1-to-5 networks, with one leader overseeing five followers. The 1-to-5 leaders were, in turn, members of the development teams covering some 30 households (see Lavers 2023).

[9] Focus groups OMF9, OMF10, Merti wereda, Oromiya, June 2018; TAF1, TAF2, Ahferom wereda, Tigray, June 2018; AGF1, Gala'elu wereda, Afar, July 2018.

[10] Focus group OMF10, Merti wereda, Oromiya, June 2018.

[11] Focus groups OMF9, OMF10, Merti wereda, Oromiya, June 2018. This implies that failure to pay these contributions and the land tax could endanger their state-owned landholdings.

[12] Focus group OMF10, Merti wereda, Oromiya, June 2018. Similar views were put forward by others that the dam would quickly translate into electricity access and employment opportunities: Focus

Beyond the delays in the GERD's construction, the potential for the dam to meet this wave of expectation created by the fundraising effort depends of course on complementary investments in the transmission and distribution grid, a topic addressed in Chapter 8.

This vast public mobilization effort has raised a significant amount of money, estimated by the GERD National Council at 13.4 billion *birr* (roughly £323 million or $399 million) by April 2020 (Ethiopian News Agency 2020). However, it should also be noted that this is a mere fraction of the originally estimated $5 billion cost of the dam, which must surely have escalated as the project was delayed. Likely more significant than public fundraising were the state's efforts to utilize its domination of the financial sector—maintained in the face of past pressure from the international finance institutions (IFIs)—to mobilize resources to enable state enterprises to invest in line with government infrastructure plans. The Industrial Development Fund was created to channel profits from state enterprises, such as Ethiopian Telecommunications, towards priority projects. Furthermore, a requirement that private banks buy National Bank of Ethiopia bills with 27 per cent of their loans, in a period of negative real interest rates, meant that the state was able to squeeze the private banking sector as an additional source of cheap finance (Oqubay 2015; Moller 2017; Ayalew 2019; Manyazewal 2019). The result was that loans to state-owned enterprises increased from 21 per cent to 62 per cent of total outstanding credit between 2007/8 and 2014/15 (Moller 2015, p. 18). Within the electricity sector, this surge in state investment and use of a wide range of concessional and non-concessional loans resulted in the accumulation of vast debts by the state utility, the Ethiopian Electric Power Company (EEPCo), which was not only tasked with making these major investments but was also constrained in its revenue generation potential by the government's retention of deliberately low tariffs as a means of subsidizing industrial and popular electricity consumption (see Chapter 8).

In this period the government also became increasingly ambitious regarding the development of domestic technical capacity. Major infrastructural investments were seen not just as necessary costs but as an opportunity to develop domestic capacity through joint ventures and collaborations with international firms. As such, the aim was to overcome the disadvantage of late developing countries in their dependence on foreign expertise. The foremost example of this strategy is the Metals and Engineering Corporation (MetEC) that was created in 2010 at Meles' instruction. MetEC brought together a number of existing military-owned engineering companies with a view to mobilizing and building upon existing expertise in the army for the benefit of the economy. For some government officials, MetEC had the potential to develop into Ethiopia's equivalent of the *chaebol* (Champion

groups OMF9, Merti wereda, Oromiya, June 2018; TAF1, TAF2, Ahferom wereda, Tigray, June 2018; AGF1, Gala'elu wereda, Afar, July 2018.

and Manek 2019)—the giant business conglomerates that played such an influential role in South Korean development (Amsden 1992). However, perhaps a more apt comparison would be the US Army Corps of Engineers, which was so influential in developing hydraulic infrastructure in the US (Reisner 1993), or Rwanda's military-affiliated conglomerate Horizon (Booth and Golooba-Mutebi 2012; Behuria 2015). Subsequently, MetEC was contracted for some of the most high-profile infrastructure projects with a view to becoming a leading engineering firm in the future. These included the electro-mechanical works in the GERD, a major fertilizer factory, and a series of enormous sugar factories (see Gebresenbet and Kamski 2019). MetEC's role within the GERD itself is discussed in Chapters 7 and 9.

In sum, then, the GTP1 period saw a major ramping up of the government's developmental ambitions, with knock-on effects for the electricity generation capacity required to meet growing demand—both domestically and for export. The result was a massive push by the government to expand the mobilization of financial resources domestically and internationally through concessional and increasingly risky commercial lending. This period also saw the first real sign of government ambition to build technical capacity in the hydropower sector, beyond a more general push for more effective planning and supervision of foreign contractors. Most notably, this involved the decision to give MetEC the GERD's electro-mechanical works in the hope that this would build its engineering capacity in line with the government's 'developmental state' narrative.

A Dams Boom on the Omo and Beyond

Having completed the first two hydropower projects in the Gibe-Omo cascade by 2010, the Omo Basin would remain the main initial focus of this expanded dam-building programme. However, the success of the Omo projects, the emergence of Salini as a trusted contractor, the government's growing developmental ambitions, and the alignment of international relations combined to drive a turn to the river basin with the greatest hydroelectric potential in the country, the Blue Nile. This section examines how this growing ambition led to a series of projects that would transform first the Omo and the Blue Nile. Chapter 5, meanwhile, analyses Salini's emergence, and Chapters 6 and 7 focus on the GERD itself.

It has not been possible to obtain a complete list of the projects originally planned to produce the additional 8,000 MW of hydropower required by the end of GTP1. However, this list would certainly have included Gilgel Gibe III (1,870 MW) and the Beles hydropower project (460 MW), both of which were already in process by 2010. It also seems likely that a dam on the Blue Nile was probably included, with Beko Abo (1,600 MW) the favoured candidate as the first in what was to be a cascade of dams as part of the collaborative Nile Basin Initiative

(NBI)-sponsored process at that time (see Chapter 6). However, the GERD, which was only announced in 2011, was certainly not among the projects. At the time of drafting GTP1, the dam, then known as Project X, was being planned in secret by a small team in MoWIE and the Prime Minister's Office without the knowledge of even the most senior officials in EEPCo.[13] As one senior official involved in planning EEPCo's work in that period noted,

> the GERD was not in the original list of projects for GTP1, but the Prime Minister's Office and the contractor [Salini] had made the decision on the project, so we have to accept it.[14]

Nonetheless, GERD—originally intended to start early generation in 2015/16—came to dominate the efforts of EEPCo and the government more broadly during GTP1.

Salini signed an engineering, procurement, and construction (EPC) contract to build Gilgel Gibe III as early as 2006 (SOGREAH 2010). Gibe III is a much larger dam than anything previously built in Ethiopia both in terms of the size of the structure—reportedly the highest roller compacted concrete dam in the world—and the installed capacity—1,870 MW—which was four times larger than any other hydropower project in Ethiopia at that point. Gibe III was conceived only partly in relation to meeting domestic demand, but also as part of the government's strategy of becoming a major energy exporter. Indeed, a key factor in the viability of the project was a new 2,000-MW transmission line that would enable electricity to be sold to Kenya and other East African countries (see Chapter 8).

Furthermore, Gilgel Gibe III became part of a broader push by the Ethiopian Government to transform the Lower Omo Valley (see Figure 3.3). Although incorporated into Ethiopian territory from the late nineteenth century, the state's presence in the Lower Omo had been very limited until recently (Markakis 2011; Turton 2011; Lavers 2016). In contrast to Gibe I and II, which had little impact on the flow of the main Omo, the 'Gibe III dam controls about 50% of the Omo catchment area, [and] about 70% of the total water runoff' (SOGREAH 2010, p. b). As such, regulation of the highly seasonal Omo River opened up the possibility of large-scale irrigated agriculture in the flat plains of the Lower Omo. The centrepiece of these plans was the government's ambition of becoming a major sugar producer, both meeting the needs of the domestic market and becoming a major source of export revenue (Lavers 2012b; Gebresenbet and Kamski 2019). The Omo-Kuraz project was the largest of all the sugar projects in Ethiopia, with irrigation works for 175,000 hectares of sugar plantations contracted to the Ethiopian Water Works Construction Enterprise (EWWCE), and four new sugar factories contracted to MetEC. Much like the Awash valley 50 years earlier, but on a much

[13] Interview EG8, senior electricity sector official, Addis Ababa, 3 October 2019, 11 February 2020.
[14] Interview EG13, senior electricity sector official, Addis Ababa, 19 February 2020.

larger scale, the government's plans amount to an intertwined project of state-building and economic modernization of the whole river basin. Meles Zenawi was quite clear in his view of the plans:

> The Gigel Gibe 3 dam is developing rapidly and when it is finished the flood, which has been a huge problem for years in this region, will end forever. It will then be possible to create a big irrigation system in this wide and fertile area of South Omo. Following the good results we have achieved in the Afar region, the government is planning, and working hard to establish, a 150,000 hectare sugar-cane development in this area starting this year. When this development work is done, we believe that it will transform the entire basis of the area ... I promise you that, even though this area is known as backward in terms of civilization, it will become an example of rapid development. (Meles, cited in Mursi Online 2011).

Senior officials at the Ministry of Water and EEPCo were not initially aware of government plans to establish large-scale irrigation in the Omo Valley (Turton 2021). Indeed, the Omo-Kuraz development would appear to have been a late addition, with no mention of the project in the 2010 sugar sector development plan, which laid out plans for many other sugar plantations and factories in the country (ESDA 2010).

Unsurprisingly, Gibe III and Kuraz were hugely controversial. Concern was related not so much to the dam itself, which flooded an unpopulated area (SOGREAH 2010), as the downstream impacts both in Ethiopia and Lake Turkana on the Kenyan border. The population of the Lower Omo Valley employed a range of livelihood strategies including flood-retreat agriculture and pastoralism. The regulation of the river flow and establishment of the sugar plantation would entail a fundamental transformation of local livelihoods, eliminating flood-retreat agriculture, cutting off vital access to the river, and displacing the local population from land that they had previously used (Turton 2011; Abbink 2012). Alongside dams and irrigation development for large-scale commercial agriculture, from about 2010 the federal government's Ministry of Federal Affairs (MoFA) conducted a villagization programme in all areas occupied by those practising mobile livelihoods in lowland areas.[15] The programme's stated intention is to promote sustainable livelihoods in the form of settled agriculture—with pastoralism and other mobile livelihoods once again framed as inherently unsustainable (MoFA 2008). For many critics, however, villagization is seen as a means of rendering pastoralists legible and governable, while appropriating land to make way for large-scale agricultural investments (The Oakland Institute 2011; Human Rights Watch 2014; Gebresenbet 2021). As such, the displacement of local populations

[15] MoFA, renamed the Ministry of Federal and Pastoral Development Affairs in late 2015, provided support to the so-called emerging regions—Afar, Benishangul-Gumuz, Gambella, and Somali—which had no experience of self-administration prior to 1991. In August 2018, MoFA was integrated into the new Ministry of Peace.

and their livelihoods is not a mere unintended consequence or an undesirable but necessary by-product of development; it is a specific policy objective to transform the 'backward' populations of the periphery. While the Gibe III impact assessment concluded this would affect approximately 84,200 people (SOGREAH 2010, p. a), many consider this to be a major underestimate with hundreds of thousands of pastoralists living in the valley (Gabbert 2021; Turton 2021).

The Gilgel Gibe III Dam therefore clearly highlights the ramifications of the EPRDF's dam building for federalism and the autonomy of Ethiopia's ethnic groups. From Haile Selassie's development of the Awash Basin to the EPRDF's development of the South Omo, Ethiopian governments have sought to avoid displacement of landholders in the politically important highlands, instead directing large-scale agriculture towards the politically marginal and relatively sparsely populated lowlands. In the EPRDF era, the focus of large-scale agricultural development shifted to the downstream reaches of the Omo (SNNPR), Baro (Gambella), and Awash (Afar region) rivers. In the Awash Basin, dams planned since the 1960s were finally built at Kessem (2014) and Tendaho (2009) by the EWWCE. Both dams were linked to downstream sugar projects, which along with expansion of existing factories at Wonji-Shoa and Metehara were contracted to Indian companies with Exim Bank finance (Kumar 2015). While federalism formally devolves considerable powers to regional administrations, rivers and dam construction remain federal responsibilities, while decision-making power regarding national development remained highly centralized. In spite of federalism, the reality, therefore, is that dam building, large-scale agriculture, and villagization have continued a longstanding process of centralized state building and economic modernization as a means of transforming the periphery. Indeed, the irony is that, despite providing ethnic groups occupying the lowland periphery with formal powers of self-determination, these groups were, in practice, even less able to contest the growing power and ambitions of the federal government than under past regimes.

The other main concern raised in relation to Gilgel Gibe III is the impact of the developments on the level of Lake Turkana and livelihoods based on fisheries as a result of the filling of the dam and the extraction of water from the river for large-scale irrigation (Stevenson 2018). Yet, the Kenyan Government's response to the dam as the downstream riparian was rather muted. While concerns were raised by Kenyan non-governmental organizations (NGOs) and some Members of Parliament (The Indian Ocean Newsletter 2009a, 2009b), the Kenyan Government made little public comment and signed Memoranda of Understanding in 2006 and 2009, paving the way for the transmission lines and power purchase agreement (PPA) (ADF 2012).[16] The Kenyan Government has its own ambitious vision for transforming the historically marginal northern frontier, including Lake Turkana,

[16] Interview EG37 with a senior official in the energy sector, Addis Ababa, 21 August 2019, 19 February 2020.

through transportation links, conservation projects, and resource exploitation (Mosley and Watson 2016). Moreover, the Kenyan Government's desire for cheap electricity from the project appears to have overcome any resistance to negative impacts on what is a politically marginalized part of Kenya. Furthermore, while the impact of dam filling is temporary, the impact of irrigation has thus far been limited. The sugar factories contracted to MetEC were subject to lengthy delays and the plantation has been significantly scaled back (Gebresenbet and Kamski 2019).

Given the severely limited political space for opposition to the 'developmental state' within Ethiopia, the campaign against Gilgel Gibe III and the sugar plantations was taken up primarily by international NGOs such as Survival International, Human Rights Watch (2012), and International Rivers (2011), reminiscent of the 'boomerang strategy' described by Keck and Sikkink (1998). The government, however, was dismissive of their concerns. For Meles, it was only through the transformation brought about by the dam and plantation that real development would occur:

> There are some people who say they are concerned for the pastoralists, but really they want the pastoralists and their lifestyle to remain as a tourist attraction forever. (Meles, cited in Mursi Online 2011)

Nonetheless, this international campaign against Gibe III and Kuraz affected the financing of the projects. Construction works for Gibe III began without finance for the whole project in place, in line with the government's new approach. However, the Ethiopian Government expected a combination of the African Development Bank, World Bank, and European Investment Bank to part-finance the dam (EEPCo 2009; SOGREAH 2010). Ultimately, however, a lack of competitive bidding in appointing Salini, concerns about the environmental impact assessments, and the international campaign against the dam led these agencies to decline. From the government's side, there remains great frustration at the 'wasted three years' spent trying to get money from these multilateral institutions (Azeb Asnake Ethiopian Electric Power (EEP) CEO, cited in Woldegebrael 2019, p. 229) and international NGOs' efforts to block access to finance, which makes them the 'best friends of backwardness and poverty' (Meles, cited in Mursi Online 2011).

Ultimately, the government made the decision to finance the works through a combination of government finance and a $235 million commercial loan from the Industrial and Commercial Bank of China (Brautigam and Hwang 2019; Woldegebrael 2019). The arrival of much-needed Chinese finance came with a requirement to hire a Chinese contractor for the electro-mechanical works—Dongfang Electric. Despite the refusal of the World Bank and African Development Bank (AfDB) to finance the dam itself, these organizations did continue to finance the transmission line to Kenya which will export electricity from Gibe III (see Chapter 8).

Throughout this period, Ethiopia continued to develop a number of projects in the Nile Basin. These included several relatively small water storage dams to support irrigation projects in the Lake Tana watershed, many based on the earlier United States Bureau of Reclamation (USBR) study, including Koga (2002–2008), Ribb (completed in 2017), and Megech (started in 2013), with several of these built by EWWCE. Furthermore, the Neshe Dam—the third in the Finchaa-Amarti-Neshe complex planned by the USBR—was completed in 2006–2011 by China Gezhouba Group Company (CGGC), largely based on Chinese Eximbank finance (Brautigam and Hwang 2019). In addition to a 95-MW hydropower plant, the dam, together with the other two built earlier, provide irrigation for some 20,000 hectares, with the Finchaa sugar estate significantly expanded as part of the government's plans to become a major sugar producer (Müller-Mahn and Gebreyes 2019, p. 6).

In parallel to Gibe III, Salini was also contracted to build the Beles hydropower plant in 2005. This project involves digging a tunnel through the western bank of Lake Tana to divert water from the main Blue Nile into the Beles River, exploiting the difference in altitude between the basins to install a 460-MW plant using Lake Tana as a natural reservoir. The Beles subsequently re-joins the main Blue Nile River near the Sudanese border, just above the site of the GERD. The project builds on a long history of similar proposals dating to the early twentieth century and detailed plans for a 168-MW capacity plant in the USBR study (1964). As with the earlier Tekeze Dam, Beles was implemented unilaterally, without the consent of downstream riparians. Reports suggest that the Egyptian Government viewed the project as an attempt to 'provoke Egypt's anger' (Salem 2010; Tawfik 2015). In itself, the project had little impact on downstream riparians since Beles does not store additional water, and the water diverted into the Beles River returns to the main Blue Nile. Of greater potential significance to the Nile, however, the government also commenced work on the Beles Sugar Development Project downstream in Amhara and Benishangul-Gumuz in 2013, partly overlapping with the former Tana-Beles scheme pursued under the Derg. Another part of the massive sugar development strategy, the project was originally intended to cover 75,000 hectares to produce sugar and ethanol at three new factories contracted to MetEC. As with other sites, the factories have suffered major delays and MetEC's contract was subsequently cancelled and years of harvests were wasted (Fantini et al. 2018; Fedeler 2021). Nonetheless, the Beles hydropower project demonstrated Ethiopia's newfound ability to finance major projects, in this case $500 million, with its own resources (Fedeler 2021), and its willingness to proceed unilaterally in Nile projects without downstream approval.

Beyond increased electricity generation capacity, this period demonstrated Ethiopia's ability to tackle ever-larger and more complex hydropower projects. Integral to this process has been the emergence of Salini as a trusted collaborator. As shown in Chapter 5, Salini's role has gone well beyond that of a standard contractor and has entailed undertaking activities throughout the project cycle from feasibility studies and design to construction, connecting the government to finance and even at points stepping in to cover financial gaps on a short-term basis. Indeed, the emergence of Salini as a trusted contractor for a series of dam projects in Ethiopia served to compensate for the lack of domestic capacity in dam construction. The Beles project was another important step in that it required Salini to establish a second team working in Ethiopia, in parallel to the existing operation working in the Omo Basin. This involved transferring some staff from Salini's long-running Omo operation to the Blue Nile and a significant scale-up of activities. Importantly, as the Beles project drew to a close in 2011/12, this Blue Nile team and their equipment was available to be deployed elsewhere, replicating the approach taken by the Omo team through the development of that basin.

Despite the government's efforts to mobilize all available financial resources and capacity towards the realization of GTP1, the plan's targets, and particularly those for electricity, proved unrealistic and were not achieved (NPC 2016). Indeed, by 2015, the Beles hydropower project commissioned in 2012 (460 MW) was the only significant addition to Ethiopia's generation capacity. This did not, as it turns out, become a major problem since the GTP1 'back-breaking' target proved an entirely unreliable indicator of future demand. Nonetheless, the GTP1 period did see the launch of a series of major hydropower projects that, when finally completed, would massively increase generation capacity. These included: Gilgel Gibe III (1,870 MW), which was originally expected to be operational before 2015, but which was finally commissioned in 2016; the CGGC-built and Chinese Eximbank-financed Genale Dawa III (254 MW), which was finally commissioned after considerable delays in 2019; and, most significantly, the GERD itself, which after several design changes will add 5,150 MW to the grid once it becomes fully operational (see Chapter 7).

The 'Green Developmental State'

As shown in Chapter 3, the almost exclusive focus on hydropower within Ethiopia's energy mix is the result of a number of factors. These include the vast hydropower potential and the legacy of past hydropower investments by the Imperial and Derg regimes for the knowledge and expertise in the sector. However, this legacy was reinforced by the EPRDF's strategy for the electricity sector which valued investments that would deliver low-cost electricity in the long run and limit Ethiopia's exposure to the foreign exchange costs of importing fossil fuels. State-owned hydropower would provide subsidized and low-cost electricity to support the development of manufacturing and mass access. In contrast, prior to GTP1 the government was silent on any possible environmental benefits of hydropower. With the rise of the climate crisis on the global agenda in the late 2000s and Meles

Zenawi's growing status internationally, however, the government seized on the purported environmental benefits of hydropower as an additional justification for its development strategy and, indeed, as a tool to be leveraged in international relations.

Reflecting his growing regional and global profile, Meles Zenawi was selected to speak on behalf of Africa at the 2009 United Nations Climate Change Conference in Copenhagen. At the conference, Meles articulated the view that since Africa had made the least contribution to climate change and is likely to suffer the most from it, it should be compensated by those responsible for large-scale emissions through funding for adaptation and mitigation:

> Every one of us knows that Africa has contributed virtually nothing to global warming but has been hit first and hardest. The fragility of our eco-system has meant that for Africans the damage of climate change is not something that could happen in the future. It is already here with us sowing misery and death across the land. Africa is indeed paying with the misery and death of its people for the wealth and wellbeing that was created in the developed countries through carbon intensive development. That is fundamentally unjust. (Zenawi 2009)

A key feature of this narrative was that Ethiopia was charting a distinct, low-carbon development path based on hydropower, providing a potential role model for the rest of the African continent and in sharp contrast to the carbon-intensive growth of the early industrializers:

> Africa is a green field that can and wants to chart a different course of development, one that is not carbon intensive. To give an example of my own country, Ethiopia, we plan to sustain our current double digit rates of growth for the next 15 years so that by 2025 we become a middle income country. We plan to do so in a manner that would allow us to have zero net-carbon emissions by 2025 ... When it comes to taking care of the environment, we occupy the moral high ground and are proud of it. (Zenawi 2009)

Indeed, the importance of renewable energy to green economic transformation became an important theme of Meles' and the government's statements in the following years:

> We in Africa have enormous untapped resources to generate power from renewable sources. We have huge hydro power and wind power potential. We have significant potential in geothermal energy and with the greening of our agriculture we will have enormous potential for modern bio-energy development. As and when the technology develops and becomes competitive with other sources of energy our abundant solar power resources will come in handy. There cannot

> be any talk of structural economic transformation without massive increase in the electricity we generate ... If we generate most or all of our energy from renewable sources then we will have by design or default embarked on a green path of economic transformation. (Zenawi 2011a)

However, Meles' statements also reveal that the underlying logic in favour of renewables continued to be based on economic as much as environmental criteria. Indeed, for Ethiopia and most other African countries without large fossil fuel deposits,

> Most people know that carbon-based energy resources are going to be prohibitively expensive even before they make our planet unlivable. It therefore makes a lot of sense for them to invest in the technologies of the future which most certainly are going to be green. (Zenawi 2011a)

Despite Ethiopia's embrace of 'green economic transformation', this did not translate into any major diversification of its energy mix beyond hydropower. As noted in Chapter 3, in addition to hydropower, Ethiopia possesses significant and, thus far, largely undeveloped potential in a range of other renewable energy sources, including geothermal, solar, and wind. While solar and wind technologies were expensive and untested in the 1990s, in the 2000s they became plausible choices as part of a strategy of energy diversification, with technological advances leading to a steep decline in the cost of solar (IEA 2020), making it competitive with hydropower over the lifespan of a project and with far lower upfront costs. However, the government's political commitment to a state-hydro model for the electricity sector prevented significant diversification of the energy mix. Since the mid-2000s there has been a growing push from private sector investors and several donor agencies for the integration of renewable energy into the Ethiopian system. However, the government initially resisted due to its political and technocratic commitment to state hydropower and the lack of domestic expertise in other energy sources. Integrating renewable technologies through private sector investment would necessarily threaten state control of the sector and thereby require revision to the tariff structure, which was set at a level that would discourage any private investor.

Ethiopia's near exclusive reliance on hydropower for both baseload and peaking power has left Ethiopia's energy sector vulnerable to periodic droughts, which result in low reservoir levels and interrupted generation, most notably in 2000, 2003, 2008–2009, and 2015.[17] As such, while there are good reasons to expand hydropower generation, there are also significant risks to exclusive dependence on

[17] Climate change also presents risks, with some predictions suggesting lower and more irregular rainfall, with likely impacts on reservoir levels (Block and Strzepek 2012; Demissie and Solomon 2016; van der Zwaan et al. 2018).

water. Respondents highlighted the severe drought and resulting load shedding in 2008/9 as something of a turning point that briefly sparked government interest in non-hydro renewables. At this time, Ethiopia theoretically had sufficient capacity to meet existing demand, but drought reduced hydropower production, leading to shortages that damaged growth, just as the economy was booming. As a MoWIE official emphasized:

> It changed in 2008/9—we had two years of drought so that showed that it is good to have a mix. That was definitely the impetus for renewables ... The government spent a lot of money at that time on diesel [for backup generators], so it definitely had an impact.[18]

The main product of this crisis was the decision to develop wind-power, resulting in the eventual commissioning of Adama 1 (51 MW) in 2012 and Adama 2 (153 MW) in 2015 built by HydroChina with Chinese Eximbank funds (Chiyemura 2019), as well as Ashegoda (120 MW) in 2013 built by French firm Vergnet with funding from the Agence Française de Développement.[19] In each case, EPC contractors were hired to install turbines that were owned and operated by EEPCo, retaining state control. However, Ashegoda has been beset with maintenance problems and is often operating well below capacity.[20]

The 2008/9 crisis also led to some progress with geothermal energy. Partly based on the poor performance of the state-owned Aluto Langano facility, it would seem EEPCo officials recognized the imperative of foreign involvement to provide the technological expertise to develop geothermal capacity in Ethiopia.[21] The government issued exploration licences to two Icelandic companies in 2009, yet negotiations on a PPA have been painfully slow (see Chapter 9). An EEPCo official centrally involved at the time highlighted the difficulty of convincing the government to allow private sector involvement, which was still seen as a threat by the political leadership:

> We pushed the government ... It was a challenge to convince the high levels. They eventually allowed us to negotiate ... The private sector is not seen as a partner, it is seen as a rent seeker to take the benefits from us.[22]

While this marked the beginning of private sector engagement in electricity generation, the dominant view within MoWIE and EEPCo remained that it would

[18] Interview EG6, senior official in the energy sector, Addis Ababa, 3 October 2019.

[19] A further EPC contract delivered a windfarm at Ayisha in Somali Region (120 MW) in 2022, built by Dongfang based on Chinese Eximbank lending (Yewondwossen 2022).

[20] Interview ED1, donor in the electricity sector, Addis Ababa, 3 June 2019.

[21] Interview EG8, senior EEP official, Addis Ababa, 3 October 2019, 11 February 2020.

[22] Interview EG13, former senior EEP official, Addis Ababa, 19 February 2020.

be better to 'just build more and larger hydro' to resolve generation problems.[23] Indeed, any investment in renewables was dwarfed by hydropower investments as the government sought to 'overwhelm' growing demand through Gilgel Gibe III (1,870 MW) and the GERD (5,150 MW). The massive increase in electricity generation planned in GTP1 (2010–2015) was to be achieved solely through hydropower (MoFED 2010). Even as late as 2014, when a new Power Sector Masterplan was developed, a consultant involved in the design process felt that 'there was no real push for diversification' and that hydropower remained the overwhelming focus.[24] While the 2008/9 drought and electricity shortages provided initial motivation for diversification, the completion of Tekeze (2009), Gilgel Gibe II (2010), Beles (2012), and Gilgel Gibe III (2016), along with several years of good rainfall, meant that this motivation fell away. As one ministry official argued, renewables

> took hold among some big-name politicians [around 2009]. But after that there was less drought ... It is because of that that the interest in renewables reduced.[25]

While the commitment to hydropower was one reason for the lack of investments in other energy sources, ideological resistance to the private sector among EPRDF officials was perhaps more important. Given the limits of state expertise, partnership with the private sector would be essential for development of renewables. And yet, 'there was no interest in private sector', at least in the short term.[26] According to one EEPCo official,

> the challenge for IPPs [independent power producers] was political ... there was no full commitment by the party leaders. It was seen more as a long-term strategy, 'in the long-run that's the solution, but for now it's not the right time'.[27]

Nonetheless, the environmental turn in the government's narrative meant casting the longstanding prioritization of hydropower as a *sustainable* and *renewable* choice. The principal statement to this effect is the 2011 Climate Resilient Green Economy (CRGE) strategy, which lays out the government's plan to achieve rapid growth and structural transformation, while limiting emissions to the 2011 annual figure of 150 Mt CO_2e, avoiding the increase to 400 Mt CO_2e by 2030 that the document estimates would be produced under 'a conventional development path' (FDRE 2011, p. 2). The existing dominance of hydropower and plans for rapid

[23] Interview EG6, senior official in the energy sector, Addis Ababa, 3 October 2019.
[24] Interview EP11, consultant to the electricity sector, by phone, 25 November 2019.
[25] Interview EG6, senior official in the energy sector, Addis Ababa, 3 October 2019.
[26] Interview EG13, former senior EEP official, Addis Ababa, 19 February 2020.
[27] Interview EG10, senior EEP official, Addis Ababa, 17 July 2019.

expansion to power an electric train network and growing industrial sector are at the centre of this strategy.[28] Indeed, the document claims that just 3 per cent of Ethiopia's emissions—themselves modest by global standards—are produced by the electricity sector (FDRE 2011, p. 13). Moreover, these emissions are purely the result of diesel plants used as back up supply and for off-grid generation, most of which would be switched off in 2012–2014 (FDRE 2011, p. 16). The implication, therefore, is that hydropower produces no emissions whatsoever. Moreover, hydropower expansion beyond Ethiopia's current domestic needs is presented as a means of helping to reduce emissions in neighbouring countries also by exporting clean hydropower (FDRE 2011, p. 25). A central focus of the document is essentially to appeal for finance to realize government plans, including in dam construction. The document's narrative is that realization of the enormous benefits of the strategy requires massive upfront costs compared to the 'conventional development path', with a financing gap of $20 billion required over 20 years to meet government plans for electricity generation and transmission alone (FDRE 2011, p. 51).

Key to the narrative of the CRGE, therefore, is that hydropower is a renewable and sustainable energy source. In this respect, there is certainly considerable debate, none of which is acknowledged in the CRGE. Ethiopia is certainly not alone in claiming hydropower as a renewable energy source and a valuable tool in the fight against climate change. Other major hydropower producers such as Brazil similarly present hydropower as a clean energy source (Atkins 2020; Hochstetler 2020), as do the World Bank (2009a) and the International Hydropower Association (IHA 2023a). Yet the construction and operation of dams certainly does produce greenhouse gas emissions. Dam construction requires vast amounts of concrete and steel, production of which requires enormous amounts of energy and associated carbon emissions. However, a greater source of emissions is likely to be found in the operation of the dams. Both in the initial filling of a reservoir and in its operation—which causes a successive rise and fall of the water level—areas of vegetation are submerged and consequently decompose anaerobically in the reservoir. The result is that atmospheric carbon dioxide is converted into methane, a gas whose greenhouse effect is approximately seven times that of carbon dioxide (Fearnside 2003). While some methane is released from the reservoir itself, the remainder is dissolved underwater in the highly pressurized, cold depths of the reservoir. The release of water from deep in the reservoir through the turbine intakes, in turn, leads to the instantaneous de-pressurization of the water and a gradual increase in its temperature, greatly reducing the solubility of the gas in

[28] A similar situation pertains with respect to the other priorities identified in the strategy regarding the intensification and productivity growth of smallholder agriculture and livestock production, and the use of efficient stoves in rural areas, thereby reducing deforestation. Like hydropower, these have been longstanding government priorities, with the green economy now superimposed as an additional justification.

the water with the consequence that almost all of the methane is released. The result has been that reservoirs have been described as 'virtual methane factories' (Fearnside 2003), with methane production particularly high in shallow, tropical reservoirs (Giles 2006; Gunkel 2009; Kuriakose et al. 2022).

To the author's knowledge, no studies have yet measured the emissions from any of Ethiopia's existing reservoirs. The result is that the few papers addressing the topic speculate based on the experience of other dams elsewhere in the world (Elagib and Basheer 2021) or use remote sensing data to estimate likely emissions (Johnson et al. 2021). Nonetheless, the location of many of Ethiopia's dams on rivers descending from the cool highlands to much hotter lowlands suggests that these processes may well be important. What is clear is that Ethiopian hydropower does not have zero emissions, as suggested in the CRGE. Quite how large they may be and what this implies for Ethiopia's goal of net-zero emissions is unclear.

The 'Developmental State' beyond Meles

Prime Minister Meles Zenawi was undoubtedly the main architect of the EPRDF's 'developmental state' and a key figure driving Ethiopia's dams boom. Meles' sudden death in 2012 therefore had important implications both for national development and the electricity sector in particular. While the post-Meles leadership initially sought to follow the path that the former premier had envisaged, they were gradually forced to confront the limitations of the existing development model, along with growing political fragmentation within the EPRDF.

Meles' death in 2012 resulted in a major shift in the balance of power within the EPRDF, accelerating the generational change in EPRDF leadership that Meles himself had initiated in his final years. The result was to bring to the fore a new leadership, including new prime minister Hailemariam Dessalegn, many of whom had not been involved in the Tigrayan People's Liberation Front's (TPLF's) liberation struggle in the 1970s and 1980s, and who were, consequently, not as deeply embedded in their predecessors' ideological commitments. Moreover, the succession marked a notable shift in the balance of power between EPRDF parties. The TPLF and, from 2001, Meles had dominated the EPRDF previously. The selection of Hailemariam, leader of the weakest EPRDF party, the Southern Ethiopian People's Democratic Movement (SEPDM), as EPRDF chairman and prime minister, represented something of a compromise between the TPLF and the increasingly assertive Amhara National Democratic Movement (ANDM) and Oromiya People's Democratic Organization (OPDO). In addition to Hailemariam's appointment as prime minister, the government created three deputy prime ministers to represent each of the more powerful EPRDF parties: Debretsion Gebremichael (TPLF), Demeke Mekonnen (ANDM), and Muktar Kedir (OPDO). The result was an inevitable reduction in elite cohesion, with the four constituent parties and their regional governments increasingly assertive in their dealings with the federal government, and greater ideological contestation within the coalition.

Rhetorically, and in many respects in policy details also, the government remained committed to Meles' version of a 'developmental state', with the Second Growth and Transformation Plan (GTP2) launched in 2015/16, building on the plans Meles had originally formulated. Despite annual economic growth rates in excess of 10 per cent during GTP1, progress in most sectors had fallen well short of the plan's enormous ambitions and sectoral targets. This was particularly the case for the industrial sector, with very little progress towards the government's long-term ambition of turning manufacturing into the main driver of the economy and source of employment. All the main targets for industrial production and exports were missed and the industrial share of formal employment increased from just 8 per cent to 9 per cent (NPC 2016 and World Development Indicators). Low rates of employment creation continued to be seen as a major political threat to the EPRDF (Lavers 2023). The post-Meles leadership once again doubled down on rapid development as a solution to their political problems, setting enormously ambitious targets across all sectors that aimed to get the economy back on track.

Despite much continuity, GTP2 heralded an important shift in the EPRDF's industrial strategy. The years since Meles' death saw internal debates between EPRDF factions regarding the appropriate role for the state and private sector in this next phase of Ethiopia's 'developmental state' (Bereket Simon on YouTube 2018; Oqubay and Kefale 2020). In contrast to the largely rural-based approach focused on domestic capital, as set out in the 2002 industrial strategy (MoI 2002a), from 2015 government priorities shifted to the state construction of a series of industrial parks to attract foreign investors (NPC 2016). Industrial policy up to that point had enjoyed moderate successes in sectors such as floriculture and cement, but progress in key priority areas such as textiles, apparel, and leather remained very limited (Oqubay 2015; Brautigam et al. 2016; Whitfield and Staritz 2021). The low capacity of the state to monitor and incentivize productivity improvements and for domestic firms to raise their productivity was identified as a major failing, as was the incompatibility of a focus on domestic capital with the requirements of global value chains dominated by international lead firms (Whitfield and Staritz 2021). The industrial parks therefore marked a major strategic shift, seeking to integrate the Ethiopian economy into global value chains by encouraging established global producers in textiles, apparel, leather, and leather products to relocate parts of their production networks to Ethiopia based on the availability of state-of-the-art 'plug and play' facilities in state-constructed parks and cheap labour (Oya and Schaefer 2021). Moreover, the parks were marketed as 'Eco-Industrial Parks', powered by cheap, 'renewable' hydropower and employing waste treatment facilities. This new strategy had important spatial implications, with infrastructural investments concentrated at key points where industrial parks were located. GTP2 therefore set out plans for a further massive increase in electricity generation to meet the needs of these new industrial parks, as well as progress towards the delayed electric railways that were to provide a key transport link to Djibouti, which monopolizes Ethiopia's foreign trade (Terrefe 2022).

Shifting intra-elite relations shaped the apportionment of ministerial positions and, in turn, the modalities and dynamics within the electricity sector itself. The key figure for the electricity sector was Dr Debretsion Gebremichael who became deputy prime minister for the finance and economy cluster in 2012, giving him authority over the economic plans in GTP2. An emerging figure in the TPLF, Debretsion was made deputy chair of the party after Meles' death in 2012 and is widely believed to have had close links with the military and intelligence services. Despite the growing fragmentation within the ruling elite as a whole, Debretsion managed to concentrate his authority over the electricity sector through his position as deputy prime minister for the economy, chair of the board of the state power company, and chair of the board of the Office for Public Participation in the GERD.

One of Debretsion's early initiatives was to unbundle EEPCo, splitting the corporation into EEP—responsible for generation and transmission—and the Ethiopian Electric Utility (EEU)—responsible for distribution. At this point, the Ethiopian Electric Agency was also renamed and re-constituted as the Ethiopian Energy Authority (EEA). These reforms were at the initiative of the government and intended to promote greater attention to distribution, which had been neglected under EEPCo (EEU is discussed in Chapter 8).[29] Although unbundling is a key part of the standard model, the reform was actually questioned by the World Bank officials at the time who felt that it was undertaken 'without good preparation' and with unclear objectives.[30] The government proceeded regardless. Indeed, the division has proven problematic in many respects, with an unclear division of functions and assets between the two new state corporations and an arbitrary division of revenues that has starved EEU, in particular, of resources.[31]

This reform was accompanied by a new push to build technical capacity in hydropower, not just supervising established foreign firms but also using massive state investment in dams to build domestic expertise, in line with the government's 'developmental state' ideology. The experience with MetEC, in which existing military engineering firms were merged to form a corporation tasked with a key part of the construction of the GERD, was but the most prominent example of a broader trend. The 'developmental state' would now be leveraged to build

[29] Interviews with senior officials in the energy sector: EG6, Addis Ababa, 3 October 2019; EG8, Addis Ababa, 3 October 2019, 11 February 2020; EG9, Addis Ababa, 23 July 2019, 17 September 2019; EG37, Addis Ababa, 21 August 2019, 19 February 2020.

[30] Interview ED16, donor representative, by phone, 5 February 2020.

[31] Interview EP17, consultant in the energy sector, Addis Ababa, 4 June 2019.

Ethiopian capacity in electro-mechanical engineering, civil engineering, feasibility studies, and design works.

EEP was identified for developing electro-mechanical expertise, and to that end the corporation formulated a 20-year capacity-building programme. EEP's long-standing training centre was to be given a major upgrade with the aim of training some 10,000 electro-mechanical technicians.[32] EEP also signed Memoranda of Understanding with Ethiopian universities who would twin with foreign universities, over five years developing the capacity within local universities to deliver the management and technical training EEP required.[33] EEP also took steps to improve recruitment and promotions—increasing the importance of qualifications and performance evaluations, based on *gimgema*, in these decisions—as well as making efforts to improve staff retention. Identifying low pay as a major issue that leads staff to move into the private sector or abroad, EEP used its autonomy from civil service pay scales to raise salaries by as much as 50 per cent in some cases, reducing, but not stopping, staff turnover.[34]

The government also took steps to expand state civil engineering capacity at this time. As noted in Chapter 3, EWWCE was created under Imperial rule and had built a series of small water storage dams under previous regimes. Under the EPRDF, EWWCE had undertaken a series of progressively larger water storage dams and irrigation projects, including the Tendaho Dam and irrigation scheme for the linked sugar estate in the Awash Basin (2010–2017), the diversion weir and vast irrigation scheme for the 175,000-hectare Omo-Kuraz sugar plantation, and water storage dams at Kessem, Ribb, and Megech. In 2015, EWWCE was merged with the Ethiopian Road Construction Corporation to form the Ethiopian Construction Works Corporation (ECWC). The new Corporation set out its ambition to move into more complex hydropower dams, ultimately developing the capacity and expertise to replace foreign contractors within Ethiopia and even to secure foreign contracts for dam projects.[35] In the words of one senior official:

> We do not [yet] have the capacity to tackle something like the GERD but we can with the others [hydropower dams] ... In the future the aim is to take EPC contracts based on our own construction, like Salini does now.[36]

Likewise, the Water Works Design and Supervision Enterprise (WWDSE) created by the EPRDF in 1998 was merged with other state enterprises, forming the Ethiopian Construction Design and Supervision Works Corporation whose remit

[32] Interviews EG12, former senior official in the energy sector, Addis Ababa, 14 February 2020; ED1, donor representative, 3 June 2019.
[33] Interview EG12, former senior official in the energy sector, Addis Ababa, 14 February 2020.
[34] Interview EG12, former senior official in the energy sector, Addis Ababa, 14 February 2020.
[35] Interview EG12, former senior official in the energy sector, Addis Ababa, 14 February 2020.
[36] Interview EG5, ECWC official, Addis Ababa, 11 February 2020.

included the design and study of dams, with plans to expand beyond their past focus on small dams and irrigation works into medium-scale hydropower projects both in Ethiopia and abroad.[37] This upsurge in ambition to develop a hydropower industry came relatively late in Ethiopia's dams boom, however. Of these newly prioritized firms, it was only MetEC that was given major responsibilities in any of Ethiopia's main dam projects. Indeed, despite these ambitions, the realization of Ethiopia's grand plans for hydropower remained dependent on foreign contractors, notably Salini and several Chinese firms.

Debretsion's outsized influence on the electricity sector shaped the planning decisions in EEP. Most of the main strategic decisions in the sector were made by the EEP board, which Debretsion chaired, with EEP management reduced to the task of implementing politically defined targets.[38] As one long-term official in MoWIE noted,

> Decisions are made by government, with details on number of connections and generation capacity ... When it comes to enforcing these decisions, the board has more power than the executive management [of EEP]. The board meets weekly, sometimes daily. The executive managers act more like line managers, they are not that powerful.[39]

These decision-making dynamics and the subordination of technocrats to politicians shaped the target setting, planning, and implementation of a number of generation and transmission projects. A new masterplan was produced in 2014 by a foreign consultancy firm and its forecast of future energy and peak demand was to feed into the GTP2 targets (Parsons Brinckerhoff 2014). However, the key inputs for the masterplan's demand forecast were economic projections that assumed the successful attainment of GTP1 targets, which had by that stage already proven far too ambitious, and even more optimistic targets set out for growth and industrial development in the draft GTP2. As a result, the 2014 masterplan was based on a massive, implausible increase in electricity demand for new eco-industrial parks operating at full capacity, an operational electric rail network, and electric-powered irrigation pumps, among many other things.[40] As an EEP official admitted,

[37] Interviews EG43, senior energy sector official, Addis Ababa, 12 February 2020; ECWC official, Addis Ababa, 11 February 2020.

[38] Interview EG2, former senior energy sector official, Addis Ababa, 3 September 2019, 13 February 2020.

[39] Interview EG2, former senior energy sector official, Addis Ababa, 3 September 2019, 13 February 2020. Or as another EEP official put it: 'Ethiopia's politicians decide for the engineers' (Interview EG9, senior energy sector official, Addis Ababa, 23 July 2019, 17 September 2019).

[40] The Djibouti–Addis Ababa link was the first and thus far only line completed in 2018. Construction of the line to Weldiya and Mekele stalled due to financial constraints and then the civil war from 2020. No progress has been made on the other lines in the planned network.

> I remember we had to push the consultants for the Power Sector Masterplan very hard to include the GTP1 projections in their forecast. Consultants are conservative, they didn't want to, but we knew that the first question we would receive from higher levels would be 'where are the GTP targets?' so we had to include it.[41]

The consultants likewise admitted that they were forced to construct the masterplan based on what they considered, correctly, to be unrealistic economic plans:

> you cannot not use their plans. You can't argue with it ... You can't say, 'we don't believe you'. We presented three scenarios based on their development plan at the time. The politicians seize on the high scenario and say, 'look we need to deliver this' ... We argued with EEPCo and they said, 'you have to do this'.[42]

Remarkably, however, even the masterplan's projections (Figure 4.2) were not considered ambitious enough by the political leadership.[43] Multiple respondents were quite clear that the key figure in translating the masterplan into targets for GTP2 was Deputy Prime Minister Debretsion. Indeed, Debretsion was open about the approach that he took in doing so:

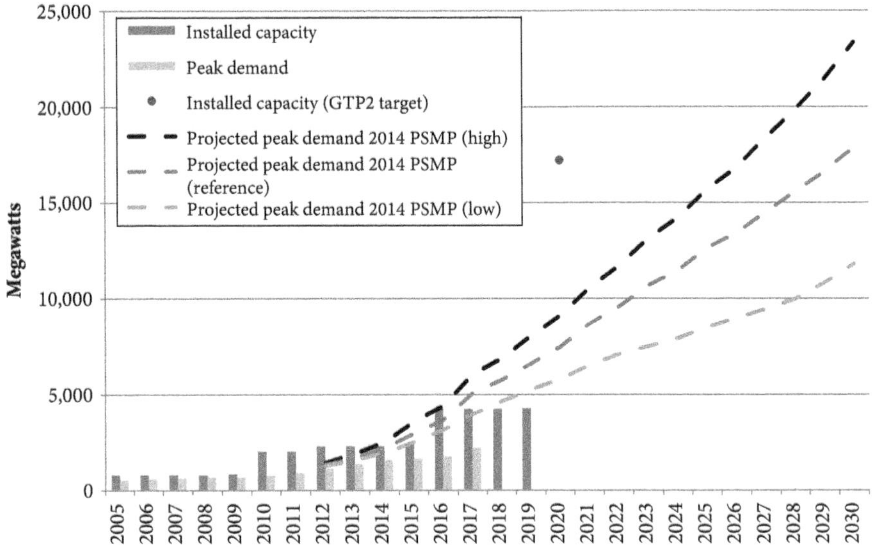

Figure 4.2 Installed capacity and targets for GTP2, 2015–2020

Data source: Parsons Brinckerhoff (2014), NPC (2016), and USAID (2019).

[41] Interview EG8, former senior energy sector official, Addis Ababa, 3 October 2019, 11 February 2020.

[42] Interview EP11, consultant to the energy sector, by phone, 25 November 2019.

[43] Interview EP11, consultant to the energy sector, by phone, 25 November 2019.

> we need to increase our generating capacity to 17,000 MW before the end of GTP II. This target is not chosen randomly. We have set this goal with due consideration to the power requirement of a middle-income country ... although we do have another ten years before Ethiopia reaches middle-income country status, we thought that we need to make power available before reaching middle-income status, and that is why we decided to expand our capacity to 17,000 MW in the next five years. (Debretsion, cited in Anberbir 2017)

At Debretsion's insistence, the high projection for 2025 from the masterplan was shifted forwards to 2020 as a target for GTP2, essentially making up for the failure of GTP1 by achieving both GTP1 and 2 within five years.[44] The latest available data show peak demand in 2017 of 2,202 MW, which is on a steady, but moderate, upward trajectory. As such, there is no indication that any more than a fraction of this target of 17,000 MW is required at present or in the medium term, while the export agreements being finalized would not come close to absorbing the surplus. As one donor official noted, GTP2 had truly 'outrageous targets'.[45]

As can be seen, EEP was nowhere near delivering the target for 2020. The delayed Gilgel Gibe III Dam was completed in 2016, nearly doubling Ethiopia's total installed capacity by adding 1,870 MW to the grid. While enormously important for national generation capacity, this barely made a dent in the GTP2 target, however. Salini was immediately contracted to build the next dam in the cascade, Koysha (or Gibe IV), which has an installed capacity even larger than Gibe III at 2,160 MW. Originally scheduled for completion in 2021, Koysha has been subject to delays due to a shortage of finance and the prioritization of the GERD (see Chapter 9). Meanwhile, construction of the GERD continued throughout GTP2, finally beginning early generation in 2022. The dam will not be fully operational until the mid-2020s at least. However, even had the GERD—at one point planned to be 6,350 MW—been completed during GTP2, EEP would still not have come close to meeting the 17,000-MW target.

Conclusion

Under the GTP1 and GTP2, the EPRDF's 'developmental state' delivered a massive boom in dam construction that raised installed generation capacity in Ethiopia to more than 4,000 MW in 2020, more than 10 times what it was when the party first took office in 1991. This is even before the largest two hydropower projects—the GERD and Koysha—are completed, with these two set to take that figure to more than 11,000 MW. The argument advanced over this and the previous chapter is that the political vulnerability of the ruling elite, ideological commitments to

[44] Interviews EG2, former senior energy sector official, Addis Ababa, 3 September 2019, 13 February 2020; EG8, former senior energy sector official, Addis Ababa, 3 October 2019, 11 February 2020.

[45] Interview ED9, donor representative, by phone, 18 October 2019.

state-led development, and the centralization of political power within a few key decision makers were the key factors shaping the government's commitment to state-led development and the particular emphasis placed on massive investment in hydropower as part of this strategy. To deliver on these political ambitions, however, the government had to secure the financial resources and technocratic capacity required to carry out these massive infrastructural investments. In terms of finance, the government became increasingly assertive in mobilizing domestic revenues from the rapidly growing economy and seeking out a range of concessional and commercial loans where available. By doing so, the government took a major gamble, accumulating large foreign and domestic debts to finance a dizzying array of infrastructural investments—including industrial parks, railways, and sugar factories in addition to hydropower dams—that, the government hoped, would pay off in terms of mass employment creation, exports, and foreign exchange earnings.

Beyond finance, the EPRDF Government also faced a challenge in accessing sufficient technical capacity to plan and implement its dam building. In terms of the planning of electricity sector development, the analysis above shows that the expansion of electricity generation was a politically driven affair, with the vanguard party and a handful of key politicians setting priorities and targets for the sector and pressing technocrats to deliver on these goals. While there were certainly efforts to build capacity within EEP, key decisions were taken by politicians at the most senior levels, with little to no consultation with electricity sector officials with relevant technical expertise. As a result, the analysis here somewhat diverges from past studies that have suggested that the expansion of the capacity and political power of EEPCo/EEP was a key factor driving the dams boom. For example, Kraak (2012, pp. 136–137) suggests that 'EEPCo is the leading hydraulic bureaucracy' and that 'the political clout of the utility is enormous', while Frezer Haile (2018, p. 185) underscores the importance of 'the growth of domestic scientific and technical capacity' in Ethiopian dam building and particularly the GERD. Contrary to the standard portrayal of the East Asian developmental states, on which Ethiopia's national development project was modelled, this chapter argues that Ethiopia's dams boom was politically driven and progressed *in spite of* limited state technocratic capacity, not because of its strengthening. Indeed, the politically driven nature of this process resulted in a series of ever-more ambitious development plans that increasingly diverged from any reasonable technical assessment of Ethiopia's energy needs or the infrastructure required to deliver it. While ambition, perhaps, has its merits, the result was that this planning process and the absence of technical inputs began to undermine the electricity sector and the development strategy more broadly, shaping the design of the dams (discussed in Chapter 7), distribution and access to electricity (Chapter 8), and the economy's exposure to foreign debt (Chapter 9). In doing so, the EPRDF dams boom from around 2010 onwards began to resemble the high modernist schemes of many past and present dam builders (Scott 1998; Dye 2016, 2018). For the EPRDF in the latter days of Meles' rule and particularly after his passing, decision making was shaped by an ideological faith among the ruling elite in the ability of ever-larger dams to master nature, deliver development, and consolidate the position of the ruling party.

The other challenge facing the government in pursuing this dams boom has been to secure the technical and engineering capacity required to actually deliver the projects themselves. As argued above, the EPRDF did latterly attempt to mobilize state investment in hydropower to build domestic capacity in MetEC and ECWC. However, these efforts arrived late in Ethiopia's dams boom and, as discussed in Chapters 7 and 9, met with little success. Rather, the capacity gap was filled primarily by the peculiar relationship between the government and Salini, a firm with longstanding interests in Ethiopia and a deep commitment to a long-term future in the country. Chapter 5 focuses specifically on the role of Salini.

5
Salini
An Ethio-Italian Story

Emanuele Fantini, Luca Puddu, Edegilign Hailu Woldegebrael, and Tom Lavers

> My company is an Ethiopian company. But it is not only an Ethiopian company, it is a company at the service of this nation and at the service of the government.
>
> Pietro Salini, chief executive officer (CEO), WeBuild (formerly Salini Impregilo)[1]

The history of dam building and hydropower development in Ethiopia is deeply interwoven with the story of a particular construction company: Salini Costruttori.[2] Started as an Italian family-owned company, Salini has been building dams and other infrastructure in Ethiopia since the 1960s, navigating different political regimes—Imperial Ethiopia, the Derg, and the Federal Republic under Meles Zenawi, Hailemariam Dessalegn, and Abiy Ahmed—and expanding its business to become a key partner of the Ethiopian Government in its most ambitious project: the Grand Ethiopian Renaissance Dam (GERD). Indeed, Ethiopia is one of the strategic bases from which Salini surged to become a global top player in the infrastructure sector, particularly after the 2014 merger with another Italian firm, Impregilo, to form Salini Impregilo, rebranded WeBuild in 2020.[3]

What explains such longstanding partnership and its success? In many respects, the story of Salini in Ethiopia is a unique one that diverges from several assumptions about multinational corporations in sub-Saharan Africa in an era of globalization. As boldly stated by its own CEO in the opening quote, Salini is not

[1] See YouTube (2022). Quote is at 2 minutes 23 seconds.

[2] In this chapter we share our respective research to explore how water and dams shapes the Ethiopian physical and sociopolitical landscape, as well as the post-colonial imaginaries and relations among Ethiopia and Italy. Emanuele Fantini wrote the introduction, conclusion, and section on Tana-Beles. Luca Puddu wrote the section on Legadadi, while Edegilign Hailu Woldegebrael wrote the section on the Gibe cascade. Tom Lavers provided additional research and writing on the Gibe dams.

[3] We refer to the company as Salini, since in Ethiopia this is the name by which the company is widely known.

Dams, Power, and the Politics of Ethiopia's Renaissance. Tom Lavers et al., Oxford University Press. © Emanuele Fantini, Luca Puddu, Edegilign Hailu Woldegebrael, and Tom Lavers (2024). DOI: 10.1093/oso/9780192871213.003.0005

simply another foreign or multinational corporation. Rather, it is also a national, Ethiopian, company with a long-run interest in consolidating its relations with the political elite and its position in the Ethiopian market. As such, the company's logic and approach cannot be reduced to that of volatile global capital constantly relocating its investments to the most lucrative and deregulated sites of production. Instead, Salini works in Ethiopia to stay in the country. At the same time, the partnership with Salini has filled a key gap in the government's dam-building strategy, namely providing the technical capacity required to undertake a series of increasingly complex engineering projects, while also demonstrating the commitment and reliability to persist with politically controversial projects amidst financial uncertainty. In doing so, Salini's dam building ties Ethiopia with another country, Italy. Salini is an Ethio-Italian story.

Stretching over 60 years and four different political regimes, this story remains largely untold. In the last years, Salini has started to narrate its own version through publications, magazines, podcasts, and cultural events, mostly relying on Italian authors and voices (Salini Impregilo 2015, 2016a, 2018; WeBuild 2023). Unsurprisingly, the firm's narrative celebrates its technical achievements, while avoiding the contentious elements that unavoidably accompany large dams. In contrast, we illustrate the peculiarities of this story through multidisciplinary research combining Ethiopian and Italian perspectives on three Salini projects across three different political regimes: the Legadadi Dam and reservoir built under Imperial Ethiopia for Addis Ababa's water supply (1964–1970); the Tana-Beles multipurpose project started in 1986 under the Derg and more recently brought new life in the 2000s; and the Gilgel Gibe cascade of three dams and four power stations along the Gibe and Omo Rivers, commissioned by the federal and 'developmental' state from 2004 onwards. The chapter considers these projects in chronological order, integrating the scarce existing literature on these projects with archival research (Legadadi), key informant interviews (Tana-Beles), and field research (Gilgel Gibe).

Three recurrent elements stand out from these three projects, and thereby illustrate the functioning of Salini's work in Ethiopia. First, in terms of political economy, Salini has acted as broker between the Ethiopian Government and international donors like the Italian Government, securing flows of capital, technology, and expertise into Ethiopia. Such a role was made possible by the unique relations Salini developed with the ruling elites of Ethiopia *and* Italy, while the projects themselves served to cement these relations. Second, from a political ecology perspective, key features of the Ethiopian landscape created the conditions for Salini's endurance in the country. Ethiopia's geomorphology, with highlands rich in water and lowlands with irrigation potential (see Chapter 2), makes it an ideal 'civil engineer's sand pit'.[4] Thus, the physical landscape shaped Salini's presence

[4] Interview, former consultant of the Italian Development Cooperation, online, February 2020.

in Ethiopia, and at the same time Salini contributed to transform this land- and water-scape. Third, these transformations happened under specific political conditions. Initial projects took place at the centre—Addis Ababa—and subsequently moved to the peripheries of the country, 'at the service of', to use Pietro Salini's words, successive Ethiopian state-building strategies. Given their symbolic and material importance, and the government's sense of the urgency of national development, these projects have been implemented in a 'state of exception' (Agamben 2005; Hagmann and Korf 2012), bypassing international and national norms on procurement and socio-environmental impact assessment.

Salini in Imperial Ethiopia: The Legadadi Project

Salini's history dates back to 1936, when Pietro Salini established his original business in Italy, with the firm re-established in 1956 by Pietro and his son Simonpietro (Salini Impregilo 2016b). Salini's involvement in the Ethiopian engineering sector, however, dates back to the 1960s. At that time, the Italian firm operated in the country through two different companies: Salini Costruttori Ethiopia, a local subsidiary created in 1967 to manage large engineering works, and Salcost, an Ethiopian firm controlled by Salini and operating in the real estate sector. The flagship project that brought Salini to prominence in the Ethiopian market was the Legadadi reservoir, which still supplies 60 per cent of Addis Ababa's water (Adugna and Cherie 2021, p. 4). The contract was signed in April 1967 and consisted of a gravity dam along with a plant for treatment, distribution, and storage of clean water to the capital.[5] The infrastructure was designed by Studio Pietrangeli, an Italian engineering firm founded in 1964 that has designed all Salini's major projects in Ethiopia. Legadadi, in turn, paved the way for the entrance of Salcost into other lucrative sectors such as private housing and hotel construction. Rapidly, the firm established itself as a leading partner of the Ethiopian state, being awarded contracts for prestigious buildings such as the Kennedy Memorial Library and the headquarters of the Lion Insurance Company in Addis Ababa.[6]

Legadadi highlights continuities in the involvement of the Italian state-business apparatus in the Ethiopian hydroelectric sector through to the present. First of all, Legadadi—and large dams in general—were associated with state-building as a symbol of modernity and technical progress, to be employed in the general struggle against hunger and poverty (Abbink 2012). This discourse was similar to that adopted by African nationalists committed to dam building during and after decolonization (Tischler 2013). Along with the development of domestic food

[5] Historical Archives of Unicredit, Banco di Roma Fund (hereafter HAUBR) XI, 4, 2, 1, f. 65, b. 4, 70,084 Salini Costruttori, Proposta di fido, 30 April 1970, p. 1.

[6] HAUBR, XI, 4, 2, 1, f. 39, b. 3, 10,050 Ethiopian Salcost, Proposta di Fido, 30 April 1970.

production (Bekele 2009), the mastery of nature through large-scale infrastructure was one of Haile Selassie's platforms for legitimizing his authority. Meanwhile, for business groups associated with the former colonial power, Italy, dam building was a perfect tool to reframe their relationship with newly independent countries, representing themselves as vanguards of an updated civilizing mission in joint venture with their African counterparts. This pattern emerged clearly from a brief description of Legadadi by Studio Pietrangeli. The company's website recalls the moral investiture received at that time by a young Giorgio Pietrangeli from Emperor Haile Selassie in person, who argued that 'every day in Ethiopia hundreds of people die because they do not have access to water' (Studio Pietrangeli 2023a).

Negotiating Finance in the International Arena

Salini's consolidation as a leading actor in the Ethiopian market was closely connected to its ability to mobilize transnational political networks in Africa and Europe, and thereby connect projects to sources of finance. Furthermore, Salini's engagement necessitated a willingness to meet additional informal conditions and to accept a low return on initial investments in return for long-term profits (Fantini and Puddu 2016, p. 109).

The early trajectory of Salini was deeply affected by the Italian Government's attempt to retain a sphere of influence in its former East African colonies. In contrast with the present, however, it was not private firms that upheld the Italian diplomatic position in Addis Ababa by virtue of their initiatives in the hydropower sector, but quite the contrary. Following the resumption of bilateral relations with the Ethiopian Empire in 1951, the Italian Government re-engineered its foreign policy to prioritize the consolidation of Italy's economic position in the region. Dam building was deemed the ideal means by which metropolitan firms could penetrate the Ethiopian market. The main purpose was to reactivate the economic links with the former colony, linking war reparations to the purchase of Italian goods and the realization of construction works directly assigned to Italian firms.[7] The Italian Government identified several promising economic sectors to this end, and hydroelectric infrastructure was top of the list.[8] The idea was that, having established a foothold in Ethiopia, Italian engineering companies would be able to claim superior technical knowledge of the territory and face lower logistics costs, putting them at an advantageous position for future competitive bids vis-à-vis other European firms.

[7] Historical Archives of the Italian Ministry of Foreign Affairs (hereafter ASMAE), Direzione Generale Affari Politici 1951–57, Busta 803, Riunione prima dell'arrivo della delegazione etiopica, 20 settembre 1952.

[8] ASMAE, Direzione Generale Affari Politici 1951–57, Busta 803, Verbale di riunione interministeriale, 15 ottobre 1952, pp. 2, 5.

Salini did not benefit directly from the war reparations package, which was reserved for engineering firms with stronger government connections in Italy. The company that was originally supposed to take the lead in the quest for domination of the hydroelectric sector was Imprese Italiane all'Estero (Impresit), which already had experience in Africa after construction of the Kariba Dam on the border of Zambia and Zimbabwe (Tischler 2013; Salini Impregilo 2016b). Impresit was awarded the contract for construction of the Koka Dam, on the Awash River, in partnership with the Italian firm Recchi (Comitato Nazionale Italiano Grandi Dighe 2016, p. 13). Impresit would also go on to be the main civil contractor on the Finchaa Dam in the 1970s (World Bank 1976). However, it was not involved in further Ethiopian dam projects until 2011 when the firm, which in 1994 merged with other Italian engineering companies to establish Impregilo SPA, was in turn purchased by Salini to produce Salini Impregilo.

Although Salini was not a direct beneficiary of war reparations, it nonetheless took advantage of other lines of credit at subsidized interest rates from state-controlled financial corporations and banking institutes such as Istituto di Credito per le Imprese di Pubblica Utilità (ICIPU) and Banco di Roma. The original financial burden of Legadadi, for instance, was supposed to be entirely covered by an Eth$25,000,000 loan from ICIPU.[9] Privileged access to the Italian financial system was probably facilitated by the fact that in the early 1960s Salini had already established a working collaboration with the Italian Government, contributing, among other things, to the construction of the Ministry of Post and Telecommunication in Rome. These connections facilitated the arrangement of a similar scheme in 1968, when the firm started negotiations with another Italian financial institution—Mediobanca—to obtain funding for Salcost to build the new Engineering College at Haile Selassie I University.[10]

The engineering groups could also advance funding through other means pending official approval of these financial arrangements. This was made possible by the privileged relationship with Banco di Roma, with Simonpietro Salini appointed to the bank's board in the early 1960s (Salini Impregilo 2016a). In theory, Banco di Roma was only authorized to support short-term commercial operations, with a primary focus on import–export trade with Italy (Puddu 2021). The Eritrean and Ethiopian subsidiaries were nonetheless instructed to do everything they could to promote Salini's expansion in Ethiopia, even going beyond the bank's statutory activities. In April 1967, for instance, Banco di Roma's agency in Asmara granted an overdraft of Eth$650,000 to Salcost under surety of a bond for the same amount released by the Rome headquarters, which was in turn backed by a private guarantee by Salini Costruttori itself.[11] A few months later, this overdraft was

[9] HAUBR, XI, 4, 2, 1, f. 65, b. 4, 70,084 Salini Costruttori, Proposta di fido, 30 April 1970, p. 1.

[10] HAUBR, XI, 4, 2, 1, f. 39, b. 3, 10,050 Ethiopian Salcost, Tel to Banco di Roma, filiale di Roma, 4 April 1968. Haile Selassie I University would later be renamed Addis Ababa University.

[11] HAUBR, XI, 4, 2, 1, f. 39, b. 3, 10,050 Ethiopian Salcost, Tel from Ministero Commercio Estero to Banco di Roma, filiale di Roma, 20 April 1967.

increased to Eth$850,000 and then to Eth$1,100,000.[12] In February 1968, finally, credit advances were raised to Eth$1,700,000, which were supposed to cover the early construction cost of the College of Engineering in Addis Ababa.[13] These loans were particularly important given that the release of Italian public funds was conditional on a bilateral agreement with the Ethiopian Government and, in theory, approval by the Ethiopian Parliament. Credit from Banco di Roma provided the opportunity to bypass these time-consuming bureaucratic procedures.

The importance of this funding to the Ethiopian ruling elite is confirmed by a telegram sent on 1 February 1968 by the president of Haile Selassie I University, Kassa Wolde Mariam, who managed the competitive bidding for construction of the Engineering College. Kassa praised Salini for the fact that its offer was among the lowest, but justified the decision to assign the contract with another argument. According to the president, 'we are interested in financing the construction by credit, and your ability to provide credit is going to be one of the decisive factors'.[14] In other words, it was Salini's capacity to expand the extraversion portfolio of Addis Ababa that gave the Italian company the upper hand in the competition with other European and American firms.

Another factor behind Salini's favour among political circles in Imperial Ethiopia was the firm's ability to take partial charge of the financial cost associated with external lending. Archival documents from the Banco di Roma suggest that, in the case of the Legadadi Dam, Salini pledged to cover the interest on the ICIPU loan. In the contract signed by Banco di Roma-Ethiopia with the Addis Ababa municipality in December 1967, the Italian bank declared itself 'primary debtor, jointly with the said Salini Costruttori, Rome, [for] the said amount of semi-annual interest for which Salini is obligated to pay according to the Plan of Reimbursement'.[15] The advantage for the municipality was not negligible because the guarantee covered a total amount of Lit. 79,417,732, or Eth$316,000.

Salini's gate-keeping position in the international financial arena and the ramification of Salini's portfolio in the Ethiopian real estate sector were also instrumental in gaining a privileged position in the allocation of scarce Ethiopian domestic financial resources. In 1970, the Salcost subsidiary became beneficiary of a line of credit amounting to Eth$2,500,000 from the state Commercial Bank of Ethiopia.[16] This generosity was connected to Salcost's work in private housing development, with the loan secured against the mortgage of the Yemaskal Tamara residential centre. Although we have no direct evidence, it is possible that this window of

[12] HAUBR, XI, 4, 2, 1, f. 39, b. 3, 10,050 Ethiopian Salcost, Ufficio partecipazioni bancarie, Roma, 8 June 1967; Appunto, 2 August 1967.

[13] HAUBR, XI, 4, 2, 1, f. 39, b. 3, 10,050 Ethiopian Salcost, Tel from Salini Costruttori to Banco di Roma, 22 March 1968, Attachment 1.

[14] HAUBR, XI, 4, 2, 1, f. 39, b. 3, 10,050 Ethiopian Salcost, Tel from Kassa Wolde Mariam to Ethiopian Salcost, 1 February 1968.

[15] HAUBR, XI, 4, 2, 1, f. 65, b. 4, 70,084 Salini Costruttori, Tel from Banco di Roma to Municipality of Addis Ababa, 2 December 1967.

[16] HAUBR, XI, 4, 2, 1, f. 39, b. 3, 10,050 Ethiopian Salcost, Proposta di Fido, 30 April 1970.

opportunity was also nurtured by a special relationship with the Ethiopian ruling class in Addis Ababa. The Ethiopian aristocracy was particularly keen to speculate in real estate in collaboration with foreign ventures, which offered access to hard currency in return for prestigious building plots in the expanding Ethiopian capital (Schaefer 2012).

What is clear, however, is that by 1970 Salini was well entrenched in the Ethiopian market, to the extent that it was awarded additional contracts for the renewal of the Jubilee Palace and the realization of a mineral water plant in Ambo. Finance, once again, came from the Ethiopian Investment Corporation, longstanding financial partner of Mediobanca and ICIPU.[17]

Negotiating Projects in the National Arena

A key to Salini's success in Ethiopia lays in its ability to exploit its position at the interface of different financial and political systems, thereby improving its bargaining position with the Ethiopian Government. This emerges clearly from the last phase of the Legadadi project, when Salini was forced to renegotiate the contract under threat of unilateral termination by the Ethiopian administration.

According to the original plan, Legadadi would be finalized in December 1969 at a cost of Eth$23,400,000, but in January 1970 the works were not yet complete. Salini argued that additional time and money were needed, and that the costs incurred to date already amounted to more than Eth$33,000,000.[18] The shortfall, according to Salini, could be met with another line of credit from ICIPU for an additional loan of Eth$15,000,000. The Addis Ababa municipality was not enthusiastic. Not only had the deadline of December 1969 been missed but the municipality also contested the balance sheet submitted by Salini. According to the British auditing company Atkins & Partners, the works to date were worth only Eth$28,000,000.[19] Ethiopian officials turned to a procrastination strategy to push Salini to comply with the original terms. They accepted the proposal of refinancing in principle, but then declared themselves ready to submit a request for Eth$7,500,000 only, with the additional condition that Salini build another hydraulic system in the capital. Moreover, they repeatedly delayed their travel to Rome, where they were expected to sign the new loan agreement. In the meantime, the municipality privately approached other engineering firms such as Impresit, suggesting that they could replace Salini in the completion of the East Reservoir.[20]

[17] HAUBR, XI, 4, 2, 1, f. 39, b. 3, 10,050 Ethiopian Salcost, Tel to Board Delegation of Banco di Roma-Ethiopia, 24 June 1970.

[18] HAUBR, XI, 4, 2, 1, f. 65, b. 4, 70,084 Salini Costruttori, Proposta di fido, 30 April 1970, p. 2.

[19] HAUBR, XI, 4, 2, 1, f. 65, b. 4, 70,084 Salini Costruttori, Tel from Banco di Roma-Ethiopia to Board delegation, 17 January 1970, p. 2.

[20] HAUBR, XI, 4, 2, 1, f. 65, b. 4, 70,084 Salini Costruttori, Tel from Banco di Roma-Ethiopia to Board delegation, 17 January 1970, pp. 2–3.

Salini was reticent to restart construction works before signature of the second loan agreement for several reasons. First, the company believed the delay was caused by errors in the geological survey on which the original timeline had been based. Secondly, Salini was confident it had the upper hand in setting the terms of the new deal, since Addis Ababa was in dire need of fresh water to satisfy its growing population. Finally, Salini was probably aware that Ethiopian attempts to find another engineering partner for Legadadi had not been successful, with Impresit declining the Ethiopian offer. In January 1970 it became clear that Salini had the bargaining power when the company suddenly opted for the unilateral termination of the contract on the grounds that the municipality had not met its financial obligations. According to Italian bankers in Addis Ababa, this show of force was a tactical move to force the municipality to compromise, since the whole reservoir would be useless without completion of the last phase.[21] The strategy proved successful. On 2 February, the mayor of Addis Ababa and the vice-minister of finance landed in Rome, where they met with ICIPU representatives and signed a preliminary agreement for the new Legadadi loan.[22] Meanwhile, the company's technicians, who were supposed to leave the country within a few days, were ordered to remain in Addis Ababa and get ready to resume works as soon as possible.[23]

On 26 February 1970, the two parties signed a new agreement. The municipality would cover part of the additional cost reportedly incurred by Salini. In addition, the Ministry of Finance would reimburse the company of all taxes paid so far, while also finalizing the Eth$7,500,000 loan agreement with ICIPU.[24] Finally, Addis Ababa pledged to adopt a friendly approach towards the resolution of the dispute for the expenses declared by Salini but not certified by Atkins, eventually recognizing the verdict of an international court of arbitration in case of disagreement.[25] On 20 April, the mayor of Addis Ababa, Haile Giorgis Workneh, and the deputy-minister of finance, Bulcha Demeksa, landed in Rome to sign the new convention with ICIPU, with the understanding that the whole sum should be spent for the finalization of the Legadadi project by Salini.[26] At the end of 1970, the project was finally completed at a total cost of Eth$37,800,000, of which Eth$30,300,000 was certified by Atkins and partners.[27]

[21] HAUBR, XI, 4, 2, 1, f. 65, b. 4, 70,084 Salini Costruttori, Tel from Banco di Roma-Ethiopia to Board delegation, 17 January 1970, p. 5.

[22] HAUBR, XI, 4, 2, 1, f. 65, b. 4, 70,084 Salini Costruttori, *The Ethiopian Herald*, 6 February 1970.

[23] HAUBR, XI, 4, 2, 1, f. 65, b. 4, 70,084 Salini Costruttori, Tel from Banco di Roma-Ethiopia to Board Delegation, 6 February 1970.

[24] HAUBR, XI, 4, 2, 1, f. 65, b. 4, 70,084 Salini Costruttori, Tel from Haile Giorgi Workneh to Salini Costruttori, 23 February 1970.

[25] HAUBR, XI, 4, 2, 1, f. 65, b. 4, 70,084 Salini Costruttori, Tel from Banco di Roma-Ethiopia to Board Delegation, 24 June 1970, p. 3.

[26] HAUBR, XI, 4, 2, 1, f. 65, b. 4, 70,084 Salini Costruttori, Tel from Banco di Roma, filiale di Roma, to Direzione Centrale, 13 May 1970.

[27] HAUBR, XI, 4, 2, 1, f. 65, b. 4, 70,084 Salini Costruttori, Nota, 31 October 1970.

Salini's ability to find a satisfactory compromise with the Addis Ababa municipality was also supported by the involvement of other institutions which performed corporate diplomacy on its behalf. One of them was Banco di Roma, which attached great importance to the agreement in light of Salini's financial exposition with the bank's headquarters. According to an internal report, Haile Giorgis Workneh was impressed by the hospitality of Banco di Roma's directors in Rome.[28] That the mission had been a diplomatic success was confirmed by the fact that the mayor of Rome, Clelio Darida, was invited by Haile Giorgis Workneh to Addis Ababa at the end of October for the inauguration of the Legadadi complex. The project realized by Salini was supposed to be the starting point of 'a new chapter in the relations between the two capitals', according to the municipality of Addis Ababa.[29]

To sum up, Salini Costruttori arrived in Ethiopia already enjoying important political and financial connections in Italy. These networks were skilfully exploited by the company to mobilize economic and diplomatic capital that would prove critical in the early and final phases of the Legadadi project. At the same time, Salini acted as an auxiliary of the Ethiopian Government in mobilizing financial resources that were not internally available and was praised for these services by the highest Ethiopian authorities. Negotiations over additional finance for Legadadi between 1969 and 1970 also show that the Ethiopian Government's trusted strategy of playing foreign donors and international firms against one another to increase its bargaining position did not work with Salini. As a gatekeeper at the interface between different financial and political systems, the engineering firm was in a powerful position. The company was, to a certain extent, an updated form of Imperial bridgehead in the post-colonial setting, but was also able to accommodate to Ethiopian demands and adapt itself to the peculiar conditions encountered on the ground. This latter aspect clearly emerges from the expansion of the company's activities into Addis Ababa's booming real estate sector. This move helped the group to create a privileged relationship with the Ethiopian political establishment, which was keen to exploit the economic opportunities arising from the lease of land and housing. Overall, the result was that by the early 1970s, Salini was well established as a leading engineering firm in Ethiopia.

Salini under the Derg: The Tana-Beles Project

A second chapter of Salini's story in Ethiopia is the Tana-Beles project.[30] The project was implemented in the second half of the 1980s in a context marked

[28] HAUBR, XI, 4, 2, 1, f. 65, b. 4, 70,084 Salini Costruttori, Tel from Banco di Roma-Ethiopia to Board Delegation, 6 February 1970.

[29] HAUBR, XI, 4, 2, 1, f. 65, b. 4, 70,084 Salini Costruttori, Il Mattino del Lunedì, Asmara, 26 October 1970.

[30] The most comprehensive analysis of the Tana-Beles project is that provided by Kristin Fedeler (2021), to which this section is indebted.

by three factors. First was the Cold War. Following the 1974 revolution, the Derg aligned with the Soviet Union (see Chapter 2). However, within the West, Italy was identified as the foreign country to retain a foothold in Ethiopia and Salini seized this opportunity to consolidate its business in the country.[31] Despite Salini's close relations with the Imperial regime, it secured the support of the revolutionary government and the contract for Tana-Beles. The second factor was the drought and famine of 1984–1985 that put Ethiopia in the international spotlight. The official goal of the Tana-Beles project was agricultural modernization, framed as a means of addressing the humanitarian emergency and promoting food security. Third was the civil war during the 1970s and 1980s. According to several commentators, the hidden goal of the resettlement programme associated with Tana-Beles was to undermine popular support for the Tigrayan People's Liberation Front (TPLF) and other insurgents (Dawit 1989; De Waal 1991). Meanwhile, the advance of the conflict towards the project area led to the eventual abandonment of Tana-Beles shortly prior to the fall of the Derg (Fedeler 2021).

As ever, Salini turned to Studio Pietrangeli to design the ambitious project (Studio Pietrangeli 1990). The full Tana-Beles plan envisaged the transformation of a vast area from Lake Tana all the way to the Sudanese border with several hydropower plants, 299,000 hectares of irrigation, and settlement of 1,470,000 people over a period of 45 years (Studio Pietrangeli 1990). The project's initial phase was on a slightly more modest scale and began in 1984, contracted to Salini Costruttori, with Italian Government funding. This component focused on infrastructure in the Beles Valley, including roads and bridges, two small dams, aqueducts and water reservoirs, housing for 48 new villages, a hospital, and even a small airport. This infrastructure was expected to support irrigated commercial agriculture and the resettlement and villagization of the population affected by the famine. The second component would entail the construction of a diversion tunnel from Lake Tana into the Beles River Basin to expand irrigation and hydropower generation, a new version of proposals that date back to British colonial surveys in the early twentieth century (see Chapter 2). However, only the first component, focused on infrastructure in the Beles Valley, was implemented at the time due to the disruption caused by the civil war. It was only during 2005–2010 under the Ethiopian Peoples' Revolutionary Democratic Front (EPRDF) that the Lake Tana diversion was finally realized.

Securing Italian Government Support

Tana-Beles was supported financially and technically through an agreement between the Italian Ministry of Foreign Affairs and the Ethiopian Government (1986). In telling the story of its involvement in the project, the company itself links Legadadi to Tana-Beles and highlights the continued importance of Salini's

[31] Interview, former consultant of the Italian Development Cooperation, online, February 2020.

political connections, and in particular the role played by a key Italian political figure, Giulio Andreotti:[32]

> Legadadi gave Simonpietro Salini a kind of diplomatic passport and a certificate of skills and efficiency. The door was open, and in the 1980s, it would be thrown open even wider thanks also to the direct impetus of the Italian government and Giulio Andreotti, then Foreign Minister. The largest project was on Lake Tana, with the hydroelectric plant on the Beles river. (Salini Impregilo 2016a, p. 42)

The financial support came from FAI (Fondo Aiuti Italiano—Italian Aid Fund), a special fund launched by the Italian Government in response to the humanitarian crisis in the Horn of Africa, recalled also in Salini's own account:

> [It was] ... one of the worst droughts in Ethiopian history. This caused a great famine that affected eight million people and killed at least one million. It was in this climate that the Italian government also decided to financially support the dam project whose initial value was 127 billion lire. For Simonpietro Salini this was the real leap forward, for a small family business ruled by corporate culture consisting of close-knit family ties, where no amount of bureaucracy can prevent a decision from being made. The challenge was a daunting one. (Salini Impregilo 2016a, p. 42)

Indeed, with Tana-Beles Salini almost doubled the volume of its business in the country. Lack of capacity on the Ethiopian Government's side, matched with the emergency context and the corporate culture described above, led to the award to Salini of an engineering, procurement, and construction (EPC) contract, in which the contractor enjoys a high degree of independence in all phases of the project. In implementing the project, Salini adopted a 'design-as-you-go' approach, justified by the need for flexibility in response to the humanitarian emergency, but also leading to a significant increase of the project's final costs.[33]

Cementing a Controversial Project of State-Building

By subscribing to the government's humanitarian relief and modernization narrative, Salini contributed to legitimize and implement the Derg's political project of state-building. The resettlement and villagization programmes, together with the land reform abolishing the previous landlord–tenant system, were a central

[32] Giulio Andreotti (1919–2013) was one of the most powerful and controversial politicians in post-war Italy. Leader of the Christian Democrat Party, he served as prime minister in seven governments and in numerous other ministerial positions. In the 1990s he was tried for criminal association with the mafia and for commissioning journalist Mino Pecorelli's murder. Andreotti was found guilty for criminal association with the mafia until the 1980s but the offence was extinguished by the statute of limitations. He was acquitted for criminal facts after 1980 and for Pecorelli's murder.

[33] Interview, humanitarian worker based in Ethiopia in the 1980s, online, March 2020.

element of the Derg's political project of top-down re-organization of the peasantry into cooperatives and collective farming. In the name of food security and agricultural modernization, Tana-Beles resettled 82,106 people from the highlands of north-central and southwest Ethiopia, considered 'drought prone' and 'overpopulated', to the Beles Valley in Metekel Zone, today part of the Benishangul-Gumuz region (Wolde-Selassie 2009). Through an ambitious plan of infrastructural development to harness natural resources like water and land, Tana-Beles sought to incorporate a periphery into the national economy (Dieci and Viezzoli 1992).

The resettlement area, the Beles Valley, was presented as a virgin land with untapped resources. In doing so, this narrative obliterated the local populations of Berta and Gumuz, whose livelihoods—based on shifting agriculture and semi-nomadic patterns—were deeply affected by the resettlement economy. Expropriated of their land, the Berta and Gumuz were pushed west into less hospitable areas towards the Sudanese border (Gebre 2009). The project was not positive for the resettled population either. Resettlement failed to achieve its goals because of a lack of 'clear conception, feasibility study, proper planning, adequate physical preparation and responsible management' (Gebre 2009, p. 93). As such, the promise of agricultural modernization did not materialize. The dismantling of the settlers' original social institutions and safety nets made it difficult for them to cope with challenging new conditions, resulting in the deterioration of their livelihoods, and, in some cases, new reliance on food aid (Wolde-Selassie 2009). Because of its top-down and forced implementation, the resettlement had a painful impact on both the settlers and the local population (Gebre 2009).

The Tana-Beles project was also controversial because of its alleged role in the government's counter-insurgency strategy and military operations. Critics argued that a hidden objective of resettlement was to undermine the insurgents' popular support by displacing the population (Clay and Holcomb 1986). Rebel groups like the Ethiopian People's Revolutionary Party (EPRP) sabotaged and raided the project sites, killing 40 people and kidnapping 39, including two Italian engineers (Salini Impregilo 2016a). These events and allegations, combined with reports about the project's negative impacts on the local and resettled populations, led to mounting international criticism. Amidst the polemic, the Italian Ministry of Foreign Affairs decided to put its support on hold (Fedeler 2021). Nevertheless, Salini continued with implementation, proving itself to be a loyal partner of the Ethiopian Government, and contributing to legitimize the government's controversial state-building project internationally, while cementing it on the ground.

A Resilient Project

With the end of the civil war, Tana-Beles was abandoned and fell into ruins, since, in the eyes of the EPRDF, it symbolized the Derg's oppression. However, in 2005, a new incarnation of the project began when the Ethiopian Electric Power Company

(EEPCo) signed a turnkey contract with Salini for the construction of the Beles Multipurpose Project, involving a tunnel from Lake Tana to the Beles Valley and a 460-megawatt (MW) hydropower project. In doing so, Ethiopia would finally put into action the century-old idea of diverting water from Lake Tana into the Beles Valley, while Salini would finally build a version of the project for which it was contracted in the 1980s.

This new project was publicly funded (Fedeler 2021), in line with the government's increasingly aggressive approach to financing infrastructure investment (see Chapter 4). The new project also diverged from the Derg iteration by omitting 'Tana' from the new name of the Beles Multipurpose Project. This change in name served both a domestic audience, to avoid links with the infamous Tana-Beles resettlement, and an international one, limiting the association with Lake Tana, source of the Blue Nile, with Egypt and Sudan increasingly alarmed about Ethiopian plans to divert Nile waters (Fedeler 2021; see also Chapter 6). Nonetheless, the Beles Multipurpose Project reveals the resilience of project ideas, and how hydrology and the physical environment, with their potentiality and constrains, can influence political choices and even convert political imaginaries.

Salini under the EPRDF: The Gilgel Gibe Projects

The enduring presence of Salini in the development of hydropower projects reached a new scale under the EPRDF in the Gibe-Omo Basin. The Gilgel Gibe projects are, therefore, particularly relevant to understanding the three factors that consolidated Salini's position as the leading firm in Ethiopia's hydropower sector: namely, the basin's geomorphology; Salini's unique partnerships with the government in its 'fast-track approach' to project management; and its role in facilitating access to project finance. In return for the preferential position given to Salini, the EPRDF acquired a trusted and locally integrated contractor that, unlike state agencies, had the required technical expertise to realize the megaprojects envisioned by the ruling elite. Moreover, unlike other international firms, Salini was trusted to stay the course in politically controversial projects in the Omo and, subsequently, Blue Nile Basins.

The Geomorphology of the Gibe-Omo River Basin

As discussed in Chapter 2, the Gibe-Omo tributaries rise in the highland plateau at an altitude of 2,000–3,000 metres, descending through step gorges to around 500 metres in the lowland plains. Moreover, relatively plentiful rainfall in its catchment area means that the Omo River has the second largest runoff in Ethiopia after the

Blue Nile. The result is that the basin has great potential for both hydropower, in the steep gorges descending from the highlands, and irrigation, in the lowlands.

The EPRDF first turned to the Gibe-Omo Basin in 1997 when it restarted the Gilgel Gibe I project. A dam at the site was proposed at least as early as a study undertaken during the Italian occupation and subsequently by the Yugoslav Electroproject Company in 1963 (EELPA 1997b).[34] Meanwhile, an initial attempt to build the dam in the 1980s with North Korean contractors was abandoned with the fall of the Derg. By 1997 when the project restarted, Salini

> started from scratch. They [the North Koreans] had been there 10 years. They excavated a bit. There was an inextricable plant which was just rusting steel. Basically nothing.[35]

The 184-MW dam was largely financed by the World Bank (US$331 million) along with contributions from the Ethiopian Government, Nordic Development Fund, and European Investment Bank. At this stage Salini was one of 12 international companies that were awarded components of the project in a competitive process, as a requirement of World Bank funding (see Chapter 3). However, Salini's involvement provided an opportunity to demonstrate its delivery capacity and to establish connections with political elites that positioned the firm for subsequent projects.

Gilgel Gibe I was completed in 2004, but before it was finished Salini had already secured the contract to build Gilgel Gibe II, now as the sole contractor rather than one of many sub-contractors and without competitive tender. Indeed, the design and contracting of Gilgel Gibe II was perhaps the key step in consolidating Salini's position as the go-to project planner and contractor for Ethiopia's dams boom. While a cascade of dams on the Gibe-Omo had long been proposed, the Gibe II project was an entirely new idea that was absent from the 1996 masterplan (Richard Woodroofe and Associates 1996).[36] Studio Pietrangeli—the designer of all Salini's dams—came up with the idea of drilling a 26-kilometre tunnel through a mountain that separates the Gilgel Gibe tributary, where Gibe I is located, from the main Omo River (see Figure 3.3), exploiting the significant drop in height of the rivers to produce 420 MW without a second dam (Pietrangeli and Pallavicini 2007). Salini and Studio Pietrangeli brought the idea to the government, convinced them of its benefits, and then went on to produce all the designs for the project (EEPCo 2004; Fantini and Puddu 2016).[37] Moreover, Salini proposed to

[34] Interview EP12, senior contractor, online, 20 November 2019, 16 February 2020.
[35] Interview EP12, senior contractor, online, 20 November 2019, 16 February 2020.
[36] Interview EP12, senior contractor, online, 20 November 2019, 16 February 2020.
[37] Interview EG37, senior official in the energy sector, Addis Ababa, 21 August 2019, 19 February 2020.

relocate staff and equipment from Gibe I, as it was completed, to the nearby Gibe II site, thereby significantly reducing the project's set-up costs. A long-serving engineer in EEPCo underscored that through the design and execution of Gibe II, 'Salini has earned the respect and admiration of the construction and engineering community as well as policymakers'.[38]

Subsequent dams in the cascade followed what became a regular pattern. Salini and Studio Pietrangeli studied the 1,870-MW Gilgel Gibe III dam downstream on the main Omo River while they were working on Gibe II.[39] The EPC contract worth more than €1.5 billion was awarded to Salini—without competition—in July 2006, enabling Salini to move staff and equipment from Gibe II, as it was completed in 2010, downstream to the Gibe III project site, reducing the time and cost of starting up operations. Likewise, the same combination of Salini and Studio Pietrangeli studied the fourth Gibe-Omo dam, named Koysha, while constructing Gibe III, with a no-bid €2.5 billion EPC contract awarded in May 2016, shortly before Gibe III was commissioned.[40] Initial studies for the fifth and final dam in the Gibe-Omo cascade with projected installed capacity of 560 MW have already been carried out by Salini as Koysha makes slow progress towards its completion (see below and Chapter 9).[41]

Thus, the particular landscape of the Gibe-Omo Basin, with its ideally suited topography and rich water resources, enabled Salini to propose repeated projects in the basin, securing close relations with the ruling elite and expanding the firm's capacities as it tackled a series of increasingly complex and controversial projects. Moreover, the potential for a cascade of hydropower projects in relatively close proximity to one another in the same basin allowed the company to conduct survey works for new dam sites in parallel with projects under implementation while reducing set-up costs by moving equipment and staff from one project to the next.[42] The result is that Salini has become a permanent dam-building operation, with equipment and staff—both Italian and Ethiopian—building expertise as they moved from project to project.[43]

Fast-Track Approach: The Ethiopian Way

The strategic partnership between Salini and the government is reflected in the 'fast-track approach' to project planning and implementation, adopted from Gibe

[38] Interview, EEP engineer, Addis Ababa, August 2021.

[39] Interview, EEP planning expert, Addis Ababa, October 2016.

[40] Interview EP12, senior contractor, online, 20 November 2019, 16 February 2020.

[41] Studio Pietrangeli (2023b). Interview EP12, senior contractor, online, 20 November 2019, 16 February 2020.

[42] For example, Salini negotiated to reduce the proposed costs for implementing the third Gibe project on the condition that the fourth Gibe would be directly awarded to the company so that it could immediately mobilize its resources to this site (interview with an EEP consultant, Gibe III project site, November 2016).

[43] Interviews EG46, former TPLF central committee member, Addis Ababa, 7 August 2019; and EP12, senior contractor in the sector, online, 20 November 2019, 16 February 2020.

II onwards. The fast-track approach seeks to bypass standard project management and competitive tendering that World Bank financing had necessitated for Gibe I. The government felt these processes slowed down the project and sought a different approach in line with its urgent need for rapid development and large-scale infrastructure development (Fantini and Puddu 2016). The fast-track approach is based on the concurrent development of all relevant phases of a large hydroelectric project, namely investigations, studies, design, financing, contracting, and construction (Ferraro et al. 2015). Civil and geotechnical engineers, and geologists from Salini and Studio Pietrangeli, have claimed that the approach allowed a reduction of the total project implementation time of at least 50 per cent (Ferraro et al. 2015).

Once this approach was tested on Gibe II, Salini replicated the same method in implementing subsequent hydropower projects.[44] Indeed, an international consultant for Ethiopian Electric Power (EEP) at the Gibe III project site argued that the approach was vital in securing the completion of the dam in 10 years, in his view a relatively short timeframe compared to conventional project cycle management.[45] The consultant proudly described the 'fast-track approach' as the 'Ethiopian way', portraying the dam as a technological triumph, which should be celebrated and emulated in other African countries:

> Steps with the usual procurement process are tedious and extremely long which is not adapted to the present needs of development. Often the process leads to a deadlock. The Ethiopian way may not be ideal and easy to manage but proved efficient and deserves attention and consideration.[46]

Despite this claimed efficiency, project management has been marked by a sense of urgency at any cost that bypassed standard procedures and operated according to the logic of a 'state of exception' (Woldegebrael 2018, drawing on Agamben's concept (2005)). For example, from the Gibe II project onwards, the government directly issued no-bid EPC contracts to Salini for successive projects in contravention of the national procurement regulation and international norms for fair competition (Woldegebrael 2018). The Ethiopian Government justified this 'exception' on the grounds of Salini's technical mastery and profound knowledge of the territory (Woldegebrael 2019). The approach also bypassed the standard norms for pre-project Environmental and Social Impact Assessments (ESIAs), with decisions on large dams made in the Prime Minister's Office before the ESIAs were completed. For instance, the ESIA for Gibe III was produced two years after the project was commenced and still excluded the downstream impact of the dam. Hence, the fast-track approach circumvented the regulation requiring dam projects of this size to undertake a 'full review' and

[44] Interview, EEP consultant, Gibe III Project Office, November 2016.
[45] Interview, EEP consultant, Gibe III Project Office, November 2016.
[46] Interview, EEP consultant, Gibe III Project Office, November 2016.

secure approval from the Environmental Protection Authority (EPA) prior to their commencement.

Thus, Salini's fast-track approach sought to reduce project completion times by bypassing Ethiopian laws and procedures in the name of a 'national energy emergency' and the need for rapid development. While certainly problematic, this approach enabled Salini to build its unique partnership with the Ethiopian Government and consolidate its position in Ethiopia's dams boom.

Brokering Project Finance

Salini's historical record of brokering project finance from international donors, notably the Italian Government, also contributed to its emergence as a leading player under the EPRDF. The growing difficulty of securing external finance for controversial dam projects and the government's increasingly aggressive approach to financing infrastructure projects led the government to first negotiate construction contracts with Salini and then seek to mobilize required financial resources.

An EEP official confirmed that one reason for directly awarding the Gibe dams to Salini was the company's ability to facilitate access to international finance.[47] As with Legadadi and Tana-Beles, Salini was able to mediate between the Ethiopian Prime Minister's Office and the Italian Ministry of Foreign Affairs to secure funding for Gibe II (Fantini and Puddu 2016). The result was the largest ever Italian Development Cooperation loan of €220 million and a further €50 million loan from the European Investment Bank, while the Ethiopian Government contributed the remaining €105 million. As hydropower projects were implemented in a closed political space, there was limited domestic debate about Gibe II (Woldegebrael 2018). Nevertheless, the direct contracting of Salini appeared to contravene not only Ethiopian but also Italian law, leading to parliamentary questions and a criminal investigation in that country (Carr 2017). The European Investment Bank, meanwhile, limited its financing to the electro-mechanical works, which were sub-contracted by Salini through a competitive, international tender.

Salini was unable to secure finance for Gibe III, however. Controversy over Gibe II and the 2008 financial crisis that adversely affected the Italian economy were among the factors for Italy's unwillingness to fund the project.[48] However, the exceptional role of Salini in Ethiopian dam building and its long-term view of the sector was such that the firm covered the costs of studies and preliminary works itself for some two years.[49] As one well-placed international consultant noted,

[47] Interview, planning expert in EEP, Addis Ababa, October 2017.
[48] Interview, EEP expert in the Gibe III Project Office, October 2017.
[49] Interview, EEP expert in the Gibe III Project Office, October 2017, and EP12, senior contractor, online, 20 November 2019, 16 February 2020.

> Salini is a contractor; they want to make money, of course. But they also do things. They leave work behind. Others start and then stop. But Salini is patient.[50]

In 2010, Gibe III finally proceeded when the government provided €448 million—30 per cent of the project costs—and made the bold decision to cover the remainder with Chinese commercial loans.[51] The loan agreement required Salini to once again demonstrate its flexibility since financing was conditional on the involvement of a Chinese firm in the project. Although Salini had originally signed an EPC contract for the entire project, the government proposed handing over the electro-mechanical and hydraulic steel works to a Chinese company, Dongfang Electric, with Salini ultimately acquiescing. Thus the original EPC contract was amended in 2010 and a tripartite contract agreement (Salini–EEP–Dongfang) was signed in which Salini continued to play the overall project coordination role.[52]

Similar dynamics played out with respect to the Koysha Dam also. Salini signed a contract for the entire project, with Italian commercial loans arranged to fund the works. However, the International Monetary Fund's (IMF's) decision to raise its assessment of the risk of Ethiopia's debt in 2017/18 led these loans to be cancelled (see Chapter 9). Once again, however, Salini stepped in, financing the costs of ongoing excavation works itself, while the project awaited a new source of finance. In the words of one respondent,

> The country's finances are in crisis ... Now the IMF has stopped the financing because the level of debt is too high. As a company we are financing the project ourselves! But we have to move slowly and we cannot start the hydro or electro-mechanical works without the assurance of finance.[53]

The result then was that Salini's role in Ethiopia's dams boom has gone well beyond that expected of a standard dam contractor. Not only does Salini design, propose, and construct dams but it has also facilitated the Ethiopia Government's access to finance and, periodically, even subsidized short-term construction costs in the anticipation of future revenues and contracts. Far more than a simple contractor, Salini is very much a fully invested partner in Ethiopian dam building.

Conclusion: The Story Continues

The development of the hydropower sector in Ethiopia cannot be fully understood without analysing the role of Salini. In this chapter we have told this story through three projects across different political regimes: the Legadadi Dam built

[50] Interview EP13, senior consultant in the hydropower sector, online, 26 November 2019.
[51] Power Technology (2021). Interview, official in EEP's finance administration, Addis Ababa, October 2017.
[52] Tripartite contract agreement document, signed on 15 July 2010.
[53] Interview EP12, senior contractor, online, 20 November 2019, 16 February 2020.

in Imperial Ethiopia (1964–1970); the Tana-Beles multipurpose project started under the Derg (1986); and the Gilgel Gibe dams complex commissioned by the federal and developmental Ethiopian state (1997–). These cases point to three elements which help to elucidate the continuity and endurance of Salini's work in Ethiopia.

First, from a political economy perspective, Salini has adopted a peculiar business model. Salini, now rebranded WeBuild, is a global player in large infrastructure projects that nonetheless considers itself also a 'national company' with significant roots and interests in Ethiopia. The result is that it has adopted a long-term approach to ensure its permanence in the country. As illustrated by all three cases, one of the keys to this strategy has been Salini's ability to act as a broker between the Ethiopian Government and international donors.

Second, from a political ecology perspective, the longstanding presence of Salini has been facilitated by the particularity of the Ethiopian landscape. As the Gilgel Gibe cascade clearly testifies, the geomorphology of the country allowed Salini to propose new projects and thereby expand its business. This was facilitated by Salini's comparative advantage in terms of local knowledge vis-à-vis other international competitors, as well as technical capacity vis-à-vis Ethiopian entities. The result is that Salini has taken the lead in proposing new projects and securing the support of political elites, designing hydro plants—always in close collaboration with its partner Studio Pietrangeli—and then implementing flagship projects.

Finally, the fact that hydropower infrastructures are mostly built at the frontier between the highlands and the lowlands in order to maximize the dams' head implies that hydropower projects also play a key role in incorporating the 'last frontiers' into the Ethiopian state and economy (Markakis 2011). Like in many other countries, dam building in Ethiopia has been a key element of state-building. As such, Salini's engineering has contributed to legitimate the presence and action of the Ethiopian state, particularly in its peripheries. Given their symbolic meaning and political sensitivity, these projects have been implemented under a state of exception, bypassing domestic and international norms on competitive bidding, and socio-environmental impact assessment, in the name of the urgency of 'development'.

Salini's role in Ethiopia's dams boom can hardly be overstated. While the 'developmental state' had ambitions of developing domestic engineering expertise to the point at which it could plan and implement major dam projects without external support, the reality is that initial efforts to build domestic capacity have fallen short. As such, the realization of the government's hydropower ambitions necessitated technical support from foreign firms. At the same time, however, dependence on foreign contractors would leave the dam-building strategy vulnerable to external influence, particularly as Ethiopia turned towards increasingly politically sensitive projects such as Gilgel Gibe III and, even more so, the Nile Basin. The unique partnership with Salini addressed this gap. While Salini has undoubtedly benefited commercially from Ethiopian dam building, the government acquired not just a technically competent contractor but an 'Ethiopian company' that has demonstrated over six decades its commitment to infrastructural development in Ethiopia, and its willingness to persist amidst great financial and political uncertainty. Speaking in 2017, then Deputy Prime Minister Debretsion underscored the government's resultant faith in Salini:

> We have seen how political pressure could be challenging for such projects while constructing Gibe III ... We have witnessed how the civil works contractor, the Italian company Salini, was pressured to abandon the project and leave Ethiopia. The pressure came from different directions: through the European Union, Italy and other countries. Fortunately, Salini understands the pressure very well and knows the country intimately as it was involved in different projects in Ethiopia for many years. You can imagine what would happen if the company was not Salini. (Anberbir 2017)

These constitutive elements of Salini's presence in Ethiopia—political economy, political ecology, and state-building—are particularly relevant as they have been brought to their apex with the construction of the GERD. Indeed, the privileged relation between Salini and the Ethiopian Government has been reaffirmed in the wake of the formation of the new government led by Abiy Ahmed. In 2022, Prime Minister Abiy Ahmed presided over the ceremony awarding an honorary PhD from Addis Ababa University to Pietro Salini, praising him as among 'the true sons of Africa' (Ethiopian Monitor 2022a). Amidst the international tensions caused by the dam, Salini clearly stood on the Ethiopian Government's side, as confirmed by Pietro Salini's words during the GERD's partial power generation ceremony on 20 February 2022:

> There are days in which your heart is so filled with joy that it is even difficult to speak. This project for us, as Ethiopians, as I feel myself, it is not a common project. It is not something that comes every day ... We faced a lot of difficulties together. This project does not come easy. There has been so many enemies. So many against it.[54]

These words once again recall how the story of Salini in Ethiopia interweaves the history of two countries, Ethiopia and Italy, through flows of money, people, and technology that have deeply transformed the Ethiopian landscape, with significant consequences for its ecology and society.

[54] YouTube (2022). Quote begins at 34 seconds.

6

Upending the Hydropolitics of the Nile

From Cooperation to Unilateralism

Tom Lavers

The victory of the Ethiopian Peoples' Revolutionary Democratic Front (EPRDF) in the civil war in 1991 revitalized Ethiopia's plans for dam development on the Blue Nile, which had stagnated since Haile Selassie's demise in 1974. Over the previous decades, relations between Ethiopia and its downstream Nile riparians had become increasingly antagonistic as the Egyptian and Sudanese stance on their 'historic rights' hardened, while Egypt had been able to block international involvement in upstream projects (Waterbury 2002, p. 167). The result was that Egypt came to be regarded as the 'hydro-hegemon' in the basin, dominating upstream countries through a combination of economic and military power, Egypt's important geo-strategic position in the Middle East resulting in strong support from global powers, and the fact on the ground of existing water infrastructure (Waterbury 2002; Zeitoun and Warner 2006; Cascão 2008, p. 20; Tawfik 2016b). For the EPRDF in the 1990s, the realization of its ambitions on the Nile would require the support of Egypt if Ethiopia were to secure access to necessary foreign finance and technical expertise. While the new government initiated its dam-building boom in other river basins, it also tackled the daunting challenge of securing Egyptian and Sudanese support for the development of the Blue Nile Basin.

This chapter examines the government's efforts to pursue a collaborative approach to building a dam on the Blue Nile through participation with Egypt, Sudan, and other Nile riparians in the Nile Basin Initiative (NBI). The NBI process was an important step in developing the proposals outlined by the United States Bureau of Reclamation (USBR) and turning them into detailed plans for particular dams and electricity trade across the Nile Basin. However, the NBI process ultimately lost momentum under familiar political pressures, with an inability to align river basin planning with the balance of political power in the basin. Unlike under past regimes, however, Ethiopia by 2011 had greatly strengthened its own economic position, as well as its capacity to build and finance major dam projects. The result was that when the collaborative process collapsed, the government acted unilaterally, launching what would become the Grand Ethiopian Renaissance Dam (GERD).

Dams, Power, and the Politics of Ethiopia's Renaissance. Tom Lavers et al., Oxford University Press. © Tom Lavers (2024).
DOI: 10.1093/oso/9780192871213.003.0006

Despite the common description of Egypt as the hydro-hegemon of the Nile Basin, this experience shows that Egypt was only a partial fit for this label. Zeitoun and Warner (2006) identify two distinct ways in which a riparian can establish dominance in a basin: through hegemony, which implies legitimate authority, and through coercion. While it could be argued that Sudanese and Ugandan regimes have, at points, accepted the legitimacy of Egyptian hegemony over the Nile, that is not true of Ethiopia and particularly Ethiopia under the EPRDF. Rather, Egypt's dominance of the Nile Basin was reliant on Ethiopia's continued internal political fragmentation and its lack of financial and technical resources. Despite the 'hegemon' label, the reality was that Egypt's position was extremely vulnerable. As the furthest downstream country on the Nile and completely dependent on that water source, Egyptian dominance depended on Ethiopia's continuing disarray. Partly as a result of Ethiopian foreign policy initiatives and Ethiopia's own economic development, and partly as a result of fortuitous factors beyond Ethiopia's control, this dominant position gradually began to erode from the 1990s. As such, the chapter examines Ethiopia's counter-strategies to contest Egyptian dominance, first through cooperation and second through unilateralism.

The chapter begins by examining the Ethiopian Government's renewed efforts to engage Egypt and Sudan during the 1990s, leading to the launch of the NBI. The following section examines efforts to pursue a collaborative project between Egypt, Ethiopia, and Sudan for a dam on the Blue Nile that would provide hydroelectricity for all three countries. Finally, the analysis turns to Ethiopia's effort to mobilize resources for construction of the GERD and the tripartite negotiations on the dam's operation, which found Egypt increasingly isolated in its opposition.

The International Dimension of Ethiopia's Dams Boom

While domestic politics and the gradual expansion of technical and financial capacity outlined in previous chapters drove the Ethiopian dam strategy, international dynamics were also vitally important in enabling the eventual turn towards the Blue Nile and construction of the GERD. These international processes have been studied more extensively, with a sizeable literature emerging in recent years. What is less evident in this work, however, is a systematic attempt to link international to domestic dynamics within Ethiopia. Notably, the Ethiopian Government was not a mere bystander to international events, but actively intervened to shape these events in its favour. Moreover, this strategy was closely connected to the EPRDF's domestic strategy for consolidating power and building the economy.

The EPRDF's ascent to power coincided with the end of the Cold War and important changes in international relations in the Horn of Africa and Middle East. The intense competition between the United States (US) and Union of Soviet Socialist Republics (USSR) for influence in the Horn, which had fuelled many conflicts in the region, came to an end. In its place, the US's regional strategy came to focus its support on key anchor states as a means of maintaining stability (Verhoeven and Woldemariam 2022). These anchors were Saudi Arabia, the United Arab Emirates (UAE), Egypt, and Ethiopia. Meanwhile, these regional powers vied to fill the gap left by declining Cold War rivalries (Verhoeven 2018; Mosley 2021). With the rise of radical Islam in Sudan and Somalia during the 1990s and particularly after 2001, Ethiopia grew further in geo-strategic importance and was seen by the US as a key source of stability in the Horn (Borchgrevink 2008; Feyissa 2011). Furthermore, from the late 1990s China's 'Going Out' strategy saw increased engagement of China in Africa, including through the availability of Chinese finance and engineering in major infrastructure projects, further unsettling the status quo (Bräutigam 2009).

The EPRDF sought to expand its influence in the Horn, projecting an image of a 'benevolent hegemon' (Le Gouriellec 2018; Verhoeven 2018; Verhoeven and Woldemariam 2022).[1] The EPRDF's key statement in this regard was the 2002 Foreign Policy, authored by Meles himself (De Waal 2013), which argued that strength internationally depends on strength of the national economy, which in turn requires regional stability (Gebreluel 2023). According to this document, Ethiopia's central concern was to avoid being drawn into the sorts of conflicts and proxy wars with neighbouring countries that had weakened past regimes and continued to do so with the 1998–2000 Eritrean War (MoI 2002b). Instead,

> our relations of friendship or otherwise should be based first of all on economic matters. We mean that we should not enter into hostilities or friendship based on matters irrelevant to our development. (MOIPAD 2001, p. 29)

Ethiopian foreign policy had two central developmental objectives, namely to secure access to ports required for trade and to make use of Ethiopia's rivers, particularly the Nile. Ethiopia became landlocked with Eritrean secession in 1993, while the subsequent Eritrean War denied Ethiopia access to the Eritrean ports of Massawa and Assab. Ethiopian trade was therefore entirely dependent on Djibouti, placing Djibouti in a favourable bargaining position (Tekalign 2019). Consequently, the Ethiopian Government has consistently sought opportunities to diversify port access in Sudan and Somaliland, while consolidating close ties with Djibouti. The economic importance of Ethiopia's transboundary rivers and therefore Ethiopia's relations with downstream riparians was also a central consideration of Ethiopian foreign policy (MoI 2002b). While the possibility of 'disagreements' with Sudan, Somalia, and Kenya was acknowledged, the view was

[1] Despite the fact that Ethiopia was at times a source of regional instability, not least through its military involvement in Somalia. In reality, Ethiopia lacked the required economic, political, and military power to dominate the region and is perhaps better described as an 'imperfect hegemon' (Le Gouriellec 2018; Gebreluel 2023).

that these 'countries can neither be obstacles for our utilization of water resources nor can they assist us to do so' (MOIPAD 2001, p. 58). In contrast, the main foreign policy challenge on the horizon 'is principally a problem with Egypt' regarding the Nile, an issue that, as a result of Egyptian influence, would affect Ethiopia's relations with the entire Arab world and beyond (MOIPAD 2001, p. 117).

Ethiopia remained limited in its ability to utilize the Nile waters during the 1990s. The government initially focused on the construction of numerous micro-dams in the Nile Basin and also signalled a major change in Nile hydropolitics by unilaterally launching the construction of Tekeze on a Nile tributary (see Chapter 3). However, Ethiopia was not in a position to build dams on the Blue Nile itself at this time. Meanwhile, Egypt continued its efforts to increase use of the river. Following the construction of the High Aswan Dam, Nasser established the narrative that land shortages and population growth necessitate the expansion of agriculture and cities into the desert based on the diversion of the Nile waters (see Chapter 2). Despite the repeated failings of past schemes, the declining role of agriculture in the economy and employment, and the ability to address Egypt's water deficit through 'virtual water' in the form of food imports, subsequent regimes have retained this basic narrative (Sims 2015). Indeed, President Mubarak insisted in 1996 that,

> Leaving the narrow [Nile] valley and fanning out, in a planned and organized manner, throughout the country, has become an unavoidable necessity. In view of these facts, the conquest of the desert is no longer a slogan or dream but a necessity dictated by the spiraling population growth. What is required is not a token exodus into the desert but a complete reconsideration of the distribution of population throughout the country. (Cited in Sims 2015, p. 19)

To this end, the Egyptian Government launched the Southern Egypt Development Project in 1996 that incorporated much of the area covered by Nasser's New Valley project into the Toshka and East 'Uwaynat schemes (Sims 2015, pp. 59–60). The project envisaged directing private investment to enable a vast expansion of irrigation, covering some 2 million feddans and the relocation of some 6 million people in the following decades. As with the New Valley scheme, the projects have only achieved a fraction of their intended targets (Sims 2015). Nonetheless, plans for a massive expansion of irrigation solidified Egypt's intent to protect its share of the Nile waters secured in 1959 and perhaps even expand this. Egypt is believed to have been using its full share according to the 1959 agreement since about 1972 and has been using part of Sudan's unused water allocation since that time (Sims 2015).

Informed by these developments, Ethiopia's 2002 foreign policy outlined Meles' reading of the Egyptian position regarding upstream Nile development, which is essentially that

> 'if Ethiopia uses the water, Egypt will be endangered. If Egypt is to use it, Ethiopia has to take her hands off the water'. The Egyptian scenario regarding the Nile is a classic example of the politics of 'I win if you lose', the zero-sum game. (MoI 2002b, p. 118)

The document continues to argue that Egypt had been using the Nile waters 'extravagantly', resulting in massive evaporation losses from Aswan and inefficient irrigation projects, while also 'systematically preventing riparian states, especially Ethiopia, from utilizing the waters of the Nile' through the 'promotion of instability in Ethiopia and the Horn' and blocking aid for Nile projects (MoI 2002b, pp. 118–121).[2] Indeed,

> Egypt's belief has been that Ethiopia, mired in poverty and embroiled in endless conflict, could not develop the basin on its own, and that with the opportunities for aid and credit closed, Ethiopians will have no choice but to sit and watch the river flow to those who can then put it to good use. (MoI 2002b, pp. 120–121)

While Egyptian concerns about upstream water extraction and protection of historic rights were as prominent as ever, the early 1990s did present something of an opening, however. The High Aswan Dam, completed in 1970, had been intended to insulate Egypt from the Nile's variable flow and therefore remove the need to engage with upstream countries regarding water infrastructure (see Chapter 2). While Aswan did maintain Egyptian water supplies during the severe drought in Ethiopia in 1984–1988, by the late 1980s the level of Lake Nasser had fallen so low that it was close to reaching dead storage, beyond which water releases are impossible. Relatively good rains in the late 1980s eased the water crisis. However, the Egyptian Government was nonetheless slightly more willing to engage in discussions regarding the Nile than in previous decades (Erlich 2002; Waterbury 2002). Meanwhile, the removal of the Derg from office offered an opportunity to reset Ethiopia's previously antagonistic relations with both Egypt and Sudan. For Ethiopia the aim was to re-frame the Nile debate in terms of the potential benefits of Ethiopian dams and water storage to Egypt—through reduced sedimentation and evaporation losses from Lake Nasser and cheap hydroelectricity—somewhat reminiscent of past British colonial plans that sought to dam the Nile in Ethiopia to the benefit of Egypt. While in the short to medium term any dam could only be pursed through collaboration on the Nile, the implication of the Ethiopian strategy was clear—Ethiopia's ability to negotiate from a position of strength and, if needed, to take unilateral action would come through economic power. Rapid economic development was the key to Ethiopia's geo-strategic interests and the development of the Blue Nile (MoI 2002b).

[2] Something acknowledged by former foreign minister, Ahmed Aboul Gheit (2020).

The EPRDF's rise to power also coincided with major political changes in Sudan. Nimeiri's breadbasket agricultural development strategy unravelled from the late 1970s with unsustainable agricultural production resulting in salinization and soil depletion, and a rapidly growing debt burden (Verhoeven 2015). By 1985, the Sudanese Government was unable to repay its debts and was overthrown by popular demonstrations. The eventual result was the formation in 1989 of the military-Islamist Al-Ingaz or Salvation regime, which combined Brigadier Omar Hassan Al-Bashir as the figurehead president and scholar-politician Hassan Al-Turabi as the main powerholder behind the scenes (Verhoeven 2015). Al-Ingaz's desire to export Islamic revolution across the region and its hosting of Al-Qaeda alienated Sudan from Egypt, most of the Arab world, and the US (Verhoeven 2018). However, Al-Ingaz supported the Tigrayan People's Liberation Front (TPLF) in the latter stages of the war against the Derg and enjoyed good relations with Ethiopia during the Transitional Government (1991–1994). Another major shift, however, occurred in 1995 when Hassan Al-Turabi was implicated in the attempted assassination of President Mubarak during a visit to Addis Ababa (Swain 2011; Verhoeven 2015). The result was a major and unprecedented break in Egyptian–Sudanese relations. Moreover, the attempted assassination led to the unravelling of ties between Ethiopia and Sudan, with the EPRDF resuming support of the Sudan People's Liberation Army (SPLA) in South Sudan and occupying the al-Fashaga contested border area, while the Sudanese renewed support for the Benishangul People's Liberation Movement (BPLM) and other insurgents in Ethiopia (Verhoeven 2015; RVI 2023).

Despite this rupture, the Ethiopian Government considered relations with Sudan to be much more promising than those with Egypt. Sudan had historically aligned with Egypt in defence of the 1959 Nile Waters agreement and Ethio-Sudanese relations had often been problematic. However, Meles was convinced that Sudanese interests were compatible with those of the upstream countries and divergent from those of Egypt. Ultimately, Meles—drawing on his reading of the literature on Nile hydropolitics—came to the conclusion that Sudan had the greatest potential to develop irrigated agriculture in the Nile Valley and would eventually exceed its 1959 allocation (e.g. Waterbury 2002; Cascão and Nicol 2016b). Indeed, during the 1990s, Sudan claimed an increased share of the Nile waters for planned irrigation projects, while making plans to heighten the Roseires Dam and to build another dam on the Blue Nile, Kajbar. The reality, however, was that in the face of Egyptian opposition and having fallen out with the Arab world and the West, Sudan lacked the resources to carry out these projects (De Waal 2015; Verhoeven 2015; Cascão and Nicol 2016b). Sudan, therefore, had much to gain from upstream regulation of the Blue Nile in Ethiopia, and when that happens,

> what becomes difficult is not reconciling the interests of Ethiopia and The Sudan but the interests of Egypt and The Sudan. (MoI 2002b, pp. 84–85)

As such, Ethiopia's relations with Sudan were to be given the 'utmost priority' (MOIPAD 2001, p. 87), attempting to peel Sudan away from its alliance with Egypt and isolate Egypt in the Nile Basin.

Soon after coming to power, the new Ethiopian Government approached downstream countries regarding a collaborative approach to the Nile.[3] Ethiopia and Sudan quickly signed a general agreement to cooperate over the Nile waters in December 1991, notably including Sudanese commitment to the principle of equitable utilization (Verhoeven 2015, p. 115). Soon afterwards, Ethiopia and Egypt also signed a 1993 accord primarily focused on the Nile. The agreement constituted a first step, recognizing the need for cooperation and the intention that the countries

> undertake to consult and cooperate in projects that are mutually advantageous, such as projects that would enhance the volume of flow and reduce the loss of Nile waters through comprehensive and integrated development schemes. (The Arab Republic of Egypt and Ethiopia 1993, para. 6)

However, in one article that has been much criticized in Ethiopia subsequently and reflects some naivety from the new government, the Transitional Government agreed to a longstanding Egyptian bargaining point in defence of its historic rights, namely that,

> Each party shall refrain from engaging in any activity related to the Nile waters that may cause appreciable harm to the interests of the other party. (The Arab Republic of Egypt and Ethiopia 1993, para. 5)

The subsequent launch of the NBI built on these initial bilateral agreements. Ethiopia had refused to fully participate in earlier Egypt- and Sudan-led efforts at collaboration on the Nile due to the belief that they would be dominated by the downstream countries. As such, Ethiopia limited its involvement to observer status in Hydromet (1967–1992), Undugu (1983), TECCONILE (1992–1998), and the annual Nile 2002 conference from 1993 to 2004 (Cascão 2009; Swain 2011). Ethiopia was, however, an active participant from the beginning in the NBI. For Ethiopia to participate in the NBI, the government required that the initiative would involve not just technical discussions but also negotiations for a multilateral legal and institutional framework (Arsano and Tamrat 2005; Cascão 2009). The result was the NBI had dual tracks: technical negotiations regarding collaborative projects under the auspices of the NBI, discussed in the following section; and a political process negotiating a Cooperative Framework Agreement (CFA) to manage the Nile waters. The Ethiopian expectation was that once the CFA was ratified,

[3] Frezer Haile also claims that there were discussions with Egypt in the 1980s while the TPLF was still fighting the Derg (Haile 2018, p. 126).

a permanent Nile Basin Commission would replace the transitional NBI and the CFA would replace the contentious 1959 agreement between Egypt and Sudan.

According to those who discussed the Initiative with him, Meles was open to exploring possible collaboration, given Ethiopia's inability to act unilaterally, but was ultimately sceptical that it would succeed. Indeed, such scepticism was reinforced during the 1990s by Egypt's unilateral announcement of the Toshka project. Ethiopia once again responded with a diplomatic note verbale rejecting Egypt's actions and insisting that this did not foreclose Ethiopia's water rights. Moreover, as discussed in Chapter 3, Ethiopia unilaterally announced two projects of its own in the Nile Basin—Tekeze and Tis Abay II—to Egypt's infuriation (Tawfik 2015). Although neither would have a discernible impact on water flows in Egypt, they were a signal of Ethiopia's intent to no longer be a mere bystander to Egyptian water development and set Ethiopia 'on a collision course' with Egypt over the Nile (Waterbury and Whittington 1998, p. 155).

The removal from power of Hassan Al-Turabi in 1999 consolidated Omar al-Bashir's power in Sudan and had important implications for Sudanese ambitions on the Nile. Al-Turabi's departure enabled a rapprochement with Egypt and thereby also the Arab states of Saudi Arabia, Kuwait, UAE, and Qatar, which provided a key source of finance. Moreover, reconciliation with Egypt paved the way for China, Malaysia, and India to invest in Sudan's oil fields after 1999, leading to a 10-fold increase in the government's budget, fuelling a decade-long economic boom (De Waal 2015; Verhoeven 2015). While new oil production provided desperately needed revenues, the Comprehensive Peace Agreement in 2005 that ended the Sudanese civil war raised the prospect of South Sudanese secession and the realization that oil deposits—largely located in South Sudan—could be exploited only for a short period. The result was that Sudan, fuelled by oil revenues and Arab finance, pursued a substantial dam-building programme of its own from the early 2000s (Verhoeven 2015). For the government and its Arab financiers, dam building aimed at massively expanding large-scale irrigated agriculture, reminiscent of the 1970s breadbasket strategy, as a means of addressing growing food insecurity across the Arab world, as well as expanding hydropower (Waterbury 2002; Whittington et al. 2014; Verhoeven 2015). Sudan contracted Chinese firm Sinohydro to build the 1,250-megawatt (MW) Merowe Dam, which was completed in 2009, and to heighten Roseires, which was completed in 2013 (Verhoeven 2015, p. 131). Sudan also developed plans for three more multipurpose dams—Kajbar, Shereik, and Dal—on the Nile.[4] As with the 1970s schemes, however, Sudan's agricultural dreams have largely been unrealized and risk a repeat of the unsustainable agricultural production pursued under Nimeiri (Verhoeven 2015).

[4] In 2021, the government announced that Dal and Kajbar would be cancelled, following several protests (Dabanga 2021).

Egyptian acceptance of Sudan's unilateral dam building appears to have been motivated by the need to consolidate the post-Islamist regime in Sudan and to secure its continued support for the 1959 agreement (Verhoeven 2015). Moreover, none of the dams provided over-year water storage and therefore only had a marginal effect on flows into Lake Nasser. However, for the Egyptian Government, the major concern was that Sudanese water extraction would grow to the point that Sudan would utilize its full water share under the 1959 agreement and perhaps even exceed it, thereby threatening Egyptian water use (Cascão 2009; Whittington et al. 2014; Verhoeven 2015; Cascão and Nicol 2016b). To a lesser degree, such concerns also applied to agricultural investments in the Ethiopian Nile Basin during this time (Tawfik 2016b; Gheit 2020). The eventual secession of South Sudan in 2011 further changed the balance of power within the Nile Basin. South Sudan represents another potential signatory to the CFA and one without much support for the 1959 agreement (Nicol and Cascão 2011). Indeed, South Sudanese independence had long been opposed by Egypt for just this reason along with concerns that any South Sudanese administration would block a renewed effort to build the Jonglei Canal.[5]

The removal of al-Turabi enabled the strengthening of Ethio-Sudanese ties, with Meles and al-Bashir enjoying good relations. These ties particularly related to trade, with Ethiopia importing petrol from Sudan, negotiating an agreement to jointly develop Port Sudan and to construct a railway linking it to northern Ethiopia, and finalizing an agreement to begin exports of Ethiopia's hydroelectricity to Sudan in 2012 (see Chapter 8) (Tawfik 2019; Gebreluel 2023). Improved relations and growing inter-dependence also enabled an agreement over the contentious al-Fashaga border region. A compromise in 2007–2008 entailed Ethiopian recognition of the formal border, but allowed Ethiopian communities to continue to farm the land they had settled and to pay taxes to Ethiopia, with Ethiopian police maintaining law and order (Berridge et al. 2022, pp. 145–146). While in many ways a constructive compromise, the secretive nature of the discussions led to rumours that the Ethiopian Government had given away Ethiopian territory (Wubneh 2015).

Amidst these shifting regional politics, the CFA negotiations began in 1997 and lasted a decade, concluding with a draft agreement circulated in 2007. All 10 riparians agreed on all but one of the articles, namely 14b on water security. All the upstream countries favoured a commitment 'not to significantly affect the water security of any other Nile Basin State'; Egypt and Sudan, in contrast, insisted on replacing this text with a commitment 'not to adversely affect the water security and current uses and rights of any other Nile Basin State' (NBI 2010). In essence,

[5] In reality, independent South Sudan has pursued something of a balancing act, utilizing agreements and Memoranda of Understanding with Egypt, Sudan, and Ethiopia to strengthen its nascent sovereignty without fully committing to any side (Verhoeven and Sennesael 2022).

and despite the slight shift in terminology, while the upstream countries continued to push for the principle of 'equitable utilization' of the Nile waters, Egypt and Sudan remained committed to defending their 'historic rights'. Following two years of frustration and deadlock—and with Ethiopia emboldened by the economic development and growing financial and technical capacity discussed in previous chapters—the upstream countries decided to act in mid-2009. Ethiopia, Rwanda, Tanzania, and Uganda signed the agreement, with the contentious clause 14b in an annex, at a joint ceremony in May 2010, shortly followed by Kenya later that month and Burundi in February 2011.[6] For the first time, the key upstream countries presented a united front that isolated Egypt and Sudan (Cascão 2009; Cascão and Nicol 2016a; Tawfik 2016c). In response, Egypt and Sudan suspended their participation in the NBI in June 2010.

Benefit Sharing and Cooperation through the Nile Basin Initiative

Alongside the legal negotiations on the CFA, the NBI oversaw a technical track that aimed to identify a set of joint projects that could be realized on the Blue Nile. Unlike the British-era schemes that prioritized Egypt's water use, the Bureau of Reclamation study that focused on Ethiopia's interests, and various unilateral initiatives along the way, the World Bank-sponsored NBI emphasized cooperation and solutions that maximized benefits to *all* riparian countries, while limiting negative impacts as much as possible.[7] At the core were three principles: 'development must benefit all three countries, be multipurpose, and lead to no regret' (World Bank 2009b, p. 3), with the aim being to identify

> the optimum cascade development scenario for integrated regional water resources management providing a high degree of regulation of Blue Nile flows, water loss reduction, drought mitigation, flood alleviation along the Blue-Main Nile and reliable energy generation. (World Bank 2009b, p. 6)

After several years laying the groundwork, the joint multipurpose (JMP) project was launched under the NBI's Eastern Nile Technical Regional Office (ENTRO) in 2005. The main focus was on projects that: increased water storage capacity to cope with droughts; stored water in the Ethiopian highlands, where cool temperatures and deep ravines would limit evaporation, enabling the reduction of storage and thereby water losses in Lake Nasser; and produced hydroelectricity that could be exported to Egypt and Sudan, providing a cheap source of power.

[6] Ratification has also proceeded, albeit more slowly, with Ethiopia (June 2013), Rwanda (August 2013), Tanzania (March 2015), and Uganda (August 2019) to date.

[7] For a discussion of the principles underpinning the World Bank's approach in the NBI, see Sadoff and Grey (2002).

From a technical and economic perspective, many have long believed—from the British colonial explorations onwards—that storing water in the Ethiopian highlands could *increase* total water availability in the river and regulate the highly seasonal flow, providing benefits to both Egypt and Sudan. While the JMP entailed extensive technical and economic studies to refine these longstanding ideas and to develop detailed plans, the central challenge has always been a political one: how to reconcile large-scale water storage and control of water flows in Ethiopia with Egypt and Sudan's dependence on the essential Nile waters, their commitment to protecting their 'historic rights', and the political importance of controlling the flow of the water. Egypt and Sudan's agreement for the studies of Ethiopian dams to be conducted was a major step in itself, and the NBI was relatively successful in securing the support of technical experts from each of the three countries for the proposed projects. However, the focus on benefit sharing ultimately failed to overcome this fundamental political challenge.

The starting point for the NBI investigations was the 1964 US Bureau of Reclamation study and its proposal for a cascade of four dams on the main Blue Nile. Given concerns about the impact of sediment on the lifespan of relatively small dams, the decision was soon made to investigate the feasibility of three slightly larger dams in place of the original four (see Table 6.1).[8] As such, pre-feasibility studies were launched in 2003 for the Karadobi, Mandaya, and Border sites identified by the USBR. Mabil, which would be flooded by a larger Mandaya reservoir, was dropped.[9] These studies were undertaken by international and Ethiopian consultants, overseen by the Hydropower Study Department in the Ethiopian Ministry of Water. The pre-feasibility study of Karadobi was very favourable, and the site was considered the top priority in the mid-2000s (World Bank 2006a, p. 29).

Table 6.1 Proposed dams in NBI-ENTRO-sponsored pre-feasibility studies

Dam	Installed capacity (MW)	Average energy (GWh/year)	Plant factor (per cent)	Water storage (billion cubic metres)
Karadobi	1,600	9,708	69	40.2
Beko Abo	1,940	12,096	71	31.7
Mandaya	2,000	12,119	69	49.2
Border	1,200	8,114[a]	77	14.4

[a] With Mandaya operating upstream to regulate the flow.
Note: Karadobi and Beko Abo were alternatives in a three-dam cascade comprising Mandaya and Border.
Data source: MoWR (2006); MoWR (2013); ENTRO (2007a); ENTRO (2007b)

[8] Interview EP14, consultant involved in the studies, by phone, 10 March 2020.
[9] Studies of the Dal dam in Sudan were also rejected due to high evaporation rates and resettlement requirements.

However, in an instance of rather poor coordination within the Ethiopian Government, an expensive new bridge over the Blue Nile—carrying the main road linking Addis Ababa and Bahir Dar—was completed in 2008 in a location that would be submerged by Karadobi's reservoir (see Figure 6.1). Subsequent investigations downstream identified Beko Abo—a site not identified by the Bureau of Reclamation and just upstream of the other bridge over the Blue Nile—as an alternative to Karadobi as the first dam in a cascade. Early investigations suggested this would be an equally, if not even more, promising site (MoWR 2007).

The sale of cheap electricity to Egypt and Sudan was a central means by which the JMP sought to secure agreement and promote benefit sharing. As such, each of the proposed dams was designed with very high plant factors—even more so than the original Bureau studies[10] —with the primary function of the dams being to provide continuous, low-cost baseload energy for all three countries. Alongside the dam studies, NBI-ENTRO also commissioned a study to investigate the feasibility of exporting much of the electricity produced to Egypt and Sudan with a view to

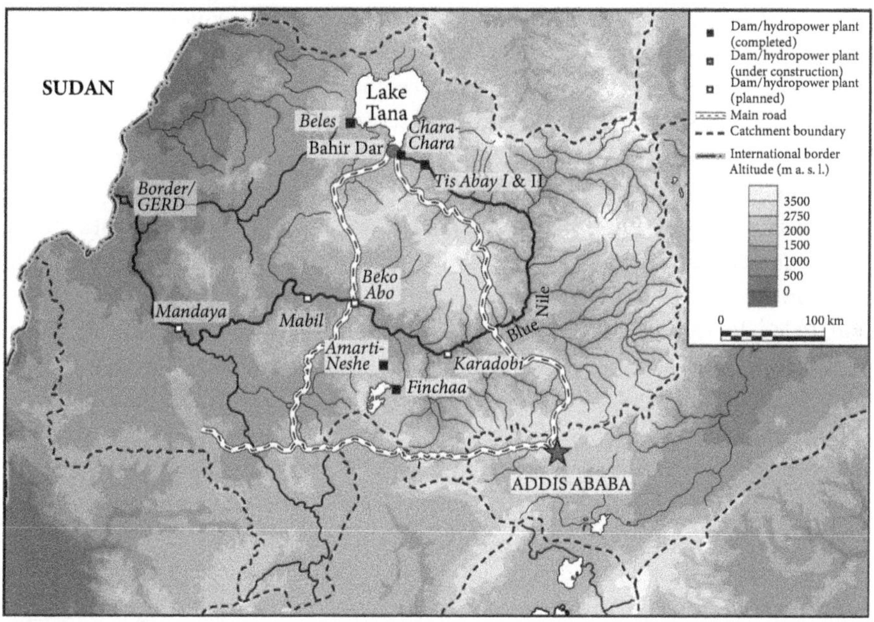

Figure 6.1 Map of the Blue Nile Dam sites

Source: Author and Manchester Cartographic Unit.

[10] Figures in Table 6.1 are for average energy, whereas those in Table 2.2 are for firm energy. Firm energy figures are not available in all the pre-feasibility studies. Plant factors for firm energy would be slightly lower than those presented, but still higher than those in the USBR study.

creating a win–win–win project. This study proposed a 1,200-MW connection to Sudan and 2,000-MW connection to Egypt, concluding on

> the economic profitability of the Egypt-Ethiopia-Sudan power interconnection. The project is characterized by good business indicators, as a short payback period and a high benefit to cost ratio under a wide range of hypothesis [sic]. (NBI ENTRO 2008, p. 2)

Based on these initial studies, the NBI continued with a view to completing full feasibility studies for the three dams in the planned cascade, which would be built from upstream to downstream: first Beko Abo; then Mandaya; and finally Border.[11] Standard practice when building a cascade of dams is to start at the top of the cascade to avoid reduced energy production at completed dams when building and filling subsequent dams upstream in the cascade. Moreover, the Border Dam design depended on upstream dams to regulate the river flow. Even though the Border Dam was slightly larger than that envisaged by the USBR, as a standalone dam it would provide insufficient storage for year-round generation and would have to overspill the majority of the river's flow.

Each of the three riparian countries, including Egypt, requested to progress with full feasibility studies for the three dams and to move towards development of a joint project, as noted in a December 2008 letter from the Egyptian minister of investment to the World Bank (World Bank 2009b, p. 4). This was not to be, however. In March 2009, Mahmoud Abu Zeid, Egyptian minister of water since 1997 and throughout the NBI process, was replaced by Mohamed Nasr Allam. Several observers noted this as an important change, with Egypt subsequently withdrawing its support for the JMP studies and hardening its position on the CFA negotiations.[12] By mid-2009 negotiations over the CFA had failed to resolve the dispute between Egypt and Sudan's 'historic rights' to the Nile waters and the upstream countries' demand for 'equitable use'. In May 2010, Ethiopia, Kenya, Uganda, Rwanda, and Tanzania signed the CFA regardless, leading Egypt and Sudan to withdraw from the CFA negotiations and the JMP. Egypt further responded by mobilizing its diplomatic power in an effort to prevent Ethiopia from securing external finance for a unilateral project (Tawfik 2015).

In retrospect, all this has an air of inevitability. It is hard to imagine that Egypt would ever have agreed to support a project on the Blue Nile or to sign a CFA that would question its 'historic rights' and replace the 1959 agreement. Yet international observers involved in the process were adamant that there was considerable optimism at the time, with all convinced that a deal was close and could have

[11] Interview EI1, senior official involved in the project, Addis Ababa, 19 September 2019, 11 February 2020.

[12] Interview ED13, senior donor representative, by phone, 1 April 2019, 7 November 2019.

materialized.[13] Nonetheless, the reality is that the unravelling of the NBI process reinforced the message to Ethiopia that any dam on the Nile would have to be built unilaterally. The numerous NBI studies provided what most would regard as a technically sound approach to river basin planning. Yet this emphasis on financial viability and shared benefits was insufficient to convince Egypt that ceding control over the water on which the country is so dependent could be in its interests. Ultimately, the process fell apart for the same basic reason as earlier initiatives to dam the Blue Nile—the technical studies failed to align with the limits of political authority and the balance of power between the riparian countries. Meanwhile, for Ethiopia, the NBI was another long process lasting more than a decade that produced ever more precise technical studies, but which ultimately failed to produce a dam.

The Grand Ethiopian Renaissance Dam

Inspired by earlier protests in Tunisia, anti-government protests against corruption, lack of freedom, and economic stagnation began in Tahrir Square in central Cairo on 25 January 2011. After weeks of protests, President Mubarak resigned on 11 February with the Supreme Council of the Armed Forces taking control prior to future elections. Shortly afterwards, plans for a massive Ethiopian dam on the Blue Nile, Project X, were leaked in the press in February 2011. The dam, originally named the Millennium Dam, was officially announced in late March.[14] In April Meles Zenawi laid the foundation stone and shortly afterwards the project was renamed the Grand Ethiopian Renaissance Dam.

The timing of the GERD's announcement led some casual observers to suggest that it was a spur-of-the-moment reaction to the Arab Spring (Fabricius 2013; Johnson 2018). To those following discussions at the time, however, the announcement that Ethiopia was to build a dam unilaterally was not such a surprise. It seems fairly clear that unilateral action was always the Ethiopian Government's plan B, once the NBI process had been given a chance to deliver results and the country had built the capacity required for unilateral action. As Cascão (2009, p. 256) noted earlier, Ethiopia had acted unilaterally through previous Nile projects, Tekeze and Beles, and was effectively giving Egypt and Sudan a choice: pursue a multilateral, negotiated solution or face unilateral action without downstream consent (see also Tawfik 2016a). Indeed, as time went on, Meles became more and more explicit in stating just this:

[13] In addition to the technical discussions, it was noted that Ethiopia made a point of notifying Egypt of its plans for the Beles hydropower project through the NBI—an exchange without prior precedent and taken at the time as a sign of good intent (interview ED13, senior official involved in the process, by phone, 1 April 2019, 7 November 2019).

[14] In reference to the recently passed Ethiopian Millennium in 2008.

> The current regime cannot be sustained. It's being sustained because of the diplomatic clout of Egypt. Now, there will come a time when the people of East Africa and Ethiopia will become too desperate to care about these diplomatic niceties. Then, they are going to act. (Meles, cited in Thomson 2005)

Available evidence suggests that the GERD was planned and designed in a relatively compressed period beginning when CFA negotiations unravelled in 2009 but well before the Tahrir Square uprising. Although the process was particularly secretive, given the sensitivities of the Nile Basin, decision making seems to have been fairly typical of that for most Ethiopian dams—the main discussions were between Meles and his advisors, and Salini, with a small team in the Ministry of Water reviewing proposals.[15] One participant in the Project X discussions estimated that planning began 'not more than two years before the dam was announced'.[16] The first available document referring to the project was an EEPCo annual plan dated August 2010 which includes a 5,000-MW Project X with contracting to be conducted in the 2010/11 year financial year (EEPCO 2010, p. 19). Meanwhile, the design document subsequently reviewed by the International Panel of Experts (IPoE) was originally submitted to the Ethiopian Government in December 2010 (IPoE 2013, p. 16). No non-NBI studies of the GERD site have yet surfaced that would provide evidence of preparatory work specific to the GERD before 2009/10. The NBI studies, meanwhile, considered a very different and much smaller Border Dam at the same site (see Chapter 7). Those involved in NBI studies were quite clear that at no point did they consider a Border Dam of anything like the size of the GERD and consequently their surveys were of limited relevance.

Alongside this secretive process, Meles began to prepare the ground politically for the dam's announcement. In July 2010, Meles gave an interview to Egyptian television in which he explained in painstaking detail his reasoning for rejecting the 1959 agreement on the Nile waters and the possibility of a solution that would benefit each of Ethiopia, Egypt, and Sudan:

> There is only one solution to the Nile problem and that solution is a win–win solution. If anybody loses, there is no solution. If Egypt and Sudan lose, there is no solution. (ETV 2010)[17]

[15] Interviews EG2, senior official in the energy sector, Addis Ababa, 3 September 2019, 13 February 2020; EG8, senior official in the energy sector, Addis Ababa, 3 October 2019, 11 February 2020; EG37, senior official in the energy sector, Addis Ababa, 21 August 2019, 19 February 2020.

[16] EG37, senior official in the energy sector, Addis Ababa, 21 August 2019, 19 February 2020. Meles also placed the discussions in this period; see comments in Amharic on YouTube (2011).

[17] The interview was subsequently shown on Ethiopian TV and the link provided in the References is to this broadcast.

Expressing his frustration about the failure of the CFA process, he insisted that Egypt was no longer able to block Ethiopian unilateral action, as had happened in the past:

> the whole policy of previous regimes in Egypt, which is based on stopping Ethiopia from utilizing the Nile water by destabilization of Ethiopia and by preventing Ethiopia from accessing loan and grant for Nile project. That approach is dead. It's finished. It's finished because Ethiopia has reached a stage where it can build its dams with its own money. (ETV 2010)

Invited to talk directly to the Egyptian people during the interview, his statement focused on addressing Egyptian fears that would arise when the dam—being planned at the time in secret—was announced some nine months later:

> I am going to tell them [the Egyptian people] no project in Ethiopia is designed to starve or fundamentally harm Egypt. Ever. This will not happen. This is not happening. Second, when some uninformed newspapers tell you that some dam is being built by this or that country in Ethiopia and you are going to starve, they are telling you absolute, total lies. Because the dams that are built in Ethiopia are also to your benefit. (ETV 2010)

All the available evidence, therefore, suggests that the GERD planning process was relatively short and commenced with the unravelling of the CFA negotiations during 2009/10, with designs and planning for the project already well advanced by the time of the Tahrir Square protests that began in late January 2011. Indeed, with Project X already well underway, it is hard to imagine that Ethiopia could have kept the project secret for much longer in any case. It may well have been that Meles decided to seize the moment in the midst of Egyptian political upheaval to announce the dam. Indeed, Alex de Waal (2015, p. 15) notes that the change in regime and the potential Egyptian approach to the Nile were at the forefront of Meles' thoughts at the time. Nonetheless, the GERD was the culmination of efforts to build financial and technical capacity, and a foreign policy strategy pursued over decades, as well as a specific design process pursued over the previous one to two years, not a knee-jerk response to the change of regime in Egypt. By 2011, Salini had emerged as a capable and trusted contractor that could be relied upon to tackle a politically controversial project like the GERD. Moreover, as Meles predicted back in 1996, the Ethiopian economy was 'running' by 2011, with rapid economic growth enhancing state revenues.[18] It may well be argued that the government's infrastructural ambitions exceeded its fiscal capacity, resulting in subsequent debt problems (see Chapter 9). However, to some degree the decision

[18] See quote on p. 1.

to pursue the GERD appears to have been a statement of belief in the ability of Ethiopia to dig deep, as much as anything else, as acknowledged by Meles in his speech launching the dam:

> the expense will be an additional and heavy burden on us. All our efforts to lighten this have been unsuccessful, leaving us with only two options. Either to abandon the project or do whatever we must to raise the required funds. I have no doubt which of these difficult choices the Ethiopian people will make. No matter how poor we are, in the Ethiopian traditions of resolve, the Ethiopian people will pay any sacrifice. I have no doubt they will, with one voice, say: 'Build the Dam!' (Zenawi 2011b)

The End of Egyptian 'Hegemony' on the Nile?

The debate on the GERD and its potential impacts on downstream countries has attracted a great deal of misinformation and hyperbole, ranging from excessively optimistic claims that the GERD will not have any negative impacts to overly pessimistic ones predicting catastrophic impacts on Egypt and Sudan. A series of recent studies provide a much more balanced view of the dam's impacts (Wheeler et al. 2020, 2022; Basheer et al. 2021). These studies show that Sudan is well placed to benefit from upstream regulation through increased hydropower generation from its existing dams and the opportunity to develop additional irrigated agriculture. In contrast, recession agriculture and the brick industry, both of which rely on the annual flood of the Nile and provide an important source of livelihoods in Sudan, will be lost, while there is a risk of downstream environmental damage, as is often the case with dams.

In terms of the impact on water availability in Egypt, studies show that in years of average or above average rainfall, the GERD can be filled and operated with little to no impact on water releases from the High Aswan Dam, albeit the Aswan reservoir will need to operate at a reduced level compared to recent years, in turn reducing hydropower production (Wheeler et al. 2020).[19] The main risk to water security concerns periods of multi-year drought, which, though relatively rare, occurred most recently in the 1970s and 1980s (Wheeler et al. 2020). These periods of multi-year drought would present a major challenge to filling the GERD and, even were a multi-year drought to start when reservoirs at Aswan and the GERD were full, could eventually lead to very low levels in both reservoirs. Following such a drought, the challenge would be how to sequence the filling of two large reservoirs situated in different countries (Wheeler et al. 2020). The resounding conclusion

[19] From a basin-wide perspective this is of course a benefit, since reduced water storage at Aswan means reduced water losses through evaporation.

therefore is that there is an urgent need to come to an agreement on data sharing and operational rules for the GERD and Aswan, thereby reducing mistrust and suspicion (Wheeler et al. 2016, 2018, 2020; Basheer et al. 2021). As always, however, negotiations regarding the Nile are not purely technical but rather a political process shaped by the dynamic power relations between the countries, and the regional and global international relations within which these are embedded.

While the process leading to the GERD was underway well before the Tahrir Square uprising brought about Mubarak's downfall, the political instability that unfolded in Egypt over subsequent years certainly impeded Egypt's response to Ethiopian unilateralism. The military interim administration moved towards quick elections, in doing so favouring already established groups such as the Muslim Brotherhood, which formed the Freedom and Justice Party led by Mohamed Morsi that won the 2012 elections (Sallam 2022). However, following a series of anti- and pro-regime protests, a military coup led by army chief General Abdel Fattah El-Sisi in July 2013, and supported by Saudi Arabia and the UAE, resulted in the imprisonment of Morsi and the Muslim Brotherhood leadership (Mosley 2021; Young and Khan 2022). The result was the restoration of military order, with the Muslim Brotherhood forced underground once more (Sallam 2022). El-Sisi won subsequent elections in 2014, 2018, and 2023 by landslides as he consolidated power. Moreover, the military leadership was at the forefront of a major investment drive, supported by Gulf investment, that once again has focused on land reclamation and new cities in the desert, further placing demands on the Nile waters (Sayigh 2022).

From 2011 to the restoration of military power under El-Sisi, the Egyptian response was divided and fragmented (Tawfik 2016a). On the one hand, the government engaged in negotiations that focused on how the GERD would be operated, implying acceptance of the reality of the GERD, and, on the other, officials periodically ramped up the rhetoric with threats of military intervention. Notably this included a leaked recording of President Morsi and his cabinet discussing options for military action against the dam (Stack 2013). The reality, however, was that once Ethiopia was able to finance the project itself and had access to the required technical expertise, Egypt's ability to contest the dam was extremely limited.

The announcement of the dam also re-shaped relations with other riparians. Sudan's position has oscillated over time with political shifts in the country. Like Egypt, Sudan initially stated its opposition to the GERD when it was announced in 2011 (Salman 2016). However, Ethiopia's long-term strategy of building ties with Sudan had borne fruit. Sudan's heightening of Roseires had enabled irrigation expansion but provided insufficient water for the country's ambitious agricultural plans, necessitating upstream water regulation in Ethiopia. As such, the GERD was seen in Sudan as the ideal means of expanding irrigation, enhancing hydropower generation, and providing flood control (Cascão and Nicol 2016b).[20] The Sudanese Government formally endorsed the GERD in March 2012 and resumed participation in the NBI, a significant challenge to the 1959 agreement (Salman 2016; Tawfik 2019). Indeed, Cascão and Nicol (2016b) claim that the Sudanese had already signalled to Ethiopia their support for the GERD as early as 2010.[21] Meanwhile, the water regulation provided by the GERD and the potential for Sudan to substantially increase water extraction for irrigated agriculture represents a major concern for Egypt.

The NBI process and the new phase of upstream assertiveness also coincided with dam building in other upstream countries. In particular, in Uganda, Salini Impregilo built the 250-MW Bujagali Dam with World Bank support during 2007–2012 (Gore 2017), while Chinese firms China International Water & Electric Corporation and Sinohydro were contracted to build the 183-MW Isimba Dam (2015–2019) and the 600-MW Karuma Dam (2013–2023). While these projects highlighted Egypt's inability to prevent upstream dam development, they also presented much less of a threat to Egyptian water security than the GERD. First, as run-of-the-river projects, they do not entail large-scale water storage. Second, situated on the White Nile, upstream of the Sudd, the impact on downstream water flows on the main Nile is minimal.

Ultimately, however, Egypt's status as the hydro-hegemon in the basin has been eroded, and Egypt has been forced to accept the reality of the GERD as a fact on the ground (Salman 2016). Sudan played a key role in mediating between Egypt and Ethiopia and initiating negotiations (Cascão and Nicol 2016b). Meanwhile, Egypt acknowledged that it was better to engage in negotiations on the project, 'even if on Ethiopian terms' (Tawfik 2015, p. 22).[22] The result is that negotiations between the countries have shifted to the filling and operation of the dam as Egypt and Sudan seek to minimize any negative effects. A key Ethiopian triumph in these early negotiations was its ability to resist repeated Egyptian attempts to broaden participation in the talks, with Egypt at various points proposing the inclusion of the US Government or Arab States as mediators. Given the long history of external support for Egypt in Nile hydropolitics, the retention of tripartite negotiations was a vitally important step. Moreover, since Sudan signalled its support for the GERD, Egypt found itself alone in opposition to the dam.

Initial discussions between the three countries in 2011 led to agreement on terms of reference for an IPoE, comprising two experts nominated by each of the

[20] Moreover, there have been suggestions that Sudanese support for the GERD was contingent on Ethiopia agreeing not to support the Sudan People's Liberation Army-North (SPLA-N) splinter group that resumed hostilities in Sudan in 2011 (RVI 2023, p. 11). The Comprehensive Peace Agreement in 2005 failed to address the issues facing Blue Nile and South Kordofan states. SPLA-N was formed in response (RVI 2023).

[21] Sudan's position was partially reversed after the 2019 military coup, as discussed in Chapter 9.

[22] To this end, Egypt offered in 2014 to contribute to the finance and management of the dam, an offer that was swiftly rejected by Ethiopia on sovereignty grounds (Tawfik 2015).

three countries and four external experts, to review the GERD's design and environment and social impacts. While broadly supportive of the dam's initial design, the panel raised several issues that required further clarification and additional study related to the design of the dam and its impacts (IPoE 2013). The subsequent agreement and signing of the Declaration of Principles by Egypt, Ethiopia, and Sudan in March 2015 was heralded by the Ethiopian negotiating team as implying that 'Egypt, for the first time, recognized Ethiopia's right to use the Nile waters'.[23] As such, the Declaration represented the culmination of a decades-long struggle by Ethiopian Governments to utilize the Nile waters, as well as the ultimate failure of the Egyptian strategy of blocking any upstream water infrastructure on the Blue Nile. Moreover, the Declaration separated the negotiations over the operation of the dam from its construction, meaning that works could progress while what turned out to be lengthy and drawn-out negotiations proceeded. Nonetheless, the Declaration was far from a full agreement on the GERD. Instead, the Declaration was 'essentially a commitment to find common ground on what had become an increasingly acrimonious dispute' but one which predictably left the hard issues of how to fill and operate the dam to future rounds of negotiations (Whittington 2016; see discussion in Chapter 9). A sign of the problems to come was that, despite the Declaration restating the need to carry out the studies recommended by the IPoE, the three countries were unable to come to an agreement on the terms of reference of these studies (Basheer et al. 2021).

Conclusion

This chapter argues that the successes of the EPRDF's dam-building programme and the ability to tackle a dam on the Blue Nile River are the result of alignment of domestic and international political dynamics, which have combined to strengthen Ethiopia's ability to pursue major projects independently and limited Egypt's ability to block unilateral Ethiopian intervention. Previous chapters have shown that domestic politics underpinned a dams boom from the early 2000s, first outside and subsequently within the Nile Basin. The centralization of power after 2001 enhanced the coherence of the political elite and the EPRDF's focus on rapid development and infrastructure investment, as part of Meles' vision of building a 'developmental state'. Along with a sustained period of economic growth from 2004, this translated into a growing belief among the EPRDF in Ethiopia's ability to self-finance major infrastructure projects, while Salini emerged as a trusted and dependable contractor with an established team ready to move from project to project.

[23] Presentation by a member of the Ethiopian negotiating team at a meeting with party political officials, 31 December 2019, Debre Damo Hotel, Addis Ababa.

This chapter shifted focus to the international dimension of Ethiopian dam building. During the 2000s, domestic politics came to align with international relations in support of a Nile dam. In particular, Egyptian dominance of the Nile Basin and the prioritization of Egypt by the global and regional powers weakened to a degree, providing an opening for an increasingly powerful and assertive Ethiopia to press first for a collaborative approach to the Nile and then, when this strategy was exhausted, to pursue a unilateral solution. In part this shift was the culmination of Ethiopia's foreign policy pursued over two decades. Ethiopia sought to isolate Egypt in opposition to upstream development, building a coalition of upstream countries on the White Nile and, of paramount importance, building ties with Sudan and securing that country's support for an Ethiopian Nile dam.

By 2010, these international and domestic dynamics aligned to the point at which the Ethiopian Government felt able to launch a dam unilaterally, just as negotiations on the CFA and attempts to identify a collaborative project on the Blue Nile collapsed. The Arab Spring and the change of regime in Egypt in early 2011 provided an opportune moment for Ethiopia to announce the dam, which had been in process for some time, taking advantage of a moment of political upheaval in Egypt that prevented any coherent response to the announcement of the project. By the time stability returned to Egypt under El-Sisi, the dam was already rapidly becoming a fact on the ground. As such, while the announcement of *an* Ethiopian dam in 2011 was not so surprising, what *was* unexpected was the scale and location of the dam that the Ethiopians announced, as discussed in Chapter 7.

7

Designing the Blue Nile Dam

Between the Hydropolitics of the Nile and an Ethiopian Renaissance

Tom Lavers

In July 2020 Ethiopia began to fill the reservoir formed by the Grand Ethiopian Renaissance Dam (GERD). Although well behind schedule due to construction delays and constrained finances, and subject to great controversy given ongoing negotiations with downstream riparians, the filling nonetheless constituted a momentous step. However, amidst fevered debate regarding the filling and operation of the dam, there remains an important question that has received relatively little attention to date: why does the GERD bear little resemblance to any previous proposal for a Blue Nile dam over the preceding century? While the GERD occupies one of the sites long identified for a Blue Nile dam, the dam is far larger—in terms of the civil structure, water storage, and installed capacity—than any other previously considered at that site or elsewhere in the basin. This chapter tackles this question, arguing that the answer lies in two main factors: first, the antagonistic hydropolitics of the Nile, and second, the politically driven nature of Ethiopia's dams' boom.

The broad outline of a technically optimal solution to the management of the waters of the Nile Basin as a whole has been known for more than a century (Collins 1990). From this technical perspective, there is a strong rationale for storing large amounts of water in the Ethiopian highlands—and relatively little downstream on the Ethio-Sudanese border, and in Egypt and Sudan—to limit evaporation and thereby maximize total water availability in the river. Upstream storage, meanwhile, enables release of a steady year-round flow of water to create low-cost hydropower in Ethiopia that could be exported across the region, while limiting flooding in Sudan, and providing a steady water supply for hydropower and irrigation in Egypt and Sudan (Guariso and Whittington 1987; Blackmore and Whittington 2008; Whittington et al. 2014). Such a scheme would not be costless. Dams on the Blue Nile change the pattern of flooding downstream which would force a change in livelihoods for those living in riverine areas in Sudan, disrupt the flow of silt, which is the basis for downstream soil fertility, and, depending on the location chosen in Ethiopia, entail some displacement of local populations.

Dams, Power, and the Politics of Ethiopia's Renaissance. Tom Lavers et al., Oxford University Press. © Tom Lavers (2024).
DOI: 10.1093/oso/9780192871213.003.0007

Moreover, dams invariably lead to a deterioration of water quality and methane emissions. Nonetheless, the fairly consistent view of engineers studying the Nile has been to favour water storage in the Ethiopian highlands.

As shown in Chapters 2 and 6, different actors, from British colonialists to the United States Bureau of Reclamation (USBR), the Ethiopian Government, and the Nile Basin Initiative, have sought to realize some variant of this basic idea, albeit that they diverged in their prioritization of the three riparians in their designs. The reality, however, is that the technical rationale for optimization at the river basin level has never aligned with the actual power relations and patterns of political authority within the basin. Past proposals for dam construction on the Blue Nile favoured first Egypt, then Ethiopia, then, under the Nile Basin Initiative (NBI), a benefit-sharing approach, yet the reality is that none of these aligned with the actual balance of political power internationally and domestically, and consequently none was realized. Instead, the antagonistic nature of Nile hydropolitics has meant that dam building—first by Egypt with the High Aswan Dam, then Sudan with Roseires and Merowe, and now Ethiopia—has been used to establish control over the river's waters within national territory and to maximize national benefits while disregarding the interests of other riparians (Waterbury 1979; Mitchell 2002; Verhoeven 2015). In a sense, therefore, the GERD is best seen as a response to and consequence of the pattern of dam building established long ago by the High Aswan Dam. Meanwhile, each successive Nile dam has shifted water management progressively further from what most would consider a technically optimal solution for the basin as a whole.

However, the GERD is not simply a reflection of the antagonistic Nile hydropolitics but has equally been shaped by the domestic political drivers of Ethiopia's dams' boom. Chapters 3 and 4 highlighted a process by which the political imperative of rapid development translated into a politically driven planning process which gradually subverted technocratic input into decision making. Moreover, as Chapter 5 showed, the establishment of Salini as the go-to contractor for Ethiopian dams meant that decision making was centralized between the Prime Minister's Office and Salini. This chapter shows that the GERD's enormous installed capacity reflects the Ethiopian Peoples' Revolutionary Democratic Front's (EPRDF's) overambitious, politically driven design process that has shaped the design of most of its dams, albeit on a larger scale.

The chapter begins by examining the GERD's design in contrast with previous proposals for a Blue Nile dam, noting the difference in choice with respect to the size of the dam, reservoir, and installed capacity, its location, and its impacts on evaporation and resettlement. The following section provides an explanation for this design choice, focusing on the hydropolitics of the Nile and the politically driven nature of decision making in Ethiopia's 'developmental state'.

The GERD: A Very Different Approach to Damming the Nile

The GERD differs markedly from the designs of earlier NBI and USBR studies and the rationale underpinning their planned cascade of dams along the Blue Nile (Tawfik 2015). The most obvious difference is that the GERD is far bigger than any dam considered by the USBR or NBI anywhere in the river basin (see Table 7.1). As Meles noted during the ceremony to lay the foundation stone, 'It is the largest dam we could build at any point along the Nile, or indeed any other river' (Zenawi 2011b).

Located at the site of the Border Dam originally identified by the USBR and subsequently studied by the NBI, the GERD is almost 70 metres taller than the NBI proposal for an 84.5-metre dam. Each of the three dams proposed by the NBI were slightly larger than the four original USBR proposals in terms of dam height and water storage in order to cope with sedimentation. However, the NBI Border proposal was still just one-fifth the water storage of the subsequent GERD and relied on upstream regulation by Mandaya to produce year-round energy. Effectively,

Table 7.1 GERD compared to previous plans for Nile dams

Dam	Installed capacity (MW)	Average energy (GWh/year)[a]	Plant factor (%)	Water storage (billion cubic metres)
USBR (1964)				
- Karadobi	1,350	5,835	49	32.5
- Mabil	1,200	5,314	51	13.6
- Mandaya	1,620	7,800	55	15.9
- Border	1,400	6,200	51	11.1
- Total	5,570	25,149	52	73.1
NBI				
- Beko Abo	1,940	12,096	71	31.7
- Mandaya	2,000	12,119	69	49.2
- Border	1,200	8,114[b]	77	14.4
- Total	5,140	32,329	72	95.3
GERD				
- 2011 design	5,250	15,692	34	74.0
- 2012 design	6,000	15,692	30	74.0
- 2017 design	6,350	15,692	28	74.0
- 2020 design	5,150	15,692	35	74.0

[a] The USBR Border plan quotes figures for firm, not average energy.
[b] With Mandaya operating upstream to regulate the flow.
Data source: USBR (1964), MoWR (2006), MoWR (2013), ENTRO (2007a), ENTRO (2007b), IPoE (2013)

the GERD combines the majority of the water storage capacity and all the installed capacity of a three-dam cascade into a single project. Moreover, the heightening of the main dam means that a 45-metre-high, 4.8-kilometre-long saddle dam is required to raise the height of one side of the GERD's reservoir (see Figure 7.1). Previously, the NBI Border study only considered the possibility of very small saddle dams that might be required in modest stretches and ruled out a higher dam due to the cost of a large saddle dam (ENTRO 2007b, section 2, p. 3; section 7, p. 1). Although the GERD utilizes the Border site studied by the USBR and NBI, it cannot be claimed that the GERD is based on those earlier studies. It is a completely different project.

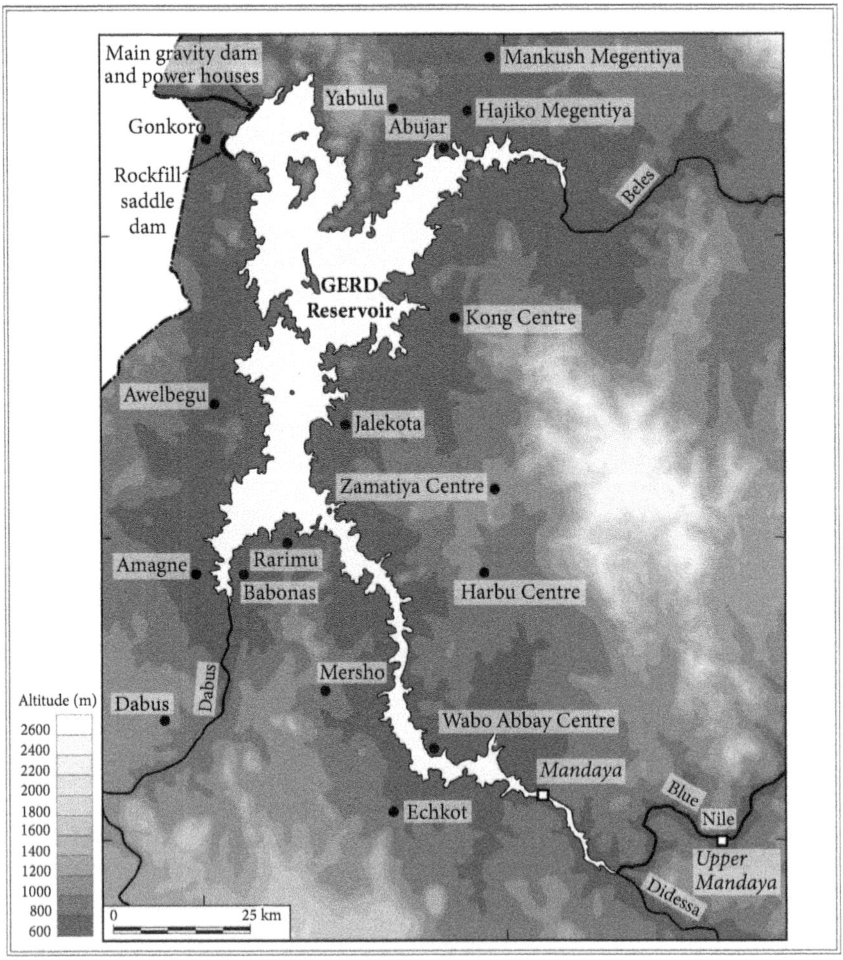

Figure 7.1 Map of the GERD, reservoir, and resettlement sites

Source: Author and Manchester Cartographic Unit.

Not only is the GERD different to the Border Dam, but the choice of the GERD also necessarily has implications for the rest of any future cascade of dams. Notably, given its size, the GERD, once full, will flood the original Mandaya site—the next dam upstream in the planned cascade (see Figure 7.1). The view amongst several consultants involved in the NBI process was that Mandaya was the best dam site in the entire cascade. As such, none of the NBI studies considered a higher dam at the Border site.[1] Indeed, some analyses show that *any* combination of dams that includes the GERD is sub-optimal compared to other possible combinations (Jeuland and Whittington 2014). When the government's plans were announced in 2011, some of those involved in the NBI studies sought to persuade officials to lower the GERD slightly to save Mandaya for future development, but to no avail (MoWE 2011).[2] After announcement of the GERD, consultants searched for an alternative site for another dam upstream of the GERD reservoir, settling on 'Upper Mandaya'. However, Upper Mandaya is upstream of the confluence of the Blue Nile and Didessa Rivers, significantly reducing water availability, and was seen as a poor substitute for the original Mandaya (MoWE 2011).

An additional challenge is that the GERD—located close to the Sudanese border—is at the bottom of any possible future cascade of Ethiopian dams. The NBI-sponsored cascade was intended to start with Beko Abo and move downstream to Mandaya and finally the Border for the simple reason that any subsequent filling of a dam upstream would result in a reduced reservoir level and hydropower production at the downstream dam. This will be a challenge should Ethiopia tackle additional upstream dams in the future: filling a dam at Beko Abo, for example, would reduce reservoir levels and electricity generation at the GERD.

The GERD also diverges from the NBI project and other previous studies, for which minimizing evaporation through water storage in the high-altitude, deep ravines of the highlands was a central priority. In contrast, the GERD maximizes water storage at a relatively low-altitude site, with much higher temperatures. Moreover, given the relatively flat topography, the GERD will create a large and comparatively shallow reservoir whose surface area is estimated to fluctuate from 703 to 1,904 kilometres^2 during regular operation (Elagib and Basheer 2021). According to one estimate, the evaporation rate from the GERD reservoir will be five times that expected at Beko Abo (Bates et al. 2013, p. 57). Meanwhile, another recent study estimated average annual evaporation losses from the GERD of 1.7 billion cubic metres (bcm), which would only be partially offset by expected lower operational levels of the High Aswan Dam and reduced evaporation losses from Lake Nasser of 1.1 bcm (Wheeler et al. 2020, pp. 3–4).[3] Given the comparatively high temperatures and shallow, fluctuating coverage of the reservoir, studies of

[1] Interviews EP8 and EP9, consultants involved in the studies, by phone, 10 October 2019.
[2] Interviews EP8 and EP9, consultants involved in the studies, by phone, 10 October 2019.
[3] Elagib and Basheer (2021) estimate evaporation at 826–1,960 Million metres^3.

other reservoirs in the world (e.g. Fearnside 2003; Giles 2006; Gunkel 2009) would suggest that the GERD is also likely to result in the production of greater methane emissions than would have been the case with upstream dams.[4] As such, the GERD potentially weakens Ethiopia's claims to green electricity production.

The other particularly noteworthy aspect of the GERD design is its electricity generation capacity. The original design for the dam announced in 2011 had an installed capacity of 5,250 megawatts (MW), vastly more than the 1,200–1,400 MW envisaged previously for the Border site and, indeed, more than the total installed capacity planned for the *entire cascade* of dams proposed by the NBI. Moreover, the installed capacity of the GERD was subsequently *increased* twice, first to 6,000 MW in 2012 and then to 6,350 MW in 2017.[5] This vast difference in installed generation capacity has provoked considerable debate. The energy generation potential of a dam is determined by the head and water flow.[6] As such, increasing the installed capacity of a dam means that the available water can be used to generate higher peaks of energy at any one point in time, but not more energy overall, reducing the plant factor of the dam. As noted in Chapter 6, the NBI studies aimed for high plant factors with a view to producing continuous and relatively low-cost baseload energy. In interviews, engineers familiar with the GERD—both international and within Ethiopian state agencies—estimated that given the water availability and topography at the GERD site, a dam could reasonably be expected to produce 1,400–1,600 MW or perhaps up to 2,000 MW year round.[7] Adding additional capacity to provide some peaking power and to allow for downtime for the maintenance of turbines, the dam's capacity should therefore be about 3,000 MW or, at a stretch, up to 4,000 MW.[8] In contrast, the extremely high installed capacity and low plant factor for the GERD are suited to a peaking plant that can provide very large amounts of energy at times of peak demand, but which can do so only for relatively short periods since operating the dam at anywhere near its full capacity would mean that the reservoir would be emptied within months.[9]

[4] Preparations for the GERD entailed an attempt to clear vegetation from the area to be flooded by the GERD's reservoir, in part to address this problem (IPoE 2013). However, as a result of construction delays, the initial clearance was conducted years before the dam filling (Vaughan and Gebremichael 2020). It is unclear whether this clearance will be repeated as the reservoir level rises.

[5] As discussed in Chapter 9, the installed capacity was subsequently reduced to 5,150 MW, effectively acknowledging that the installed capacity was excessive.

[6] Head is the difference in water elevation between the reservoir and the turbines and therefore dependent on the height of the dam and the drop in altitude of the existing watercourse. Since the GERD site is relatively flat, the head is provided by the height of the dam and therefore reservoir.

[7] Interviews EA4, academic familiar with the project, by phone, 2 April 2019; and EG11, senior engineer involved in the project, Addis Ababa, 21 February 2020.

[8] Interviews EP14, consultant involved in the NBI studies, by phone, 10 March 2020; EA4, academic familiar with the project, by phone, 2 April 2019; EP13, senior consultant involved in the project, by phone, 26 November 2019.

[9] Recent technical studies have raised similar concerns about the excess of installed capacity at the GERD given available water (Basheer et al. 2018; Wheeler et al. 2018; Eldardiry and Hossain 2021).

The design of the GERD therefore raises the question of what the electricity produced will be used for. In the short to medium term at least, utilization of the full installed capacity of the dam to produce peaking power, even for short periods, would require export to Sudan and/or Egypt since the installed capacity of the GERD comfortably exceeds total peak demand within Ethiopia. For example, in 2017 peak demand was just 2,202 MW (USAID 2019), far less than the GERD's capacity, even disregarding all other existing sources of power. Moreover, the main demand for electricity within Ethiopia lies in central areas of the country, particularly Addis Ababa and a growing number of industrial consumers in the highlands. For domestic use, an upstream dam such as Beko Abo would be far preferable given the reduced cost of building transmission lines and the significant energy losses in long-distance transmission. In terms of location, the choice of the GERD, near the Sudanese border, is consistent with the NBI's focus on exporting significant amounts of electricity. However, the ability to export electricity will depend of course on export agreements with Sudan and Egypt for peaking power, which are tied up in the tense negotiations over the dam filling and operation (see Chapter 8).

Alternatively, operating GERD as a baseload plant would mean that much of the energy could be used domestically, but that the majority of the GERD's installed capacity would be unused. As such, the consensus amongst engineers is that the GERD has far more installed capacity than is justified by the water availability or the potential market for electricity. Indeed, as the International Panel of Experts, established by the three countries to examine the design of the dam, concluded,

> The GERD is economically attractive. The economic justification is not given with respect to the installed capacity of 6000 MW. Particularly with consideration to the apparent low load factor and the cost of transmission to the main load centre, the economic considerations are not clear as far as the installed capacity is concerned. (IPoE 2013, p. 38)

Alternatively, as one international engineer summed up, 'they certainly don't need so much capacity in terms of turbines. They won't be able to use all of them'.[10]

Another challenge with the GERD concerns displacement of local populations and the resulting resettlement programme. While one advantage of all the dams along the Blue Nile valley is that population density is relatively low, the GERD, as a result of its location and the vast size of the resulting reservoir, requires resettlement of many more people than would be the case with upstream sites, such as Beko Abo, which are located in deep and largely unpopulated gorges. The GERD primarily affects Gumuz populations living in the reservoir area who previously practised shifting cultivation, supported by fishing, livestock rearing, and gold

[10] Interview EA4, academic, by phone, 2 April 2019.

panning.[11] Their displacement takes place in the historical context of past attacks and slave raids in the Imperial era and, more recently, displacement to make way for highland populations resettled in the Tana-Beles project (see Chapter 5). The result has been to force the Gumuz progressively further west out of the Ethiopian highlands over previous centuries (James 2002b).

The resettlement programme began in 2013 and was run by Ethiopian Electric Power's (EEP's) federal project office, meaning that it was conducted separately from the ongoing villagization programme and with little involvement of the regional government or Abay Basin Authority (Vaughan and Gebremichael 2020).[12] The programme will resettle everyone living below 645 metres above sea level (masl), the expected maximum height of the reservoir. Despite low population density, the vast size of the reservoir means that a total of 5,391 households, approximately 20,000 people, were to be moved into 17 newly built settlements at a cost of 815 million *birr* for capital expenses and a further 890 million *birr* for livelihood development (Vaughan and Gebremichael 2020, pp. 13–14; see Figure 7.1). GERD resettlement has been subject to 'strong continuity of top-down, distant, elitist and exclusionary decision making which continues to shape Ethiopian resettlement policy making' more broadly (Vaughan and Gebremichael 2020, p. 7). The result was that local officials were put under pressure to move people quickly, in line with the original, implausible timeline for the dam construction. Consequently, people were moved years before the reservoir was finally filled (Vaughan and Gebremichael 2020). Moreover, the locations of the new resettlement sites were identified by *wereda* administrations, without discussion with the local population, and there was no flexibility, even when key resources such as springs and groundwater were later found to be lacking. The result has been a crisis of water supplies in many of the resettlement sites (Vaughan and Gebremichael 2020). In addition, the purpose-built concrete housing and offices in the resettlement sites are poorly suited to the high temperatures in the area, while, ironically, most of the sites lack any electricity supply. Displaced households received financial compensation, though this was far below most people's expectations, while there appears to have been very little planning regarding livelihoods or the potential opportunities provided by the reservoir, such as fishing or tourism (Vaughan and Gebremichael 2020). As such, the GERD appears to follow a longstanding pattern of dam building and resettlement, disregarding and further exploiting politically marginal populations in the interests of 'development'.

[11] Details on resettlement draw on Sarah Vaughan and Mesfin Gebremichael's (2020) paper which provides, to our knowledge, the only primary research on the GERD resettlement sites. Like this book, their paper was part of the FutureDAMS project. It is available at: https://hummedia.manchester.ac.uk/institutes/gdi/publications/workingpapers/futuredams/futuredams-working-paper-010-vaughan.pdf.

[12] The villagization programme is attempting to settle populations practising mobile livelihoods into planned settlements across Benishangul-Gumuz, as well as Afar, Gambella, Somali, and Southern Nations, Nationalities, and Peoples Region (SNNPR).

Despite undoubted limitations to the GERD's design, there are also some advantages of the GERD's location and its enormous size. Most important is that as the furthest downstream site possible within Ethiopia, the GERD will capture and store the maximum possible volume of water. This includes the Beles River—which has increased flow since the Beles hydropower project began diverting water from Lake Tana—and the Dabus River, which both join the Blue Nile below the Mandaya site upstream (see Figure 7.1). The result is that 17 bcm or 34 per cent of the annual flow of the Blue Nile at the GERD site is added to the river after Mandaya (ENTRO 2007b, pp. 4–15). An additional advantage of the GERD's size is the ability to cope with sedimentation. The highly seasonal rains cause massive erosion and the river carries a very large amount of sediment downstream. Historically the basis of fertile soils in Egypt and Sudan, sedimentation has caused major problems at the High Aswan Dam and Roseires in Sudan, significantly reducing storage and hydropower capacity (Waterbury 2002). The NBI study of the Border site noted a lack of reliable data on sediment loads, but estimated a dam would trap 318 million tonnes of sediment per year, which could have reduced the storage of the much smaller Border Dam by 70 per cent over 50 years (ENTRO 2007b, pp. 4–39). According to one estimate, the GERD's massive storage capacity will enable the dam to trap 100 years' worth of sediment without loss of energy production (IHA n.d.). However, the IPoE (2013) report found that sedimentation had not been adequately studied.

The GERD as a Product of Nile Hydropolitics and the EPRDF's Developmentalism

Overall, therefore, it is clear that the GERD design and location is based on a very different rationale to the technical optimization process at the river basin level employed by the NBI studies. This begs the question then of why the dam is so different to past proposals. The following analysis underscores the view that dam design and construction is rarely a purely technical process, but rather one that is fundamentally shaped by politics. In particular, the GERD's design is the result of two main factors: geo-strategic concerns in the context of the antagonistic relations with Egypt; and the politically driven ambitions of Ethiopia's 'developmental state'.

Interviews with people who discussed the Nile dams with Meles over several years make it clear that geo-strategic concerns—principally the challenge presented by Egypt and the inevitable confrontation that would follow unilateral action—were at the forefront of his thinking over more than a decade leading up to 2011.[13] In terms of relations with Egypt, the GERD offers a number of

[13] Interviews ED13, senior donor official, by phone, 1 April 2019 and 7 November 2019; EA5, academic, London, 8 April 2019.

potential advantages over other possible dams in the Blue Nile cascade. First and foremost, a complete GERD with a full reservoir puts to an end more than a century of debate with Egypt over the regulation of the Nile and definitively ends Egypt's so-called 'hydro-hegemony' over the river (Cascão 2008; Cascão and Zeitoun 2010; Haile 2018). Having repeatedly found Egypt to be unwilling to revise the 1959 agreement and to compromise on a Blue Nile dam, the Ethiopian Government changed tack. The GERD is the dam that maximizes Ethiopia's control over the Nile waters, enabling Ethiopia to command 59 per cent of the annual flow of the Nile at Aswan on completion. In contrast, Beko Abo—the proposed first dam in the NBI cascade—would command approximately half of this volume of water (MoWR 2013, p. 11–10). The GERD is therefore uniquely positioned to undermine the power relations through which Egypt dominated the river basin in the past. Prior to and since the announcement of the dam, Meles and other Ethiopian Government officials have been at pains to stress that the GERD will have positive impacts on, not harm, Egypt and Sudan, continuing the NBI's 'benefit-sharing' narrative (MoI 2002b; ETV 2010; Zenawi 2011b). Whatever the downstream impacts of the dam, however, what is incontestable is that the GERD places all operational decisions regarding regulation of the flow of the majority of the Nile waters and thereby massive political influence in Ethiopian hands.

Furthermore, while commencing a potential cascade of dams with the GERD at the bottom does not make sense from a technical perspective, it does offer potential benefits in terms of negotiating strategy. Certainly, some officials in Ethiopia expected that an agreement about the operation and releases from the GERD between Egypt, Ethiopia, and Sudan could mean that any further upstream dam construction in Ethiopia would be an internal issue of water management between Ethiopian dams, rather than an issue to be re-negotiated with Egypt. One can easily imagine that had the Ethiopian Government decided to commence the cascade with Beko Abo, proceeding to Mandaya and then the Border, the result would have been three separate, protracted negotiations with Egypt and Sudan over the releases from each additional dam in the cascade. As one former EEP official put it, however, with the GERD, 'there will not be a quarrel in the future. It will kill the conflict'.[14]

In addition, the GERD supports Ethiopia's long-term aim of winning Sudan's support for the development of Blue Nile dams. As discussed in Chapter 6, for Meles, the central political challenge regarding the Nile was between Ethiopia and Egypt. In his view, Sudanese interests on the Nile were actually in close alignment with Ethiopia's (MoI 2002b) since dams in Ethiopia would limit sedimentation

[14] Interview EG13, former senior EEP official, Addis Ababa, 19 February 2020. A similar view was expressed by a former senior Ministry of Water official, EG2, Addis Ababa, 3 September 2019. As discussed in Chapter 9, however, attempts to define water releases in relation to inflows to the GERD reservoir have brought future Ethiopian dams into the purview of negotiations.

and flooding, regulate seasonal fluctuation in the Nile flow, and thereby enable increased irrigation and hydropower production from existing Sudanese dams. While any of the proposed dams would have benefitted Sudan in this way, the size and location of the GERD maximizes each of these benefits to Sudan. In contrast, one of Egypt's central concerns is that the GERD will enable Sudan to increase water utilization through a major expansion of irrigation, perhaps beyond its quota in the 1959 agreement (Tawfik 2016a). It may well have been that Meles recognized the potential of the GERD to split Egypt and Sudan in subsequent negotiations, further isolating Egypt in opposition to the dam. Indeed, this turned out to be the case once the Sudanese Government signalled its support for the GERD in March 2012 (Tekle 2012) and re-started participation in the NBI in 2013.[15]

A final geo-strategic advantage of the GERD site concerns its proximity to the Sudanese border. Egypt has threatened military action against upstream water infrastructure from Sadat in the 1970s through to leaked discussions by President Morsi's cabinet in 2013 (see Chapters 2 and 6). Indeed, Meles acknowledged the possibility of Egyptian military action:

> When we assess it scientifically, the risk of Egyptian invasion of Ethiopia is small. It is not zero. But it is very small. Thus, we should not lose sleep over a minor risk. However, as it is not zero, we should do our level best to be more prepared to meet this risk given our resources.[16]

For some observers, the strategic advantage of the GERD is that any attack on the completed dam would result in relatively little damage in Ethiopia, but catastrophic impacts on Sudan and potentially even Egypt as a result of the flood released downstream. As such, destroying the dam once it is complete and filled becomes unthinkable.[17] The antagonistic hydropolitics of the river basin therefore provide a strong rationale for focusing on the furthest downstream dam and the largest possible reservoir as a starting point for a Blue Nile cascade, contrary to the technically optimal solution for basin-wide water management. By doing so, Ethiopia is in the process of undermining Egypt's hydro-hegemony, while also strengthening its bargaining position with Egypt and Sudan regarding the dam's operation.

In addition to Nile hydropolitics, the GERD's design has also been fundamentally shaped by the top-down decision-making process that has driven Ethiopia's dams' boom and marginalized technical input into planning. While the GERD's

[15] This position was partially reversed after the 2019 military coup, after which the military returned the Sudanese position to its historic alignment with the Egyptians.

[16] YouTube (2013), minutes 14–20.

[17] One analysis of the potential failure of the GERD when full found that the resulting flood would put Khartoum under 10–15 metres of water and wash away all Sudanese dams on the river, potentially even threatening the High Aswan Dam (Soliman et al. 2019, p. 170). While the accuracy of these predictions is unknown, destroying the full dam is clearly an impossibility.

vast installed capacity and very low plant factor make it stand out in comparison to the earlier USBR and NBI studies, the GERD design is actually in keeping with that of other Ethiopian dams. As discussed in Chapters 3 and 4, decision making within the electricity sector was highly centralized under first Meles and then, after his death in 2012, Debretsion Gebremichael as deputy prime minister for the economy and chair of the board of EEP. Decisions on project design were largely made by these senior officials in discussion with Salini, which proposed many of the new projects, with limited input from technocrats in EEP or the Ministry of Water. Driven by Ethiopia's 'developmental state' ideology, which increasingly verged on high modernism, and the growing ambitions for rapid development that this demanded, the result has been something of a fixation on maximizing the installed capacity of individual dams and the electricity system, rather than considering the most efficient way of meeting a realistic assessment of future energy demand.

The same political elites that drove the national planning process towards ever more unrealistic targets were also responsible for selecting individual projects and pushing for the maximization of installed capacity, largely bypassing technical expertise in EEP and the Ministry of Water, Irrigation, and Energy (MoWIE). While MoWIE undertakes feasibility studies for hydropower projects and EEP uses these studies to propose a list of projects to meet ambitious development targets, the decisions to pursue Gilgel Gibe II, Gilgel Gibe III, Koysha, and the GERD were all taken by the Prime Minister's Office in discussion with Salini. These new projects were outside the plans developed by EEP and MoWIE, and the decision to proceed was made apparently without the knowledge of EEP leadership. While the secrecy surrounding the planning process for the GERD might explain the decision making for that project, respondents insisted that this process was typical of past projects also.[18] In the words of one former senior EEP official: 'the Prime Minister's Office and the contractor had made the decision on the project, so we have to accept it', whereas in EEP, 'we have no control'.[19]

Several respondents at MoWIE, EEP, and independent contractors reiterated the point that politicians repeatedly pressed them to increase the installed capacity of particular dams. One senior MoWIE official involved in the GERD lamented that

> in this country there is a misconception, they [politicians] look at the size in terms of megawatts and assume that big megawatts is what matters. There is this misconception amongst the politicians. [But b]y increasing the installed capacity they have just increased the unit cost of the energy.[20]

[18] Interviews EG2, senior official in the energy sector, Addis Ababa, 3 September 2019, 13 February 2020; EG8, senior official in the energy sector, Addis Ababa, 3 October 2019, 11 February 2020.
[19] Interview EG13, former energy sector official, Addis Ababa, 19 February 2020.
[20] Interview EG11, senior energy sector official, Addis Ababa, 21 February 2020.

Equally, a long-time contractor in the sector involved in several projects noted:

> The idea throughout was to maximize the megawatts of a single project ... The focus was on maximizing power generation—the installed capacity in megawatts. This was the decision of the highest levels.[21]

As Table 7.2 shows, the main hydropower projects undertaken during the EPRDF's dams' boom have been adapted from earlier feasibility studies that sought to meet requirements for baseload power and modest peak generation capacity, resulting in relatively high plant factors. In each case, the final design significantly increased the installed capacity of the dams, resulting in a series of projects with low plant factors. Indeed, most of Ethiopia's dams are able to produce energy at maximum capacity for little more than one-third of the time. Moreover, respondents were quite clear that in each case—for Gilgel Gibe III, Beles, Koysha, and the GERD[22]—this decision to increase installed capacity was made

Table 7.2 Details of key hydropower projects

	Installed capacity (MW)	Average energy generation (GWh)	Plant load factor (%)
Gilgel Gibe III (original design)[a]	1,200	6,500	62
Gilgel Gibe III (actual)	1,870	6,500	40
Beles (original design)[b]	220	998	52
Beles (actual)	460	1,720	43
Border Dam (NBI)[c]	1,200	6,011	57
GERD (original 2011 design)	5,250	15,692	34
Koysha (original design)[d]	1,472	6,460	50
Koysha (current design)	2,160	6,460	34

[a] Interview EG8, former senior energy sector official, Addis Ababa, 3 October 2019, 11 February 2020.
[b] Interview, consultant to the energy sector, by phone, 10 March 2020 and Acres International (2003, p. 37). Similarly, a 1989 study by Studio Pietrangeli commissioned as part of the Derg's Tana-Beles project proposed a 270-MW plant that would produce 1,860 gigawatt hours (GWh)/year with an 80 per cent plant factor (Studio Pietrangeli 1989).
[c] ENTRO (2007a, p. E3). It should be noted that since the Border Dam was to be part of a cascade, with upstream dams regulating the flow into the reservoir, it is not directly comparable with the GERD.
[d] As listed in the 2014 Power Sector Masterplan (Parsons Brinckerhoff 2014, pp. 4–9).
Data source: USAID (2019), except where otherwise specified in table notes.

[21] Interview EP12, private contractor in the energy sector, by phone, 20 November 2019, 16 February 2020.

[22] Interviews EG8, former senior energy sector official, Addis Ababa, 3 October 2019, 11 February 2020; EP14, member of the original feasibility study team, by phone, 10 March 2020; EP12, private contractor in the energy sector, by phone, 20 November 2019, 16 February 2020; and EG11, senior official in the energy sector, Addis Ababa, 21 February 2020.

by the political leadership. At points the focus on maximizing installed capacity has been questioned by contractors and consultants to the sector. One recalled asking,

> Why do you want so much installed capacity? They said, 'we want to be the power supply of Africa'. That's their vision. They always wanted the maximum installed capacity possible. Is that a good decision? Time will tell. I cannot blame the decision. I struggled with them several times, but I didn't convince them![23]

Indeed, there is no doubt that technical officials were aware of the limitations of the dam designs, with several current and former officials in EEP and MoWIE highlighting these issues. As one foreign consultant noted, 'EEPCo [the Ethiopian Electric Power Company] people must know, but they decided not to say anything'.[24] Indeed, EEP officials were clear that they understood the limitations but that, in a situation in which power was highly centralized amongst a political elite, there was little space for technical input into decision making. One official recalled that 'the technical people tried to resist but they were strongly pushed to accept'.[25] While the political centralization of decision-making power meant that technocrats had limited leeway, it is also important to acknowledge the complexities of their position. Politicians' demands for ever higher installed capacity targets translated into the massive investment of resources and prestige in EEP, in particular through the pursuit of high-profile megaprojects. Furthermore, inflated targets for installed capacity were included in the annual performance assessments for relevant MoWIE and EEP officials.[26] The result is that inflating the installed capacity of a particular dam would have helped technocrats make progress towards their challenging performance targets, undermining the incentive to resist political pressure. As such, there would have been strong personal and career incentives for senior officials in EEP and MoWIE to go along with politicians' plans, and senior technocrats' retrospective claims to have resisted should perhaps be viewed with some caution.

In terms of the specific process leading to the GERD, the selection of the Border site as the preferred option on the Nile was based on a proposal by Salini, which by now was well accustomed to the government's preferences. According to one participant in the Project X discussions,

> Meles called Salini and requested for a project on the Nile. We didn't think that the Border Dam was important enough to engage on as it was only 1,200 MW. It was

[23] Interview EP13, consultant to the energy sector, by phone, 26 November 2019.
[24] Interview EP14, consultant to the energy sector, by phone, 10 March 2020.
[25] Interview EG8, former senior energy sector official, Addis Ababa, 3 October 2019, 11 February 2020.
[26] Interviews EG2, senior official in the energy sector, Addis Ababa, 3 September 2019, 13 February 2020; EG12, official in the energy sector, Addis Ababa, 14 February 2020.

> relatively small, so was not in our thoughts. We rather were more interested in the upper dams, with higher generation capacities, such as Beko Abo and Mandaya. But Salini suggested that a saddle dam could be used to increase the generation at the site of the Border Dam from 1,200 to 5,000 MW.[27]

Indeed, this chimes with statements made by Meles also, who argued that the Border site was chosen because it is the only available site at which an installed capacity of 5,250 MW would be possible.[28] Moreover, another official centrally involved in the GERD project stated that Salini originally proposed two options for the GERD, with the government—as had consistently been the case with other dams—choosing the one with higher installed capacity and lower plant factor:

> With the GERD there was a preliminary design proposed by the contractor, Salini. In that they gave two options—3,500 megawatts or 5,250 megawatts.[29]

A dam of 3,500-MW capacity would have been broadly in keeping with estimates of an optimal size for the GERD provided by several experts interviewed for this research and would have resulted in a plant factor of approximately 49 per cent, reflecting a balance of baseload and peaking power. In contrast, the choice of 5,250 MW and the subsequent increase in installed capacity exemplified the over-ambition of politicians in the electricity sector and the bypassing of technical inputs into decision making.

As noted earlier, the GERD's design has evolved in important respects since 2011, in particular regarding the installed capacity which was increased still further on two separate occasions. A particularly important factor in these changes was the decision to sub-contract the electro-mechanical work for the dam to the military-owned Metals and Engineering Corporation (MetEC). Salini was initially contracted for the entire GERD project, which would have required Salini to sub-contract the electro-mechanical work. As with Gibe III, however, the government subsequently revised the contract in November 2011, removing the electro-mechanical work from Salini's contract and contracting MetEC in its place.[30] The central motivation for this change was the government's desire to build domestic capacity in line with its 'developmental state' agenda. To this end, the government sought to negotiate with international turbine manufacturers to facilitate a joint venture arrangement with MetEC to enable technology transfer and learning, but to no avail.[31] However, an additional motivation for turning to MetEC was the fear that international companies contracted for the dam might be

[27] Interview EG13, senior official in the energy sector, Addis Ababa, 21 August 2019.
[28] See Meles' interview with ETV (in Amharic) (YouTube 2011).
[29] Interview EG11, senior official in the energy sector, Addis Ababa, 21 February 2020.
[30] Interview EP13, senior consultant involved in the project, by phone, 26 November 2019.
[31] Interviews EP8 and EP9, international consultants involved in the project, by phone, 10 October 2019.

pressured to drop their involvement by Egypt and their allies. Debretsion, deputy prime minister after Meles' death, was clear in highlighting government concerns:

> had we decided to put a foreign company in charge of this project, the challenges we could have faced would be unimaginable. For one, given the nature of the project, the level of diplomatic pressure we could have been subjected to, would be quite considerable. We had no guarantee that foreign contractors would carry out the work in the face of intense diplomatic pressure from their governments and other countries. Worst case scenario, they could have abandoned the project midway. (Anberbir 2017, n.p.)

MetEC was at the centre of both increases in the installed capacity of the dam, further reducing the plant factor. The original design for the dam announced in 2011 had a capacity of 5,250 MW, with 15 turbines each rated at 350 MW. In March 2012 the installed capacity was increased to 6,000 MW—with the addition of one turbine and the upgrading of all 16 turbines to 375 MW. Then in 2017 generation capacity was further raised to 6,350 MW—by upgrading 14 of the 16 turbines from 375 MW to 400 MW.[32] The first increase to 6,000 MW in March 2012 occurred in the final months of Meles' life and could only have taken place with Meles' approval. The reason for this increase is unclear, though Debretsion subsequently claimed that it was based on a study by MetEC (McDubus 2016). Meles' approval for the increase came despite the fact that he had earlier stated that an initial design of more than 6,000 MW was rejected based on the cost and time required.[33] This new design was imposed by the Prime Minister's Office on EEP—in theory, the owner of the project—in the face of opposition from at least some of the key technical people managing the construction, leading to the removal of several from the project, including the current head engineer who was only reinstated several years later (see Chapter 9). One former EEP official noted:

> The technical people tried to resist but they were strongly pushed to accept. When the proposal to raise GERD from 5,250 to 6,000 megawatts was made there was a big complaint from EEP, with some managers removed as a result.[34]

The second increase involved raising the installed capacity from 6,000 MW to 6,350 MW by upgrading most of the turbines. This change took place in February 2017, several years after Meles' death and at a time when Deputy Prime Minister

[32] After 2017 the installed capacity of the GERD was frequently cited in the press and by some government officials to be 6,450 MW (Deputy Prime Minister Debretsion, cited in Anberbir 2017; Tadesse 2019; Embassy of Ethiopia n.d.; IHA n.d.). This does not ever appear to have been the case, however. At its maximum, the dam was to have had 14 turbines rated at 400 MW and two rated at 375 MW, giving a total of 6,350 MW.

[33] See interview on YouTube (2011).

[34] Interview EG8, former senior EEP official, Addis Ababa, 3 October 2019, 11 February 2020.

Debretsion had assumed a central role in the electricity sector. Comments made by Debretsion attribute both the changes to studies and innovations by MetEC, with these 'improvements' to the dam held up explicitly as 'the fruit of recruiting local partners' (Debretsion, cited in Anberbir 2017, n.p.). Debretsion, who had enormous influence over the electricity sector given his positions as deputy prime minister for the economy, chair of the EEP board, and member of the GERD board, took credit for convincing the rest of the government to go ahead with the changes (Champion and Manek 2019). Debretsion is also reported to have had close links with the military leadership, including senior figures in MetEC, while the director-general of MetEC, Major General Kinfe Dagnew, was also a member of the EEP board while EEP was, in theory, overseeing MetEC's delivery of its work on the GERD and approving its plans to expand the installed capacity.

Yet key officials in EEP and those overseeing the GERD itself have never seen the studies supposedly carried out by MetEC to justify the increase in installed capacity, while no technical expert interviewed for this research could offer any reasonable explanation for adding generation capacity to an original design that was already considered excessive. The design changes merely added unnecessary capacity to the dam at significant additional cost. Indeed, ironically, the involvement of MetEC—intended to build Ethiopia's capacity to carry out large infrastructure projects—actually served to marginalize further the technical capacity that already existed within EEP.

The decision to choose the GERD as Ethiopia's first dam on the Blue Nile was made by Meles and his exact reasoning was lost with his death. However, the clearest explanation for the GERD's design lies not in the technical calculations regarding the costs and benefits of different dams but in the political processes analysed over previous chapters, namely the political pressure to deliver a series of ever larger dams to meet the EPRDF's developmental ambitions and the antagonistic relations between the Nile riparians.

Conclusion

This chapter reinforces a point commonly made in the literature, namely that dam design—on the Nile, as with any other river—is far from a purely technical process, but is necessarily shaped by politics, and the needs and priorities of those making proposals. Over the past century there have been repeated initiatives to build a dam on the Blue Nile, with the Ethiopian highlands seen to offer important advantages for river basin management. Yet in each case, from British colonialists promoting cotton production in Egypt to the NBI's benefit-sharing rationale, these dam proposals and their distribution of benefits failed to align with the prevailing constellation of political forces. In contrast, the GERD follows in a line of unilateral dam building on the Nile that can be traced back at least as far as the High

Aswan Dam. Decades earlier, the Egyptian Government veered away from river basin planning, pursuing the High Aswan Dam based on Egypt's desire to consolidate its control of the Nile waters and insulate Egypt from the rest of the river basin. Likewise, whatever its technical strengths and limitations, the GERD can be best understood as an attempt to wrest control back to Ethiopia, while insulating Ethiopia against Egypt's inevitable opposition to the dam.

The GERD's design is the product of these adversarial relations in the Nile Basin and Ethiopia's developmental ambitions that prioritized expansion of installed capacity over technical expertise. The centralization of decision-making power among a few key figures in the Ethiopian Government was essential to the dams' boom and the launch of the GERD, but it was also responsible for many of the inefficiencies in electricity planning and dam design. Clearly, Meles' single-minded focus over many years on a Blue Nile dam and his centralization of power were vitally important in the mobilization of the Ethiopian state and people to build the GERD. Yet the centralization of power and the secretive nature of the decision-making process directly contributed to the marginalization of technical expertise and the decision to give free rein to MetEC, which lacked the expertise required to carry out such a challenging project.

8

Electrifying Ethiopia, Consolidating Power

The Challenge of Distributing Electricity

Tom Lavers and Fana Gebresenbet

The Ethiopian Peoples' Revolutionary Democratic Front's (EPRDF's) dams boom has resulted in a major expansion of generation capacity, whatever the limitations of the planning and design process. Moreover, the eventual completion of the Grand Ethiopian Renaissance Dam (GERD) and Koysha will massively enhance this capacity. As argued in Chapters 3 and 4, this dam-building strategy was undertaken as part of a national development strategy tasked not only with socioeconomic development but also with securing the political position of the ruling party. Hydroelectric dams were expected to support industrialization, initially through rural-based industrialization and latterly concentrated in urban industrial parks, to secure popular compliance through mass electricity access and to boost foreign exchange earnings through electricity exports. Meanwhile, fundraising for the GERD not only exploited nationalist sentiment but also cultivated the expectation of imminent mass access to electricity in exchange for financial contributions towards the dam's construction. The challenge facing the EPRDF therefore was not just expanding generation capacity but also ensuring that hydroelectricity reached key users.

On taking power in 1991, the transmission and distribution infrastructure was woefully inadequate.[1] At that time, the electric grid was focused primarily on Addis Ababa, while electricity access in rural areas, where the majority of Ethiopia's population lived, was almost non-existent. The World Bank estimated that only 4 per cent of the population had an electric connection in 1996, while Ethiopia's per capita electricity consumption was 'among the lowest in the world' (World Bank 1996, pp. i, 3). The challenge of electricity distribution was enhanced by the EPRDF's almost exclusive focus on hydropower, which resulted in a series of ever larger dams located primarily in the south and west of the country in locations where there is very little demand for electricity. Moreover, low rates of

[1] An electric grid comprises high-voltage transmission lines used for long-distance transmission from sources of generation to major centres of demand and low-voltage distribution lines to supply electricity to end users. Sub-stations step down the electricity from high to low voltage.

Dams, Power, and the Politics of Ethiopia's Renaissance. Tom Lavers et al., Oxford University Press. © Tom Lavers and Fana Gebresenbet (2024). DOI: 10.1093/oso/9780192871213.003.0008

urbanization and the government's initial focus on rural-based industrialization meant that expanding popular and industrial access required a massive grid expansion across national territory, much of which is extremely mountainous. The result is that realization of the government's political-economic objectives for the electricity sector confronted a transmission and distribution challenge just as daunting as that of expanding generation.

The burden of grid expansion was one that fell solely on the shoulders of the state as a result of the state-hydropower model envisaged for the sector. As argued in Chapter 3, the government's strategy was based on massive state investment in hydropower that, in the long run, would provide relatively cheap electricity, enabling low tariffs to support industry and mass consumption. In doing so, low tariffs removed any incentives for private sector investment. Moreover, subsidized tariffs meant limited electricity revenues, constraining the resources available for investment in generation, transmission, and distribution. The government's ability to realize its objectives for the electricity sector were, in turn, shaped by the political prioritization of: electricity relative to other vital sectors; spending on generation relative to transmission and distribution within the electricity sector; the spatial distribution of the grid in the context of a federal system that increasingly politicized competition between ethnic regions; and, finally, in a context in which growth in demand often outstripped supply, between electricity supplies for industry, export markets, and domestic consumers.

This chapter examines how the EPRDF wrestled with these challenges and assesses the extent to which it succeeded in realizing its political-economic goals. On the face of it, the government was very successful. As the World Bank (2019a) noted in a recent study, under the EPRDF, the government 'launched one of the most successful electrification programs in Sub-Saharan Africa, expanding the grid to nearly 60 percent of the country—from only 667 towns and villages to approximately 6000'. Moreover, a series of eco-industrial parks and a hydroelectric-powered railway have been promoted as a model of sustainable development. Digging beneath the surface, however, provides a more mixed picture in which important progress was undermined by poor planning and political pressures. Indeed, in many respects the challenges of distributing electricity are similar to those that undermined the planning and implementation of generation, discussed in previous chapters. First, grid expansion was based on politically determined targets that led to problematic decisions to focus on transmission lines to towns and villages, but not actual connections to households. Meanwhile, massive investment in generation capacity meant that resources for transmission and distribution lagged behind, to the detriment of reliable provision. Second, overambition and political fragmentation undermined efforts to provide electricity to new industrial parks, constituting a major barrier to efforts to promote foreign investment. Third, the goal of large-scale electricity exports remains dependent on demand from countries in the region, many of whom share Ethiopia's goal of becoming an energy exporter, while those in the Nile Basin are caught up in the politically fraught negotiations regarding the GERD's operation. Consequently, despite major progress, the EPRDF ultimately failed to realize any of its key objectives of using electricity to support industrialization or mass access, or to boost foreign exchange earnings.

The chapter begins by focusing on electricity tariffs, which have long been a subject of contention and an entry point for a broader debate between the government, donors, and other critics about electricity sector governance. For the government, low tariffs were key means of subsidizing industrial and mass consumption. However, to do so required a massive expansion of the electric grid to bring new hydropower production to dispersed industrial and domestic consumers. The next section therefore examines the government's efforts to realize universal electrification. The chapter then considers regional inequality in electricity access, a topic that has become increasingly politicized as a result of the growing salience of ethnicity in Ethiopian politics. Partly in response to the challenges of universalization efforts, from the mid-2010s the government changed its industrial strategy in an attempt to accelerate structural transformation. New industrial parks were intended to concentrate infrastructural development in specific locations to integrate Ethiopia into global circuits of production. The following section examines efforts to supply the industrial parks with reliable electricity supplies in a context of growing political fragmentation. The final section turns to exports, showing how international negotiations and infrastructure development have failed to keep pace with the government's characteristically huge ambitions for turning electricity into foreign exchange earnings.

Subsidizing Development through Electricity

Ever since the EPRDF came into office, the government and donors have been involved in a struggle regarding the electricity sector, with two competing visions of how the sector should be run. Tariffs have constituted a central point of contention. For the government, the sector should be integrated under state ownership, using tariffs to subsidize key priorities in line with the government's political and economic objectives: notably industry and mass consumption, particularly for the rural population (see Chapter 3). Indeed, for the government, state ownership and subsidized tariffs were essential precisely because necessary investment in grid expansion would not be considered economically viable by private investors.

Donors, among whom the World Bank has been particularly vocal and influential, have contested the government's approach on both ideological grounds and in relation to its claims to be promoting equality. For opponents, state subsidies lead to inefficient electricity usage by customers and inefficient production by producers, as well as starving the state of resources for investment and favouring wealthier groups that are more likely to have electricity connections and use more electricity (Cardenas and Whittington 2019). Instead, the World Bank has repeatedly pushed for cost-reflective tariffs and an end to state subsidies, enabling state utilities to fund investment from their own revenues. The financial independence of state corporations would be the first step towards allowing the private sector to compete with state entities in generation, and ultimately distribution and transmission, with the end point being the Standard Model of electricity sector governance (see Chapter 1). While the World Bank occasionally secured limited concessions from the government at moments of fiscal weakness and as a condition for external support, ultimately its pressure for reform was resisted.

By the mid-1990s, there had been no adjustment in electricity tariffs since 1986, when the Derg was in power, with the result that tariffs had fallen to around half the cost of generating and distributing electricity (World Bank 1996). With the government heavily dependent on donor support at this time, it was forced to negotiate with the World Bank regarding reforms as part of its efforts to secure finance for the Gilgel Gibe I dam (see Chapter 3). In 1996, along with the corporatization of the state electric utility, the government agreed to a 60 per cent increase in electricity tariffs over five years, with the aim of strengthening the finances of the newly created Ethiopian Electric Power Company (EEPCo). However, this compromise fell well short of the World Bank's desire to move towards cost-reflective tariffs that would lead to 'the elimination of all subsidies', enabling EEPCo to operate as a corporate entity (World Bank 1997, p. 5). As a World Bank document at the time stated,

> While most welcome, the tariff increase, especially in its first phase (20%), represents only slow progress toward meeting economic and financial requirements. The average first phase tariff of Birr 0.23/kWh is only 50% of LRMC [long-run marginal cost] while, even at the end of the scheduled five year implementation period, the average tariff of Birr 0.33/kWh would be no more than 72% of LRMC. Larger and more rapid tariff increases are required if the tariff is to do its economic job of guiding overall consumption and allocating it to the most efficient uses, and its vital financial job of mobilizing adequate domestic resources for investment in the sector. (World Bank 1996, p. iv)

However, the government did not fully implement even these modest changes. There was a one-off increase in the late 1990s, but no subsequent increases were implemented from 1999 until 2006, leading the World Bank to repeatedly signal its concern about EEPCo's financial position (World Bank 2006b). This tariff freeze only changed when the government again approached the World Bank for financial support for a major electrification project in 2005 (discussed in the following section). In return for World Bank support, the government implemented a 22 per cent tariff increase in 2006 and signalled its acceptance that 'further tariff adjustments will be required over the next several years' (World Bank 2006c, p. 4). However, having secured World Bank funding and despite its promises, the government subsequently refused further tariff increases, leading the Bank to rate the government's project performance as 'Moderately Unsatisfactory' (World Bank 2013, p. 25). Indeed, with declining dependence on the World Bank after 2005, it would be another 13 years, until the demise of the EPRDF, before tariffs would again be increased (see Chapter 9). It is hard to avoid drawing the conclusion that the government only agreed to modest concessions to secure World Bank finance, and that it never had any intention of a significant move towards cost-reflective tariffs or the World Bank's Standard Model. Instead, EEPCo relied on state subsidies and debt accumulation to finance massive infrastructural investments in generation and distribution. Much to the World Bank's frustration, but in line with the government's political-economic strategy, by 2018, the 'average domestic tariff rate, last revised in 2006, sits at US$0.03 per kWh, one of the lowest in Sub-Saharan Africa' and well below the cost-reflective level, estimated at $0.07–0.08 per kWh (World Bank 2018a, p. 3).

While the main point of contention with the World Bank concerned average tariffs, it should be noted that the government adopted differential tariffs for different users. In line with the government's priorities, domestic consumers using very small amounts of electricity and industrial users with high-voltage supplies paid the lowest tariffs, while high-usage domestic and commercial users paid the most (see Figure 8.1). Nonetheless, Cardenas and Whittington's (2019, p. 791) study of Addis Ababa found that the richest quintile of the population received 37 per cent of the total subsidy to the electricity sector while the poorest received just 7 per cent (see also World Bank 2015). Despite the attempt to support low-income households, overall high-income groups benefited most because all users were subsidized and high-income groups use the most electricity. Furthermore, prices did not vary between rural and urban locations, despite the fact that grid extension and maintenance in rural areas make the cost of distribution much higher.

The government's ambition of turning Ethiopia's hydropower industry into a major source of electricity exports from the mid-2000s onwards is also relevant here. While political and economic priorities necessitated low tariffs for domestic users, there remained potential for export tariffs to be negotiated at much higher levels, providing valuable revenue that could go some way towards offsetting loss-making domestic provision. Electricity exports and tariffs are discussed later in this chapter.

Ultimately, the EPRDF managed to resist pressure from the World Bank to revise its electricity tariffs, a change that would have endangered key political

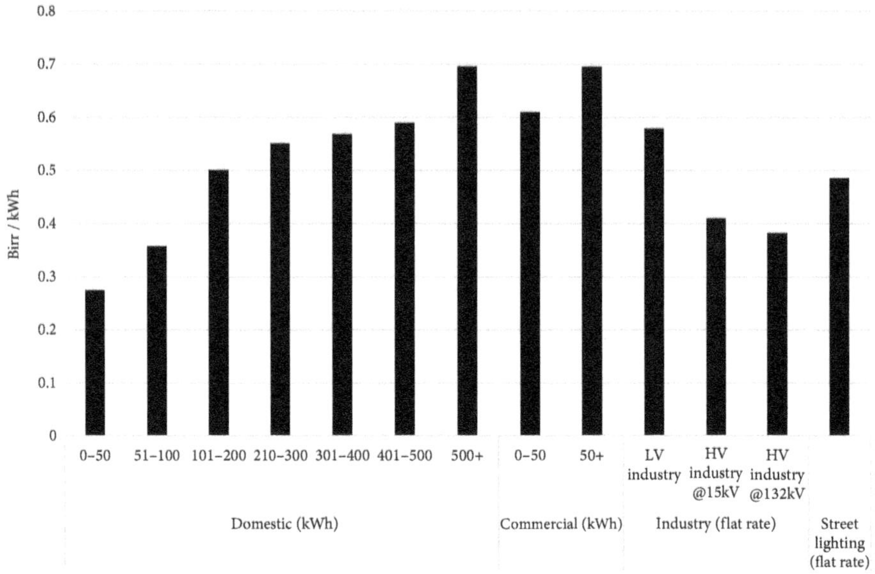

Figure 8.1 Electricity tariffs in 2016
Data source: Author based on Beyene (2018, p. 42).

and economic objectives and entailed a fundamentally different approach to governing the sector. The result, however, was that massive state investment in the context of limited revenues meant massive accumulation of debt in state electric companies.

Distributing Hydropower, Delivering Development

For a government seeking to use hydropower to provide mass access to electricity for a predominantly rural population, as well as to promote largely rural-based industry, a massive expansion of the electric grid was essential. The main part of the Ethiopian electric grid is the interconnected system (ICS), which in 1991 was focused on Addis Ababa and the Rift Valley as far as Dire Dawa, and was supplied by the five hydropower plants built under Haile Selassie and the Derg (Figure 8.2). In addition, there were a number of self-contained systems (SCSs), which consisted of small power plants—either diesel-powered or hydroelectric—supplying particular towns, separate from the main grid. By 1993, there were 25 SCSs. The largest, comprising Tis Abay I and Bahir Dar, was integrated into the main grid in 1994 (World Bank 1996, p. 41).

From very early on, the new government signalled its desire to expand access through the grid. In particular, the EPRDF launched the Ethiopia National Rural Electrification Project (ENREP) in the 1990s with the goal of doubling the

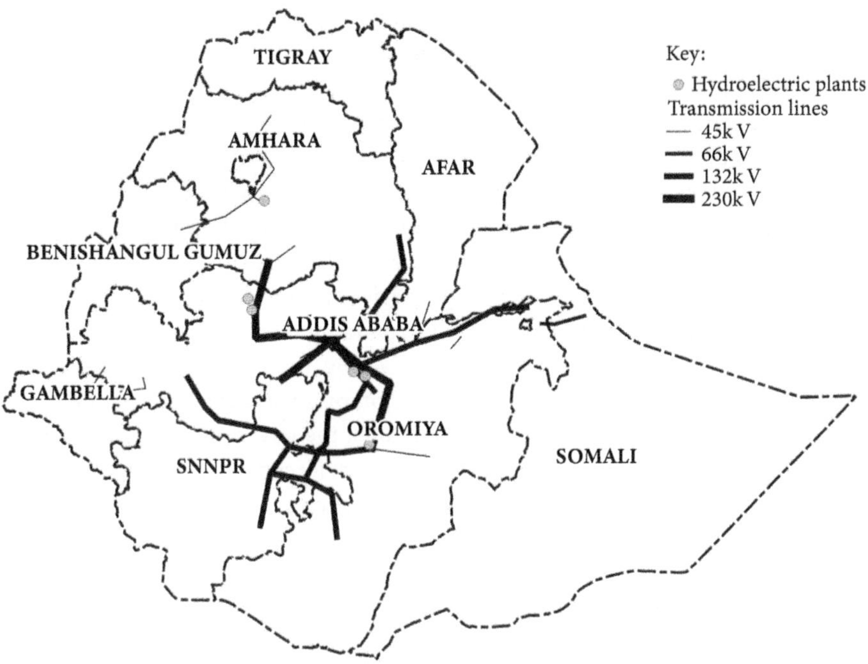

Figure 8.2 Ethiopian electric grid in 1991
Source: Author and Manchester Cartographic Unit.

connected population by 2011 (World Bank 1996). Compared to later plans, this was a relatively modest goal that would be outpaced by the rate of population growth, leading to a declining proportion of the population with an electric connection. However, progress towards even this modest goal during the 1990s was slow. One challenge was limited generation capacity, which made it difficult to expand access when supplies were insufficient for existing customers. Moreover, a major barrier was the shortage of domestic resources and the government's reliance on international donors such as the World Bank, which were promoting an altogether different model for the sector. Indeed, the World Bank's focus on eliminating subsidies and promoting financial sustainability was directly at odds with the government's goal of expanding rural grid connections. Given the dispersed population, the high cost of grid expansion, low tariffs, and low electricity demand from each user, expanding access could never be justified from a purely economic perspective. The Bank was explicit in arguing that

> prudent management requires EELPA [Ethiopian Electric Light and Power Authority] to proceed slowly with the expansion of rural services where every consumer connected and kWh sold leads to a worsening of the utility's financial position. (World Bank 1996, p. vii)

The political crises of the early 2000s resulted in important changes for transmission and distribution, as with generation. In the wake of the 2001 split in the Tigrayan People's Liberation Front (TPLF), urban protests, and the 2005 elections, the government redoubled its efforts to promote structural transformation and mass service delivery as a means of securing popular acquiescence (Lavers 2023). Electricity distribution was a central requirement for each of these priorities. At this point, the government's Agricultural Development-Led Industrialization (ADLI) strategy prioritized agricultural development and rural-based industry to process agricultural products and supply agricultural producers (MoFED 2002, 2003; MoI 2002a). As such, the goals of expanding electric supplies to support industry and irrigated agriculture and delivering mass electricity access were largely compatible through a general expansion of the electric grid. As the economy began a period of rapid growth from 2004, the government could draw on increased domestic resources and autonomy from foreign donors to invest in the electricity sector. Furthermore, as major projects such as Gilgel Gibe II and Tekeze began operation, there was greater space for new connections thanks to increased supply.

The first step towards grid expansion was the Rural Electrification Project launched as part of the Sustainable Development and Poverty Reduction Programme (SDPRP) in 2002, which aimed at electrifying 164 *wereda* towns and prioritized achieving equality in electricity access between regions (MoFED 2002, p. 63). However, these plans were massively expanded in 2005 in the wake of the elections that year with the announcement of the Universal Electrification Access Programme (UEAP). By 2005, still only 6 per cent of the population had an electric connection and 15 per cent lived in areas with an electricity supply (World Bank 2006c, p. 2). The UEAP aimed to expand electricity access to 50 per cent of the population by connecting 6,000 towns to the grid within five years and virtually every town and village in the country by 2015 (World Bank 2005a). The programme was initially launched with government resources. However, having negotiated a modest tariff increase and promised further rises, the government secured two World Bank loans to the tune of $263 million (World Bank 2006c, 2007a).[2] Additional financial support for UEAP was subsequently secured from the African Development Bank, Kuwait Fund, the Arab Bank for Economic Development in Africa (BADEA), and the Indian Government.

Respondents report that officials in the Ministry and EEPCo spent quite some time discussing different definitions of electricity access that would be used to measure the programme's performance, ultimately settling on the comparatively lesser challenge of electrifying towns, rather than individual connections:

[2] The loan agreements state that government commitments to the programme amounted to $92 million.

> there are different ways of reporting access. The tendency was to say that if there is a line passing within 10 kilometres of a household then they have theoretical access, they can pay to get connected.[3]

Despite the pro-poor narrative of government policy, this decision effectively prioritized productive activities—particularly irrigation and small manufacturing in line with ADLI—and social services, rather than individual users (World Bank 2005a). As one official underscored,

> In the 2005 UEAP the target was not really connections, it was reaching the centre of the town ... Our aim was to focus on productive uses. Once you reach the town, people can ask for connections for water pumps, grinding mills, schools, clinics. This was our top priority, not individuals. Once you have done this, the people can benefit.[4]

A central challenge was that government resources were severely constrained and there simply was not enough money to cover the huge additional expense of connecting households en masse, especially since most would use relatively little electricity and therefore generate little revenue.[5] Instead, the government began with the optimistic view that once a town was connected to the grid, 40 per cent of households would pay to connect within one year and an additional 10 per cent each year until connection rates reached 70–75 per cent (World Bank 2006c, pp. 4–5).

In certain respects, UEAP was hugely successful. The programme spearheaded a major expansion of transmission and distribution lines to previously unconnected areas, with the total length of transmission lines more than trebling, albeit progress was, perhaps unsurprisingly, slower than the hugely optimistic targets in national development plans (Figures 8.3 and 8.4). More than 5,000 additional towns and villages were connected to the grid by 2010[6] and electricity access, measured by the percentage of people living within 10 kilometres of the grid, increased to 60 per cent by 2015 (Figure 8.5). This massive grid expansion also led to a trebling of the number of domestic, commercial, and industrial customers (Figure 8.6) and a massive increase in energy consumption (Figure 8.7). However, the optimistic prediction that large numbers of households would quickly connect to the grid as soon as a town was connected proved unfounded (Figure 8.5). Instead, connection rates lagged far behind access rates, with an estimated 21 per cent of households

[3] Interview EG2, senior energy sector official, Addis Ababa, 3 September 2019, 13 February 2020.
[4] Interview EG2, senior energy sector official, Addis Ababa, 3 September 2019, 13 February 2020.
[5] Interview EG2, senior energy sector official, Addis Ababa, 3 September 2019, 13 February 2020.
[6] Interview EG19, UEAP official, Addis Ababa, 1 October 2019.

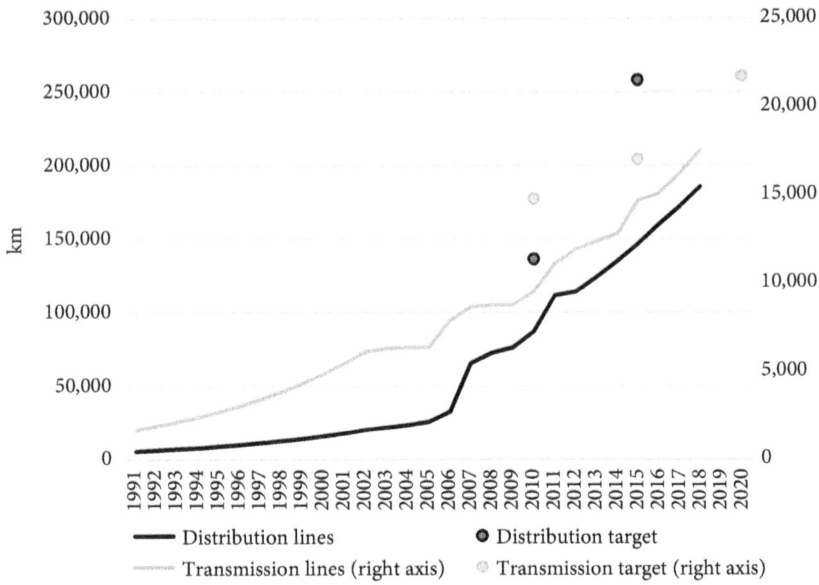

Figure 8.3 Length of transmission and distribution lines

Data source: Author based on EEP and EEU data, MoFED (2002), MoFED (2005), MoFED (2010), and NPC (2016).

having a registered grid connection by 2017 (MoWIE 2019, p. xvii).[7] The result, as one UEAP official underscored, was that despite the huge investment connect towns and villages, very few connections were made:

> Only 20–30 per cent of the population [in electrified areas] used electricity. We would construct 70–80-kilometre medium-voltage lines, low-voltage lines for 14–15 kilometres but then there would be less than 50 customers![8]

There are many reasons for the UEAP's limitations, both in terms of the slower-than-hoped-for progress with access and the modest progress with electricity connections. Foremost among these is that despite growing attention to grid expansion after 2000, this continued to pale in comparison to the political emphasis placed on expanding generation. The result was that finance for transmission and distribution remained limited. EEPCo's planned investment from 2006/7 to

[7] Many households have informally connected to those with registered connections, a practice known as meter loading. In 2017, 33 per cent of the population received electricity from the grid, including those with informal connections. An additional 11 per cent had some access to off-grid electricity, mainly solar lanterns and small solar home systems, many of which were insufficient to provide a minimum service of four hours per day (MoWIE 2019).

[8] Interview EG18, UEAP official, Addis Ababa, 3 October 2019.

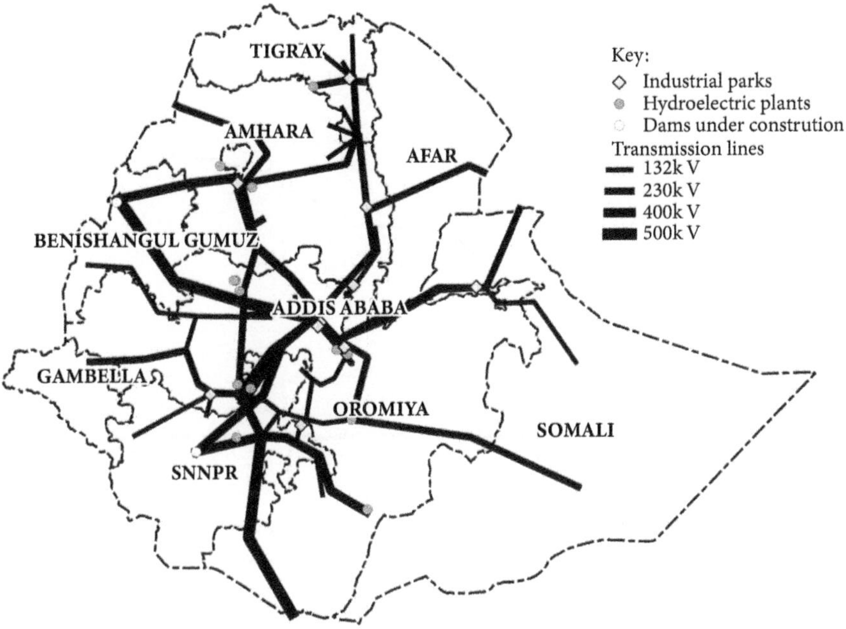

Figure 8.4 Ethiopian electric grid in 2019

Source: Author and Manchester Cartographic Unit.

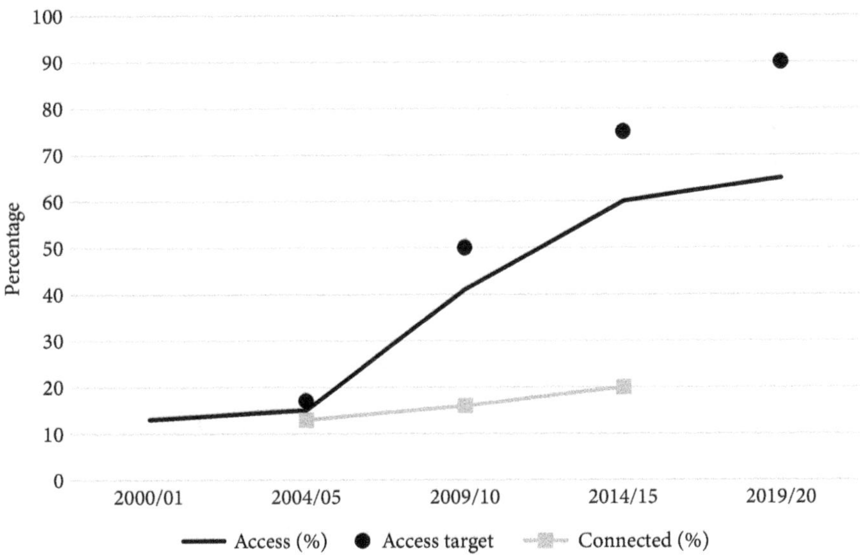

Figure 8.5 Electricity access and connection rates

Data source: Author based on MoFED (2002), MoFED (2005), MoFED (2010), NPC (2016), and MoWIE (2017).

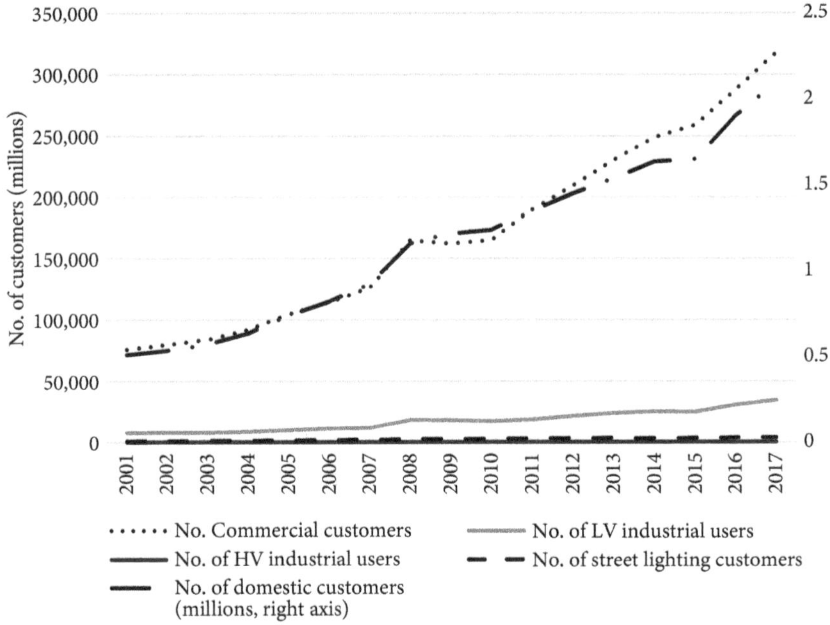

Figure 8.6 Number of electricity customers by type of user

Data source: Author based on USAID and PowerAfrica (2018).

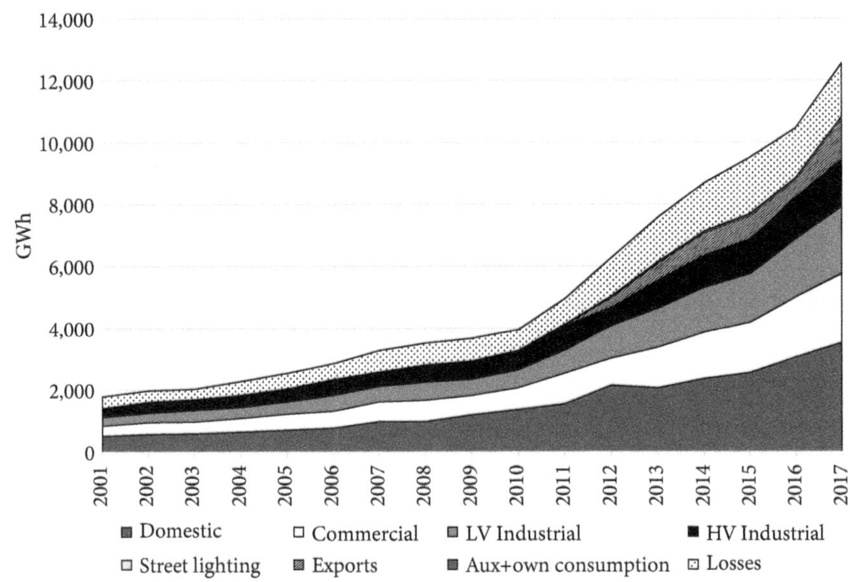

Figure 8.7 Electricity generated by end purpose

Data source: Author based on USAID and PowerAfrica (2018).

2015/16 allocated 68 per cent of resources to generation, while transmission, distribution, and UEAP combined received just 22 per cent (World Bank 2007b, p. 36). As one senior official at the time noted,

> The logic of investing in generation at the time was 'we will do that [transmission and distribution] at a later stage'. The task of building dams was seen as the burden of generations ... [while those responsible for the grid] were starved of resources. Every cent went into new generation, that was the priority.[9]

One result of this prioritization is the neglect of maintenance of the existing grid, leading to large-scale losses in transmission and distribution. Government plans repeatedly highlight transmission losses of some 20 per cent, with ambitious goals for reducing these to minimal levels within five years. However, to date there has been little progress. Moreover, many believe that these estimated losses may significantly underestimate the problem. According to some sources, Ethiopian Electric Utility (EEU) has unofficially acknowledged distribution losses as high as 40 per cent of supply.[10] The result has been that even with the major increase in generation capacity since the mid-2000s, the transmission infrastructure was unable to support this increased supply, with sub-stations often overloaded at times of peak demand (MoWIE 2017, 2019). Indeed, by 2018 when installed capacity had reached more than 4,200 megawatts (MW), well-placed respondents estimated that the 'substations and transformers could [only] support some 2,500 MW'.[11] The limited availability of electricity was compounded by periodic reductions in hydroelectric generation capacity due to drought. Notably, in 2008/9 severe drought reduced hydropower generation, leading the government to impose a moratorium on new electric connections in 2009–2010, slowing the pace of UEAP. This moratorium was only removed once Tekeze, Gilgel Gibe II, and Beles were operational (World Bank 2013, pp. 5–6).

The political emphasis placed on generation rather than transmission or distribution is also evident in the governance of the sector. Before 2013, EEPCo was an integrated utility responsible for generation, transmission, and distribution. In practice, however, multiple respondents confirmed that EEPCo's priorities reflected those of the political leadership in focusing on generation and high-profile dams.[12] In 2013, EEPCo was divided into Ethiopian Electric Power (EEP), responsible for generation and transmission lines of 66 kilovolts (kV) and above, and the EEU, responsible for lines less than 66kV, including individual connections. EEPCo's division served to exacerbate existing financial and staffing

[9] Interview EG2, senior energy sector official, Addis Ababa, 3 September 2019, 13 February 2020.
[10] Interview ED10, donor representative, Addis Ababa, 6 June 2019.
[11] Interviews EG2, senior energy sector official, Addis Ababa, 3 September 2019, 13 February 2020; ED1, donor representative, Addis Ababa, 3 June 2019; and MoWIE (2019).
[12] Interview EG21, EEU official, Bahir Dar, 10 March 2020.

problems, and resulted in increased coordination challenges. When the companies were split, Debretsion Gebremichael, then deputy prime minister and chair of the EEPCo board (see Chapter 4), made the decision to divide revenues for the electricity sector according to an apparently arbitrary formula and without consultation with sector officials, with 60 per cent going to EEP and 40 per cent to EEU. Despite their separation, the two new firms have never adequately separated their infrastructure and lack the meters to accurately measure how much electricity is passed from EEP to EEU. The consequence is that both utilities complain that they are starved of resources.[13]

Staffing and management have been an additional challenge, particularly for EEU. Given the political prioritization of major dam projects managed by EEP, when the two firms split,

> the big boys all moved to EEP. They had the incentives there, the big projects, the study abroad. EEU was left without someone to fight for them.[14]

Debretsion's initial response was to contract out EEU management to Power Grid Corporation, an Indian firm, for two years.[15] Having used a similar, and apparently successful, management arrangement for Ethiopian Telecommunications,[16] Debretsion's plan appears to have been to strengthen management with outside expertise while training Ethiopian staff to gradually take over operations. The experience is uniformly regarded as a disaster by government and donor officials, with various respondents pointing to divisions in the Indian management team, poor relations with Ethiopian staff, and unclear objectives as the main problems.[17] The cumulative result has been that the common challenge across the electricity sector of retaining competent staff given low public sector salaries has been particularly acute for EEU, which is bluntly regarded by many donors as 'a flipping disaster'.[18]

Although the UEAP had always prioritized connection of towns and villages, rather than individuals, the expectation was, nonetheless, that demand for individual connections would follow and that the electric utility would have the capacity to meet this demand. One obvious problem is that the cost to customers of an electric connection was \$50–100, more than the annual income for many households (World Bank 2005a). Moreover, the focus on expanding electricity

[13] Interviews EP17, consultant to the energy sector, Addis Ababa, 4 June 2019; and EG9, senior energy sector official, Addis Ababa, 23 July 2019, 17 September 2019.

[14] Interview EP17, consultant to the energy sector, Addis Ababa, 4 June 2019.

[15] Interview EG37, senior energy sector official, Addis Ababa, 21 August 2019, 19 February 2020; FBC (2013).

[16] France Telecom-Orange was contracted to restructure and manage ETC from 2010 to 2012 (Maasho 2010).

[17] Interview EG37, senior energy sector official, Addis Ababa, 21 August 2019, 19 February 2020. See also World Bank (2018a, p. 5). PowerGrid did not respond to multiple interview requests.

[18] Interview ED9, donor representative, by phone, 18 October 2019.

access led to the setting and pursuit of a narrow set of development targets, which were subsequently adopted as performance targets for departments and officials. From the perspective of these officials, setting targets based on the lesser challenge of access rather than connections would give the impression of better performance:

> You could say the definition of access was manipulated or widened to capture larger groups and suggest better performance ... There was lots of playing with the definitions.[19]

As is a common challenge with performance evaluation, once targets had been defined, however, officials focused solely on the narrow targets that were to be assessed, rather than any broader conceptualization of the ultimate objectives of the programme. Consequently, access targets at the national level were translated into five-year and annual performance targets for electrified towns, while actual connections received minimal attention. In the words of one official, once the national targets were set,

> afterwards everyone sat down to derive the BSC[20] for five years and to divide responsibility for the targets between teams ... I remember lots of Excel spreadsheets to track progress.[21]

Another source of delays in UEAP was the decision, in line with the broader 'developmental state' narrative within government, to utilize the major investments involved in UEAP to build domestic manufacturing capacity and to create jobs. One example of this was the decision to switch from using wooden poles for electricity cables to concrete ones, from about 2013.[22] While wooden poles were cheaper, they did not last as long as concrete ones, which could be contracted to micro and small enterprises (MSEs) as a means of creating work opportunities for young people. More problematic was the decision to contract the Metals and Engineering Corporation (MetEC) for equipment ranging from transformers and compact sub-stations to smart meters.[23] Limited capacity within MetEC meant that it was no more capable of delivering on these contracts than it was for the electro-mechanical works in the GERD. The resulting delay in production of electric meters, in particular, was highlighted by the World Bank as a major factor delaying electricity connections in towns newly incorporated into the grid (World Bank 2013, pp. 24–25).

[19] Interview EG2, senior energy sector official, Addis Ababa, 3 September 2019, 13 February 2020.
[20] Balanced scorecards (BSCs) are a tool used to assess performance. BSCs were adopted in many state agencies, drawing on ideas from New Public Management, and as a complement to *gim gema*.
[21] Interview EG2, senior energy sector official, Addis Ababa, 3 September 2019, 13 February 2020.
[22] Interview EG15, energy sector official, Addis Ababa, 24 July 2019.
[23] Interview EG33, MetEC official, Addis Ababa, 28 November 2019.

The end result then was that despite the massive expansion of generation capacity and the grid after 2005, and a huge accumulation of debt by the state electric companies, this investment fell short of meeting the government's political and economic objectives for the sector. The majority of the population continued to lack a grid connection, while electricity provision for those with connections remained unreliable with frequent instances of load shedding. As an illustration, in Addis Ababa—the best-served area in the country—many of the distribution lines and transformers are old and in poor condition, resulting in an average of 42 power outages per week (JICA 2018, pp. 2–11). Meanwhile, newly connected towns tended to have few consumers, while many were frustrated by being able to see the grid but not connect to it.

In comparison to the focus on grid expansion, attention to off-grid electricity has been marginal under the EPRDF, with some donor officials going so far as to describe off-grid as 'taboo' before the change of government in 2018.[24] Nonetheless, in 2005 the government did establish a Rural Electrification Fund in the Ministry of Water, Irrigation, and Energy (MoWIE) with funding from the World Bank and Global Environment Facility to support rural energy access in areas outside EEPCo's expansion plans for the next decade (World Bank 2005b). This Fund provided concessional loans to the private sector to invest in some 40,000 solar home systems in isolated areas (MoWIE 2017, p. xxi). Furthermore, the Development Bank of Ethiopia (DBE) provided credit to microfinance organizations lending to private solar providers (MoWIE 2017, p. xxi).

These challenges eventually forced a change in approach. As discussed later in this chapter, the government adapted its industrial strategy to focus on new industrial parks, in part to lower the challenge of providing reliable electricity and other infrastructure to industrial firms. Furthermore, the failure to translate improved access into connections was acknowledged from 2016 with a National Electrification Strategy that prioritized connections over grid expansion. As discussed in more detail in Chapter 9, the focus switched to densification—prioritizing connecting customers who are already situated close to the grid—as well as expanding off-grid solutions for those living beyond grid expansion plans.

Ethnic Politics and the Regional Distribution of Electricity

The growing politicization of ethnicity in Ethiopia since the introduction of federalism and the dominance of the TPLF within the EPRDF has led to increasingly intense competition for resources between ethnic regions, and frequent claims that

[24] Interview ED2, donor representative, Addis Ababa, 10 June 2019.

regions are not treated equally in the allocation of federal resources. The massive expansion of the electric grid under the EPRDF therefore raises questions about the spatial distribution of electricity infrastructure. Unfortunately, data on the regional allocation of resources and the decision-making process leading to this distribution are limited. This section reviews the available evidence. While some inequality is clear, only tentative conclusions can be drawn about the complex processes leading to this.

A recent World Bank study provides a rare insight into regional variations in electricity connections and use, suggesting significant variation. Unsurprisingly, Addis Ababa has by far the highest rates of grid access, with close to universal connections. Among the four highland regions, however, Tigray stands out for its relatively high rates of grid access (51 per cent) and off-grid access (37 per cent), with just 12 per cent of the population estimated to lack any access to electricity (see Figure 8.8). In contrast, the Southern Nations, Nationalities, and Peoples Region (SNNPR) is the poorest performer, with 62 per cent of the population lacking any access to electricity. Although data are unavailable, connection rates in Afar, Benishangul-Gumuz, Gambella, and Somali are likely lower still.[25] A similar picture is evident with respect to the percentage of secondary schools that have electricity connections (Figure 8.9). Unsurprisingly, the vast majority of secondary schools in the cities of Addis Ababa, Dire Dawa, and Harar have

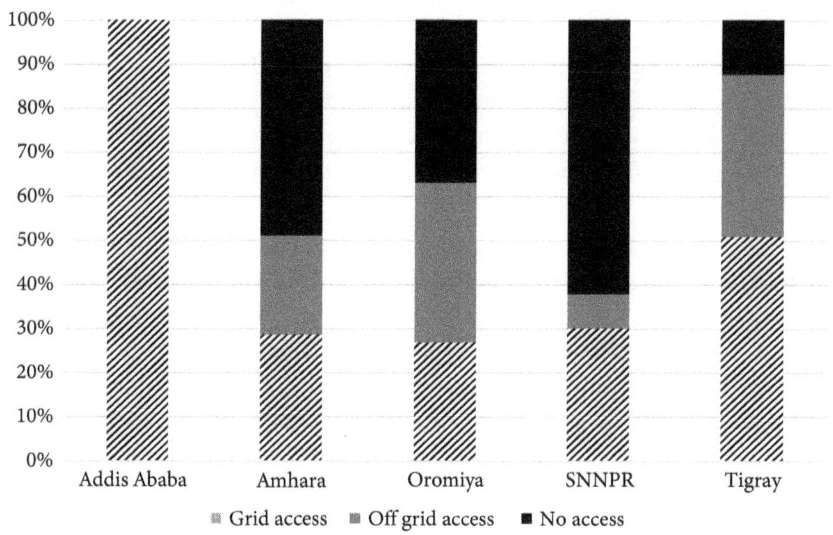

Figure 8.8 Electricity access by region

Data source: Author based on Padam et al. (2018).

[25] As Figure 8.4 shows, grid penetration into these regions remains very limited and largely focused on regional capitals and transmission lines for exports.

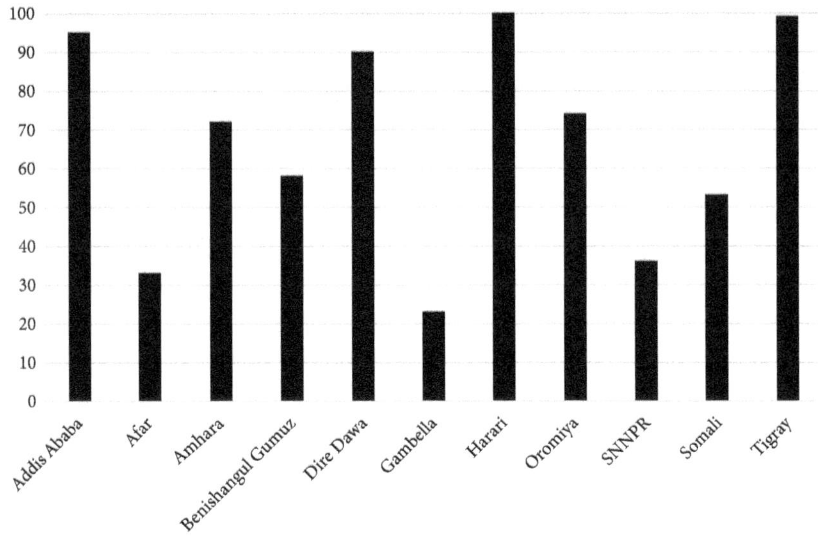

Figure 8.9 Electricity connection rates for secondary schools by region
Data source: Author based on MoWIE (2019, p. 87).

connections. However, Tigray is exceptional among the larger regions with near universal access. At the other extreme, just 36 per cent of secondary schools in SNNPR have access to electricity.

One potential source of this variation would be UEAP itself and the possibility that the programme disproportionately favoured Tigray in electrification of new towns since 2005. Available data suggest that this is not the case, however. One of UEAP's stated ambitions, in line with the EPRDF's justification of federalism in general, was to

> redress the regional imbalances in infrastructure, especially in the less-developed regions. In some cases, this will not be cost-effective, because of low concentrations of population, or the high costs of reaching remote areas, but to the extent that it is possible within available resources, efforts will be made to expand the connection of these areas. (MoFED 2005, pp. 138–139)

As such, UEAP provided justification for concentrating its efforts on regions that were previously under-served by the grid, including Tigray, but also SNNPR and others. In doing so, grid expansion would necessarily reduce the concentration of connections in Addis Ababa and surrounding areas of Oromiya as a proportion of the national total. According to officials, the federal UEAP office calculates a quota of the number of towns to be connected and a proportional share of the budget for each region based on a formula determined by the House of Federation using regional population figures.[26] Once the region has been allocated its quota, the regional Presidents' Offices are responsible for deciding which towns are selected for electrification, usually beginning with the zonal towns and then proceeding to *wereda* and then smaller urban centres.[27]

Official figures from UEAP partially support the claim that the programme has sought to address regional inequality, albeit with some exceptions. Figure 8.10 shows the 'bias' in electricity connections in 2004 and 2014, where 'bias' is calculated as the region's share of the total number of electrified towns in the country minus the region's share of the total population, excluding Addis Ababa. In 2004, just before UEAP began, Oromiya had a share of electrified towns that comfortably exceeded its share of the country's population (see Figure 8.10). The first 10 years of UEAP to 2014, however, extended the grid beyond Oromiya with the result that Oromiya's share of electrified towns fell marginally below its share of the national population by 2014. Amhara in contrast was relatively under-served in 2004, but its share of electrified towns somewhat exceeded its population share by 2014. The other main outliers are SNNPR and Somali regions

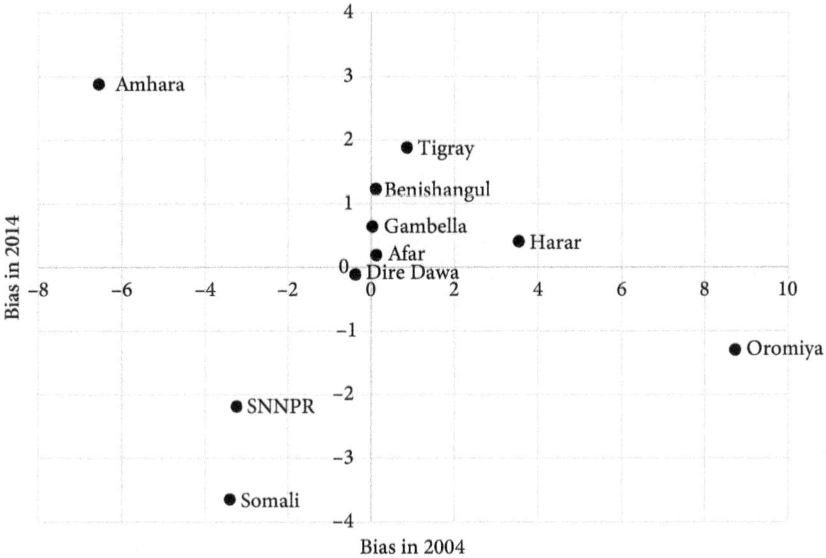

Figure 8.10 Regional distribution of electrified towns in 2004 and 2014

Data source: Author based on data provided by UEAP for towns and the 2007 Census for population shares (CSA 2008b).

[26] Interviews EG18, UEAP official, Addis Ababa, 3 October 2019; EG22, UEAP official, Bahir Dar, 11 March 2020.

[27] Interviews EG19, UEAP official, Addis Ababa, 1 October 2019; EG22, UEAP official, Bahir Dar, 11 March 2020; EG23, UEAP official, Addis Ababa, 14 February 2020; EG24, UEAP official, Addis Ababa, 21 February 2020; EG37, senior energy sector official, Addis Ababa, 21 August 2019, 18 February 2020.

which were under-served in 2004 and remained so in 2014. The highly dispersed population and long distances between populated centres in Somali and parts of SNNPR provide a likely explanation for the low electrification rates there.[28]

Tigray's electrification rates under UEAP slightly exceeded its population, but only to a modest degree. As such, UEAP does not provide an obvious explanation for the disproportionately high rates of electricity access in the region. Instead, high electricity access rates appear to be the result of higher grid connections in areas that were electrified, as well as greater uptake of off-grid solutions in Tigray. It is far from clear why EEU was able to achieve higher connection rates in Tigray, though it is worth noting that the challenge of electrification in Tigray—a relatively small region in which the majority of the population is concentrated in the east and central areas—pales in comparison to the task of electrifying the vast Oromiya region, for example. As such, geography may provide a partial explanation for the variation. It is also unclear what has caused variation in off-grid electricity access. However, the involvement of microfinance organizations in off-grid solar systems may provide a partial explanation. The Ethiopian microfinance sector is dominated by EPRDF-affiliated organizations, organized along ethno-regional lines, which accounted for 89 per cent of loans in 2014/15 (NBE 2015, p. 54). Notably, the TPLF-linked Dedebit Credit and Savings Institution was by far the largest of these microfinance organizations and perhaps therefore better placed to provide loans for off-grid access.

EEP's investment in the regional distribution of sub-stations exhibits a somewhat similar pattern to UEAP's investment in electrification of towns (Figure 8.11).[29] Sub-stations are used to step down high-voltage electricity used in transmission to the low voltages used by consumers. They are therefore a critical part of the grid infrastructure. Once again, Addis is, unsurprisingly, over-supplied with sub-stations relative to its population. In contrast, SNNPR, Somali, and, on this occasion, Amhara are relatively undersupplied. Indeed, the lack of new sub-stations in Amhara was raised with EEP leadership by regional officials back in 2017, arguing that this has impeded electricity supplies and was a barrier to investment in the region.[30]

Given the limited data available, it is clear that the EPRDF Government did not eliminate regional inequality in electricity access. The massive grid expansion reduced the concentration of electricity access in Addis and surrounding areas in Oromiya. However, progress in Tigray and, to a degree, Amhara has not been matched by that in SNNPR and Somali, which continue to lag behind in every measure. Based on this limited analysis, it is not possible to draw any definitive

[28] Interview EG37, senior energy sector official, Addis Ababa, 21 August 2019, 18 February 2020.

[29] EEP, responsible for transmission infrastructure, including sub-stations, is one of the few state organizations still organized along geographical rather than ethnic regions.

[30] See YouTube (2017).

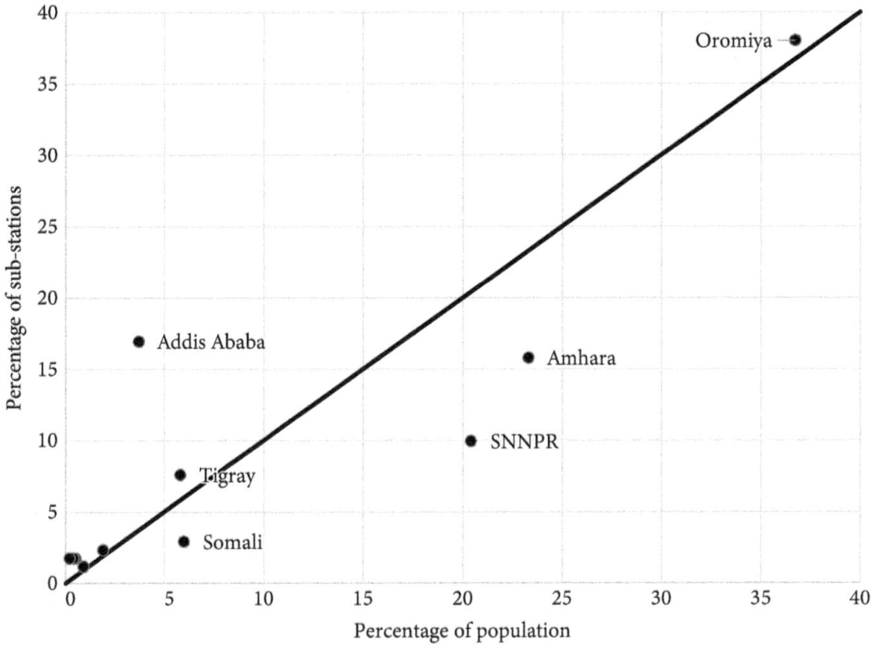

Figure 8.11 Distribution of electricity sub-stations by region

Data source: Author based on EEP sub-station data from Ambaw (2020, pp. 289–290) and the 2007 Census for population shares (CSA 2008b).
Note: The line indicates a one-to-one relationship, so, for example, any region below the line is relatively under-served with sub-stations compared to its population.

conclusions about the causes of this variation. Electricity access is shaped by a range of factors including topography, urbanization, and population density, and proximity to generation sources and load centres, alongside any possible political influence on infrastructure investment. Nonetheless, the comparatively strong performance of Tigray has been seized upon by critics and opponents of the TPLF to promote what are at least plausible claims of ethnic favouritism. Particularly following the change of government in 2018, politicians from other regions argued that Tigray received preferential treatment as part of a general attempt to blame the TPLF for the challenges facing the country. As an example, one Member of Parliament reported that in contrast to the lack of access and electricity shortages elsewhere in the country,

> Of course with exaggeration, there was a saying that 'Tigray's cattle graze at night using electric lamps'.[31]

[31] Interview EG29, Member of Parliament involved in the energy committee, Addis Ababa, 27 August 2019.

Powering a New Centre of Global Manufacturing?

Industrial policy in the ADLI era prioritized rural-based industry through support and subsidies to domestic capitalists. This strategy met with limited success during the 2000s for a number of reasons, as discussed in Chapter 4. Among these problems was the challenge of large-scale grid expansion, resulting in unreliable electricity supplies. New customers had to wait 195 days on average to be connected to the grid due to a lack of capacity in EEU (MoWIE 2019, p. 40), while for existing customers power cuts remained a routine occurrence. Past studies show how unreliable electricity supplies caused major problems for key priority industrial sectors. This includes the cement industry, which uses vast amounts of electricity. Mugher, the state-owned cement producer, reported losing 119 days of production due to power cuts in 2009, the worst-affected year (Oqubay 2015, pp. 142–143). Likewise, floriculture requires continuous electricity to maintain stable greenhouse temperatures or risk damage to crops (Oqubay 2015, p. 181), while power cuts cause lengthy and costly production delays for textile firms.[32] The result is that power cuts have regularly been identified as one of the main problems faced by industrial firms in Ethiopia (UNDP 2018; MoWIE 2019). In many instances, this led firms to invest significant resources in costly diesel backup generators, undermining profitability (Abdisa 2018). From the mid-2010s, the government's industrial policy evolved and sought to attract established foreign firms to relocate production to Ethiopia by providing state-of-the-art industrial parks. Among the incentives for investors was a guaranteed, reliable supply of low-cost 'renewable' electricity written into the contracts with foreign firms.[33]

Rather than pursuing a spatially dispersed agro-industrial strategy in an attempt to limit urban migration and spread job creation around the country, as previously, the industrial park strategy instead concentrated industrial production in particular locations to pursue agglomeration effects to allow learning and subcontracting between firms (Oqubay and Kefale 2020). As such, the change in industrial strategy had very important implications for infrastructure, including electricity. Instead of a general expansion of the grid across national territory, the industrial parks required high-quality infrastructure connecting generation sources to particular localities. Indeed, this reduced requirement for electricity and transport infrastructure expansion was highlighted as one of the advantages of the new strategy by its main architect, Arkebe Oqubay:

> Our capacity to provide utilities and infrastructure is quite limited, and it is very expensive. We have to concentrate on how to minimize the efforts by focusing

[32] Whitfield and Staritz (2021) and interview ARP1, manager of a textile factory, Bahir Dar, 19 March 2010.

[33] Interview EG27, senior EIC official, Addis Ababa, 5 June 2019.

> on limited clusters; instead of, for example, attempting to distribute electricity all over the place, it is wise to do so effectively in one place. (Arkebe Oqubay, cited in Mihretu and Llobet 2017, p. 28)

In doing so, the transmission and distribution plans for the industrial parks diverged from the goal of mass electrification that, like ADLI previously, required a general grid expansion.

The Industrial Parks Development Corporation (IPDC) was established in 2014 to oversee park construction, which was contracted out to Chinese firms. Meanwhile, the Ethiopian Investment Commission (EIC), whose board is chaired by the prime minister, was given responsibility for promoting investment and overseeing the IPDC. The IPDC was initially led by Arkebe with the direct support of the prime minister. Once adopted as a political priority, the government pursued industrial park development with characteristic ambition, using a 10-year $1 billion Eurobond to finance an initial eight industrial parks (Manyazewal 2019). The industrial parks were a key priority for Growth and Transformation Plan 2 (GTP2) with the target of creating 2 million jobs by 2025, while raising manufacturing from 4 to 20 per cent of gross domestic product (GDP) and increasing the manufacturing export share to 40 per cent (NPC 2016). Hawassa Industrial Park, the largest industrial park in Africa, was built in just nine months by 2016, with construction on the remaining seven beginning soon after. Similar to the fast-track approach adopted by Salini to speed up construction of Ethiopia's dams, the IPDC adopted a 'design-build' process in which planning proceeded alongside construction to compress the timeline and meet the deadlines imposed by GTP2 (Wondimu 2023).

The challenges faced by the industrial parks are, in many respects, comparable to those affecting planning in the electricity sector in general. Selamawit Wondimu's (2023) recent study of the industrial park planning process and its implications for urban planning is illuminating in this respect. Like this book, her analysis highlights the top-down nature of decision making as a defining feature of EPRDF policymaking. Hugely demanding targets were set by the federal government, with lower levels of state bureaucrats assessed based on their ability to deliver on these ambitions. She argues that while Meles Zenawi monopolized political power, he was able to ensure some degree of coordination between agencies, which were forced to work together towards key national priorities. However, after 2012, growing political fragmentation within the EPRDF leadership undermined this forced coordination. As discussed in Chapter 4, Meles' death left a political vacuum, while the selection of Hailemariam Dessalegn as EPRDF chairman and prime minister was a compromise between the once dominant TPLF and the increasingly assertive Amhara National Democratic Movement (ANDM) and Oromiya People's Democratic Organization (OPDM). The result was growing political fragmentation as federal decision making became subject to negotiation and bargaining between factions, while regional administrations became increasingly assertive in demanding their share of national resources. This led to both enormous pressure to reach unobtainable targets and an inability to bring together necessary agencies to work towards a common goal.

Given the desire to reduce the challenge of infrastructure provision, the obvious choice would have been to concentrate industrial parks in the corridor between Addis Ababa and Djibouti where there is a plentiful supply of labour, existing road, rail, and electricity infrastructure is already relatively good and comparatively easy to upgrade, and there is good access to the port of Djibouti for imported inputs and export of final products. However, the industrial park strategy took a very different approach, with ethno-regional administrations each demanding their own park, leading to a dispersal of industrial parks across the country, undermining their efficiency and enhancing the infrastructural challenge (see Figure 8.4).[34] Moreover, regional pressures led to the addition of a further three industrial parks in 2018 in order to provide Afar, Benishangul-Gumuz, and Somali regions with their share of this new national priority. As one senior official involved in the process underscored,

> The first generation of parks was not so much based on feasibility but political considerations. Currently the political system cannot support decision making based on feasibility studies. But now there is recognition of the huge costs and the waste of money.[35]

Moreover, the IPDC, empowered by the prime minister to deliver on this ambitious industrial park strategy, proceeded to 'bulldoze' through, largely ignoring the implications of its actions for other sectors and agencies, and failing to conduct meaningful consultations (Wondimu 2023). In particular, the selection of sites for industrial parks ignored EEP's plans for upgrading transmission infrastructure as well as the existing transport plan which had already commenced construction of new rail links (Wondimu 2023). The accelerated industrial park strategy therefore placed huge demands on the state agencies responsible for necessary infrastructure, including, of course, the state electric utilities responsible for building the transmission and distribution infrastructure required to connect the parks. The government estimated that the 11 industrial parks would require dedicated supplies of some 1,400–1,500 MW, with the largest requiring 200–300 MW each (Wondimu 2023, pp. 6, 141).

The result of this rushed and fragmented process has been a series of missteps that have undermined electricity provision to the industrial parks and, in turn, threatened their attractiveness to foreign investors. The initial approach in IPDC

[34] As Arkebe acknowledged, this spatial distribution also undermined the intended agglomeration effects of the parks (Oqubay and Kefale 2020).

[35] Interview EG26, senior EIC official, Addis Ababa, 5 June 2019.

appears to have been extremely naïve, expecting that the parks, despite their large additional demand, could just draw on the existing infrastructure of neighbouring cities. As one senior official with insight into the challenges noted,

> They thought they could just connect the industrial park to the nearest city, but when they did that in Hawassa it seriously disrupted power in the city. By then they had six to seven parks already under construction. And then they realized the need for sub-stations.[36]

Indeed, Hawassa, the first industrial park, initially took dedicated access to one of the existing lines from the city leading to electricity shortages across the city as the park was prioritized (Wondimu 2023). Another challenge was the decision to add a recycling plant—excluded from the original plans—at Hawassa in line with Ethiopia's 'green developmental state' framing of its eco-industrial parks. The addition of the recycling plant added to the power requirements and the pressure on electricity infrastructure.[37]

The IPDC's strategy has subsequently switched to building a dedicated sub-station for each park, with mobile sub-stations used to address short-term needs.[38] However, these mobile sub-stations have lower capacity than the requirements of the parks, can be unreliable, and are only a temporary stop gap. Hawassa was initially connected with a mobile sub-station, while a permanent sub-station was constructed and finally completed in 2019. However, the cost of constructing these sub-stations—estimated at some $1.8 billion—has raised questions about which state agency is responsible and exposed the growing fragmentation between state agencies post-2012. In theory, EEP should provide transmission infrastructure up to and including the sub-station, while EEU connects the sub-station to the industrial park and IPDC has responsibility for the facilities of the park itself. IPDC, with strong political backing, expected that EEP and EEU would finance the connections, in effect continuing the longstanding practice under the EPRDF in which the electric utilities were expected to subsidize other priority sectors. As construction of the parks proceeded, however, growing indebtedness constrained the electric utilities and forced them to limit their exposure (see Chapter 9). As one EEU official noted,

> IPDC is asking us to bring power. They say 'everything outside our compound is you', but we are a company and they have to pay. They think that we are both the government, so there is no need to pay from one pocket to another pocket! At the Prime Minister's Office they say both are sister offices. IPDC tells us to go to the

[36] Interview ED6, donor representative, Addis Ababa, 10 February 2020.
[37] Interview ED6, donor representative, Addis Ababa, 10 February 2020.
[38] Interview EG20, EEU official, Addis Ababa, 4 October 2019.

> Ministry of Finance, the Ministry of Finance says go to IPDC. They say EEU has to work for free.[39]

Likewise, the growing view in EEP was that where the transmission lines and sub-stations were dedicated to the industrial parks, it should be the IPDC, not EEP, that pays for construction.[40] In Hawassa, even after the permanent sub-station had been constructed, contention around finance initially prevented it from being connected. According to an EEU official,

> After three years the permanent sub-station is now completed. But the problem is the distribution line, there is a financial problem. According to EEU procedures, the financial solution is from the customer: IPDC ... But they didn't pay so we are waiting for that money. We cannot construct the line before payment. The sub-station with capacity of 200 MW is completed ... We want to move the temporary sub-station from Hawassa now that the permanent one is complete, but we cannot until it is connected.[41]

In turn, this failure to relocate the temporary sub-station meant that Adama Industrial Park, which was by now completed, was left without any electricity supply, forcing the investors there to invest large amounts of money in diesel generators.[42]

By 2018/19, the electricity supply situation was dire with only Hawassa and Debre Birhan having a dedicated sub-station, while others relied on a patchwork of mobile sub-stations or lacked electricity connections altogether. As one senior official involved in the planning process summarized, the 'industrial parks have no power ... [and] without power industrialization cannot happen'.[43] Indeed, the lack of supporting infrastructure, of which electricity was foremost, has been a major deterrent to would-be investors. Dire Dawa Industrial Park—in some respects the best location for a park given its proximity to the port of Djibouti—has been particularly badly affected, as have Kombolcha, Adama, and Mekele.[44] According to a senior official from the EIC responsible for investment promotion,

> It [electricity] is number one. The question we couldn't answer. They [investors] like everything but then they see that there is no power, no water, no road ... with

[39] Interview EG20, EEU official, Addis Ababa, 4 October 2019.

[40] Interview EG10, EEP official, Addis Ababa, 17 July 2019.

[41] Interview EG20, EEU official, Addis Ababa, 4 October 2019.

[42] Interview EG20, EEU official, Addis Ababa, 4 October 2019. The fragmentation of the state agencies and lack of coordination from higher levels is also evident outside the industrial parks. When established, EEU was to be the exclusive supplier of electricity, with EEP limited to generation and transmission. However, EEP has subsequently sought to bypass EEU, selling electricity directly to the largest consumers of electricity, such as cement factories. In effect, this cuts EEU out of lucrative bulk electricity sales (interviews EG20, EEU official, Addis Ababa, 4 October 2019; EP17, consultant to the energy sector, Addis Ababa, 4 June 2019).

[43] Interview EG25, former EIC official, Oxford, 21 May 2019.

[44] Interviews EG26 and EG27, EIC officials, Addis Ababa, 5 June 2019.

a full supply we would have more investment, certainly. Dire Dawa is complete, the labour is almost ready, the park, the road is nearly there, but there is no power. So nobody goes there.[45]

The result then is that despite huge investment and the political prioritization of the industrial parks, industrialization still made modest progress, with electricity supplies among the principal challenges. Indeed, in many respects the problems are familiar ones, with over-ambition from the federal government, top-down decision making, and political fragmentation undermining coherent planning.

From an Ethiopian Renaissance to Powering Africa?

Electricity exports were seen as a means of ameliorating an increasingly acute foreign exchange crisis as industrial development and manufacturing exports repeatedly failed to live up to expectations in the 2000s. Moreover, large-scale exports offered the possibility of balancing out the finances of the electricity sector, with relatively high export tariffs compensating for the loss-making domestic electricity sector. As the government's dam-building plans grew in ambition, generation capacity in the 2010s was set to exceed existing domestic demand, with export markets becoming increasingly important as a means of absorbing excess capacity in the short to medium term. Western donors and international finance institutions (IFIs) had been hesitant to support Ethiopia's hydropower projects due to their political, social, and environmental impacts, while support for the electricity sector in general often led to contention regarding liberalization and privatization reforms. However, promoting international power trade clearly aligns with the objectives of these external actors. The result has been that financial and technical support for transmission infrastructure has been readily forthcoming, particularly from the World Bank and the African Development Bank (AfDB). Despite support for electricity exports, however, progress has been slow, with the government's ambitions undermined by construction delays, the competing power ambitions of neighbouring countries, and the international relations of the region.

The first steps towards turning Ethiopia into a major source of electricity exports were taken in the 2000s, with deals struck to supply relatively small amounts of electricity to Djibouti and Sudan. In 2004, the African Development Fund (ADF) agreed to provide $52 million to build a 230-kV transmission line with a capacity of 180 MW from Dire Dawa to Djibouti (ADF 2011). The power purchase agreement (PPA) signed in 2006 provided for the sale of 243 GWh annually at a tariff of $0.06–0.07 per kWh (ADF 2012). Djibouti was facing an electricity supply shortage and the deal was expected to provide 36–72 per cent of the country's

[45] Interviews EG26 and EG27, EIC officials, Addis Ababa, 5 June 2019.

annual supply (ADF 2011). While the deal, which sold electricity for roughly double domestic tariffs, would boost Ethiopia's foreign exchange earnings, perhaps at least as important was the need to solidify relations with what was Ethiopia's sole means of accessing a port. The transmission line was completed in 2011, albeit energy exports have tended to fall below levels originally envisaged.[46]

The other early export agreement was with Sudan, with the World Bank providing $41 million towards construction of a 300-km, 230-kV line with 200 MW capacity from Bahir Dar to Metema on the Sudanese border (World Bank 2007b). As with the Djibouti deal, however, the Sudanese interconnector had much broader significance than the export of a relatively modest amount of electricity. The project was part of the Nile Basin Initiative (NBI), coordinated by the Eastern Nile Technical Regional Office (ENTRO). In 2004, the Eastern Nile countries decided to fast-track several projects, including the Ethio-Sudan interconnector, while the more complex negotiations about water rights and dams on the Blue Nile were ongoing. As such, the interconnector was seen as a means of building trust between the Nile riparians. The project was

> one of the first tangible investments to flow from the NBI, and as such is an important step in converting the collaborative intentions of the countries into physical investments and benefits which, in turn, should reinforce increased cooperation. Although the Project does not touch water issues directly, it is the fruit of the cooperation around the Nile and specifically among the Eastern Nile countries. (World Bank 2007b, p. 8)

In addition to the broad objective of Nile cooperation as a step towards a joint project on the Blue Nile, the project also directly served Ethiopia's foreign policy objectives, building interdependence between Sudan and Ethiopia, and Sudanese support for hydroelectric production within Ethiopia. In parallel to the construction of the Bahir Dar-Metema line, the NBI also launched a feasibility study for larger-scale electricity trade in an attempt to promote a win-win deal between the countries. Completed in 2008, this study proposed construction of a 500-kV interconnector from the proposed Mandaya Dam in Ethiopia with the capacity to export 1,200 MW to Sudan and 2,000 MW to Egypt (NBI ENTRO 2008).

The Bahir Dar-Metema interconnector was completed, slightly behind schedule, in 2012 (IEG 2014). The initial agreement with Sudan was to supply a minimum of 100 MW or 832 GWh per year, and up to 200 MW, at a price of $0.05–0.06 per kWh (World Bank 2007b, pp. 18–19). However, supply was interrupted soon after the connection became operational and Ethiopia sought to renegotiate the price of electricity to $0.07 per kWh, in line with the Djibouti

[46] More recently there have been discussions about building a second connection to Djibouti, with the ADF again discussing finance.

deal (IEG 2014). Exports resumed in 2013, but volumes have been consistently below forecasts and have occasionally been interrupted entirely due to shortages in Ethiopia.[47] However, one senior EEP source claimed that the PPA governing the sales was never actually signed, enabling this interruption:

> We negotiated a firm energy agreement with penalties [for failure to supply the agreed electricity], but it was never signed. In the end Meles and Al-Bashir just agreed to sell electricity at a very low price without any agreement in place. So now we can stop supply without a penalty.[48]

A more substantive deal to export electricity to Kenya and, from there, across East Africa was negotiated soon afterwards. Ethiopia and Kenya signed Memoranda of Understanding regarding energy development and integration of their grids in 2006 and 2009 (ADF 2012). These were followed by feasibility studies for a 1,000-kilometre, 500-kV, 2,000-MW capacity line from Sodo to Nairobi, with ADF, the World Bank, and the Agence Française de Développement providing the vast majority of the $1,260 million funding (ADF 2012). The transmission line was integral to the plan for Gilgel Gibe III, located close to Sodo, with dam construction beginning around this time. Moreover, the promise of relatively cheap electricity to ease supply constraints appears to have been influential in securing Kenyan acquiescence for the dam, despite the potential impacts on Lake Turkana. The project also held further significance since it was the first meaningful step towards realization of the Eastern African Power Pool (EAPP), established in 2005, which aims to integrate the electric grids of Ethiopia, Kenya, Rwanda, Tanzania, and Uganda and, subsequently, those of countries as far north as Egypt and Libya all the way to South Africa to the south (EAPP 2014). The Ethiopia–Kenya connection is referred to as the 'backbone' of this integrated system (World Bank 2012b, p. 5) and essential to 'position Ethiopia as the main powerhouse and Kenya as the main hub for power trade in the East African region' (ADF 2012, p. iv). Underpinning the investment in the transmission line is a PPA signed in 2012, which commits the two countries to the sale of at least 400 MW of electricity for 25 years at a cost of $0.07 cents per kWh (ADF 2012, p. 8; MoWIE 2019, p. 7). As such, the exports should generate some $200 million per year for Ethiopia (World Bank 2012b, p. 7). Beyond this minimum amount, the expectation was that Kenya would require up to 1,000 MW by 2022 (World Bank 2012b) and that a subsequent agreement would be reached with Tanzania to export electricity via Kenya.

The interconnector was originally expected to be completed in November 2017 (ADF 2012). However, the project has been repeatedly delayed, primarily on the

[47] Interview EG15, EEP official, Addis Ababa, 24 July 2019.
[48] Interview EG14, senior EEP official, Addis Ababa, 3 October 2019.

Kenyan side.[49] Among the main challenges were that part of the Kenyan line was delayed due to a legal case concerning compensation for those displaced by the project and, subsequently, by Covid restrictions that interrupted construction works. The line finally began test exports in November 2022 (Capital Newspaper 2022; Tadesse 2022). The delays to the project meant that the long-stop date in the original PPA had elapsed by 2022 (World Bank 2020). Consequently, the two countries had to negotiate a revised PPA signed in July 2022 (Ethiopian Monitor 2022b).[50]

Beyond Kenya, the next step in realizing Ethiopia's export goals and the EAPP mission is to connect the Kenyan and Tanzanian grids, and subsequently Tanzania to Rwanda and Uganda. An agreement for the ADF and the Japanese International Cooperation Association (JICA) to fund a $200 million project to connect Kenya to Tanzania with a 440-kV line was reached in 2015 (AfDB 2015). Nonetheless, the completion of the project, originally expected in 2019, has been repeatedly delayed, with commissioning of the line expected during 2024 (AfDB 2022). In the meantime, Ethiopia and Tanzania have held extensive negotiations over a 400-MW PPA, with one of the main sticking points being the charge that Kenya imposes for transmitting the electricity.[51] Following the Kenya–Tanzania connection, the next priority for EAPP, and undoubtedly for Ethiopia, is to build a much larger connection between Ethiopia and Sudan (EAPP 2014). As noted above, feasibility studies for the connections to Sudan and Egypt were carried out in the 2000s as part of the NBI. However, for the time being, any possibility of electricity trade with Egypt or Sudan remains dependent on the tense negotiations regarding the filling and operation of the GERD (Tawfik 2019) (see Chapter 9).

Overall, then, Ethiopia's push to be an energy giant in East Africa has made slow progress. Exports to Djibouti began in 2011 with Sudan following shortly afterwards. Hopes for far larger sales have yet to be realized, however. The 2014 Power Sector Masterplan, which provided key inputs into the targets in GTP2, set the expectation of much more rapid progress, with aims to begin sales of electricity from the GERD to Sudan and Egypt from 2015, while Kenya would follow in 2017 and Tanzania in 2020 (Parsons Brinckerhoff 2014, p. 5). Indeed, GTP2 forecast export revenues of $640 million a year by 2020 (NPC 2016, p. 104), while exports were expected to reach 45 per cent of total electricity sales (World Bank 2012b, p. 44). As Figure 8.12 shows, the reality has fallen far short. While precise data after 2017 are unavailable, the fact that exports remained limited to the modest amounts

[49] Interview EG10, EEP official, Addis Ababa, 17 July 2019.

[50] It would appear that this renegotiation enabled the revision of one of the more contentious aspects of the deal. The original PPA fixed the electricity tariff for the entire 25-year deal, with the inevitable result that the value would erode over time to Ethiopia's disadvantage (Parsons Brinckerhoff 2014, p. 64). Reports now suggest that the revised PPA will enable a revision of the price after the first five years (Capital Newspaper 2022).

[51] Interview EG14, senior EEP official, Addis Ababa, 3 October 2019.

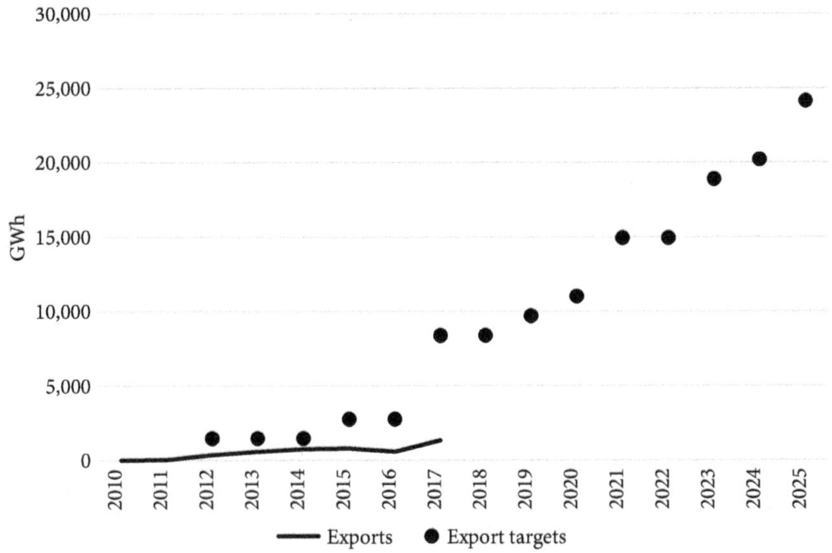

Figure 8.12 Electricity exports and export targets

Data source: Author based on Parsons Brinckerhoff (2014) and USAID and PowerAfrica (2018).

provided to Djibouti and through the original Sudan interconnector until late 2022 means there is no reason to suggest that there has been any significant increase in sales.

The slow progress with these initial export agreements reinforces doubts about the feasibility of Ethiopia's export strategy (Cuesta-Fernández 2015). In particular, political instability within Ethiopia, a lack of trust between countries in the region, and tense international relations all make realization of the EAPP's grand plans and Ethiopia's export ambitions very challenging. The main immediate targets for Ethiopian exports are the relatively small markets in East Africa to the south. However, Kenya, Rwanda, Tanzania, and Uganda have all made significant investments in electricity generation themselves, often involving major hydropower projects, that will go some way to addressing domestic demand and will dampen enthusiasm for Ethiopian electricity.[52] More speculatively, the Ethiopian Government has hinted at supply agreements with Eritrea, Somaliland, and South Sudan, yet none of these are likely to require large amounts of electricity any time soon. The bigger prize for Ethiopia is to secure access to the much bigger markets of Egypt, Sudan, and South Africa (Cuesta-Fernández 2015). Realization of these ambitions, however, will require additional massive infrastructure investments and trading

[52] These include Tanzania's ongoing construction of the 2,100-MW Stiegler's Gorge or Nyerere Dam, Uganda's construction of the Bujagli, Karuma, and Isimba Dams (Gore 2017), and several electricity projects, including dams in Rwanda (Dye 2018).

agreements between multiple countries, which are largely beyond Ethiopia's influence, as well as a resolution to the tense and complex negotiations on the GERD and the Nile waters. There is little sign that these challenges will be resolved any time soon.

Conclusion

The dam-building boom unleashed under the EPRDF did not merely seek to build dams as an end in itself, but was motivated by the belief that a massive increase in electricity production was a pre-requisite for the coalition's political and economic strategy for retaining power. In particular, electricity was seen as a key means of supporting industrialization and mass employment creation outside agriculture. In doing so, low-cost electricity supplies for industry and mass consumption would secure the position of the ruling party. In addition to a major increase in generation capacity, the EPRDF also made significant progress in extending the grid infrastructure to bring this electricity to new consumers, both industrial and domestic. Yet, ultimately, progress fell short of government ambitions, and the electricity sector failed to play the key roles envisaged by the EPRDF leadership. In particular, industrial users—inside and outside industrial parks—continue to face an unreliable electricity supply that disrupts production and discourages further investment. Moreover, connection rates in Ethiopia remain among the lowest in the world, while electricity exports, for the time being, remain minimal and have made little contribution to foreign exchange earnings. All of these challenges can potentially be resolved and it may be that in the future the major investments made under the EPRDF will be seen as undertaking the envisaged 'burden of generations', laying the infrastructural ground work for mass access to electricity. For the time being, however, massive investments undertaken by EEP and EEU, while subsidizing electricity consumers, have meant the accumulation of vast debt burdens, with comparatively little progress in terms of electricity provision.

These limitations are indicative of the general policymaking process under the EPRDF and mirror problems identified in previous chapters regarding generation planning. In particular, the top-down planning process has entailed political leaders setting unobtainable targets that reduce technocrats to the implementation of a politically defined, rather than technically feasible or efficient, plan. While emphasizing the urgency of progress, this top-down decision-making process has led to problematic incentives, with officials needing to be seen to be making progress towards performance targets, regardless of whether this contributes to the ultimate objective of electricity provision, as with the rapid expansion of electricity access despite limited progress in grid connections. The rushed process has also inevitably led to coordination challenges between state agencies in the pursuit of collective goals. In a context of growing political fragmentation since 2012, these coordination challenges have only increased, with the coordination failures between EEP, EEU, and the IPDC resulting in a particularly problematic electricity shortage at new industrial parks. Moreover, like the construction of dams on transboundary rivers, the goal of making Ethiopia an electricity provider to East Africa and beyond is contingent on international relations to open up major export markets. In particular, the markets of Egypt and Sudan remain dependent on securing an agreement on the management of the Blue Nile waters.

With the GERD edging gradually towards completion, the government sought to build popular support for the dam, creating a narrative in which the dam was not only an embodiment of Ethiopian nationalism but also the solution to the country's electricity shortages. In doing so, the implication has been that the dam's eventual completion will immediately eliminate power outages and directly lead to mass electrification. While increased generation capacity is undoubtedly a necessary step in this regard, it is not sufficient on its own. Even with a fully operational GERD, massive challenges remain in terms of upgrading the existing transmission and distribution infrastructure to improve reliability and reduce load shedding, and to expand the grid, connecting vast numbers of Ethiopian households who remain without a grid connection. Indeed, the remaining challenge of transmission and distribution is perhaps at least as large as that of building the dams in the first place.

9

Beyond the 'Developmental State'

Prosperity and Conflict after the EPRDF

Tom Lavers, Biruk Terrefe, and Fana Gebresenbet

Ethiopia launched a dams boom under the Ethiopian Peoples' Revolutionary Democratic Front (EPRDF) based on a high degree of political elite cohesion in response to the perceived existential threat of mass unrest.[1] The construction of hydropower dams was seen as essential to deliver increased electricity supplies, which, in turn, would underpin the government's industrialization drive and address increasingly acute foreign exchange shortages. In doing so, the government's state-hydropower model for the electricity sector was seen as a crucial means of maintaining the position of the ruling party. Moreover, this high degree of political cohesion was vital to resolving the internal and external barriers that had inhibited dam construction in the past, particularly in the Nile Basin. For Meles and the EPRDF, internal political strength was essential to the promotion of economic growth to build fiscal capacity and to building the technical capacity to deliver these projects. Of equal importance, internal political cohesion underpinned Ethiopia's foreign policy that sought enhance Ethiopia's position within the region, prioritizing strong relations with any external actors able to support the country's developmental efforts. The culmination of this decades-long strategy was the beginning of the construction of the Grand Ethiopian Renaissance Dam (GERD), Sudan's expression of support, and Egypt's eventual acceptance of the GERD in the 2015 Declaration of Principles.

In retrospect, however, 2015 marked a high-water mark in Ethiopia's dams boom, and the beginning of a political and economic crisis that would unravel the EPRDF's state-hydro model and the foreign policy that underpinned Ethiopia's Nile ambitions. Popular protests gathered pace from 2015, eventually forcing the EPRDF into reform by 2018, while the failure of the EPRDF's megaprojects to deliver economically led to an increasingly unsustainable debt burden. This internal political and economic crisis was compounded by external shifts within the Nile Basin, the Middle East, and globally. The result has been severe

[1] Biruk Terrefe and Fana Gebresenbet contributed to the sections in this chapter on liberalization of the electricity sector and private sector investment.

Dams, Power, and the Politics of Ethiopia's Renaissance. Tom Lavers et al., Oxford University Press. DOI: 10.1093/oso/9780192871213.003.0009

political instability within Ethiopia, leading to the outbreak of civil war in 2020, and a greatly weakened position from which to negotiate the operation of the GERD. Construction of the final megaprojects of the EPRDF era—the GERD and Koysha—has continued, but at a slow pace as financial and capacity constraints have become apparent. Furthermore, the debt crisis and regime change led the new government to abandon the state-hydro model of the past, with Western donors instead pressing for private investment and renewable technologies to expand electricity generation.

This chapter examines the political economy dynamics shaping dam building and the electricity sector since Abiy Ahmed's rise to power in 2018. To do so, it begins by tracing the political and economic crisis that brought Abiy to power and subsequently led to the unravelling of the EPRDF and Ethiopia's descent into a catastrophic civil war. The analysis then turns to the impacts of this political and economic crisis: first, on dam building and the international negotiations over the operation of the GERD; second, on the liberalization of the electricity sector and efforts to attract foreign investment; and finally on renewed plans for universal electrification.

The End of the 'Developmental State'

The fragmentation of political power after 2012 precipitated a political and economic crisis that has undermined Ethiopia's dam-building efforts and developmental ambitions. Furthermore, political upheaval across the Nile Basin and heightened competition for external influence within the Horn of Africa has meant that Ethiopia and the Nile Basin have increasingly become embroiled within global and regional power struggles. This chapter begins by analysing this political and economic upheaval before turning to the implications of these dynamics for dam building and the electricity sector in subsequent sections.

Meles Zenawi's dominance in the EPRDF after 2001 was such that leadership succession was always going to be a challenge. Meles' death in 2012 and the compromise choice of Hailemariam Dessalegn as his replacement resulted in a dispersal of political power and the beginning of an ideological evolution within the ruling coalition (see Chapter 4). Among other things, the transition provoked internal debates regarding the appropriate role for the private sector in the next phase of Ethiopia's 'developmental state'. These political shifts were reinforced by growing economic challenges. By the time the second Growth and Transformation Plan (GTP2) was drafted in 2015/16, it was clear that past state investments in hydropower dams and other infrastructure had failed to stimulate a major increase in export revenues, resulting in a foreign exchange squeeze. This growing challenge was highlighted in September 2015, when the International Monetary Fund's (IMF's) annual consultation classified Ethiopia as being at moderate risk of debt distress, after one of the IMF's risk indicators crossed its threshold (IMF 2015). While Ethiopia's overall debt level was not particularly problematic (Figure 9.1), the IMF's concerns related to the ability to service external debt given weak export growth (Figure 9.2).

The government's developmental ambitions were only reinforced by this foreign exchange challenge, and the spectre of mass unemployment and landlessness as population growth outpaced employment creation (Lavers 2023). For the post-Meles administration, further massive investments in infrastructure and industry to accelerate employment creation and export performance were perceived as the only possible way out. Nonetheless, GTP2 marked an important departure from past strategies in several ways. First, rather than nurturing domestic capitalists, the new industrial strategy sought to attract global lead firms to relocate production to newly built state industrial parks (see Chapters 4 and 8). Second, GTP2 acknowledged that state finances were insufficient to realize GTP2's enormous ambitions, necessitating that 'the private sector ... plays its role in infrastructure development following the existing policies of the country' (NPC 2016, p. 169). This would include electricity generation where the private sector could narrow 'the gap in the areas of technology, finance and project administration' (NPC 2016, p. 178).

The debt situation deteriorated further after 2015. In October 2016, the Ministry of Finance issued 'a directive to strictly control external borrowing by

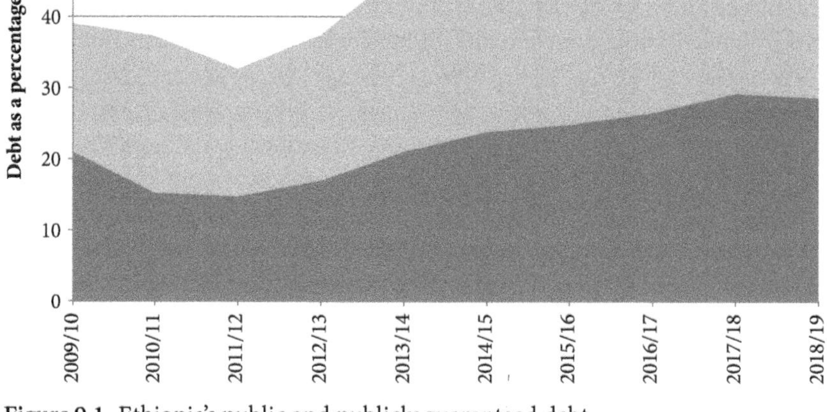

Figure 9.1 Ethiopia's public and publicly guaranteed debt
Data source: Various IMF Staff Article IV consultations.

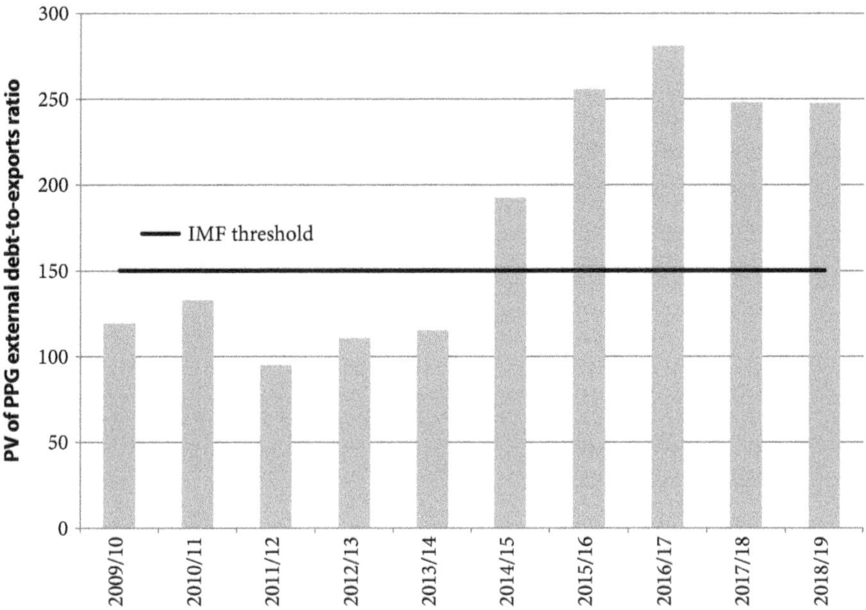

Figure 9.2 Present value of public and publicly guaranteed external debt-to-exports
Data source: Various IMF Staff Article IV consultations.

public enterprises, especially non-concessional borrowing' (IMF 2018, p. 36). Meanwhile, GTP2 investments failed to translate into improved export earnings, including with respect to electricity exports (Chapter 8). Consequently, the IMF's 2017 assessment, published in January 2018, downgraded Ethiopia to a high risk of external debt distress when a second indicator crossed the IMF's threshold (Figure 9.3). The electricity sector was a major source of this debt, with the two utilities combined holding debt of about $10 billion or 15 per cent of gross domestic product (GDP) (World Bank 2019b, p. 9). Ethiopia's debt liabilities to Chinese lenders for several infrastructure projects also became a major issue at this time, with the government forced to restructure its debt obligations to the Eximbank, among others (Acker et al. 2020; Chen 2021). As such, Chinese finance did not provide an alternative means of continuing Ethiopia's debt-financed infrastructure development.

In parallel to growing debt problems, the delicate political bargain struck in 2012 also began to unravel. Protests first arose in western Oromiya in April 2014 in relation to expansion plans for Addis Ababa, which many Oromo viewed as an attempt to seize Oromo territory and displace Oromo farmers. The security services' typically heavy-handed response subdued these initial protests. However, in late 2015 another, larger wave of protests began, spreading across Oromiya,

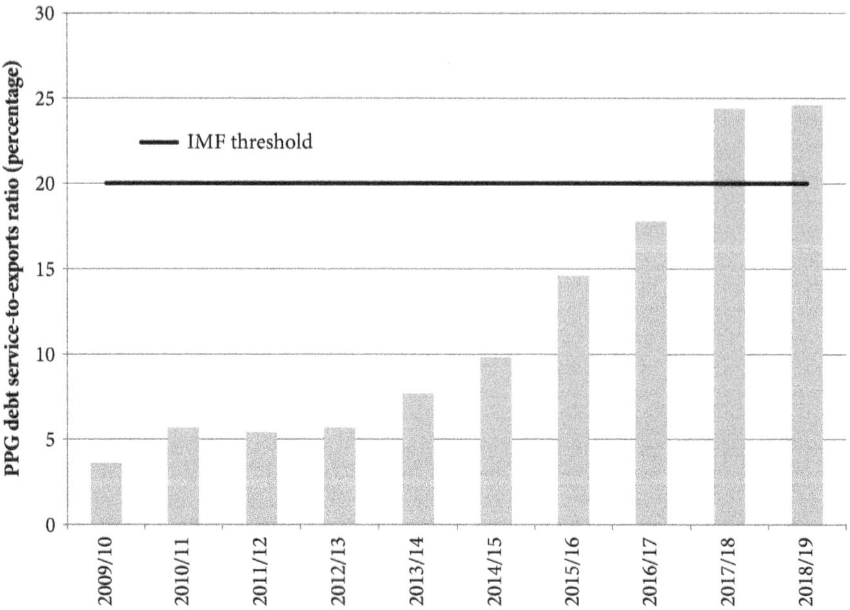

Figure 9.3 Public and publicly guaranteed debt service-to-exports ratio
Data source: Various IMF Staff Article IV consultations.

and in 2016 into Amhara and other regions.[2] While initially focused on the Addis Ababa expansion plans, the protests were sustained by widespread landlessness and unemployment among the young adults (known as *qeerroo* in Oromiya and *fano* in Amhara) that led the protests, along with corruption, the democratic failings of the ruling party, and a range of local grievances (Lavers 2023). Notably in Amhara, protestors focused particularly on the contested territory of Welkait and Raya, part of Tigray region, but claimed by many as an integral part of Amhara.

Popular protests eventually combined with elite political dynamics to bring about regime change (Lavers 2023). From late 2015, factions of the Oromiya People's Democratic Organization (OPDO) and Amhara National Democratic Movement (ANDM) supported and encouraged the protests, using the protests to strengthen their bargaining position within the ruling coalition, which had previously been dominated by the Tigrayan People's Liberation Front (TPLF) (Davison 2016; Lefort 2016; Hassen and Ademo 2017). Reformist leaders Lemma Megersa and Abiy Ahmed came to power in Oromiya in 2016, and by the end of 2017 the ANDM and OPDO had forged an alliance to drive change in the EPRDF. In January 2018, the federal government finally made concessions, promising reforms, and released some 6,000 political prisoners, including leaders

[2] The spread of the protests is discussed at length in Lavers (2023, chapter 10).

of opposition parties. However, by this point protestors were unsatisfied with anything short of regime change. Hailemariam Dessalegn finally resigned in February 2018, and Abiy Ahmed of the reformist OPDO was selected by the EPRDF as his replacement, taking office as prime minister in April.

Prosperity and Conflict under Abiy Ahmed

Abiy Ahmed took office in challenging circumstances, following years of mass protests and popular disenchantment with the ruling EPRDF, with growing divisions within the ruling elite, and an increasingly severe debt crisis that threatened the economic gains of recent years. The new prime minister's response was to launch a dizzying array of political and economic reforms, marking a major shift from the previous administration in both domestic and foreign policy, with vital implications for governance of the electricity sector and the completion of the GERD.

Abiy's rise to power within the EPRDF came about through the support of his party, the OPDO, and the ANDM, but against the wishes of the once dominant TPLF (Fekade and Lemma 2018; Fisher and Gebrewahd 2018). The main TPLF officials left Addis in this period, instead taking up key positions in the Tigray regional government in Mekele, consolidating the party's control of that region. Meanwhile, Abiy sought to dissociate himself from the EPRDF, dismissing the economic achievements of the EPRDF era as '27 years of darkness' (Walsh and Marks 2020), while curtailing the influence of the once dominant TPLF within the ruling coalition. Opponents of Abiy's reform agenda were labelled 'daytime hyenas', widely interpreted as an ethnic slur for Tigrayans (Plaut and Vaughan 2023). The remaining TPLF officials were removed from their political posts, as were the Tigrayan heads of the armed forces and security services in June 2018. Subsequently, the Tigrayan leadership of the Metals and Engineering Corporation (MetEC) was arrested on corruption charges (discussed below). The growing division between Abiy and the TPLF was confirmed in late 2019 when Abiy dissolved the EPRDF and formed the Prosperity Party, merging the former ANDM, OPDO, and the Southern Ethiopian People's Democratic Movement (SEPDM), along with other affiliated parties, into a single party. The TPLF refused to join.

For Ethiopia's development partners, whose prior influence over the EPRDF's economic strategy was limited, the debt crisis and political transition presented a major opportunity to promote long advocated reforms and, for the United States (US), to consolidate Ethiopia as a regional anchor state (Verhoeven and Woldemariam 2022). To this end, the World Bank committed $1.2 billion in the first part of its 'Growth and Competitiveness' budget support in October 2018, with an additional $500 million in February 2020, and a third tranche expected in 2021, while the US International Development Finance Corporation promised

$5 billion over three to five years (Pilling 2020). Subsequently, the IMF pledged the maximum amount it could under its rules with a financing package of $2.9 billion over three years in December 2019 (IMF 2019). World Bank budget support was conditional on adopting new investment and competition proclamations to expand opportunities for foreign and private sector investment, providing telecommunications licences for foreign companies, and reforms to the electricity sector, as discussed below (World Bank 2018b). Moreover, the World Bank and US hired Ethiopian and diaspora economists and energy sector specialists who were posted to advisory positions in key ministries, a notable shift from the past when the EPRDF actively sought to limit technical assistance to maintain policy autonomy (Furtado and Smith 2009). Donors forged a tight-knit relationship with a new cohort of relatively young technocrats appointed by Abiy to replace the displaced stalwarts of the EPRDF era. Many of these new appointees were former World Bank and International Finance Corporation employees, and took key strategic positions in the Ministry of Finance, National Bank, and Investment Commission.

The EPRDF's Executive Committee announced sweeping reforms in June 2018 including the part privatization of state-owned enterprises, previously considered the sacred 'commanding heights' of the economy under the 'developmental state', including Ethiopian Airlines, Ethio Telecom, and energy generation (discussed below).[3] References to the 'developmental state' were dropped and in December 2019 Abiy Ahmed expressed his government's preference for IMF and World Bank loans in stark contrast to Meles Zenawi's regular criticism of these agents of 'neo-liberalism' (Wade 2001; Stiglitz 2003; Zenawi 2006a; Feyissa 2011):

> taking loan from IMF and the World Bank is like borrowing from one's mother. It is not a loan. It is not a loan. Because after they give us a 1 billion *birr* [loan], we will have 20–30 years to repay at 2, 3 or 4 per cent interest. What harmed Ethiopia is borrowing from companies and some countries, before borrowing from these institutions.[4]

The Prosperity Party's subsequent economic programme was named 'A Home-grown Economic Reform Agenda: A Pathway to Prosperity' in an apparent attempt to address widespread concern about the growing influence of these international financial institutions.

In parallel to economic reforms, the new administration continued to open political space by removing the terrorist classification of opposition groups the Oromo Liberation Front (OLF) and Ginbot 7, and facilitating their return to Ethiopia during 2018, along with Jawar Mohammed, a diaspora activist and vocal supporter of the Oromo protests. Furthermore, in June 2018, the government

[3] The administration subsequently rolled back the decision to privatize Ethiopian Airlines.
[4] See YouTube (2019). Quote is from 27 minutes onwards.

announced the normalization of relations with Eritrea and the opening of the Eritrean border for the first time since 2000.[5] This move was made without consultation with the TPLF, despite the fact that Tigray occupies the majority of the border with Eritrea. Eritrean reconciliation was facilitated by US allies Saudi Arabia and the United Arab Emirates (UAE), who saw an opportunity to strengthen their position in the Horn of Africa as part of their regional power struggles with Iran, Qatar, and Turkey (Verhoeven 2018; Mosley 2021; Verhoeven and Woldemariam 2022). Indeed, the UAE also transferred $1 billion to the National Bank of Ethiopia to support balance of payments and promised a further $2 billion in future investment (Young and Khan 2022).

Abiy therefore seemed set to end the EPRDF's authoritarian tendencies, while embracing economic liberalization domestically and peace internationally. The resulting hysteria was such that he was awarded the Nobel Peace Prize in 2019 for making peace with Eritrea. However, the situation facing the new government remained perilous, with the political transition resulting not in peace and stability but an explosion of violence across the country. The EPRDF's coercive control had previously placed a lid on numerous longstanding grievances, while the transition provided the opportunity for ethno-political elites to advance local claims on territory and resources. As such, inter-ethnic conflicts erupted across the country, including: between the Guji Oromo and Gedeo in Southern Nations, Nationalities, and Peoples Region (SNNPR); between the Somali and their neighbours in Oromiya and Afar; in Benishangul-Gumuz between the Berta, Gumuz, Amhara, and Oromo populations; and between the Sidama and Wolayita in Hawassa. Indeed, the political opening in the context of ethnic federalism and the return of previously exiled politicians led to a sharp ethno-nationalist turn in Ethiopian politics. This was particularly evident in Amhara, involving both the Amhara branch of the ruling party and the new opposition National Movement of Amhara (NaMA) (Tazebaw 2021; Workneh 2021). A central focus of this Amhara nationalism concerns irredentist claims to territory held by Tigray, Oromiya, Benishangul-Gumuz, and Sudan.

The new government soon began to close the political space that it had briefly opened. Abiy removed the Somali regional president and TPLF ally, Abdi Illey, in August 2018,[6] and installed favourable regional administrations in Gambella and Afar. By 2019, the TPLF administration in Tigray was the sole remnant of the EPRDF era that had not aligned with Abiy. Meanwhile in western Oromiya, an Oromo Liberation Army (OLA) faction that refused to join the OLF-negotiated

[5] The border was closed again in December 2018, likely to stem the flow of Eritreans out of the country and to limit the impact on the Eritrean economy.

[6] Abdi built powerful regional special forces that persecuted the brutal counter-insurgency campaign against the Ogaden National Liberation Front (ONLF) (Hagmann and Korf 2012) and were subsequently involved in attacks on Oromo populations living along the Oromiya–Somali border in 2017 (Hassen Hussein 2017; Lefort 2017).

demobilization process launched an expanded insurgency that led to a brutal counter-insurgency campaign from early 2019 (Abebe 2023). Subsequently, the July 2020 assassination of Hacaalu Hundessa, an Oromo singer whose songs provided the soundtrack to the Oromo protests, further sparked mass unrest and led to the detention of the Oromo Federalist Congress (OFC) leadership, including Jawar Mohammed. The result was that by the end of 2020 political space for opposition to the ruling party had once again closed.

The period after 2018 saw a steady build-up of federal and regional armed forces, which gathered pace as tensions increased with the TPLF during 2020 (Plaut and Vaughan 2023). Meanwhile, it soon became clear that reconciliation with Eritrea was not solely about peace but, in part, also an anti-TPLF alliance. The TPLF and Eritrean leadership had had a problematic relationship throughout the civil war in the 1970s and 1980s (Berhe 2008), and the Eritrean Government harboured great resentment about the outcome of the 1998–2000 war and the international isolation imposed on Eritrea subsequently. Abiy and Eritrean president Isaias Afeworki held numerous meetings in 2018–2020 with unprecedented visits to military installations in each country in July and October 2020 giving the impression of joint military planning (Plaut and Vaughan 2023).

A major flashpoint in the deterioration of relations between the federal and Tigray governments concerned national elections, originally slated for May 2020. Elections were delayed past the constitutional limit in September 2020 due to the Covid pandemic. Dismissing the federal government as illegitimate and in contravention of the constitution, the TPLF organized and resoundingly won regional elections in September. The federal government ruled these regional elections illegal and cut all federal transfers in October (Plaut and Vaughan 2023). War finally broke out on the night of 3–4 November in the midst of the US presidential elections. The exact details of how the conflict began remain subject to much debate. The federal government claims that the Tigrayan forces launched an unprovoked attack on the army's Northern Command in Mekele, seizing weaponry and murdering non-Tigrayan officers. An alternative account claims that the federal government sent commandoes by plane to Mekele to eliminate or capture the TPLF leadership (Plaut and Vaughan 2023). Whatever the exact sequence of events, both sides had clearly been preparing for war. The Tigray Defence Forces (TDF) found themselves fighting on multiple fronts as the Ethiopian National Defence Force (ENDF), accompanied by the Amhara regional special forces, and Amhara militia attacked from the south, while the Eritrean Defence Forces attacked from the north, supplemented by UAE drone support operating from Assab, Eritrea (Verhoeven and Woldemariam 2022). In the face of this onslaught, the TDF were rapidly displaced from the main urban centres by the end of November, retreating to the mountains to begin a guerrilla campaign.

The war exacerbated Ethio-Sudanese tensions. Ethiopia and Sudan built close relations during the 2000s, culminating in Sudan's declaration of support for the GERD from 2012. However, Ethio-Sudanese relations deteriorated from 2018. The Eritrean peace deal prompted Sudanese concerns about the potential regional dominance of an Ethio-Eritrean alliance (Verhoeven and Woldemariam 2022; Gebreluel 2023). Moreover, the ousting of al-Bashir through popular protests in 2019 following an extended economic crisis and the subsequent military takeover in Sudan strengthened ties with the Egyptian military and led the Sudanese Government to adopt a more nationalist stance (Mosley 2021; Berridge et al. 2022; RVI 2023). Just prior to the war, the Ethiopian Government asked their Sudanese counterparts to close the Sudan–Tigray border to deny the TPLF/TDF external access (Manek 2021; Berridge et al. 2022). However, the Sudanese military seized the opportunity to enhance its nationalist credentials by taking control of the long-contested Al-Fashaga triangle (Manek 2021). Meles and al-Bashir had come to a common understanding that enabled Ethiopian and Sudanese farmers to cultivate the land side by side (see Chapter 6). However, Sudan's seizure of the area displaced thousands of predominantly Amhara farmers and low-level conflict between the Sudanese, Amhara militia, and ENDF threatened to spill over into war (Berridge et al. 2022; RVI 2023).

The conflict in Tigray shifted to a guerrilla campaign in which the TDF sought to replicate the tactics employed to such good effect by the TPLF decades previously. The TDF launched surprise attacks on ENDF and Eritrean forces, while the occupying militaries launched reprisal attacks targeting both the TDF and the civilian population suspected of harbouring and supporting them. The result was widespread human rights abuses including systematic rape, extrajudicial killings, and the use of famine as a weapon of war. While both sides in the conflict have undoubtedly committed offences, the Tigrayan population was particularly exposed to a brutal campaign at the hands of Ethiopian, Eritrean, and Amhara forces.[7]

After Joe Biden took office as president in January 2021 and amidst growing evidence of widespread human rights violations, the US pressured the UAE to withdraw drone support, threatened to cut aid to Ethiopia in spring 2021, and removed Ethiopia from the list of countries benefiting from the African Growth and Opportunities Act (AGOA) in November 2021 (Gebre and Marks 2021; Whitfield and Maile 2021). In so doing, Ethiopia lost tariff-free access to the US market, severely damaging the business case for its industrial parks and adding to the economic crisis. US intervention, meanwhile, was used by the government to fuel a nationalist, anti-imperialist popular response within Ethiopia.

[7] Catalogued by Nyssen (2023).

Delayed federal elections were finally held in June 2021, and having suppressed much of the opposition, Abiy Ahmed's Prosperity Party secured the vast majority of parliamentary seats. However, in the days following the election the regrouped TDF launched a massive assault that killed or captured thousands of ENDF soldiers. Within days of the election, the TDF had retaken Mekele in triumph, while the ENDF retreated in disarray, leaving the TPLF once more in control of the vast majority of Tigray, with the exception of Amhara-occupied western Tigray. The TDF then sought to break the siege on the region during the second half of 2021 through offensives to the west and south into Amhara and to the east into Afar. The most successful of these was along eastern route from Tigray to Addis, capturing the Amhara towns of Weldiya, Dessie, and Kombolcha, before finally being forced back as they approached Debre Sina around 100 miles from Addis Ababa in late 2021.

In the absence of support from the US and UAE, the Ethiopian Government turned to other global and regional powers for support, securing significant numbers of Chinese, Iranian, and Turkish drones to aid the war effort (Donelli 2022, p. 2; Plaut and Vaughan 2023). These drones and renewed conscription turned the tide once more. The TDF retreated northwards, re-establishing a front line around the Tigrayan border by the end of 2021. Amidst another massive Ethiopian and Eritrean assault on Tigray in late 2022, the TPLF finally negotiated a Cessation of Hostilities in Pretoria, with Tigrayan forces agreeing to demobilize and restore federal authority (Gebresenbet and Tariku 2023). Ultimately, two years of conflict had resulted in massive loss of life, widespread human rights abuses, famine, and destruction of infrastructure particularly in Tigray, though also to a lesser degree in Amhara and Afar. On the face of it, the peace deal was a triumph for Abiy's administration, finally bringing a rogue region to heel, but the cost—in human lives, economic resources, and political capital—has been immense.

As more and more Ethiopian soldiers were moved north to fight the TDF, this provided the opportunity for other armed groups across the country to expand their activities (Abebe 2023). In particular, the OLA expanded its insurgency throughout much of western and central Oromiya from 2020 onwards (Abebe 2023). The peace agreement between the federal government and the TPLF meant that the Ethiopian army turned its attention to Oromiya, and the OLA retreated to strongholds in Wellega. Likewise, the Benishangul People's Liberation Movement (BPLM)—allegedly with Sudanese and Egyptian support (Bekele 2021; RVI 2023)—has been increasingly active in Benishangul-Gumuz, the location of the GERD (Vaughan and Gebremichael 2020; Manek 2021; RVI 2023).

The result is that after 2015 the political cohesion that underpinned Ethiopia's developmental push has unravelled. Widespread political instability has heightened the growing economic crisis with important implications for Ethiopia's dams boom and the governance of the electricity sector.

From Dams Boom to Bust

Amidst this political and economic upheaval, the new Ethiopian Government sought to complete the major infrastructure projects left to it by the EPRDF, including Koysha and the GERD. While the EPRDF dams boom was underpinned by political cohesion and rapid economic growth, the crises of recent years have presented major challenges to both the construction and international negotiations over the GERD's operation. Initial generation of the GERD's first turbines was originally supposed to commence by 2015. In keeping with the planning process for the electricity sector, this proved wildly optimistic. Significant delays resulted from unexpected additional excavation required for the dam's foundations. Moreover, after 2015 progress was also disrupted by a shortage of funds, insecurity in surrounding areas due to the OLA and BPLM insurgencies (Vaughan and Gebremichael 2020; RVI 2023) and, most importantly, the unravelling of MetEC's role in the dam.

When the GERD was launched in 2011 and even when Koysha began construction around 2015, the government was bold and ambitious in its belief that it could finance major infrastructure projects through a combination of domestic revenue generation, concessional, and, where required, commercial lending. However, growing debt concerns soon forced a re-think. The government had arranged commercial loans to finance the Koysha Dam when the project was initiated. However, in 2016 the Ministry of Finance's directive to limit non-concessional lending removed the financing for Koysha.[8] From that point onwards, the government sought to prioritize the more prestigious GERD with the limited resources available, while Koysha was starved of resources.[9] One Ethiopian Electric Power (EEP) official concisely summarized the change:

> [in the past] we'd be told to do something, and we'd have to do it: 'don't worry about finance. Just build'. But this has changed now. We have to deal with financial issues.[10]

The result is that Koysha has progressed far more slowly than intended, with Salini maintaining a minimal level of operations, at times subsidizing construction costs itself, while the government searched for additional funds to complete the project. Massive military spending on the Tigray War and the conflict's disruption of the economy further exacerbated the financial crisis, in turn slowing progress with the GERD.

Just as problematic as financial issues was the decision to sub-contract the GERD's electro-mechanical works to MetEC. The original intention of including

[8] Interview EP12, long-term contractor in the electricity sector, by Skype, 20 November 2019, 16 February 2020.

[9] Interview EG14, senior EEP official, Addis Ababa, 3 October 2019.

[10] Interview EG10, senior EEP Official, Addis Ababa, 17 July 2019.

MetEC in the GERD and other major infrastructure projects was to reduce costs, build the technical expertise of an Ethiopian firm, and ensure that key works were contracted to a firm that would not be subject to external pressure to withdraw from the project. The reality, however, is that MetEC's involvement was a mistake, causing costly delays. Ultimately, the scale of the problems was only revealed after the political transition in 2018 and the purge of TPLF figures from the government and security services, including the military-owned MetEC.

Before 2018, the government gave the impression that construction was going to plan and, as late as early 2017, Deputy Prime Minister Debretsion insisted that early testing of the first two turbines would soon begin (Anberbir 2017). However, shortly after Abiy came to power in April 2018 the director-general of MetEC, Major General Kinfe Dagnew, resigned, and in July Abiy was widely quoted as stating that the dam might not be finished for another decade (Davison 2018). Two days later, the GERD's head engineer, Semegnew Bekele, was found shot and dying in Meskel Square in central Addis. Although subsequently ruled a suicide, rumours inevitably abound about the cause of death (Africa Confidential 2018a). MetEC was stripped of its contract for the GERD in August 2018, along with those for sugar factories and a fertilizer plant (Mohammed 2018; Nazret 2018), and state media released a documentary alleging corruption and enormous wastage of state resources across the projects in which it was involved (Africa Confidential 2018b). In late 2018 some 27 MetEC officials were arrested and charged with corruption related to procurement and contracting, including Major General Kinfe and his deputy, Brigadier General Tena Kurunde (Africa Confidential 2018c; Fasil and Tsegaye 2018). In the midst of this upheaval, EEP's chief executive officer (CEO), Azeb Asnake, was also dismissed and charged with corruption (Reuters 2019).

For the time being, little evidence has been presented to support corruption charges and legal processes are ongoing. For some of Abiy's critics, the removal of Tigrayans from the MetEC leadership has been part of a broader attempt by Abiy to consolidate power and marginalize the TPLF. In contrast, the government insists that removing MetEC from the construction effectively saved the dam because MetEC was doing so much damage. Abiy was clear during his first press conference as prime minister that

> Salini is completing its part of the project on time and now it is demanding huge payment because the project is lagging from the side of MetEC. We have handed over a complicated water dam project to people who have not seen a dam in their life and if we continue in that direction, the project may never see the light of day. (Abiy cited in Egypt Today 2019)

While allegations of corruption remain unproven at the time of writing, those interviewed for this research were adamant that MetEC had indeed taken on work that was far beyond its capacity. No one willing to be interviewed defended MetEC.[11] One consultant involved over several years reflected,

> It was a terribly wrong decision. Building MetEC's capacity is great, but pick something small, not the GERD. When you are teaching a kid to eat, you do not put a great big plate in front of them with lots of different foods, you start with small things, easy.[12]

MetEC's limitations for the highly complex electro-mechanical works in the dam were apparently clear from very early on. As one respondent involved in the construction noted,

> We realized since the early stages, at the time of the river diversion [May 2013]. The diversion required steel work, but it did not come on time. So we asked—'if they have problems with something this simple, what is going to happen with the complex works?' We just got no feedback from their side as to what was happening. Again, we completed the main dam structure to the extent possible, but then we needed the penstocks to be completed, but there was nothing from MetEC and the progress stalled.[13]

Despite Salini highlighting problems, however, the government took no action:

> Salini repeatedly warned the government that MetEC was going wrong from very early on. But no one believed them. They took timelapse photos showing Salini's progress and the absence of work from MetEC ... They failed to even do the penstocks—anyone can do that. But they didn't.[14]

Similar concerns were raised by a state official closely involved in the dam construction:

> The intention was good with the capacity building, this was effective in Egypt, China, and the US. But you have to build the capacity. You cannot let anyone fly a plane or drive a car—the results would be disastrous. Equally you cannot let someone who had never even seen a hydro plant before. And MetEC was given one of the most complex parts of the project in coordinating the electro-mechanical work.[15]

[11] This is perhaps unsurprising given that fieldwork was conducted in a period in which MetEC was being publicly vilified.
[12] Interview EP13, senior consultant involved in the project, by Skype, 26 November 2019.
[13] Interview EP13, senior consultant involved in the project, by Skype, 26 November 2019.
[14] Interview with EP12, longtime contractor in the energy sector, by Skype, 20 November 2019, 16 February 2020.
[15] Interview EG11, senior engineer involved in the project, Addis Ababa, 21 February 2020.

Reflecting on the delays at a public consultation in 2020, Minister of Water Seleshi Bekele highlighted the failings of MetEC's work:

> When the employer representative [Tractebel] visited, 70 per cent failure was recorded for the first culvert. Welding was 70 to 30 per cent failure, while the tolerable failure level is 0 to 2 per cent.[16]

None of the supervisory arrangements in place to monitor the work of the contractors was able to address MetEC's limitations until it was too late. When Salini's original contract was revised to allocate the electro-mechanical works to MetEC, Salini was given no supervisory power. Instead it fell to EEP, as the owner of the dam, advised by the owner's engineer, Tractebel, an international engineering firm of Belgian origin, to supervise the work of both Salini and MetEC. Some respondents pointed to this, in itself, as a problem, since it can easily lead to the lack of accountability and finger-pointing between contractors that in time materialized.[17]

Ultimately, however, the power dynamics between the different parties prevented any oversight of MetEC. When MetEC was originally contracted, Meles was still prime minister and unrivalled in his authority. While MetEC's limited capacity would have been a problem in any case, it is possible that Meles would have been able to challenge their lack of progress. After his death, however, the fragmentation of political power within government meant that no one could hold them to account. The director-general of MetEC sat on the board of EEP, which was responsible for overseeing MetEC as a sub-contractor, a clear conflict of interest. Moreover, the MetEC leadership was closely aligned with the military and senior figures in the TPLF, while the prime minister, Hailemariam, was caught in the middle. Respondents claim that the owner's engineer—supposedly advising EEP regarding the dam's progress—also raised concerns, but got nowhere:

> What were they doing all through this? They wrote a lot of letters. But they were instructed not to go deep into it. How can you oversee someone who has a gun in their hand?[18]

Following the removal of MetEC in 2018, much of the metalwork was replaced, causing major delays. MetEC had subcontracted turbine manufacture to GE France and Voith—world-leading firms whose contracts were retained. Chinese firm Sinohydro, meanwhile, was brought in to handle pre-commissioning activities (CGTN Africa 2019). Furthermore, after the death of the head engineer,

[16] Seleshi Bekele, minister of water, irrigation, and energy, public conference held at the Hyatt Regency Hotel, Addis Ababa, 6 February 2020.

[17] Interview EP13, senior consultant involved in the project, by Skype, 26 November 2019.

[18] Interview EG11, senior engineer involved in the project, Addis Ababa, 21 February 2020. Requests for an interview with Tractebel were declined, citing their contractual obligations.

Semegnew Bekele, Kifle Horo—one of the EEP officials removed from the GERD due to his opposition to MetEC's original proposal to increase the dam's installed capacity in 2012 (see Chapter 7)—returned as head engineer. In January 2020, the dam's installed capacity was reduced by 1,200 megawatts (MW) to 5,150 MW. At this point, officials acknowledge that the 'the increase [in installed capacity] by MetEC was just meaningless' and three 400-MW turbines, which had not yet been contracted, were cancelled, a saving of some $210 million.[19] Nevertheless, many respondents acknowledged that this reduced capacity is still too large given the availability of water. However, since all the other turbines had been contracted already, the decision was made to install them. The result is that the GERD will ultimately have 11 turbines rated at 400 MW and two rated at 375 MW. Meanwhile, MetEC has been reformed and renamed Ethio Engineering Group.

Negotiating a New Order on the Nile

In the meantime, the Blue Nile riparians have engaged in lengthy negotiations about the GERD's operation. Repeated attempts to build on the 2015 Declaration faltered and discussions became deadlocked. The key stumbling block, once again, was not so much technical as political, and Ethiopia's political crisis and internal fragmentation significantly weakened its bargaining position.

The central focus of the technical negotiations has been the timeline for the filling of the dam and the rules for its operation, particularly concerning water releases during drought years. Egypt and Sudan have pushed for a legally binding agreement, including guaranteed releases to ensure a minimum level in the reservoir behind the High Aswan Dam. This would constrain the GERD's operation and Ethiopia has instead proposed a system of non-binding guidelines and data sharing. These different stances on the nature of the agreement translate into significant differences in proposals for minimum annual water releases from the GERD and, in turn, have important implications for the length of time it will take to fill the GERD reservoir, the operation of the dam during drought years, and the distribution of water storage between the GERD and Aswan (Mada Masr 2020).

However, as Fana Gebresenbet and Dawit Wondemagegnehu argue, the two countries' divergent positions on technical issues are entrenched within distinct historical narratives and state identities, making concessions and compromise all but impossible:

> Egyptian and Ethiopian elites have so far framed their ontological security around the River Nile in a mutually incompatible fashion. Both countries (though

[19] Interview EG11, senior engineer involved in the project, Addis Ababa, 21 February 2020.

> to varying levels), view a change in the status quo as a threat to their biographical continuity, which cannot be addressed through dispute resolution mechanisms centered on transboundary water sharing norms and principles alone. (Gebresenbet and Wondemagegnehu 2021)

The GERD was initiated at a moment of political crisis within Egypt, contributing to an inconsistent response by the Transitional Government and the brief Freedom and Justice Party administration. Since the 2013 coup that brought El-Sisi to power, however, Egypt has adopted a more coherent strategy to re-engage with Nile Basin countries (Tawfik 2019), attempting to unpick the upstream coalition that Ethiopia had carefully assembled under Meles Zenawi, while engaging regional and global allies to pressure Ethiopia into make concessions. The apparent 'kingmaker' in negotiations is Sudan, which had long aligned with Egypt, but which signalled its support for the GERD in 2012, a major diplomatic success for Ethiopia (Cascão and Nicol 2016b). The removal of al-Bashir, who had forged close ties with Addis Ababa in 2019, the subsequent coup, and Ethiopia's decision to begin unilaterally the filling of the GERD, however, resulted in a further pendulum shift. The Sudanese military—which retains close ties to its Egyptian counterpart—dominated the Sovereign Council that took power and hardened its stance on the GERD, signalling its support for Egypt's demand for a binding agreement on the GERD (Mosley 2021; RVI 2023). Border conflict over Al-Fashaga since 2020 further soured relations with Addis Ababa and complicated negotiations. More broadly, Egypt has sought to re-engage with upstream countries on the White Nile in its effort to strengthen its bargaining position, continuing a longstanding strategy of assisting Nile Basin countries to develop water resources outside the Nile Basin (Waterbury 2002; Tawfik 2015). This has included the award of the contract to build Tanzania's 2,100-MW Julius Nyerere Hydropower Station to Egyptian state-owned firm, Arab Contractors, in 2018 (GCR 2018), as well as initiatives to build hydropower projects in Burundi (Takouleu 2018) and solar projects in Uganda (Tabikha 2023). Egypt also engaged with South Sudan following its independence, supporting water projects and reviving discussions regarding the Jonglei Canal (Tawfik 2015; Monodanga 2022; Verhoeven and Sennesael 2022). Egypt's diplomatic offensive is likely among the reasons why only four countries have ratified the Cooperative Framework Agreement (CFA) to date (Tawfik 2015).

Soon after taking power in 2018 and in the midst of domestic reforms, Abiy visited Cairo to re-start stalled negotiations regarding the GERD. In doing so, Abiy appeared to go well beyond the standard Ethiopian position that the dam would not cause significant harm to Egypt by stating that Ethiopia would preserve Egypt's share of the Nile, implying support of the 1959 agreement:

> We will take care of the Nile and we will preserve your share and we will work to increase this quota and President Sisi and I will work on this. (Abiy, cited in Reuters 2018)

Moreover, when urged by El-Sisi, he reassured his guests that, 'I swear to God, we will never harm you'. In May 2018, the three countries established the National Independent Scientific Research Group (NISRG) made up of researchers from each of the countries that have provided technical input into the negotiations.

Egypt has long sought to bring third-party facilitators into the negotiations, in particular the US and Arab states that have historically supported Egypt's position. In contrast, Ethiopia had sought to limit negotiations to the three riparians directly affected. In late 2019, Ethiopia finally found itself backed into a corner due to its weakened financial position and some slightly naïve diplomacy. In October 2019, Abiy Ahmed attended the Russia–Africa Summit in Sochi and in a bilateral meeting with El-Sisi agreed to trilateral talks hosted by the US, apparently against the advice of his own foreign ministry (Berridge et al. 2022, p. 131). Given the ongoing debt crisis and the importance of the US in providing financial support, Ethiopia's ability to refuse these negotiations was extremely limited.

Several rounds of talks took place in Washington, DC in late 2019 and early 2020 with US Treasury and World Bank observers in a concentrated push to reach an agreement.[20] While broad agreement was achieved on the filling and operation of the dam under normal hydrological conditions, the negotiations faltered regarding the definition of drought conditions and the procedures to be followed once a drought was declared. Ethiopia refused initial Egyptian and US proposals to define a drought in relation to the water level in the High Aswan Dam or the average historical flow of the Nile due to the concern that this would imply acceptance of Aswan and the 1959 water agreement. A subsequent US proposal to base drought classifications solely on the water flows into the GERD reservoir, in contrast, brought Ethiopia's planned future upstream projects, which had previously been excluded from discussion, into negotiations (Helal and Bekhit 2023). While the Egyptian team felt that the US favoured Ethiopia on several points (Helal and Bekhit 2023), the Ethiopian Government and popular perception in Ethiopia was that the US was not a neutral observer, but was intervening in favour of Egypt and President Trump's 'favourite dictator', El-Sisi (Verhoeven and Woldemariam 2022, p. 638). Certainly, the US role went well beyond that of an 'observer', pushing the countries to sign a final deal that the US team had drafted in March 2020. In response, the Ethiopian team skipped the final meeting (Maru 2020; Meseret 2020; Berridge et al. 2022). Egyptian members of the negotiating team drew the conclusion that

> Ethiopia was driven by a desire to conclude a legal instrument that consecrates and codifies its control over the Blue Nile ... [and] a policy of seeking to establish itself as a de facto hydro-hegemon. (Helal and Bekhit 2023, p. 32)

[20] Some of the Egyptian negotiators have subsequently provided a fascinating account of the negotiations in Helal and Bekhit (2023). By their own admission, this is necessarily an Egyptian perspective of events.

The US responded in August 2020 by pausing $270 million in aid commitments because it felt the Ethiopians had been too inflexible (Verhoeven and Woldemariam 2022, p. 639), while in October Trump was filmed on a phone call with the Sudanese and Israeli prime ministers stating that Egypt would eventually 'blow up' the dam (Al-Jazeera English 2020). US intervention fuelled a nationalist, anti-imperialist response in Ethiopia including the social media campaign #itsmydam, resisting international interference in negotiations and raising funds for the GERD's construction.

By May 2020, nine years after construction began, the GERD was finally ready to begin filling, impounding an initial 4.9 billion cubic metres (bcm) in 2020. Egypt responded to the filling by appealing to the United Nations Security Council and expressing its outrage that Ethiopia was unilaterally filling the dam without agreement (Geneva Water Hub 2023). In this context, African Union sponsored negotiations in 2020–2021 were 'doomed to fail' from the beginning, perpetuating the stalemate (Tawfik 2023, p. 13; Geneva Water Hub 2023; Magome 2020). There were subsequently reports of secret talks sponsored by the UAE—an important source of finance for both Egypt and Ethiopia—in 2022–2023 (Sudan Tribune 2022; The New Arab 2023). At the time of writing, the talks appear no closer to resolving differences. Moreover, the outbreak of civil war in Sudan in April 2023 between the Sudanese Armed Forces and the Rapid Support Forces weakened Egypt's efforts to press for a deal.

In the absence of an agreement, Ethiopia continues to raise the middle section of the dam and fill the reservoir in annual phases each rainy season in June to September. Meanwhile, Egypt has little leverage in its efforts to slow progress and shape operation of the dam. By mid-2023, Ethiopia carried out the fourth annual filling, raising the reservoir height to 620 metres above sea level (masl), with the potential to store about 42 bcm.[21] Moreover, the first turbines (750 MW) finally began generating electricity in 2022 (The Reporter 2022). At the present rate of progress the dam should reach its full height of 640 masl by about 2025/2026, depending on the availability of finance. Since filling began in 2020, rainfall has been above average, with the result that it has been possible to fill the GERD without downstream shortages. Yet the risk remains that future droughts in the absence of a water-sharing agreement will lead to coordination challenges between the GERD and Aswan (Basheer et al. 2021). While the GERD may not have been the most efficient choice of dam on the Blue Nile, it is nonetheless finally set to deliver on its promise to provide a massive boost to electricity generation in Ethiopia and, potentially, the East African region. The GERD alone will not solve the challenges of universal electrification, industrial development, and export earnings. However, it will be an important step towards these goals.

[21] The base of the dam is at 495 masl, so the middle section of the dam would be 125 metres high.

Liberalization and the Pursuit of Prosperity through the Standard Model

The EPRDF long resisted pressure from the World Bank to implement tariff increases and to implement reforms that would have clashed with the government's efforts to use subsidized electricity to support industrialization and mass consumption. However, the debt crisis and political transition to Abiy Ahmed's Prosperity Party have opened the way for donors to press for significant electricity sector reforms towards the Standard Model.[22]

The key reforms to be undertaken in the electricity sector were specified in the 'indicative triggers' for release of budget support agreed in 2018. One of these requires the electricity sector to achieve 'full cost recovery' through 'a multi-year electricity tariff-increase framework' (World Bank 2018b, p. 19). To this end, in September 2018 the Council of Ministers approved the move towards cost-reflective tariffs in four annual increments (MoWIE 2019). The government sought to frame these changes as a 'tariff adjustment', rather than an increase, in an apparent attempt to downplay their significance (MoWIE 2019, p. 8).[23] Yet the proposed changes involve major increases for almost all consumers, with up to four-fold increases for high consumption domestic users (see Figure 9.4). The only tariff that remains unchanged is for households that consume the least electricity, an attempt to continue 'to support the lower class, the poorest of the poor', in line with previous EPRDF policy.[24] Likewise, while industrial tariffs increased two to three times, they remain lower than those for domestic and commercial users, to support industrial investment. This includes foreign investors in state industrial parks who were asked to renegotiate their contracts to bring them in line with government policy.[25] Unlike unfulfilled commitments to tariff increases under the EPRDF, the Prosperity Party Government—desperate for foreign exchange and financial support—has implemented these increases, triggering release of World Bank funds.[26] While a major increase, some observers still doubt that the tariffs actually reflect the cost of delivering electricity, however, arguing for further increases.[27]

In part, the tariff revision is aimed at addressing the electric utilities' rising debts. However, the changes are also a pre-requisite for the broader goal—long advocated by donors and apparently now internalized by the government—of creating an attractive electricity market for private investors to compete with state utilities. As

[22] As discussed in Chapters 1 and 3, the Standard Model comprises unbundling, corporatization, and commercialization of state utilities, independent regulation, opening to private investment and market competition, and, ultimately, divestiture of state-owned generation and distribution.
[23] Interview EG15, EEP official, Addis Ababa, 24 July 2019.
[24] Interview EG15, EEP official, Addis Ababa, 24 July 2019.
[25] Interview EG27, EIC official, Addis Ababa, 5 June 2019.
[26] The latest tariffs advertised on the EEU website match those planned for 2021 (EEU 2023).
[27] Interview ED10, donor representative, Addis Ababa, 6 June 2019.

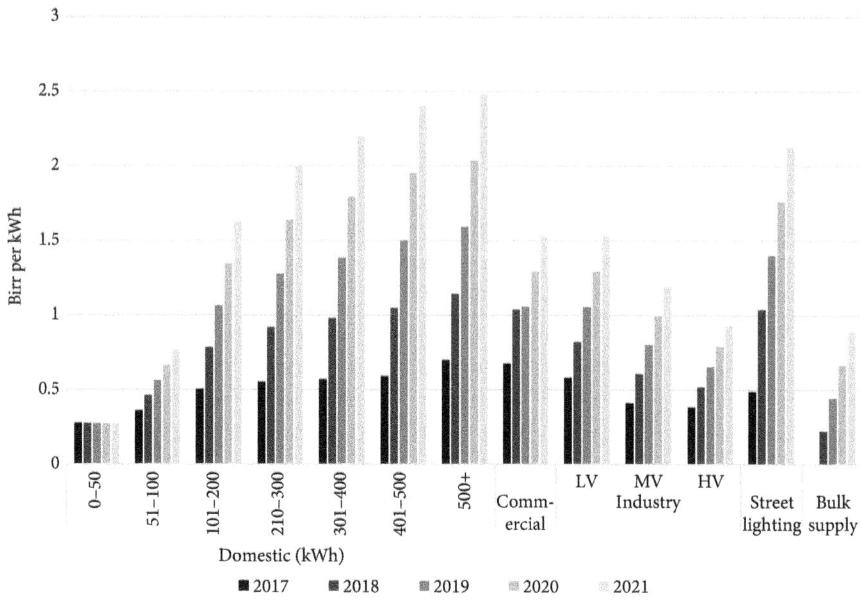

Figure 9.4 Committed electricity tariff increases
Data source: Author based on ESMAP (2018).

such, another 'indicative trigger' for World Bank finance requires the government to produce a 'roadmap for institutional reform in the power sector including recommendations for potential unbundling and privatization of selected power companies' (World Bank 2018b, p. 19). This reform will require strengthening the Ethiopian Energy Authority's (EEA's) capacity, clarifying the division of assets between EEP and the Ethiopian Electric Utility (EEU), installing meters to record electricity sales from EEP to EEU, and improving EEU's metering and billing to increase revenues.[28] These changes are essential to ensure that EEU can pay providers for the electricity it receives, to balance the books at EEP, and to integrate private providers into the system.

Plans are also being made for further unbundling of EEP, with the expectation that EEP will focus on electricity generation, while a new off-taker—which the World Bank (2019b, p. 99) provisionally named Ethiopian Electric Transmission—will be created, responsible for buying electricity from EEP and independent power producers (IPPs), and operating transmission infrastructure. At the time of writing the final decision has yet to be taken by government, though this change is a vital step to level the playing field between EEP and private

[28] Interview ED15, senior donor official in the electricity sector, by Skype, 26 June 2019.

investors.[29] Likewise, debt restructuring is considered an absolute necessity before EEP can be unbundled and this constituted another of the World Bank's 'indicative triggers' (World Bank 2018b, p. 19). To this end, the government established the Liability and Asset Management Corporation in January 2021 to absorb the vast debts accrued by state-owned enterprises at the centre of the EPRDF's 'developmental state' project, including Ethiopian Electric Power, Ethiopian Railways, Ethiopian Sugar Corporation, and MetEC, of which the largest share was accrued by EEP with 370 billion *birr* (Tadesse 2021). The Corporation will draw on revenues from the remaining state enterprises and proceeds of privatization to repay these debts (Endale 2022).

This first stage of restructuring will therefore introduce competition into electricity generation. However, early discussions have taken place about possible future reforms that would create a fully competitive electricity market with private investment in transmission and distribution also.[30] Indeed, the World Bank has already sketched out a potential structure for 'a fully competitive power market' in line with the Standard Model of electricity reform (World Bank 2019b, p. 99). Moreover, the new regulation that accompanied the 2020 Investment Proclamation—another trigger point specified by the World Bank (2018b, p. 24)—removes barriers to domestic private investment in the transmission and distribution of electricity (FDRE 2020, para. 4). The extensive World Bank role in these reforms and limited ownership within EEP was neatly summed up by one senior official centrally involved in the public–private partnership (PPP) process when asked about the reform trajectory:

> try to get someone in the World Bank to tell you more. Nobody in EEP really knows exactly what is happening ... The World Bank is very involved in Ethiopia and the energy sector, too many projects are managed and financed by them.[31]

It is hard to imagine any state official in the EPRDF era making such a statement. Yet the period since 2018 has brought major changes to Ethiopia's electricity sector. In doing so, the new government has begun to dismantle the EPRDF's 'developmental state' and, in its place, has tentatively turned to the private sector to pursue its electric ambitions. While the outbreak of civil war in 2020 slowed this impetus, the peace agreement in late 2022 and subsequent return of donor involvement seem likely to rebuild momentum.

[29] Interviews EG37, senior official in the electricity sector, Addis Ababa, 21 August 2019, 19 February 2020; EG38, senior MoWIE official, Addis Ababa, 16 August 2019.
[30] Interview ED15, senior donor official in the electricity sector, by Skype, 26 June 2019.
[31] Interview EG16, senior EEP official, Addis Ababa, 30 September 2019.

From 'Parasitic Rent Seekers' to Partners in Prosperity: Private Sector Investment in Ethiopia's Electricity Sector

Under the Prosperity Party, there has been a sharp change in the discourse on the private sector, which is no longer framed as a threat to development but as a key partner for the government's economic strategy. However, one area of continuity with the EPRDF is the new government's high ambitions for rapid development and headline-grabbing projects (Terrefe 2020). This is evident in the electricity sector, with a new generation strategy—produced with United States Agency for International Development (USAID) support (USAID 2019)—that is almost as ambitious as the implausible projections set out in the 2014 masterplan (see Figure 9.5). While the plan for increased generation includes the completion of the legacy projects of the EPRDF's state-hydro model—GERD and Koysha—all new generation projects will instead be funded by private sector investment. This shift towards the private sector as the main engine of new electricity generation capacity will, in turn, necessitate a growing role for non-hydro renewables and therefore some diversification of the energy mix.

The first sign of opening to private investment in generation took place in the final years of the EPRDF Government. This partial shift was driven by necessity,

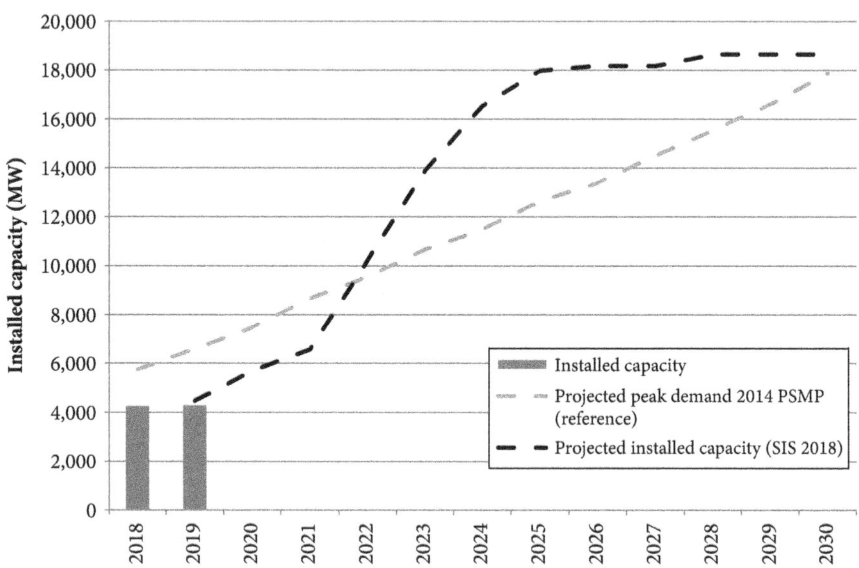

Figure 9.5 Plans for expansion of generation capacity to 2030

Data source: Parsons Brinckerhoff (2014); USAID (2019).

rather than an ideological sea change.[32] The 2016 GTP2 set the unrealistic target of raising installed capacity from just 2,300 MW in 2015 to 17,000 MW by 2020 at the same time as the government acknowledged that its ambitions exceeded state resources. While state-hydropower investment remained the central pillar of the electricity strategy during GTP2, the government also signalled growing openness to non-hydro renewables. EEP considered all possible options to expand generation to meet the government's huge target, with non-hydro renewables expected to provide 2,882 MW of the 17,000 MW target by 2020. This renewable energy production would have to be realized through private sector investment, rather than state resources.

The result was that in 2015/16 the government began the design of a policy and legal framework for PPPs with strong support from the World Bank and USAID. The new PPP policy was approved in 2017 and a proclamation issued in February 2018, establishing a PPP directorate in the Ministry of Finance, which would oversee a centralized process for project approval. The PPP process was therefore initiated well before the political transition in 2018 that brought Abiy Ahmed to power. However, the political transition cleared many of the political barriers to further reform and brought to power an economic team for whom economic reforms were not just a grudging necessity, but desirable. Within state agencies, however, there remains considerable diversity of opinion regarding the role for hydropower in future energy plans. Growing numbers, particularly in the Ministry of Water, Irrigation, and Energy, believe that excessive hydropower dependence is a risk and that diversification of the energy mix is essential.[33] In contrast, many EEP technocrats with years of hydropower experience remain convinced of the benefits of hydropower and risks of renewable technology.[34]

The government's initial request for expressions of interest in PPPs in 2019 continued to favour hydropower, with six projects totalling 3,358 MW (see Table 9.1). Despite government hopes, however, the reality is that PPP-financed dams are rare in low- and lower-middle-income countries due to investors' assessment of the risks involved (Markkanen et al. 2020). Indeed, Ethiopia's proposal of dams on transboundary rivers in the midst of political turmoil, conflict, and corruption scandals would tick almost every box for high-risk investments that would stop any possibility of financing (Plummer Braeckman and Markkanen 2021). These investment risks also apply to a degree to renewable energy investments. However, solar and wind-power have much lower upfront costs and shorter payback periods for investors, with the result that they are better positioned to take on the kind of political risks that would block long-term financing for a dam project. Moreover,

[32] Interviews EG8, senior EEP official, Addis Ababa, 3 October 2019, 11 February 2020; ED15, senior donor official in the electricity sector, by Skype, 26 June 2019; EP7, lawyer in the electricity sector, Addis Ababa, 30 September 2019.

[33] Interview EG40, senior MoWIE official, Addis Ababa, 1 October 2019.

[34] Interview EG14, senior EEP official, Addis Ababa, 3 October 2019.

Table 9.1 Candidate projects for future hydropower PPPs

Basin	Name	Installed capacity	Estimated cost ($m)
Blue Nile	Chemoga Yeda 1	162	492
	Chemoga Yeda 2	118	
	Dabus	304	984
Baro	Tams	2,000	3,360
Genale Dawa	Genale Dawa 5	100	387
	Genale Dawa 6	250	793
Omo	Halele Werabessa	424	1,200

Data source: MoF (2021)

the key difference between hydropower and renewables is that renewables have received strong financial support from multilateral and bilateral donors aiming to create an energy market in Ethiopia and demonstrate the viability of PPPs, while promoting a market-led renewable energy transition (World Bank 2019b). In line with what has been described as 'development as de-risking' (Gabor 2021), multilaterals and Western donors have provided investment guarantees for renewable energy, but have no intention of providing similar backing for hydropower. The result is likely to be some diversification of Ethiopia's energy mix and the possibility of finally exploiting some of Ethiopia's vast non-hydro renewable potential (discussed in Chapter 3). Figure 9.6 shows the 2018 projections for the energy mix, with a significant expansion of solar and other renewables expected in the short term and geothermal in the medium to long term. The completion of Koysha and the GERD dwarfs all other investments. However, excluding these two legacies of the EPRDF era, new investments strongly favour renewables (see Figure 9.7).[35]

Despite this change in narrative, progress with private sector generation projects has been slow and drawn out with little in the way of results. These delays have a number of causes, primarily related to the significant institutional and ideological changes involved in switching from a state-led model to the embrace of the private sector as partners.

Several projects currently under negotiation pre-date the 2018 PPP proclamation. Two geothermal exploration licences were issued, without competitive tender, in 2008/9 in the wake of the drought that disrupted hydropower production at the time. Both projects—Corbetti and Tulu Moye—combine Icelandic geothermal companies, private sector investors, and donor investment and guarantees to

[35] In October 2019 an agreement was also signed with Russia to establish a nuclear programme (Global Construction Review 2019). While many officials were sceptical, Abiy Ahmed appears to have personal interest, dating back to his time as minister of science and technology.

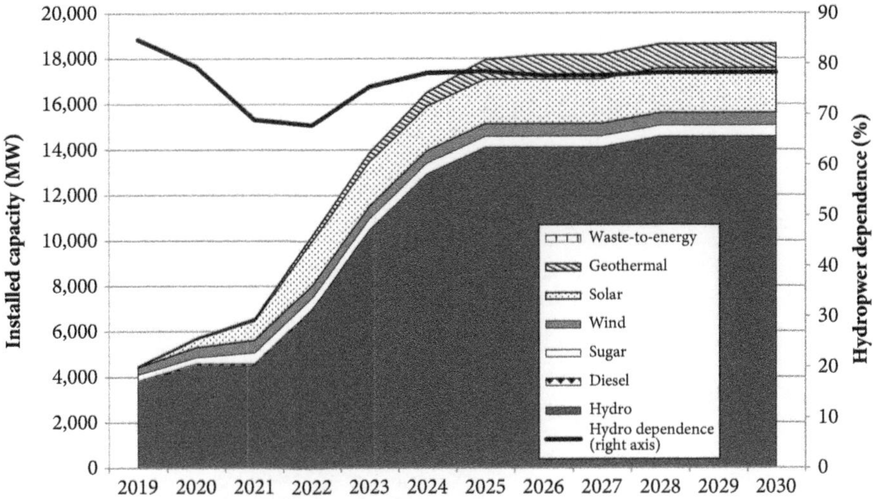

Figure 9.6 Projection of installed capacity by source

Data source: Author based on USAID (2019).

underwrite the projects. Support from the British Government's CDC Group,[36] the US's Power Africa, and the Geothermal Risk Mitigation Facility (GRMF)—a joint initiative of the African Union, the German Government (BMZ) and development bank (KfW), the European Union (EU), and the UK's Department for International Development (DfID)—has been vital to enable private sector involvement and maintain interest through what has proven to be a tortuous negotiation process. Corbetti and Tulu Moye finally signed a power purchase agreement (PPA) and implementation agreement in late 2017. In each case the agreement was for a 500-MW development on 600 hectares of land with the tariff set at $0.07 per kWh, what the investors consider to be the cheapest geothermal rate in the world.[37] By 2019 and in the midst of severe debt problems, the government renegotiated the contracts, however, requesting a reduction from 500 MW to 150 MW, while insisting on maintaining the same tariff. Not only does this reverse an agreement that the investors had considered to be closed, but it also ignores their financing, which was in part based on the economy of scale in the investment.[38] In 2020, the firms agreed PPAs for 150 MW. However, at the time of writing the final outstanding legal issues are yet to be resolved and the projects have not reached financial close.

[36] The Commonwealth Development Corporation, which has since been renamed British International Investment.

[37] Interview EP16, investor in geothermal energy, Addis Ababa, 19 August 2019.

[38] Interviews EP16, investor in geothermal energy, Addis Ababa, 19 August 2019; EG29, Member of Parliament, Addis Ababa, 27 August 2019; ED5, donor official involved in the electricity sector, Addis Ababa, 12 February 2020.

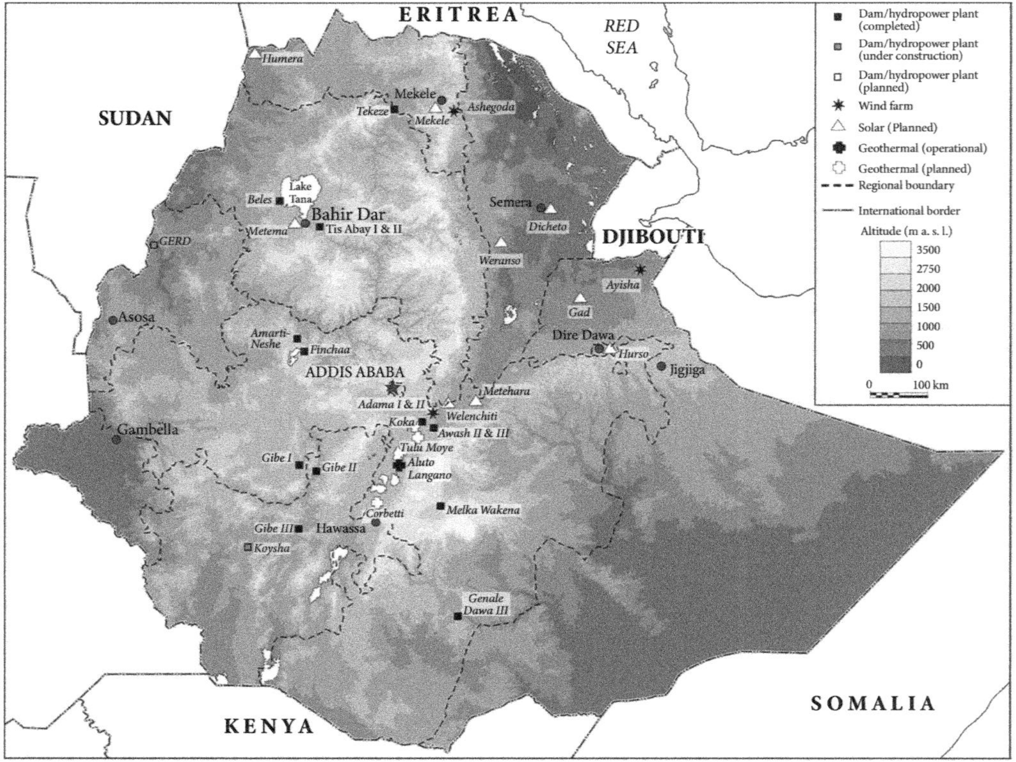

Figure 9.7 Ethiopia's existing generation and renewable energy sites

Source: Author and Manchester Cartographic Unit.

Negotiations for Ethiopia's first solar IPP have been only marginally less protracted. The US Government's Power Africa programme supported a competitive tender for the Metehara solar plant, which will provide 100 MW over a period of 20 years, won in 2017 by a joint venture of Enel Green Power (a major Italian energy firm) and Orchid Business Group (an Ethiopian company). A key step in the development of the Metehara project was the World Bank's approval of its Renewable Energy Guarantee Programme (REGREP) that provides a partial risk guarantee for non-payment by EEP and loan guarantees for commercial lenders (World Bank 2019b). However, the government's willingness to renegotiate the tariff has again proved problematic. The tariff originally negotiated in 2017 of $0.05898 per kWh was considered to be internationally competitive, yet having subsequently secured a lower tariff for another deal, the government raised the possibility of renegotiation (World Bank 2019b).[39]

The deal in question was originally part of the International Finance Corporation's (IFC) Scaling Solar initiative that aims to promote private sector investment in solar technology in developing countries. Like Metehara, these projects are covered by the World Bank's REGREP. The first phase of Scaling Solar was for two 125-MW projects, Gad in Somali Region and Dicheto in Afar (Table 9.2). However, two weeks before the deadline in 2019, the IFC pulled out because the government refused to agree to the IFC's standard foreign exchange convertibility guarantees. Foreign exchange shortages have been a major problem in Ethiopia, with strict rationing in place. For the other renewable projects, the National Bank of Ethiopia (NBE) agreed to give priority in the allocation of foreign exchange, but stopped short of a guarantee. To avoid setting a precedent for the future, the NBE insisted on continuing with the same approach. The IFC considered this to be insufficient and withdrew, leaving the five qualified investors with just two weeks to secure alternative financing.[40] Ultimately, only one bidder—the Saudi-Chinese firm ACWA Power—proceeded and was awarded the contract with the lowest tariff in Africa at just $0.02560 cents per kWh.[41] However, the failure of ACWA to make progress with the plant, initially due to Covid and subsequently due to the civil war, led the government to cancel the agreement in 2022 (Fentaw 2022). Moreover, this episode disrupted the second phase of Scaling Solar, which would have comprised six solar projects totalling 750 MW, as well as plans to apply the same IFC-sponsored process to wind-power.

[39] Interview EG13, former senior EEP official, Addis Ababa, 19 February 2020.

[40] Interviews EG16, senior EEP official, Addis Ababa, 30 September 2019; ED18, donor official involved in the electricity sector, Addis Ababa, 2 October 2019; EP7, lawyer in the electricity sector, Addis Ababa, 30 September 2019. Another area in which the government has been forced into reform is regarding ratification of the New York Convention on arbitration. While this is considered important to address foreign investors' concerns, it constrains the government powers over the private sector.

[41] Interviews EP7, lawyer in the electricity sector, Addis Ababa, 30 September 2019; ED18, donor official involved in the electricity sector, Addis Ababa, 2 October 2019.

Table 9.2 Planned Scaling Solar projects

	Project	Installed capacity (MW)	Estimated cost (US$ million)
Scaling Solar 1	Gad	125	150
	Dicheto	125	150
Scaling Solar 2	Mekele	100	120
	Humera	100	120
	Welenchiti	150	165
	Weranso	150	165
	Metema	125	125
	Hurso	125	150

Data source: MoF (2021)

The PPP process to date has raised serious concerns among the private sector regarding the government's ability to commit to contracts, a basic requirement for private investment. To a degree, the challenges to date can be attributed to a lack of capacity and expertise in government, and the typical decision to pursue so many tenders at the same time, stretching state capacity thin (Ayele et al. 2021). Until very recently, there was no experience whatsoever of private sector finance within state agencies, which had been accustomed to engineering, procurement, and construction (EPC) contracts that provide the government with considerable flexibility with contractors:

> The government is still in the process of learning. Their previous assumption is that IPP is similar to EPC. There has been a gradual change in approach with the technical people. But at higher levels—the senior management and the PPP board, the state ministers—they still don't understand the difference.[42]

Likewise, one investor in renewable energy expressed their frustration:

> I am not sure the government is really aware of the concepts of time or value for money… It's this sort of EPC mentality that they are used to and a project finance deal is so different to an EPC. Ethiopia will always get investors, but with this kind of behaviour, you'll lose value for money and you won't get competitive offers.[43]

Beyond issues of capacity, however, longstanding scepticism about the private sector from the Derg's nationalization of the main means of production to the EPRDF's concerns about 'parasitic rent seekers' is, inevitably, proving slow to change. One international official involved in these processes has concluded that

[42] Interview ED5, donor official involved in the electricity sector, Addis Ababa, 12 February 2020.
[43] Interview EP16, investor in geothermal energy, Addis Ababa, 19 August 2019.

> the government has a paranoia about being taken for a ride with privatization and getting it wrong … They believe that private sector success is a sign they got it wrong rather than successful privatization. They still believe they can continually renegotiate terms on signed contracts as with geothermal.[44]

Ultimately, however, the result is to provide 'seriously negative messaging to the private sector'.[45] In spite of the significant steps taken towards liberalization and significant donor support to de-risk private sector investment, for now, the result is well short of the creation of a viable energy market. As one investor summed up the situation,

> If you think about it, we are taking the risk, in a sector that has never done an IPP, with a customer that has never done one. Most people are looking at us, asking us if we are crazy. We don't have an informed customer.[46]

Questions about the risk of investment in Ethiopia have been enhanced by the civil war that shook the country from late 2020. The conflict affected area included several of the planned solar sites in Tigray, Afar, and Amhara, leading to their suspension (Fentaw 2022). More generally, the war and threat of its spread has served as a disincentive to would-be investors. Despite the major change in rhetoric towards the private sector, to date this has not yet been matched by the realization of private sector energy projects.

Power to the People? Political Reforms and Mass Electrification

The changes in the electricity sector also have implications for distribution. In particular, a new approach to rural electrification, which was in process before the 2018 political transition, was incorporated within a new political narrative of improved governance and service delivery under the Prosperity Party. The initial step was the 2016 National Electrification Strategy, which acknowledged the limitations of the Universal Electrification Access Programme. This led to two versions of a National Electrification Programme (NEP) issued in 2017 and 2019. Drawing on study tours to Indonesia and Vietnam (MoWIE 2019, pp. 36–37), NEP planned out the 'least-cost' approach to universal electrification based on a donor-funded Geographic Information System (GIS) mapping of the electric grid and population, and the World Bank's Multi-Tier Framework (MTF) that was used to estimate the amount of electricity required by different types of household. The result is a dual emphasis, on the one hand, on connecting the vast numbers of people who live near the existing grid but lack a connection, and on the other, a new emphasis

44 Interview ED18, donor official involved in the electricity sector, Addis Ababa, 2 October 2019.
45 Interview EP16, investor in geothermal energy, Addis Ababa, 19 August 2019.
46 Interview EP16, investor in geothermal energy, Addis Ababa, 19 August 2019.

on off-grid solutions for households that have little prospect of a grid connection in the medium to long term.

NEP's main focus remains the electric grid and the distribution of Ethiopia's growing hydropower capacity. Having made major investments in connecting urban centres under the Universal Electrification Access Programme (UEAP), the surveys underpinning the strategy found that 44 per cent of households live within 1 kilometre of the grid, while a further 16 per cent live 1–2.5 kilometres away (MoWIE 2019, p. 15). As such, the NEP proposes a 'strategic shift from infrastructure development to service delivery' focusing on what is described as 'densification' by building the 'last mile' of electric connections to consumers (MoWIE 2019, p. 15).[47] The strategy is framed as a means of addressing the grievances associated with the UEAP. As one senior official argued,

> The universal electrification plan started in 1998 [EC, 2005] and lasted for 11 or 12 years. It mainly targeted town centres ... This raised expectations and grievances ... [People would say] 'the line passes over us, but we don't get electricity'.[48]

Alongside this change in strategy, there has also been a reform of the organizational structure of electricity distribution. This began in 2016 when UEAP, previously focused on transmission lines to connect towns and based in EEP, was moved to EEU, with its remit of distribution and connections. Moreover, first UEAP and then EEU in 2018 underwent a process of decentralization creating regional offices accountable to regional governments. In the long term, one possibility is that the federal EEU is entirely replaced by fully independent regional utilities.[49] Numerous respondents from federal and regional governments argued that these reforms offered the prospect of improved governance and accountability, an implicit, and sometimes explicit, criticism of the previous system and regime. In line with the standard expectations of the good governance agenda, respondents asserted that decentralization would increase responsiveness of decentralized utilities and their accountability to regional administrations.[50]

While the NEP is framed as a 'least-cost' approach to universal electrification, it is nonetheless a massive undertaking given the numbers of connections involved. The Ministry of Water, Irrigation, and Energy (MoWIE) estimates that

[47] As with the national economic strategy, the NEP asserts that it is a 'homegrown strategy' (MoWIE 2019, p. xv). Yet it is clear that donors such as the World Bank and USAID had a major role in its design.

[48] Interview EG2, senior energy sector official, Addis Ababa, 3 September 2019, 13 February 2020.

[49] Interview EG37, senior energy sector official, Addis Ababa, 21 August 2019, 19 February 2020.

[50] Interviews EG29, Member of Parliament, 27 August 2019; EG2, senior energy sector official, Addis Ababa, 3 September 2019, 13 February 2020; EG21, EEU official, Bahir Dar, 10 March 2020.

capital expenditure on the grid would require $10.4 billion[51]—or roughly double the original budget for the GERD—by 2025 to achieve its contribution to universal access (MoWIE 2019, p. 29). As such, government resources and revenues from increased tariffs will need to be heavily supplemented by donor funding if the NEP is to get anywhere near its targets.

An even more marked change in the NEP is a new focus on off-grid access for households living more than 2.5 kilometres from the grid. As noted in Chapter 8, the EPRDF prioritized grid expansion and made only modest efforts to expand off-grid access. In contrast, NEP plans a very rapid expansion of off-grid infrastructure, providing access to electricity for the remaining 35 per cent of the population who will not be connected to the grid by 2025 and thereby reaching the goal of universal electrification. As NEP acknowledges, this will require a 'dramatic acceleration' in off-grid rates to 1 million new connections per year (MoWIE 2019, p. 22). Nevertheless, off-grid technology continues to be seen as an 'interim solution' for most households (MoWIE 2019, p. 16). Indeed, in the following five years to 2030 NEP plans a further grid expansion, incorporating new mini-grids into the main grid, with just the 4 per cent of the population living more than 25 kilometres from the current grid in the most remote areas retaining off-grid access in the long term (see Figure 9.8).

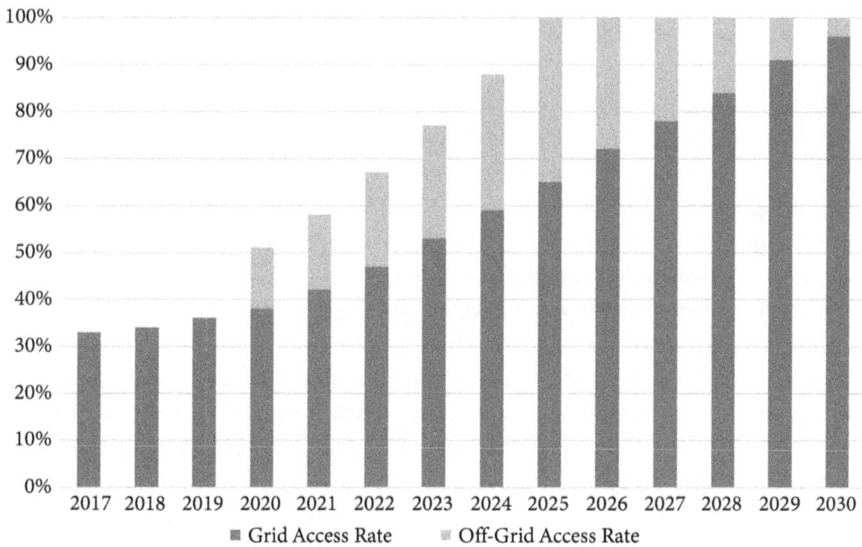

Figure 9.8 Plans for grid and off-grid expansion under NEP, 2017–2030
Data source: Author based on MoWIE (2019).

[51] That is, $3.2 billion to connect those within 2.5 kilometres of the existing grid and another $7.2 billion for transmission lines to areas up to 25 kilometres from the grid.

Another major shift is that the private sector is now expected to take the lead in the major investments required to expand off-grid access. Yet, the few private sector firms already involved in off-grid technologies remain very sceptical about government plans. For mini-grids to be commercially viable, they require a relatively high concentration of customers, yet with the highly dispersed rural population, there are relatively few locations in which this is present.[52] Moreover, the NEP's plans for grid expansion—however implausible they may be—undermine the viability of private investment in mini-grids.[53] In particular, the major planned grid expansion between 2025 and 2030 would integrate most mini-grids into the grid, so

> if you believe the NEP, no one will invest. You are required to have 10 to 15 years for the return on investment with a mini grid. But in the NEP there is only seven years before the grid arrives. When you go to MoWIE—a different part of the same ministry—they ask for 15- to 20-year return plans, but that is inconsistent with the grid expansion plan.[54]

While there are signs of a significant change in the governance of the electricity sector, one thing that does not appear to have altered is the government's recurrent setting of ambitious—or rather implausible—targets. Despite the recurrent narrative of mass electrification associated with GERD fundraising efforts, the goal of universal electrification still seems to be many years away from being achieved.

Conclusions

The period since 2015, and particularly since the change of government in 2018, has seen the almost complete unravelling of the 'developmental state' and the political economy that underpinned Ethiopia's dams boom. Previously, massive state investment in hydropower was expected to provide subsidized access to cheap electricity for mass consumers and industry as a means of consolidating the position of the ruling party. In the midst of a debt and political crisis, donor agencies have pressed for a complete change in approach, one that appears to resonate with at least elements within the Prosperity Party Government. While government plans continue to be impeded by recurrent over-ambition and a shortage of capacity, as well as the recent conflict, the result is that the current direction of travel in the electricity sector is towards liberalization and private sector investment in generation and distribution. In turn, donor investment guarantees intended to

[52] Interviews ED12, donor representative, Addis Ababa, 7 August 2019; EP4 and EP5, representatives of an off-grid electricity firm, Addis Ababa, 6 June 2019.

[53] A longstanding problem according to Asress et al. (2013).

[54] Interviews EP4 and EP5, representatives of an off-grid electricity firm, Addis Ababa, 6 June 2019.

support creation of an electricity market intersect with the objective of pursing a market-led energy transition. Consequently, prospective new investments are primarily in renewable electricity, raising the prospect of a degree of diversification away from hydropower in Ethiopia's energy mix. The result is the abandonment of the central tenets of the EPRDF's state-hydro model for the electricity sector.

Meanwhile, the Prosperity Party administration continues to labour towards the completion of the final legacies of the EPRDF era: GERD and Koysha. Resources have been constrained given the debt crisis and the civil war, greatly delaying construction as a result. Moreover, the unravelling of Ethiopia's foreign policy that had previously isolated Egypt in the GERD negotiations has significantly complicated matters. Nonetheless, the reality is that Ethiopia holds most of the cards and with each passing year edges closer to the completion of the massive Blue Nile Dam. While the GERD and, likely, Koysha will eventually be completed, it is far from clear quite what the future holds for Ethiopian dam building. Certainly, Ethiopia's hydropower potential is nowhere near being exhausted, with numerous potential dam sites in the Blue Nile, Baro, and Omo Basins. However, it is likely to be some time before Ethiopia once again possesses the key factors that underpinned the EPRDF's dams boom, namely political cohesion, financial capacity, and technical capacity.

10

Ethiopia's Renaissance, Dams, and State-Led Development in the Twenty-First Century

Tom Lavers

The utilization of Ethiopia's rivers for hydropower and irrigation, thereby spurring national development, has been a central objective of Ethiopian Governments, at least since the reign of Haile Selassie. The reality, however, was that dam building under the emperor and his military successors, the Derg, was limited to relatively small dams in the river basins with the least potential for hydropower along with increasingly grand but largely unrealized plans to take advantage of the western basins. Ethiopia's hydro ambitions were constrained by internal political fragmentation, the financial weakness of one of the poorest economies in the world, and a marginal position on the global stage which translated into minimal external support for dam building that would threaten the key geo-strategic prize in the region—Egypt.

It was only with the ascent to power of the Ethiopian Peoples' Revolutionary Democratic Front (EPRDF) that concrete steps were taken towards realizing Ethiopia's hydraulic mission, particularly in the most politically challenging river basin—the Blue Nile. The EPRDF came to power with a long-term vision for the structural transformation of the country and a perception of political vulnerability among its leadership that made developmental progress an imperative. For the EPRDF, the only way to achieve the political consolidation of the regime was to grow the economy and distribute these economic gains—in the form of land, increased agricultural yields, and manufacturing employment—through party-state structures to secure the compliance of the masses (Lavers 2023). The imperative of economic progress directly translated into the necessity of increased electricity generation to meet ever-growing demand from domestic, agricultural, and industrial users. This sense of urgency was further reinforced in the early 2000s with a series of 'Armageddons'—a party split, food crisis, and urban protests—that threatened the EPRDF's hold on power. The crises reinforced the sense of urgency of developmental progress, and the concentration of political power around Meles Zenawi from this point led to a massive upscaling of ambitions for rapid development and, in particular, a series of ever-larger hydroelectric

Dams, Power, and the Politics of Ethiopia's Renaissance. Tom Lavers et al., Oxford University Press. © Tom Lavers (2024).
DOI: 10.1093/oso/9780192871213.003.0010

dams. The centralization of political power and the EPRDF's long-term strategy was essential to overcoming the barriers that had held back Ethiopia's hydraulic mission in the past. After 2003, a booming economy gave the government greater fiscal room for manoeuvre and autonomy from external donors. At the same time, stability internally translated into improved international relations with key states in the region and the major global powers—both the United States (US) and China. Improved relations with upstream Nile riparians and vitally Sudan meant the growing isolation of Egypt in defence of the status quo, and an increasingly influential upstream coalition in favour of reform.

The political imperative of rapid expansion of electricity generation and the government's long-term strategy—along with the remnants of Marxist ideology—were also key determinants of the state-hydro model pursued in the electricity sector. The government's central priority was to support the creation of a vibrant manufacturing sector that would provide mass employment and thereby stabilize the regime. For this purpose, the government required not just improved access to large amounts of electricity but also *cheap* electricity that would subsidize the production costs of the nascent industrial sector. State control of the electricity sector was seen as essential to providing the required investment and subsidies that would not be feasible through 'rent-seeking' private sector investors in the electricity sector.

Ethiopia's considerable hydropower potential was seen as the only means of fulfilling this ambition, providing the cheapest long-run source of power and avoiding external dependence on fossil fuel imports. Although motivated primarily by material concerns, hydropower also offered the potential to be wrapped in a narrative of 'green development' and sustainable energy generation. The resulting dam-building strategy faced considerable financial challenges to mobilize sufficient resources to provide the required investment and subsidies. However, it also faced the challenge of securing the technical and bureaucratic capacity to deliver a series of increasingly complex engineering projects. In line with its 'developmental state' ideology, the government envisaged a process in which Ethiopian firms would gradually acquire the necessary competence and experience to take on large-scale projects themselves through learning from foreign contractors and engaging in joint ventures. In the meantime, however, the missing piece in Ethiopia's dam-building strategy was filled by Salini, an Italian firm with deep Ethiopian roots, which through a series of projects in the Omo Basin demonstrated its ability to deliver on complex projects, while persisting in the face of considerable political controversy surrounding the Gilgel Gibe III Dam.

The high point of the EPRDF's developmental push and its dams boom arrived around 2015–2016. By this point, the Gilgel Gibe III Dam—at 1,870 megawatts (MW), the largest in the country—had brought installed capacity to more than 4,000 MW, a 10-fold increase on that inherited from the Derg in 1991. Moreover, Ethiopia's political cohesion, financial capacity, and foreign relations had enabled the beginning of construction of the Grand Ethiopian Renaissance Dam (GERD) and, in 2015, the Declaration of Principles effectively signalled for the first time Egypt and Sudan's acceptance, however grudging, of Ethiopia's Blue Nile Dam. The opening of a series of industrial parks and a new railway from Addis Ababa to Djibouti, all powered by hydroelectricity, appeared to signal the triumph of the EPRDF's 'green developmental state'.

The political upheaval of subsequent years has, however, served to highlight that this dams boom was symbolic not only of the successes but also of the many failings of the EPRDF's 'developmental' project. The key factor driving the dams boom—namely, the political pressure for rapid progress—ultimately turned out also to be its key failing. While the ruling elite's political centralization and perceived vulnerability translated into the urgency of rapid economic development and dam building, it also meant a series of politically driven targets that warped the planning process, bypassing available technocratic capacity. Likewise, while Salini's elevation to go-to contractor and a key figure in the proposal and design of dams was a vital component of the dam-building strategy, the relationship with Salini was also problematic. Salini remains a private company with commercial interests that could never fully replace the role of an empowered and competent technocracy in holding the government to account. Moreover, Salini's 'fast-track approach' to project delivery accentuated these weaknesses, delivering rapid progress perhaps, but at the cost of standard planning and project management processes that might otherwise have placed constraints on the ambitions of the political leadership.

The result is that, despite the undeniable progress that has been made, the EPRDF's dam-building programme failed to deliver on the regime's key political economic objectives. Many of Ethiopia's dams, including the GERD, were designed to maximize installed capacity and largely ignored energy generation, with the result that they are a rather costly and inefficient way of addressing Ethiopia's electricity needs. In addition, in the case of the GERD, the attempt to build domestic capacity by contracting Metals and Engineering Corporation (MetEC) for the electro-mechanical works massively backfired, exacerbating other construction delays with the result that the dam construction has proceeded far behind schedule and, presumably, considerably over budget. Moreover, this dam building has thus far failed to deliver low-cost, reliable access to electricity for key end users, as envisaged by the political leadership. The initial strategy for electricity distribution planned a massive expansion of the electric grid to connect remote hydropower plants to towns and villages across the country, meeting the needs of rural-based manufacturing and mass access. However, the cost and time required for this grid expansion was one of several factors that contributed to a new industrial strategy from the mid-2010s that focused instead on state-constructed industrial parks, concentrating required infrastructure in particular locations to entice foreign firms to relocate production to Ethiopia. Yet, the top-down decision-making process and rushed implementation of these parks has, once again, undermined coordination, with the result that many parks lack reliable access to electricity, discouraging investment.

Meanwhile, vast numbers of Ethiopians still lack any access to electricity and, contrary to the official narrative, even the impending completion of the GERD will not quickly lead to universal access. Rather, the massive challenge of densification and grid expansion remains. Finally, the aim of turning the electricity sector into a major source of foreign exchange earnings remains unrealized. While modest exports have begun and there are prospects for future growth, thus far the government's grand ambitions have been constrained by neighbouring countries' own ambitions of electricity generation, delays in the construction of transmission infrastructure, and the difficulty of negotiating international agreements for electricity sales, particularly in the Blue Nile Basin. The overall result, then, is that the electricity sector has fallen short of its key objectives, while accumulating vast debts from state investment and subsidies.

In 2024, Ethiopia's dam-building programme is at a moment of considerable uncertainty. The internal political cohesion and external coalitions that the EPRDF had crafted fell apart spectacularly as mass protests spread across Oromiya and subsequently nationwide from 2014. By 2018, political reform was essential and the EPRDF's nomination of Abiy Ahmed as prime minister marked the Tigrayan People's Liberation Front's (TPLF's) loss of dominance and the growing influence of the Amhara and Oromo branches of the ruling coalition. Political elite fragmentation coincided with acknowledgement of the growing debt crisis and a rush from foreign donors to press for reform of the state-led development model. Major steps have now been taken to begin the liberalization of the electricity sector, raising tariffs and promoting private investment as a means of further generation expansion. In doing so, donor guarantees to reduce investor risks have been selectively applied, prioritizing non-hydro renewables, thereby pushing a degree of diversification away from hydropower. The combined result has been to pick apart the EPRDF's state-hydro model for the electricity sector.

The political and debt crisis has also had important implications for the GERD directly. The political transition facilitated the removal of MetEC from the project and exposed the firm's limitations for such a complex undertaking. The subsequent fallout with the TPLF and descent into war further drained limited state resources for the GERD, while instability in Benishangul-Gumuz has disrupted transportation and thereby the dam's construction. Moreover, internal political fragmentation and indebtedness since 2018 have exposed Ethiopia to external influence, undermining its autonomy regarding influential regional and global actors. The result is that while the GERD is slowly creeping towards completion, Ethiopia has been subject to intense external pressure to negotiate with Egypt and

Sudan, and to come to an agreement that would shape operation of the completed dam. These negotiations have thus far resulted in a political stalemate, with the three countries manoeuvring for advantage while posturing to domestic audiences, frequently through nationalist stances. Ultimately, all three have a direct interest in securing some sort of deal, however. Most directly, Egypt and Sudan need security and predictability of their vital water supplies. However, for Ethiopia, a deal stipulating releases from the GERD is surely a key requirement of any future prospect of electricity sales to Sudan or Egypt, both potentially lucrative markets. Finally, all three countries would benefit from clear operating procedures to address future multi-year droughts that might otherwise lead to escalation of the dispute. To date, none of the three countries has been willing to move far from their initial entrenched and incompatible positions in the bargaining process. However, the pending completion of the dam construction may sharpen the focus and the incentives to compromise.

An outstanding question concerns what will become of Ethiopia's dam building in the future. While the GERD was the largest single project in the EPRDF's plans, it is by no means the end to Ethiopia's hydropower ambitions. Beyond Koysha, there are preliminary plans for a smaller fifth project in the Gibe-Omo cascade, as well as other dams on the Omo's tributaries; several projects have been planned on the Baro River that feeds into the White Nile; and there is potential for another two dams on the Blue Nile itself, upstream of the GERD. The prospects for these dams in the short to medium term appear limited, however. It is likely to be some time before state finances recover to the point of supporting another wave of dam building. Moreover, the government is unlikely to find private finance for hydropower projects any time soon due to the high political and economic risks involved. While the prospects for further dam building in Ethiopia seem limited for the time being, a common feature of dam building worldwide has been that project proposals are rarely definitively rejected, but rather await the next propitious combination of political and economic drivers that lead decades-old studies to be dusted off and given concrete form.

The Multi-Scalar Politics of Dam Building

Chapter 1 proposed a multi-scalar framework used throughout the book to analyse the dynamics of Ethiopian dam building. The starting point for this framework was that large dam construction, and particularly the construction of a series of large dams as has been the case in Ethiopia over the past three decades, requires a combination of: elite cohesion that enables the ruling coalition to adopt a long time horizon and to mobilize available resources; the necessary technical capacity to design and implement projects; and access to sufficient sources of finance. Political cohesion, technical capacity, and financial resources are in turn shaped by the material interests and ideational commitments of key political and technical actors and the relations between them. However, dams are inherently multi-scalar phenomena, bringing together, for example, national governments and their developmental ambitions, cooperation and conflict between riparians, local impacts on displaced populations, and international relations, finance, and expertise. The preceding analysis of the Ethiopian dams boom demonstrates both the complexity of the processes at play and the utility of this broad analytical framework.

First, for a late-developing country—lacking established technical expertise and state resources—relations with global powers exert a major influence on the ability of national governments to secure the financial and technical expertise to build dams and other major infrastructure projects. Despite the EPRDF's developmental ambitions, it was not able to develop a capable domestic dam-building industry and remained reliant on external expertise and finance to supplement domestic resource mobilization. Ethiopia's early dam-building ambitions under Haile Selassie and the Derg were constrained by the Cold War rivalry between the US and Soviet Union, with both global powers prioritizing relations with Nile riparian Egypt. The end of the Cold War changed this dynamic and the advent of the US's 'war on terror' strengthened Ethiopia's position as an important anchor state for the US in the Horn of Africa. More recently, competition for influence in the Horn of Africa between the US and China has complicated the picture further, providing new sources of financial support, but also enmeshing the country within complex international relations. While these shifts have not translated into financial support for Ethiopian dams on the Blue Nile, they have somewhat weakened the previous straightforward prioritization of Egypt by the global powers.

The second level of analysis is the river basin and surrounding regional political economy. Ethiopia is an extreme example of a country which is the upstream riparian on every major transboundary river, while Egypt is a particularly extreme example of a downstream country—completely reliant for fresh water on a single river. Consequently, the river basin has been a particularly important factor shaping Ethiopian dam building. Moreover, the Nile and the Red Sea have been vitally important factors linking two Regional Security Complexes, namely the Horn of Africa and the Middle East.[1] In doing so, Nile hydropolitics are inevitably shaped by regional power shifts and alliances. Egypt's strategy for maintaining its dominance of the Nile Basin involved using its global and regional influence to deny Ethiopia the financial and technical capacity to build dams, while provoking political instability within Ethiopia and on its borders. The result was to force past Ethiopian Governments to focus dam building instead on river basins with

[1] One future possibility is that linkages between these regions, in terms of military alliances and flows of troops and weapons; inter-dependence of port and other transport infrastructure; and agricultural and industrial investments develop to the point at which the Horn is effectively incorporated into the Middle East Regional Security Complex, as noted by Buzan and Wæver (2009).

much less potential in the eastern half of the country. This included the Awash, the one river that remains entirely within Ethiopian territory, and the Wabe Shabelle and Omo, whose downstream riparians Somalia and Kenya either had little ability or interest in resisting upstream dam construction. Despite Egypt's success in preventing any major dam on the Blue Nile for several decades, its position was inherently vulnerable, however, and political cohesion and economic development under the EPRDF presented a major threat to the status quo on the Nile. Ethiopia's eventual move to build the GERD—the largest possible dam on the Blue Nile—reinforced a pattern of dam building established with the High Aswan Dam whereby unilateral actions are used to consolidate power and pursue national priorities, undermining anything resembling 'optimal' river basin planning in the process.

While the international sphere certainly shaped the potential for Ethiopian dam building, a central argument put forward in this book is that the key factor driving Ethiopia's dams boom, and the third level of analysis in the framework, is national-level politics. The EPRDF Government both responded to and, through diplomatic initiative, sought to reshape international relations to its advantage. As noted above, the motivation for Ethiopian dam building was the ruling coalition's sense of vulnerability and its belief that structural transformation, powered by hydroelectricity, was the key to regime maintenance. As such, the dams boom is rooted in the material interests of the ruling party. However, the 'developmental state' framing adopted by the regime soon became a guiding ideology—strongly resonating with high modernism—justifying the pursuit of ever bigger projects, ever more megawatts, and the contracting of domestic firms to fulfil key engineering roles against all reason. Likewise, while the decision to focus on hydropower over other sources of electricity is rooted in material concerns regarding foreign exchange, long-run costs, and local expertise, Ethiopia's hydropower dominance was subsequently wrapped within a discourse of green developmentalism and sustainable energy generation. As such, both material interests and ideas are essential analytical tools to understanding the motivations and limitations of Ethiopian dam building.

A full understanding of the domestic politics of dam building cannot be limited to national political elites, however. Indeed, the fourth level of sub-national political elites has proven an important influence at times. Early efforts to build a dam at Lake Tana by British colonialists and Haile Selassie were held up, in part, by powerful regional lords and competitors for the Imperial throne in Gojjam and Begemdir. Meanwhile, dam ambitions during the Derg era were hamstrung by conflict with ethno-nationalist insurrections that drained state resources through protracted military conflicts. In contrast, the political centralization and state-building undertaken first by Haile Selassie and the Derg, and subsequently by the EPRDF, was an important underlying factor that enabled the EPRDF's eventual dam programme. Despite creating an ethnic federal system, the EPRDF-era constitution established federal control over all rivers and water bodies, and the party-state enhanced the government's control over regional administrations. The result was that for the first time the national dam-building programme faced little organized opposition from influential sub-national actors. Whether that remains the case is open to question, however. In the final years of the EPRDF and after 2018, regional autonomy has grown as the centre fragmented, and regions have increasingly contested federal initiatives. While there seems no prospect of the federal government's constitutional authority over rivers being weakened, future phases of dam building may well confront regional administrations with greater de facto power than was the case under the EPRDF.

The fifth and final level of analysis concerns the local level, at which dams take material form and have the most direct impacts on the populations living in the vicinity of the dam and its reservoir. The combination of physical and political geography in Ethiopia is such that the main dam sites are located in river valleys descending from the central highlands—where political power has long been concentrated—into the lowland periphery—which was more recently incorporated into Ethiopia. As such, a recurrent theme in Ethiopia, as elsewhere (McCully 1996), from Haile Selassie to the Derg, the EPRDF, and beyond, has been that politically marginal ethnic minorities in lowland regions have been negatively affected by Ethiopian dam building. Affected populations have been displaced in the name of transformation and modernization with little to no compensation for lost livelihoods and housing, and lost access to key land and water sources. In many instances government efforts at rehabilitation have focused on transforming people who had previously practised mobile livelihoods—whether forms of pastoralism or shifting cultivation—into settled agriculturalists. These schemes have rarely been successful. While the most recent resettlement programme to make way for the growing GERD reservoir sought to address some past failings and avoid the controversy associated with disrupted livelihoods in the South Omo, the familiar limitations of a top-down implementation process were nonetheless apparent. Given the constraints on political organization in Ethiopia, where resistance was quickly cast by the ruling party as being 'anti-development', the ability of affected populations to contest dam projects and associated plantations directly has been limited. Instead, the most prominent example of resistance is the campaign against the Gibe III Dam, which along with some local support was taken up by international advocacy organizations. This campaign played a part in blocking Western finance for the project, but at the high point of EPRDF dominance was not able to stop the dam.

The result is that understanding of the timing and pace of the EPRDF's dams boom as well as the spatial dynamics of dam building over successive regimes requires this broad, multi-scalar analytical framework. It was only when distinct political economy dynamics at each of these five levels of analysis came into alignment during the EPRDF era that the government was able to draw on the required political cohesion, technical capacity, and financial resources to pursue the hydraulic mission on the Blue Nile. Even then, this alignment was fleeting, with political fragmentation, economic crisis, and external intervention putting an end to the dams boom and forcing the Ethiopian Government in new directions to expand electricity generation capacity.

The Significance of Ethiopian Dam Building

Ethiopia's dams boom is of great importance to the political economy of development in Ethiopia and across the Nile Basin. However, this particular case has broader significance to debates regarding the role of the state in development, the politics of dam building, and the political economy of energy transitions, as discussed in Chapter 1. The final task of this chapter is to return to these themes and to highlight the contribution of this study to those literatures.

State-Led Development and Governance of the Electricity Sector

The EPRDF bucked the dominant global trend of recent decades towards market-led development. Drawing on a mixture of socialist ideology and the East Asian developmental states, the government placed the state at the centre of its development efforts in agriculture, industry, and infrastructure. In doing so, Ethiopia became something of an exemplar for those arguing for state-led development and a more active approach to industrial policy (Oqubay 2015; Cheru et al. 2019; Hauge 2019). The electricity sector was an important feature in this development model, and here also the EPRDF rejected external pressure for unbundling, liberalization, and privatization as part of the World Bank's Standard Model, retaining an integrated state utility to deliver key government priorities of increased generation and supply of low-cost hydroelectricity.

Broadly in line with Doner et al.'s (2005, 2009) theory of 'systemic vulnerability', the main driver of state-led development in Ethiopia was elite perceptions of threat and vulnerability. The EPRDF came to power as a minority ethnic group that was unable to consolidate control through patronage or electoral politics. As such, the government instead pursued rapid, broad-based development as a means of binding the population to the regime, first through access to land and agricultural livelihoods, and subsequently through industrial policy and employment creation (Lavers 2023). In turn, this necessitated a massive increase in electricity provision providing access to industry and the masses. At the same time, however, the Ethiopian experience also signals a limitation of Doner and colleagues' theory regarding the connection between elite vulnerability and economic development. According to Doner et al.'s work, where the threat to ruling elites is sufficiently severe, elites invest in the state capacity required to deliver on politicians' developmental objectives. As such, the more parsimonious reading of their theory is rather ahistorical, ignoring pre-existing levels of state capacity. In the Ethiopian case, the EPRDF inherited from the Derg a relatively low level of state capacity, particularly in the technical expertise required to plan and implement hydroelectric projects. The result was that the regime's growing infrastructural ambitions and development targets quickly outpaced the government's subsequent attempts to build the state capacity to deliver on these. As a consequence of this rush to advance and the centralization of decision-making power, many projects and priorities in the electricity sector and beyond were identified by politicians before being imposed on the technocracy. Frequently, this resulted in poorly thought-out and inefficient projects that only partially delivered on their objectives. One conclusion to be drawn from the Ethiopian case is that some minimum level of existing technical and bureaucratic capacity is required in advance of elite threats. Where this is the case, developmentally orientated politicians may be more likely to empower technocrats, rather than bypassing them, while these technocrats may be better placed to challenge poorly thought-out political projects.

Given that Ethiopia has become such a central case for debates about state-led development, what then are the implications of Ethiopia's experience for other countries currently tackling the challenge of late development? On the one hand, the EPRDF's development model delivered the longest sustained period of economic growth in Ethiopia's history, fuelled by massive state investment in economic infrastructure, alongside increased access to social services and large-scale poverty reduction. It is hard to believe that comparable progress could have been achieved had the EPRDF acquiesced to donor pressure for liberalization and privatization in the 1990s. Yet, the legacy of this period and the prospects for further progress at the current juncture are decidedly mixed. The state-led development model accumulated massive debts that will be a burden for many years to come, while many megaprojects in transport, industry, and electricity have not fully delivered. In certain respects, this all feels rather predictable and reminiscent of the post-World War II phase of state-led development, which too often led to a series of high modernist infrastructure projects that failed to meet expectations (Scott 1998; Mold 2012).

The Ethiopian case is also an important one concerning debates about electricity sector governance. In retaining an integrated state utility, Ethiopia differed markedly from the direction of travel globally. Once again, the performance in the electricity sector is rather mixed, with a major expansion of generation capacity, yet modest improvements in electricity access for industrial and domestic users. Had Ethiopia followed World Bank policy prescriptions of unbundling and liberalization, would the Standard Model have performed better? It is far from clear that it would. There is little evidence to suggest that massive private sector investment would have been forthcoming without major support from donors in the form of co-investment and risk guarantees. Indeed, comparable reforms in other countries have failed to deliver the expected benefits (Zhang et al. 2008). Examples in this regard include Uganda, probably the African country that has gone furthest towards implementation of the Standard Model, where, two decades later, electricity access remains extremely low and electricity tariffs are among the highest in the world (Gore 2017). Likewise, somewhat more modest liberalization in Ghana has resulted in a hugely costly over-supply of expensive contracts with independent power producers (IPPs) amidst recurrent load shedding (Dye 2023), despite the Ghanaian Government prioritizing a major expansion of electricity access ever since independence (MacLean, Bob-Milliar et al. 2016; MacLean, Gore et al. 2016). Indeed, the limitations of the Standard Model have even been acknowledged by some within the World Bank, who identify the 'ambiguous' impacts of such a one-size-fits-all approach (see Lee and Usman 2018). Beyond this, donor efforts to crowd in private finance in infrastructure also transfers significant risk to the state through take-or-pay clauses in power purchase agreements (PPAs) and partial risk guarantees, which if triggered, transfer into World Bank loans (Gabor 2021). As such, while liberalization and privatization are currently presented by donors and some in government in Ethiopia as necessary steps in the light of the country's debt burden, these reforms are by no means magic bullets and are certainly not without major risks.

For decades, the EPRDF Government routinely dismissed the private sector as 'parasitic rent seekers', effectively barring them from playing any role in key sectors such as electricity generation. Since 2015, however, Ethiopia has initiated a number of public–private partnerships (PPPs) in renewable electricity generation and commenced a series of reforms that would take the electricity sector some way towards the Standard Model that had long been resisted. Indeed, some have—rather prematurely—proclaimed Ethiopia as an emerging success story for private sector investment in renewable technologies (Tsafos and Carey 2020). In several respects, Ethiopia's reforms echo Gore et al.'s (2019) conclusions regarding the drivers of electricity sector reform in other African countries, with indebtedness and close relations with the World Bank proving influential, along with an absence of civil society mobilization to resist reforms. Indeed, there is a certain irony here. While Ethiopia's 'developmental state' was explicitly framed as an alternative to the 'neo-liberalism' of the World Bank and International Monetary Fund (IMF) (Zenawi 2006a, 2006b, 2012), it was ultimately the excesses of this state-led infrastructure boom that exposed Ethiopia to debt vulnerability and provided the World Bank with the leverage required to push reforms. The Ethiopian case, moreover, highlights another vitally important factor, overlooked by Gore et al., that first enabled the EPRDF's resistance to reform and subsequent led to the embrace of reforms under the Prosperity Party: intra-elite relations. Ethiopia first came under pressure from the World Bank to reform the electricity sector in the late 1990s, but this was strongly resisted by an ideologically opposed and coherent political elite. Following years of growth under a state-led development model, from 2015 onwards, Ethiopia faced a dual economic and political crisis. Not only did high levels of debt force a turn to the World Bank and IMF for support, but the political transition within the ruling party also removed many of the main ideologues who had resisted liberalization in the past, while political fragmentation divided the remaining opposition. The result has been greater internal openness to economic reforms, including liberalization of the electricity sector.

The Third Wave of Dam Building

The extent of Ethiopia's dam building over the past three decades stands out within Africa.[2] While the GERD understandably attracts attention, the reality is that with 4,000 MW installed over the past three decades, Ethiopia already had the most installed hydropower capacity of any country in Africa even before the GERD and Koysha come online (IHA 2023b). The eventual completion of these dams will put Ethiopia out on its own as the main source of hydropower on the continent. Elsewhere in Africa, the late colonial and early independence periods produced a handful of large dams including: the 1,626-MW Kariba Dam completed in 1959 on the Zambezi between Zambia and Zimbabwe, which has the largest reservoir in the world by volume (Tischler 2013); Ghana's 1,038-MW Akosombo Dam built in 1965 which has the largest reservoir by surface area; the 2,075-MW Cahora Bassa Dam built on the Zambezi in Mozambique in 1974 (Isaacman and Isaacman 2013); and, of course, the 2,100-MW High Aswan Dam completed in 1970. However, none of these countries launched a dam-building programme of anything approaching the scale undertaken by the EPRDF. More recently, the third wave of dam building since 2000 has seen substantial dam programmes in Sudan, with the 1,250-MW Merowe Dam and the heightening of Roseires (Verhoeven 2015), and Angola, with construction of the Capanda (520 MW, completed in 2004), Laúca (2,070 MW, 2020), and Caculo Cabaça dams (2,172 MW, intended completion in 2024) (Dye and Alencastro 2020). Yet none of these compares to the range and size of dam projects undertaken in Ethiopia.[3]

So what does the Ethiopian case tell us about this latest dam resurgence? Large dams have long been associated with high modernism, namely an ideological

[2] The one country whose hydropower potential rivals, and perhaps exceeds, that of Ethiopia is the Democratic Republic of the Congo. To date the only completed dams are Inga I (351 MW 1972) and Inga II (1,424 MW 1982). Both have fallen into disrepair and operate well below their nameplate capacity. Plans to build the Grand Inga project which would amount to some 39 GW have not been implemented due to the reasons identified in the analytical framework guiding this book, notably political fragmentation and instability, a lack of technical and financial capacity, and concerns around the market for the electricity produced.

[3] It should be noted that Ethiopia's dam building pales in comparison to the largest earlier dam builders, such as the United States, with 102 GW of installed capacity, and the most prolific recent dam builders such as China (391 GW) and Brazil (109 GW) (IHA 2023b).

commitment and uncritical belief in the ability of science and planning to conquer nature and to deliver human progress (Scott 1998). High modernism in many instances closely connects to the pursuit of the hydraulic mission in which nature must be controlled and turned to human advantage, often with the result that dams do not merely provide a possible tool for expanding electricity generation but become the objective, synonymous with development itself. Past studies have underscored the importance of high modernism in shaping decision making in the first wave of dam building in the US and elsewhere, the second wave in newly independent countries following World War II (Tischler 2013; Sneddon 2015; Miescher 2022), and, in some cases, amidst the ongoing third wave of dam building (Dye 2016). The result has often been poorly planned and over-optimistic projects that neglect the complexity of political ecologies and generally fail to deliver claimed benefits. Clearly Ethiopia is not an exception to this trend, with the EPRDF's ideology of 'developmentalism' resonating in important ways with high modernism and playing an important role in driving over-ambition in the electricity sector and the attempt to transform the lowlands through irrigated plantations and resettlement. Yet, there is also a risk in over-emphasizing the importance of high modernist ideas in the EPRDF's developmental project. The EPRDF's dam building was not primarily motivated by ideological commitments to modernization. Rather, the starting point for the EPRDF's developmental push lay in the political leadership's assessment of the situation in which it found itself on taking power and following the Armageddons of the early 2000s. Their assessment was that the only way of maintaining political stability and retaining power was to pursue rapid development and structural transformation, underpinned by hydroelectricity. As such, the EPRDF's dams boom was an attempt to outpace the vulnerability and growing political crisis that the leadership faced. Ethiopian dam building was shaped by high modernist tendencies but was also rooted in the balance of power between state and society. As such, the Ethiopian case reinforces the need to integrate a focus on materiality and ideology in the conceptualization and analysis of dam building.

Having embarked on its dam-building mission, Ethiopia, like other late-developing countries, faced the central challenge of how to secure the technical capacity to plan and implement projects. One possibility is to establish and develop a domestic dam industry, usually beginning from scratch. Doing so confronts common industrial policy challenges, requiring extended periods learning how to use existing technology and building capabilities before advancing towards the technological frontier. This was the case with early dam builders such as the US (Reisner 1993), as well as later-comers such as China, Brazil, and Norway (Tendler 1968; Midttun 1988; McDonald et al. 2009). As with industrial policy in other areas, developing a domestic dam industry is likely to be slow and costly initially, with the challenge becoming harder and harder as the technological frontier advances and the gap between the technological frontier and domestic firm capabilities expands (Amsden 1992). Given these challenges, by far the most common choice by late-developing countries in the third wave has been to rely on external expertise, hiring foreign contractors from the earlier dam builders who developed expertise domestically before going global.

Ethiopia sought to buck this trend, setting out to build its own engineering capacity, partly inspired by its 'developmental state' ideology and partly due to the fear that foreign contractors would be pressured to abandon any project on the Nile. As such, the hope was that favoured domestic firms—most notably MetEC, but also the Ethiopian Construction Works Corporation, Ethiopian Electric Power (EEP), and several companies in the Endowment Fund for the Rehabilitation of Tigray (EFFORT) conglomerate—would build their capacity and expertise such that Ethiopia would be able to build its own dams without external support and even begin to export its expertise to other countries. The reality, however, was that government support to domestic engineering firms was too inconsistent and the perceived urgency of progress such that the dams boom could not wait for the necessarily slow process of building domestic expertise. EEP was regularly bypassed in the planning and decision-making process, while MetEC was rushed in to tackle the most complex parts of the GERD for which it was woefully unprepared. Ultimately, the government instead cultivated ties with Salini, a peculiar Ethio-Italian firm, which demonstrated its long-term commitment to working in Ethiopia, rather than the short-run economic calculations of other contractors. Salini gradually proved itself capable of meeting the government's ambitions and willing to persist in politically challenging projects. While this addressed the immediate challenge of finding a contractor willing to tackle the politically charged Blue Nile, it leaves open the question as to whether it is viable for late-developing countries such as Ethiopia to build a new dam-building industry from scratch. To what extent are MetEC's failings purely the result of poor planning and accountability failures, or do they also highlight the inherent difficulty of late industrialization?

The Ethiopian experience is also relevant to debates about the financing of dams. The funding possibilities for dams has shifted markedly since the post-World War II period when the World Bank and some other Western donors were the main source of finance. Western donors have now moved away from direct finance of projects with the World Bank instead providing investment and foreign exchange guarantees as a means of de-risking private infrastructure investments (Gabor 2021). Yet, investors view dam projects in low-income countries as excessively high risk, particularly those on politically charged transboundary rivers, with the result that this funding option is only really open to middle-income countries (Plummer Braeckman and Markkanen 2021). Instead, China's willingness to finance major dam projects has seen it emerge as perhaps the main actor in the dam resurgence. However, once again, China was not forthcoming to finance the GERD directly, given the hydropolitics of the Nile. Where foreign finance is not available, as was the case for Ethiopia on the Blue Nile, a country has little choice but to raise funds itself if it is to proceed. Much has been made of Ethiopia's mobilization of resources for the GERD through a wide range of popular initiatives (Menga 2017; Abtew and Dessu 2019). While certainly a useful supplement to state finances, the reality, however, is that these mass mobilization efforts likely contributed a relatively modest proportion of the total funding of the dam. The bulk of the construction costs have instead been met in more traditional ways—state revenues, bolstered by economic growth and rising tax receipts, and commercial loans, which bring risk and exposure to interest rate fluctuations. Indeed, the debt crisis in which Ethiopia has subsequently become embroiled suggests that the EPRDF's model for financing major infrastructure projects had major limitations.

The GERD is also of vital significance to the literature on the international relations shaping river basin politics. Prior to the launch of the GERD, the hydropolitics of the Nile Basin were frequently viewed through the lens of hydro-hegemony (Zeitoun and Warner 2006). From this perspective, Egypt had long established its hegemony over the river basin, a situation of 'leadership buttressed by authority' in which subordinate actors come 'to accept not just the hegemon's authority, but to adopt and internalize its values and norms' (Zeitoun and Warner 2006, p. 438). This hegemony was underpinned by Egypt's greater military and economic power, established claims based on existing water infrastructure, the support of global and regional powers, and a convincing narrative about Egypt's dependence on the Nile and the extreme threat of upstream water use (Cascão and Zeitoun 2010).

While Egyptian influence over the Nile Basin may have appeared hegemonic, the reality is that stability is always subject to challenge (Cascão 2008). Despite the label, Egypt was never truly a hegemon in the sense of having established legitimate authority and the consent of all riparians. Rather, the Egyptian position was more aptly described as dominance, 'defined as leadership buttressed by coercion' (Zeitoun and Warner 2006, p. 438). Arguably, governments in Sudan and Uganda may have, at times in the past, internalized the Egyptian position on the Nile (Waterbury 2002). That was not the case for Ethiopia, however, with successive regimes contesting the validity of the 1959 agreement, Egypt's unilateral downstream water projects, and their potential to damage Ethiopia's future water use. Instead of hegemony, Egypt's dominance of the Nile Basin was based on its leverage of ties to global and regional powers to cut Ethiopia off from access to international finance and technical support for dam projects. This dominance was inherently vulnerable since, as Meles Zenawi noted in the opening quote in Chapter 1, once the Ethiopian economy had started 'running' it would be able to forgo international finance. Ethiopia's counter-resistance to Egyptian dominance was multi-faceted, contesting Egypt's historic rights with the counter-narrative of equitable distribution, enhancing its influence with global and regional powers, and building alliances with upstream riparians. However, it was primarily through enhancing its own economic power that Ethiopia was able to challenge Egyptian dominance. Following a period of rapid growth during the 2000s and the accompanying growth in state revenues, by 2011 the Ethiopian leadership came to the conclusion that it had the resources to launch construction unilaterally. The weakness of the Egyptian position has been evident in the protracted negotiations since construction began. Egypt has sought to defend its historic rights and to build mechanisms for doing so into the rules for the operation of the GERD. In the face of Ethiopian refusal, however, there is very little that Egypt can do and construction creeps slowly forward with every passing year.

The Political Economy of Energy Transitions

The final contribution of this study is to the growing literature on the political economy of energy transitions in developing countries (Baker et al. 2014; Scoones et al. 2015; Newell and Phillips 2016; Power et al. 2016; Hochstetler 2020). The Ethiopian case reinforces the conclusion of a growing body of work that the energy mix is not merely a technical choice or one determined by natural resource endowments, but rather a reflection of political economy, including material interests, ideological commitments, and institutional arrangements (Hochstetler 2020). The energy mix is subject to path dependence whereby entrenched interests, dominant power relations, and ideological commitments result in self-reinforcing institutional 'lock-in' (Baker et al. 2014; Gore et al. 2019; Hochstetler 2020). Energy transitions therefore require not just new technology but the disruption of the existing political economy, allowing for a new set of actors with expertise and know-how to enter the sector. In the case of late-developing countries, where existing generation capacity is limited, the question arises as to the circumstances under which countries adopt renewable energy sources at an early stage, potentially locking in a renewable energy pathway.

Of course, Ethiopia's focus on hydropower partly reflects the considerable potential for dams on the many rivers that flow from the central highlands. However, the decision to focus exclusively on dams to power Ethiopia's developmental push was to an important degree also a reflection of the EPRDF's strategy for maintaining power, and the material interests and ideological commitments which shaped it. The EPRDF perceived a need for rapid economic development and structural transformation, necessitating a major expansion of electricity generation and access. During the 1990s, the World Bank, among others, pressed the government to prioritize thermal plants as the quickest means of addressing rising electricity demand. However, the government rejected these proposals. Having emerged victorious from the civil war, the EPRDF adopted a long-term vision for transforming the economy and this long-term planning underpinned the focus on hydropower as the cheapest energy source, albeit one with a long lead time for individual projects. In contrast, the leadership concluded that thermal plants risked exposing Ethiopia to the risk of reliance on costly fossil fuel imports. Furthermore, the EPRDF leadership retained a high degree of scepticism of the private sector based on its socialist and, subsequently, developmentalist ideology. The desire to maintain the electricity sector within state hands meant favouring and reinforcing the modest levels of technocratic expertise in dams and hydropower, while resisting the move to non-hydro renewables that would require foreign expertise and investment.

Ethiopia's hydropower focus was therefore a reflection of the EPRDF's political and economic strategy for ruling Ethiopia, rather than a deep ideological commitment to environmental sustainability. Nonetheless, as environmental issues rose on the global development agenda, the EPRDF and Meles, in particular, were able to position Ethiopia within these debates. According to this framing, Ethiopia was not just a 'developmental state' but a 'green developmental state', bucking the trend of unsustainable development in the early industrializers that had caused the growing climate crisis and demonstrating a model of sustainable development for other late developers. The government's environmental credentials were, in turn, used as a means of mobilizing resources, for Africa as the continent that had done the least to cause the climate crisis but which is most negatively affected by it, but also for Ethiopia, supporting the investments that would drive forward its green developmental project. However, Ethiopia's development trajectory may not be quite as sustainable as the government claims. While electricity generation does not rely on fossil fuels, the environmental credentials of its dams are open to question. Repeated studies have catalogued the wide array of negative environmental impacts of dam building in general (Adams 1992; McCully 1996; Khagram 2018) and there is little reason to suggest that Ethiopian dams are any exception to this general pattern. More specifically, there is a growing body of evidence that many dams, particularly in tropical climates, produce vast amounts of methane, a greenhouse gas far more problematic than carbon dioxide (Fearnside 2002, 2003; Giles 2006; Gunkel 2009; Kuriakose et al. 2022). Research on the greenhouse gas emissions from Ethiopian dams should therefore be a priority.

Ethiopia's tentative steps towards diversification away from hydropower also underscore the deeply political nature of energy transitions. Ethiopia's potential to develop large-scale solar, wind, and geothermal power has been known for many years. While relatively expensive and untested in the 1990s, technological improvements in wind and solar translated into rapidly falling prices in subsequent years. Moreover, studies suggest that solar, wind, and geothermal are highly compatible with Ethiopia's hydropower production, enhancing energy security by diversifying energy sources (Asress et al. 2013; Mondal et al. 2017). Yet for years, there was no significant push to develop renewable energy. The central obstacle was not any adversity towards renewable electricity, but rather the challenge that it represented to Ethiopia's state-controlled electricity sector. Ethiopia had no real expertise in these renewable technologies and, as such, a renewable energy transition would necessitate the liberalization of the electricity sector and the promotion of private investment. This in turn was incompatible with the EPRDF's central political economic objective for the sector: to support industry through the provision of low-cost electricity.

The initial steps that have been taken towards the embrace of renewables and diversification of the energy mix, meanwhile, have resulted directly from the political transition from the EPRDF to the Prosperity Party. The economic and political crisis since 2015 has disrupted the prevailing political economy in the sector, opening the way for reform and a degree of change in the energy mix. An initial process of generational change within the EPRDF from about 2010 began to remove many ideologues from the ruling coalition, a process that was reinforced by the 2018 change in leadership, with a clear-out of TPLF officials and many of the old guard in the other EPRDF parties. In their place, a new generation of appointees rose to prominence, many of them with past experience in international finance institutions and the finance industry. The result was a much greater openness to the private sector and foreign investment throughout the Ethiopian economy, including the electricity sector, which had previously been completely off-limits. This ideological shift was reinforced and enabled by the debt crisis that brought the previous state-hydro model for the electricity sector into doubt. The IMF had long expressed its concerns about the fiscal sustainability of Ethiopia's development model. The decisions to raise its risk assessment of Ethiopia's debt in 2015 and 2017 reduced Ethiopia's access to commercial lending and precipitated a debt crisis that became apparent in the midst of the political transition. The World Bank, IMF, US, and other Western lenders seized the long-awaited moment to press for the liberalization of the Ethiopian economy, offering large-scale debt relief in exchange for specific reforms to the EPRDF's cherished 'commanding heights' of the economy: telecommunications, logistics, and electricity.

The debt crisis and the pressure exerted by foreign donors, accompanied by the removal of the political figures most committed to the previous state-hydro model, have enabled some tentative but significant steps towards liberalization and, as a by-product, diversification of the energy mix. A key objective of these reforms is to bring private sector investment into generation. To do so, the government has been required to raise electricity tariffs closer to cost-reflective levels and has begun preparations to strengthen regulatory authorities, enabling EEP to operate in competition with private generation. Donor efforts to create a market for electricity generation have involved not only legal reforms but also financial support aimed at de-risking private sector investments in what is considered a high-risk context. As such, while some state officials remain committed to further expanding hydropower, the donors' financial backing of other renewables has meant that initial PPPs have focused on geothermal, solar, and wind. The Ethiopian case therefore reinforces the message that energy transitions are driven by political economy concerns and inevitably tied up with the dynamics of global capitalism.

In sum, then, the story of Ethiopia's dams boom is one in which the history of water and electricity is interwoven with the dynamics of political and economic power. Moreover, the successes and failures of Ethiopian dam building are illustrative of the strengths and limitations of the EPRDF's 'developmental state'. Over the past three decades, Ethiopia has experienced the most sustained period of economic growth in its history and improvement in almost every socioeconomic indicator. A massive expansion of economic infrastructure, including a series of major dams, has been at the heart of this progress. Yet, as the key symbol of the EPRDF's developmental project—the GERD—grinds slowly to completion, Ethiopia is mired in economic crisis and massive debt, and little closer to the structural transformation of the economy long prioritized by the EPRDF. In the aftermath of the dams boom, the new Prosperity Party Government appears set to take a very different path with the private sector pressed to the fore and non-hydro renewables preferred for future generation expansion. In the light of these contrasting fortunes, the Ethiopian case has equally mixed implications for the prospects of state-led development in other late-developing countries, the dams resurgence of the past two decades, and efforts to promote a renewable energy transition in response to the gathering climate crisis.

Glossary

Abay The Amharic name for the Blue Nile.

abun The head of the Ethiopian church.

belg The short rainy season in the Ethiopian highlands from March to April.

birr The Ethiopian currency.

Chaebol South Korea business conglomerate.

Derg Literally a committee (in Amharic), the name given to the committee of junior military officers that overthrew Haile Selassie in 1974.

distribution The supply of low-voltage electricity from sub-stations to end users.

Fano Youth in Amhara. *Fano* first emerged as a protest movement from 2016 to 2018. The term came to be used for a militia involved in subsequent conflicts.

firm energy The guaranteed energy generation of a dam, regardless of the inter-annual variability of river flow.

gimgema A system of evaluation used by the TPLF and then extended to the civil service. Involves critique and self-critique undertaken by individuals in front of their superiors and subordinates.

head The difference in water elevation between the reservoir level and the turbines, therefore dependent on the height of the dam and the drop in altitude of the existing watercourse.

iddir A burial association.

kilil The ethno-linguistic regions introduced under the federal system in 1994.

meher The long rainy season in the Ethiopian highlands from June to September.

penstock A pipe in a dam that carries water from the reservoir to the turbine.

plant factor The plant load factor (or capacity factor) is the actual energy generation of a plant over a year divided by its maximum potential energy generation. A high plant factor indicates that a power plant is operating continuously at near full capacity, while a low plant factor indicates that the plant operates at full capacity for only short periods, usually coinciding with peak demand.

qeerroo An Afaan Oromo term meaning an unmarried young man, approximately 20–36. *Qeerroo* emerged as an Oromo protest movement in 2014–2018.

rist A descent-based land tenure system common in much of northern Ethiopia prior to the 1974 revolution.

sub-station Sub-stations step down the electricity from high voltage used in transmission to low voltage used for distribution.

transmission The use of high-voltage lines to bring electricity from sources of generation to major centres of demand.

turbine A mechanical device that turns energy in a stream of fluid into useable energy.

wereda An administrative district.

References

Abate, Z., 1994. *Water Resources Development in Ethiopia: An Evaluation of Present Experience and Future Planning Concepts*. Ithaca, NY: Cornell University Press.

Abbink, J., 2012. Dam controversies: Contested governance and developmental discourse on the Ethiopian Omo River dam. *Social Anthropology*, 20 (2), 125–144.

Abdisa, L.T., 2018. Power outages, economic cost, and firm performance: Evidence from Ethiopia. *Utilities Policy*, 53, 111–120.

Abebe, D., 2023. Western Oromiya. *RVI Conflict Trend Analysis*.

Abtew, W. and Dessu, S.B., 2018. *The Grand Ethiopian Renaissance Dam on the Blue Nile*. Cham: Springer.

Abtew, W. and Dessu, S.B., 2019. Financing the Grand Ethiopian Renaissance Dam. In: W. Abtew and S.B. Dessu, eds. *The Grand Ethiopian Renaissance Dam on the Blue Nile*. Cham: Springer International Publishing, 161–169.

Acker, K., Brautigam, D., and Huang, Y., 2020. Debt relief with Chinese characteristics. *China Africa Research Initiative Working Paper*, 39.

Acres International, 2003. *Power Sector Masterplan Study*. Addis Ababa: Ethiopian Electric Power Corporation (EEPCo).

Adams, W.M., 1992. *Wasting the Rain: Rivers, People and Planning in Africa*. London: Earthscan.

ADF, 2011. *Ethiopia-Djibouti Power Interconnection Project: Completion Report*. African Development Fund.

ADF, 2012. *Ethiopia-Kenya Electricity Highway: Project Appraisal Report*. African Development Fund.

Adugna, T. and Cherie, D., 2021. A review on reservoirs sedimentation problems in Ethiopia. *Asian Journal of Advanced Research and Reports*, 15 (3): 1–8.

AfDB, 2015. *Multinational: Kenya–Tanzania Power Interconnection Project Appraisal Report—Revised Version*. Abidjan: African Development Bank (AfDB).

AfDB, 2022. *Implementation Progress and Results Report (IPR): Kenya–Tanzania Interconnection*. Abidjan: African Development Bank (AfDB).

Agamben, G., 2005. *State of Exception*. Chicago, IL: Chicago University Press.

Al-Jazeera English, 2020. Trump says Egypt may 'blow up' Ethiopia dam [online]. YouTube. Available from: www.newarab.com/news/egypt-may-withdraw-uae-based-nile-talks-ethiopia [Accessed 8 May 2023].

Ambaw, D., 2020. Infrastructure Equity for State- and Nation-Building Processes: The Case of Ethiopia. PhD thesis. Addis Ababa University, Addis Ababa.

Amsden, A.H., 1992. *Asia's Next Giant: South Korea and Late Industrialization*. Oxford: Oxford University Press.

Anberbir, Y., 2017. Nuts and bolts of Ethiopian power sector [online]. *The Reporter*. Available from: www.thereporterethiopia.com/content/nuts-and-bolts-ethiopian-power-sector [Accessed 8 June 2020].

Ang, Y.Y., 2016. *How China Escaped the Poverty Trap*. Ithaca, NY: Cornell University Press.

Ansar, A., Flyvbjerg, B., Budzier, A., and Lunn, D., 2014. Should we build more large dams? The actual costs of hydropower megaproject development. *Energy Policy*, 69, 43–56.

The Arab Republic of Egypt and Ethiopia, 1993. *Framework for General Co-operation between the Arab Republic of Egypt and Ethiopia*. Cairo: The Arab Republic of Egypt and Ethiopia.

Arriola, L.R., 2008. Ethnicity, economic conditions, and opposition support: Evidence from Ethiopia's 2005 elections. *Northeast African Studies*, 10 (1), 115–144.

Arsano, Y., 2007a. *Ethiopia and the Nile: Dilemmas of National and Regional Hydropolitics.* Zurich: Center for Security Studies, Swiss Federal Institute of Technology.
Arsano, Y., 2007b. *Ethiopia and the Nile: Dilemmas of National and Regional Hydropolitics.* Zurich: ETH.
Arsano, Y. and Tamrat, I., 2005. Ethiopia and the eastern Nile Basin. *Aquatic Sciences*, 67 (1), 15–27.
Ashami, M.G., 1985. The Political Economy of the Afar Region of Ethiopia: A Dynamic Periphery. PhD thesis. University of Cambridge, Cambridge.
Asress, M.B., Simonovic, A., Komarov, D., and Stupar, S., 2013. Wind energy resource development in Ethiopia as an alternative energy future beyond the dominant hydropower. *Renewable and Sustainable Energy Reviews*, 23, 366–378.
Atkins, E., 2020. Contesting the 'greening' of hydropower in the Brazilian Amazon. *Political Geography*, 80, 102179.
Ayalew, Y., 2019. Ethiopian financial sector development. In: F. Cheru, C. Cramer, and A. Oqubay, eds. *The Oxford Handbook of the Ethiopian Economy.* Oxford: Oxford University Press, 159–174.
Ayele, S., Shen, W., Worako, T.K., Baker, L., and Hadush, S., 2021. Renewable energy procurement in Ethiopia: Overcoming obstacles in procurement from independent power producers. *IDS Research Report*, 87.
Baker, L., Newell, P., and Phillips, J., 2014. The political economy of energy transitions: The case of South Africa. *New Political Economy*, 19 (6), 791–818.
Basheer, M., Wheeler, K.G., Ribbe, L., Majdalawi, M., Abdo, G., and Zagona, E.A., 2018. Quantifying and evaluating the impacts of cooperation in transboundary river basins on the water–energy–food nexus: The Blue Nile basin. *Science of the Total Environment*, 630, 1309–1323.
Basheer, M., Nechifor, V., Calzadilla, A., Siddig, K., Etichia, M., Whittington, D., Hulme, D., and Harou, J., 2021. Collaborative management of the Grand Ethiopian Renaissance Dam increases economic benefits and resilience. *Nature Communications*, 12 (5622).
Bates, A., Tuncok, K., and Klimpt, J.-É., 2013. Strategic perspectives and options assessment of Blue Nile multipurpose development. *NBI-ENTRO JMP1 Working Paper*, 2.
BBC News, 2005. You asked Ethiopia's PM Meles Zenawi [online]. *BBC News.* Available from: http://news.bbc.co.uk/1/hi/talking_point/4149925.stm [Accessed 15 May 2019].
Behnke, R. and Kerven, C., 2013. Counting the costs: Replacing pastoralism with irrigated agriculture in the Awash Valley. In: A. Catley, J. Lind, and I. Scoones, eds. *Pastoralism and Development in Africa: Dynamic Change at the Margins.* London: Routledge, 57–70.
Behuria, P., 2015. Between party capitalism and market reforms: Understanding sector differences in Rwanda. *The Journal of Modern African Studies*, 53 (03), 415–450.
Behuria, P., 2020. The politics of late late development in renewable energy sectors: Dependency and contradictory tensions in India's National Solar Mission. *World Development*, 126, 104726.
Bekele, G., 2009. Food matters: The place of development in building the post-war Ethiopian state, 1941–1974. *International Journal of African Historical Studies*, 42 (1), 29–54.
Bekele, M., 2021. The involvement of external forces behind Metekel conflict [online]. *The Reporter.* Available from: www.thereporterethiopia.com/11049 [Accessed 3 April 2023].
Bennett, A. and Checkel, J.T., 2014. *Process Tracing.* Cambridge: Cambridge University Press.
Berhe, A., 2008. A Political History of the Tigray People's Liberation Front (1975–1991): Revolt, Ideology and Mobilisation in Ethiopia. PhD thesis. Vrije Universiteit, Amsterdam.
Berhe, M.G., 2020. *Laying the Past to Rest: The EPRDF and the Challenges of Ethiopian State-Building.* London: Hurst & Company.
Berridge, W., De Waal, A., and Lynch, J., 2022. *Sudan's Unfinished Democracy: The Promise and Betrayal of a People's Revolution.* Oxford: Oxford University Press.
Beyene, G., 2018. The Challenges and Prospects of Electricity Access in Ethiopia. Master's thesis. Addis Ababa University, Addis Ababa.

Blackmore, D. and Whittington, D., 2008. *Opportunities for Cooperative Water Resources Development on the Eastern Nile: Risks and Rewards.* Report to the Eastern Nile Council of Ministers, Nile Basin Initiative, Entebbe. Entebbe: Nile Basin Initiative.

Block, P. and Strzepek, K., 2012. Power ahead: Meeting Ethiopia's energy needs under a changing climate. *Review of Development Economics*, 16 (3), 476–488.

Blyth, M., 2002. *Great Transformations: Economic Ideas and Institutional Change in the Twentieth Century.* Cambridge: Cambridge University Press.

Boone, C., 2003. *Political Topographies of the African State: Territorial Authority and Institutional Choice.* Cambridge: Cambridge University Press.

Booth, D. and Golooba-Mutebi, F., 2012. Developmental patrimonialism? The case of Rwanda. *African Affairs*, 111 (444), 379–403.

Borchgrevink, A., 2008. Limits to donor influence: Ethiopia, aid and conditionality. *Forum for Development Studies*, 2, 195–220.

Bosshard, P., 2009. China dams the world. *World Policy Journal*, 26 (4), 43–51.

Brautigam, D., 2009. *The Dragon's Gift: The Real Story of China in Africa.* Oxford: Oxford University Press.

Bräutigam, D., Fjeldstad, O.-H., and Moore, M., eds., 2008. *Taxation and State-Building in Developing Countries.* Cambridge: Cambridge University Press.

Brautigam, D. and Hwang, J., 2019. Great walls over African rivers: Chinese engagement in African hydropower projects. *Development Policy Review*, 37 (3), 313–330.

Bräutigam, D. and Tang, X., 2012. An overview of Chinese agricultural and rural engagement in Ethiopia. *IFPRI Discussion Paper*, 01185.

Brautigam, D., Weis, T., and Tang, X., 2018. Latent advantage, complex challenges: Industrial policy and Chinese linkages in Ethiopia's leather sector. *China Economic Review*, 48: 158–169.

Bush, R., 2007. Politics, power and poverty: Twenty years of agricultural reform and market liberalisation in Egypt. *Third World Quarterly*, 28 (8), 1599–1615.

Buzan, B. and Wæver, O., 2009. *Regions and Powers: The Structure of International Security.* Cambridge: Cambridge University Press.

Capital Newspaper, 2022. Second power transfer tests to Kenya to start next week [online]. *Capital Newspaper.* Available from: www.capitalethiopia.com/2022/11/27/second-power-transfer-tests-to-kenya-to-start-next-week [Accessed 14 February 2023].

Cardenas, H. and Whittington, D., 2019. The consequences of increasing block tariffs on the distribution of residential electricity subsidies in Addis Ababa, Ethiopia. *Energy Policy*, 128, 783–795.

Çarkoglu, A. and Eder, M., 2010. Domestic concerns and the water conflict over the Euphrates-Tigris River Basin. *Middle Eastern Studies*, 37(1): 41–71.

Carr, C.J., 2017. *River Basin Development and Human Rights in Eastern Africa: A Policy Crossroads.* Cham, Switzerland: Springer.

Cascão, A.E., 2008. Ethiopia: Challenges to Egyptian hegemony in the Nile basin. *Water Policy*, 10 (S2), 13–28.

Cascão, A.E., 2009. Changing power relations in the Nile river basin: Unilateralism vs. cooperation? *Water Alternatives*, 2 (2): 245–268.

Cascão, A.E. and Nicol, A., 2016a. GERD: New norms of cooperation in the Nile basin? *Water International*, 41 (4), 550–573.

Cascão, A.E. and Nicol, A., 2016b. Sudan, 'kingmaker' in a new Nile hydropolitics: negotiating water and hydraulic infrastructure to expand large-scale irrigation. In: E. Sandstrom, A. Jagerskog, and T. Oestigaard, eds. *Land and Hydropolitics in the Nile River Basin.* London: Routledge, 89–116.

Cascão, A.E. and Zeitoun, M., 2010. Power, hegemony and critical hydropolitics. *Transboundary Water Management: Principles and Practice*, 27, 42.

CGTN Africa, 2019. Ethiopia contracts Chinese companies to complete GERD construction. CGTN Africa.

Champion, M. and Manek, N., 2019. Death on the Nile haunts Ethiopia's rebirth. Bloomberg.com.

Chang, H.-J. and Hauge, J., 2019. The concept of a 'developmental state' in Ethiopia. In: F. Cheru, C. Cramer, and A. Oqubay, eds. *The Oxford Handbook of the Ethiopian Economy.* Oxford: Oxford University Press, 824–841.

Cheesman, M.R.E., 1936. *Lake Tana and the Blue Nile: An Abyssinian Quest.* 1st edition. London: Macmillan and Co.

Chen, G.C. and Lees, C., 2016. Growing China's renewables sector: A developmental state approach. *New Political Economy*, 21 (6), 574–586.

Chen, Y., 2021. Laying the tracks: The political economy of railway development in Ethiopia's railway sector and implications for technology transfer. *China Africa Research Initiative Working Paper*, 43.

Cheru, F., 2016. Emerging Southern powers and new forms of South–South cooperation: Ethiopia's strategic engagement with China and India. *Third World Quarterly*, 37 (4), 592–610.

Cheru, F., Cramer, C., and Oqubay, A., eds., 2019. *The Oxford Handbook of the Ethiopian Economy.* Oxford: Oxford University Press.

Cheryachukin, A.P. and Sitnin, O.V., 2000. Malka Wakana hydroproject on the Webi Shebeli river in Ethiopia. *Hydrotechnical Construction*, 34 (8), 485–489.

Chiengkul, P., 2018. The degrowth movement: Alternative economic practices and relevance to developing countries. *Alternatives*, 43 (2), 81–95.

Chiyemura, F., 2019. The Winds of Change in Africa-China Relations? Contextualising African Agency in Ethiopia-China Engagement in Wind Energy Infrastructure Financing and Development. PhD thesis. Open University, Milton Keynes.

Clapham, C., 1988. *Transformation and Continuity in Revolutionary Ethiopia.* Cambridge: Cambridge University Press.

Clapham, C., 2002. Controlling space in Ethiopia. In: W. James, D.L. Donham, E. Kurimoto, and A. Triulzi, eds. *Remapping Ethiopia: Socialism and After.* London: James Currey, 9–32.

Clay, J.W. and Holcomb, B.K., 1986. *Politics and the Ethiopian Famine: 1984–1985 (Vol. 20).* Piscataway, NJ: Transaction Publishers.

Collier, D., 2011. Understanding process tracing. *PS: Political Science & Politics*, 44 (4), 823–830.

Collins, R.O., 1990. *The waters of the Nile: Hydropolitics and the Jonglei canal, 1900–1988.* Oxford: Clarendon Press.

Collins, R.O., 1999. Smoothing the Waters. Part II of II: The Nile Conflict. *IGCC Policy Brief* 11(2).

Comitato Nazionale Italiano Grandi Dighe, 2016. *Italian Dam Engineering Abroad.* Rome: ITCOLD.

Africa Confidential, 2018a. A flood of rumours. *Africa Confidential*, 59 (16): 6.

Africa Confidential, 2018b. Deep waters. *Africa Confidential*, 59 (18): 8–9.

Africa Confidential, 2018c. Rounding up the suspects. *Africa Confidential*, 59 (23): 7–8.

Cosme, I., Santos, R., and O'Neill, D.W., 2017. Assessing the degrowth discourse: A review and analysis of academic degrowth policy proposals. *Journal of Cleaner Production*, 149, 321–334.

Coyne and Bellier, Howards Humphreys Consulting Engineers, and Rust Kennedy and Donkin, 1996. *Tis Abay II Hydropower Project.* Addis Ababa: Ministry of Water Resources.

CSA, 2008a. *Report of the 2007 Population and Housing Census: Statistical Tables.* Addis Ababa: Central Statistical Agency.

CSA, 2008b. *Summary and Statistical Report of the 2007 Population and Housing Census: Population Size by Age and Sex.* Addis Ababa: Central Statistical Agency.

Cuesta-Fernández, I., 2015. Mammoth dams, lean neighbours: Assessing the bid to turn Ethiopia into East Africa's powerhouse. In: S. Scholvin, ed. *A New Scramble for Africa? The Rush for Energy Resources in Sub-Saharan Africa.* London: Routledge, 107–124.

Dabanga, 2021. Sudan to cancel controversial Nile dams after years of resistance [online]. *Dabanga.* Available from: www.dabangasudan.org/en/all-news/article/sudan-to-cancel-controversial-nile-dams-after-years-of-resistance [Accessed 7 September 2023].

Dasandi, N. and Esteve, M., 2017. The politics–bureaucracy interface in developing countries. *Public Administration and Development*, 37 (4), 231–245.

Davison, W., 2016. Ethnic tensions in Gondar reflect the toxic nature of Ethiopian politics. *The Guardian*, 22 December.

Davison, W., 2018. Shock death intensifies dam debate: Was Abiy pessimistic or realistic about GERD? *Medium*.

Dawit, W.G., 1989. *Red Tears*. Trenton, NJ: Red Sea Press.

Death, C., 2016. *The Green State in Africa*. New Haven, CT: Yale University Press.

Demissie, A.A. and Solomon, A.A., 2016. Power system sensitivity to extreme hydrological conditions as studied using an integrated reservoir and power system dispatch model, the case of Ethiopia. *Applied Energy*, 182, 442–463.

De Waal, A., 1991. *Evil Days: Thirty Years of War and Famine in Ethiopia (Vol. 3169, No. 69)*. New York: Human Rights Watch.

De Waal, A., 2013. The theory and practice of Meles Zenawi. *African Affairs*, 112 (446), 148–155.

De Waal, A., 2015. *The Real Politics of the Horn of Africa: Money, War and the Business of Power*. Bristol: Polity Press.

Dieci, P. and Viezzoli, C., eds., 1992. *Resettlement and Rural Development in Ethiopia*. Milan: FrancoAngeli.

Donelli, F., 2022. The Ethiopian crisis: A dangerous precedent for future conflicts? *Al Sharq Strategic Research Expert Brief*.

Doner, R.F., 2009. *The Politics of Uneven Development: Thailand's Economic Growth in Comparative Perspective*. Cambridge: Cambridge University Press.

Doner, R.F., Ritchie, B.K., and Slater, D., 2005. Systemic vulnerability and the origins of developmental states: Northeast and Southeast Asia in comparative perspective. *International Organization*, 59 (2), 327–361.

Donham, D.L., 2002. Old Abyssinia and the new Ethiopian empire: Themes in social history. In: D.L. Donham and W. James, eds. *The Southern Marches of Imperial Ethiopia*. London: James Currey, 3–50.

Dupuis, C., 1904. Part III. Report upon Lake Tsana and the Rivers of the Eastern Sudan. In: W. Garstin, ed. *Report upon the Basin of the Upper Nile: With Proposals for the Improvement of That River*. Cairo: National Printing Department.

Dye, B., 2016. The return of 'high modernism'? Exploring the changing development paradigm through a Rwandan case study of dam construction. *Journal of Eastern African Studies*, 10 (2), 303–324.

Dye, B., 2021. Meeting Africa's latest dam builders: The Indian ExIm Bank, 'entrepreneurial' companies and the outcomes of South–South cooperation. *FutureDAMS Working Paper*, 16.

Dye, B., 2023. When the means become the ends: Ghana's 'good governance' electricity reform overwhelmed by the politics of power crises. *New Political Economy*, 28 (1), 91–111.

Dye, B.J., 2018. The Politics of Dam Resurgence: High Modernist Statebuilding and the Emerging Powers in Africa. PhD thesis. University of Oxford, Oxford.

Dye, B.J. and Alencastro, M., 2020. Debunking Brazilian exceptionalism in its Africa relations: Evidence from Angola and Tanzania. *Global Society*, 34 (4), 425–446.

EAPP, 2014. *EAPP Regional Power System Master Plan: Executive Summary*. Addis Ababa: Eastern Africa Power Pool (EAPP).

EEC, 1985. *Ethiopia–EEC Relations*. Brussels: Commission of the European Communities.

EELPA, 1997a. *Gilgel Gibe Hydroelectric Project: Environmental Assessment*. Addis Ababa: Ethiopian Electric Light and Power Authority (EELPA).

EELPA, 1997b. *Gilgel Gibe Hydroelectric Project*. Addis Ababa: Ministry of Mines and Energy.

EEPCo, 2004. *Gilgel Gibe II Hydroelectric Project Environmental Impact Assessment*. Addis Ababa: Ethiopian Electric Power Corporation (EEPCo).

EEPCo, 2006. *Ethiopian Power System Expansion Master Plan Update*. Addis Ababa: Ethiopian Electric Power Corporation (EEPCo).

EEPCo, 2009. *Gibe III Hydroelectric Project: Environmental and Social Management Plan*. Addis Ababa: Ethiopian Electric Power Corporation (EEPCo).

EEPCo, 2010. *Corporate Plan for the Year 2003 (EC)* [Amharic original: *የ2003 በጀት ዓመት የኮርፖሬት መሪ ዕቅዱ*]. Addis Ababa: Ethiopian Electric Power Corporation.

EEU, 2023. Monitor your meter reading each month. If not, apply to our service center immediately [online]. Ethiopian Electric Utility. Available from: www.ethiopianelectricutility.gov.et/contents/postpaid [Accessed 9 March 2023].

Egypt Today, 2019. Ethiopia's Abiy Ahmed blames military contractor for GERD delay [online]. *EgyptToday*. Available from: www.egypttoday.com/Article/1/56616/Ethiopia-s-Abiy-Ahmed-blames-military-contractor-for-GERD-delay [Accessed 2 March 2019].

Elagib, N.A. and Basheer, M., 2021. Would Africa's largest hydropower dam have profound environmental impacts? *Environmental Science and Pollution Research*, 28 (7), 8936–8944.

Eldardiry, H. and Hossain, F., 2021. Evaluating the hydropower potential of the Grand Ethiopian Renaissance Dam. *Journal of Renewable and Sustainable Energy*, 13 (2), 024501.

Embassy of Ethiopia, n.d. Facts on GERD [online]. Available from: https://ethiopianembassy.be/facts [Accessed 24 August 2020].

Endale, A., 2022. LAMC earmarks 176.3 billion birr for debt payment [online]. *The Reporter*. Available from: www.thereporterethiopia.com/26135 [Accessed 13 March 2023].

ENTRO, 2007a. *Pre-Feasibility Study of Mandaya Hydropower Project, Ethiopia*. Addis Ababa: Eastern Nile Technical Regional Office (ENTRO).

ENTRO, 2007b. *Pre-Feasibility study of Border Hydropower Project, Ethiopia*. Addis Ababa: Eastern Nile Technical Regional Office (ENTRO).

EPRDF, 1990. *Report of the 1st Congress of the EPRDF, 1983* [Ethiopian Calendar] [in Amharic]. Unpublished manuscript.

EPRDF, 1993. *Our Revolutionary Democratic Goals and the Next Step*. Addis Ababa: Ethiopian Peoples' Revolutionary Democratic Front.

EPRDF, 2006. *Development, Democracy and Revolutionary Democracy* [in Amharic: Limat democracy ena Abiyotawi Democracy]. Addis Ababa: Birhanena Selam Printing Press.

EPRDF, 2010a. *EPRDF Program*. Addis Ababa: EPRDF.

EPRDF, 2010b. *The Tehadso Mesmer and Ethiopia's Renaissance*. Addis Ababa: Mimeo.

Erlich, H., 1994. *Ethiopia and the Middle East*. Boulder, CO: Lynne Rienner.

Erlich, H., 2002. *The Cross and the River: Ethiopia, Egypt, and the Nile*. Boulder, CO: Lynne Rienner.

ESDA, 2010. *Five Years (2010–2015) Sugar Industry Sub-Sector Development Plan*. Addis Ababa: Ethiopian Sugar Development Agency.

ESMAP, 2018. ESMAP Ethiopia-Revised Electricity Tariff December 2018 [online]. ESMAP. Available from: https://rise.esmap.org/data/files/library/ethiopia/Electricity%20Access/Ethiopia-Revised%20Electricity%20Tariff%20December%202018.xlsx [Accessed 9 March 2023].

Esteban, J., Stiglitz, J., and Lin Yifu, J., eds., 2013. *The Industrial Policy Revolution II: Africa in the Twenty-First Century*. Basingstoke: Palgrave Macmillan.

Ethiopian Herald, 2015. GERD music album launched [online]. AllAfrica. Available from: https://allafrica.com/stories/201509240365.html [Accessed 7 July 2023].

Ethiopian Herald, 2016a. Ethiopia launches lottery to finance Grand Renaissance Dam [online]. AllAfrica. Available from: https://allafrica.com/view/group/main/main/id/00041349.html [Accessed 7 July 2023].

Ethiopian Herald, 2016b. Adama raises 5 million birr for GERD [online]. AllAfrica. Available from: https://allafrica.com/stories/201610250843.html [Accessed 7 July 2023].

Ethiopian Monitor, 2022a. AAU confers honorary doctorates on WeBuild CEO, AfDB president [online]. Available from: https://ethiopianmonitor.com/2022/05/14/aau-confers-honorary-doctorates-on-webuild-ceo-afdb-president [Accessed 20 June 2023].

Ethiopian Monitor, 2022b. Ethiopia signs power purchase agreement with Kenya [online]. *Ethiopian Monitor*. Available from: https://ethiopianmonitor.com/2022/07/27/ethiopia-signs-power-purchase-agreement-with-kenya [Accessed 15 February 2023].

Ethiopian News Agency, 2018. Ethiopia to Enhance diaspora's support to GERD through lottery [online]. *AllAfrica*. Available from: https://allafrica.com/view/group/main/main/id/00041349.html [Accessed 7 July 2023].

Ethiopian News Agency, 2020. Public raises over half billion birr for Grand Ethiopian Renaissance Dam [online]. Available from: www.ena.et/web/eng/w/en_14039 [Accessed 7 July 2023].

Ethiopian Technical Experts, 1996. Nile basin integrated water resource management: A strategy for cooperation. In: M. Abu-Zeid and A.K. Baswas, eds. *River Basin Planning and Management.* Calcutta: Oxford University Press, 66–74.

ETV, 2010. PM Meles Zenawi interview with Egyptian TV on Nile sharing [online]. YouTube. Available from: www.youtube.com/watch?v=2zzXLFKU0HM [Accessed 25 August 2020].

Evans, P.B., 1995. *Embedded Autonomy: States and Industrial Transformation.* Princeton, NJ: Princeton University Press.

Everard, M., 2013. *The Hydropolitics of Dams: Engineering or Ecosystems?* London: Bloomsbury Academic & Professional.

Fabricius, P., 2013. Egypt's transitional government prepares for battle over Ethiopia's giant dam on the Nile *Institute for Security Studies Weekly Issue* 93.

Fantini, E. and Puddu, L., 2016. Ethiopia and international aid: Development between high modernism and exceptional measures. In: T. Hagmann and F. Reyntjens, eds. *Aid and Authoritarianism in Africa: Development Without Democracy.* London: Zed Books, 91–118.

Fantini, E., Muluneh, T., and Smit, H., 2018. Big projects, strong states? Large-scale investments in irrigation and state formation in the Beles Valley, Ethiopia. In: F. Menga and E. Swyngedouw, eds. *Water, Technology and the Nation-State.* London: Routledge, 81–96.

FAO, 1965. *Report on Survey of the Awash River Basin.* Rome: Food and Agriculture Organization of the United Nations (FAO).

Farer, T.J., 1979. *War Clouds on the Horn of Africa: The Widening Storm.* Washington, DC: Carnegie Endowment for International Peace.

Fasil, M. and Tsegaye, Y., 2018. Inside Ethiopia's trial of grand corruption. Who is accused of what? *Addis Standard.*

FBC, 2013. EEPCo split official, two new entities go operational [online]. ethioconstruction.net. Available from: www.ethioconstruction.net/?q=news/eepco-split-official-two-new-entities-go-operational [Accessed 11 July 2023].

FDRE, 2002. Re-enactment of the investment proclamation. *Federal Negarit Gazeta Proclamation,* 280/2002.

FDRE, 2011. *Ethiopia's Climate-Resilient Green Economy: Green Economy Strategy.* Addis Ababa: Federal Democratic Republic of Ethiopia.

FDRE, 2020. Investment regulation. *Federal Negarit Gazeta Proclamation,* 474/2020.

Fearnside, P.M., 2002. Greenhouse gas emissions from a hydroelectric reservoir (Brazil's Tucuruí Dam) and the energy policy implications. *Water, Air, and Soil Pollution,* 133 (1), 69–96.

Fearnside, P.M., 2003. Greenhouse gas emissions from hydroelectric dams: Controversies provide a springboard for rethinking a supposedly 'clean' energy source. *Change,* 66 (1–2), 1–8.

Fedeler, K., 2021. Reshaped Rivers, Ruins and Renaissance: The Politics of Hydro-Developmentalism in the Case of Tana-Beles Ethiopia. PhD thesis. University of Edinburgh, Edinburgh.

Fekade, L. and Lemma, T., 2018. Dr Abiy Ahmed becomes a prime minister the legacy EPRDF fought against to the bitter end. What went behind closed doors and how could that shape his premiership? *Addis Standard.*

Fentaw, M., 2022. Ethiopia terminates $300 million solar power project with Saudi firm [online]. *The Reporter.* Available from: www.thereporterethiopia.com/23824 [Accessed 13 March 2023].

Ferraro, B., Bezzi, A., Rossini, C., and Mastrofini, P., 2015. Fast track approach to design and construction at Grand Ethiopian Renaissance Dam. *GERDP – HydroVision paper,* 0115.

Feyissa, D., 2011. Aid negotiation: The uneasy 'partnership' between EPRDF and the donors. *Journal of Eastern African Studies,* 5 (4), 788–817.

Fiseha, A., 2006. Theory versus practice in the implementation of Ethiopia's ethnic federalism. In: D. Turton, ed. *Ethnic Federalism: The Ethiopian Experience in Comparative Perspective.* London: James Currey, 131–164.

Fisher, J. and Gebrewahd, M.T., 2018. 'Game over'? Abiy Ahmed, the Tigrayan People's Liberation Front and Ethiopia's political crisis. *African Affairs*, 118 (470), 194–206.

Flyvbjerg, B., Garbuio, M., and Lovallo, D., 2009. Delusion and deception in large infrastructure projects: Two models for explaining and preventing executive disaster. *California Management Review*, 51 (2), 170–193.

Foster, V., Butterfield, W., Chen, C., and Pushak, N., 2009. Building bridges: China's growing role as infrastructure financier for sub-Saharan Africa. *World Bank Trends and Policy Options*, 5.

Fourie, E., 2012. New Maps for Africa? Contextualising the 'Chinese Model' within Ethiopian and Kenyan Paradigms of Development. PhD thesis. University of Trento, Trento.

Furtado, X. and Smith, J., 2009. Ethiopia: Retaining sovereignty in aid relations. In: L. Whitfield, ed. *The Politics of Aid: African Strategies for Dealing with Donors.* Oxford: Oxford University Press, 131–155.

Gabbert, E.C., 2021. Introduction. Futuremaking with pastoralists. In: E.C. Gabbert, F. Gebresenbet, J.G. Galaty, and G. Schlee, eds. *Lands of the Future: Anthropological Perspectives on Pastoralism, Land Deals and Tropes of Modernity in Eastern Africa.* New York: Berghahn Books, 1–39.

Gabbert, E.C., Gebresenbet, F., Galaty, J.G., and Schlee, G., 2021. *Lands of the Future: Anthropological Perspectives on Pastoralism, Land Deals and Tropes of Modernity in Eastern Africa.* New York: Berghahn Books.

Gabor, D., 2021. The Wall Street Consensus. *Development and Change*, 52 (3), 429–459.

Garretson, P.P., 2002. Vicious cycles: Ivory, slaves, and arms on the new Maji frontier. In: D.L. Donham and W. James, eds. *The Southern Marches of Imperial Ethiopia.* London: James Currey, 196–218.

Garstin, W., ed., 1904. *Report upon the Basin of the Upper Nile: With Proposals for the Improvement of That River.* Cairo: National Printing Department.

GCR, 2018. Tanzania awards $3.6bn Stiegler's Gorge dam to Egyptian state contractor [online]. *Global Construction Review.* Available from: www.globalconstructionreview.com/tanzania-awards-36bn-stieglers-gorge-dam-egyptian [Accessed 8 May 2023].

GDPC, 2022. Chinese loans to Africa database [online]. Available from: www.bu.edu/gdp/chinese-loans-to-africa-database [Accessed 1 July 2022].

Gebre, A., Getachew, D., and McCartney, M., 2008. *Stakeholder Analysis of the Chara Chara Weir, Lake Tana.* Colombo, Sri Lanka: International Water Management Institute (IWMI).

Gebre, S. and Marks, S., 2021. U.S. to restrict economic aid to Ethiopia over Tigray war [online]. *Bloomberg.* Available from: www.bloomberg.com/news/articles/2021-05-24/u-s-to-restrict-economic-aid-to-ethiopia-over-tigray-war#xj4y7vzkg [Accessed 2 May 2023].

Gebre, Y., 2009. Why did resettlement fail? Lesson from Metekel. In: A. Pankhurst and F. Piguet, eds. *Moving People in Ethiopia: Development, Displacement and the State.* London: James Currey, 119–129.

Gebreluel, G., 2023. Ideology, grand strategy and the rise and decline of Ethiopia's regional status. *International Affairs*, 99 (3), 1127–1147.

Gebresenbet, F., 2014. Securitisation of development in Ethiopia: The discourse and politics of developmentalism. *Review of African Political Economy*, 41 (sup1), S64–S74.

Gebresenbet, F., 2016. Land acquisitions, the politics of dispossession, and state-remaking in Gambella, western Ethiopia. *Africa Spectrum*, 51 (1), 5–28.

Gebresenbet, F., 2021. Villagisation in Ethiopia's lowlands: Development vs. facilitating control and dispossession. In: E.C. Gabbert, F. Gebresenbet, J.G. Galaty, and G. Schlee, eds. *Lands of the Future: Anthropological Perspectives on Pastoralism, Land Deals and Tropes of Modernity in Eastern Africa.* New York: Berghahn Books, 210–229.

Gebresenbet, F. and Kamski, B., 2019. The paradox of the Ethiopian developmental state: Bureaucrats and politicians in the sugar industry. *Journal of Contemporary African Studies*, 37 (4), 335–350.

Gebresenbet, F. and Tariku, Y., 2023. The Pretoria Agreement: Mere cessation of hostilities or heralding a new era in Ethiopia? *Review of African Political Economy*, 50 (175): 96–106.
Gebresenbet, F. and Wondemagegnehu, D.Y., 2021. New dimensions in the Grand Ethiopian Renaissance Dam negotiations: Ontological security in Egypt and Ethiopia. *African Security*, 14(1): 80–106.
Geels, F.W., 2002. Technological transitions as evolutionary reconfiguration processes: A multi-level perspective and a case-study. *Research Policy*, 31 (8), 1257–1274.
Geels, F.W., 2014. Regime resistance against low-carbon transitions: Introducing politics and power into the multi-level perspective. *Theory, Culture & Society*, 31 (5), 21–40.
Geneva Water Hub, 2023. A drama of GERD negotiations [online]. *Geneva Water Hub*. Available from: https://gerd.controversy.genevawaterhub.org [Accessed 3 May 2023].
George, A.L. and Bennett, A., 2004. *Case Studies and Theory Development in the Social Sciences*. Cambridge, MA: MIT Press.
Gheit, A.A., 2020. *Egypt's Foreign Policy in Times of Crisis: My Testimony*. Cairo: American University in Cairo Press.
Giles, J., 2006. Methane quashes green credentials of hydropower. *Nature*, 444 (7119), 524–526.
Gizachew, A., 2017. Refining the impoverishment risks and reconstruction (IRR) model: A study of the model's 'overlooked' risks, evidences from the impacts of Tekeze Dam, North East Ethiopia. *Journal of Development and Agricultural Economics*, 9 (4), 66–79.
Global Construction Review, 2019. Russia signed up to help Ethiopia start its first nuclear plant by 2029 [online]. *Global Construction Review*. Available from: www.globalconstructionreview.com/news/russia-signed-help-ethiopia-start-its-first-nuclea [Accessed 24 March 2021].
Goldemberg, J., 1998. Leapfrog energy technologies. *Energy Policy*, 26 (10), 729–741.
Gore, C.D., 2017. *Electricity in Africa: The Politics of Transformation in Uganda*. Woodbridge: Boydell & Brewer.
Gore, C.D., Brass, J.N., Baldwin, E., and MacLean, L.M., 2019. Political autonomy and resistance in electricity sector liberalization in Africa. *World Development*, 120, 193–209.
Grabham, G.W. and Black, R.P., 1925. *Report of the Mission to Lake Tana, 1920–1921*. Cairo: Government Press.
Gratwick, K.N. and Eberhard, A., 2008. Demise of the standard model for power sector reform and the emergence of hybrid power markets. *Energy Policy*, 36 (10), 3948–3960.
Guariso, G. and Whittington, D., 1987. Implications of Ethiopian water development for Egypt and Sudan. *International Journal of Water Resources Development*, 3 (2), 105–114.
Gunkel, G., 2009. Hydropower: A green energy? Tropical reservoirs and greenhouse gas emissions. *CLEAN—Soil, Air, Water*, 37 (9), 726–734.
Hagmann, T., 2007. Fighting for the Desert? Pastoral Conflict and Resource Management in Ethiopia's Somali Region. PhD thesis. University of Lausanne, Lausanne.
Hagmann, T. and Korf, B., 2012. Agamben in the Ogaden: Violence and sovereignty in the Ethiopian–Somali frontier. *Political Geography*, 31 (4), 205–214.
Haile, F.G., 2018. Unravelling the Gift of the Nile: Examining the Domestic and International Determinants of Ethiopian Counterhegemony in the Eastern Nile River Basin. Kings College London, London.
Halcrow, 1989. *Master Plan for the Development of Surface Water Resources in the Awash Basin*. Draft Final Report: Volume II, Main Report. Addis Ababa: Ethiopian Valleys Development Studies Authority (EVDSA).
Hanna, R. and Allouche, J., 2018. Water nationalism in Egypt: State-building, nation-making and Nile hydropolitics. In: F. Menga and E. Swyngedouw, eds. *Water, Technology and the Nation-State*. London: Routledge, 81–95.
Harbeson, J.W., 1978. Territorial and development politics in the Horn of Africa: The Afar of the Awash Valley. *African Affairs* 77 (309), 479–498.
Hassen, H. and Ademo, M., 2017. Ethiopia: Is OPDO the new opposition party? An Appraisal [online]. OPride.com. Available from: www.opride.com/2017/11/11/ethiopia-is-opdo-the-new-opposition-party-an-appraisal [Accessed 3 February 2021].

Hassen Hussein, M., 2017. Ethiopia: Oromo and Amhara MPs boycott parliament as winds of change and a bitter power struggle reaches legislature [online]. OPride.com. Available from: www.opride.com/2017/12/22/ethiopia-oromo-amhara-mps-boycott-parliament [Accessed 9 December 2021].

Hauge, J., 2019. Should the African lion learn from the Asian tigers? A comparative-historical study of FDI-oriented industrial policy in Ethiopia, South Korea and Taiwan. *Third World Quarterly*, 40 (11), 2071–2091.

Hechter, M. and Brustein, W., 1980. Regional modes of production and patterns of state formation in western Europe. *American Journal of Sociology*, 85 (5), 1061–1094.

Helal, M. and Bekhit, H., 2023. So near, yet so far: An Egyptian perspective on the US-facilitated negotiations on the Grand Ethiopian Renaissance Dam. *Water International* 48(5): 580–614.

Herbst, J., 2000. *States and Power in Africa: Comparative Lessons in Authority and Control.* Princeton, NJ: Princeton University Press.

Hickel, J. and Kallis, G., 2020. Is Green Growth Possible? *New Political Economy*, 25 (4), 469–486.

Hirschman, A.O., 1967. *Development Projects Observed.* Washington, DC: The Brookings Institution.

Hoben, A., 1973. *Land Tenure among the Amhara of Ethiopia: The Dynamics of Cognatic Descent.* Chicago, IL: University of Chicago Press.

Hochstetler, K., 2020. *Political Economies of Energy Transition: Wind and Solar Power in Brazil and South Africa.* Cambridge: Cambridge University Press.

HRW, 2012. *'What Will Happen if Hunger Comes?': Abuses against the Indigenous Peoples of Ethiopia's Lower Omo Valley.* New York: Human Rights Watch.

Human Rights Watch, 2014. Ethiopia: Omo sugar plantations [online]. Available from: www.hrw.org/video-photos/interactive/2014/02/10/ethiopia-omo-sugar-plantations [Accessed 10 December 2015].

Hurst, H.E., Black, R.P., and Simaika, Y.M., 1946. *The Nile Basin. Volume VII: The Future Conservation of the Nile.* Cairo: Ministry of Public Works.

Hussein, A. El S.A., 2018. Water Balance of the Aswan High Dam Reservoir. PhD thesis. Kiel University, Kiel.

IBRD, 1969. *Report and Recommendation of the President to the Executive Directors on a Proposed Loan to the Ethiopian Electric Light and Power Authority with the Guarantee of the Empire of Ethiopia.* Washington, DC: International Bank for Reconstruction and Development (IBRD).

IEA, 2020. *World Energy Outlook 2020.* Paris: International Energy Agency.

IEG, 2014. *Completion Report: Ethiopia/Nile Basin Initiative: Ethiopia-Sudan Interconnector.* Washington, DC: World Bank.

IHA, 2023a. Clean energy systems [online]. International Hydropower Association. Available from: www.hydropower.org/what-we-do/clean-energy [Accessed 20 June 2023].

IHA, 2023b. Hydropower worldwide [online]. Available from: www.hydropower.org/discover/hydropower-around-the-world [Accessed 16 May 2023].

IHA, n.d. Ethiopia: Grand Ethiopian Renaissance Dam (GERD) [online]. Available from: www.hydropower.org/case-studies/ethiopia-grand-ethiopian-renaissance-dam-gerd [Accessed 24 August 2020].

IMF, 2015. The Federal Democratic Republic of Ethiopia: Staff report for the 2015 Article IV consultation. *IMF Country Report*, 15 (300).

IMF, 2018. The Federal Democratic Republic of Ethiopia: Staff report for the 2017 Article IV consultation—Press release; staff report; and statement by the executive director for the Federal Democratic Republic of Ethiopia. *IMF Country Report*, 18 (18).

IMF, 2019. IMF reaches staff-level agreement on a US$2.9 billion financing package with Ethiopia [online]. IMF. Available from: www.imf.org/en/News/Articles/2019/12/11/pr19450-ethiopia-imf-reaches-staff-level-agreement-on-a-us2-9-billion-financing-package [Accessed 24 March 2021].

International Rivers, 2011. *Ethiopia's Gibe III Dam: Sowing Hunger and Conflict.* Berkeley, CA: International Rivers.

IPoE, 2013. *Grand Ethiopian Renaissance Dam Project (GERDP): Final Report*. Addis Ababa: International Panel of Experts (IPoE).

Isaacman, A.F. and Isaacman, B.S., 2013. *Dams, Displacement, and the Delusion of Development: Cahora Bassa and Its Legacies in Mozambique, 1965–2007*. Athens, OH: Ohio University Press.

Jackson, T., 2011. *Prosperity without Growth: Economics for a Finite Planet*. London: Routledge.

James, W., 2002a. No place to hide: Flag-waving on the western frontier. In: W. James, D.L. Donham, E. Kurimoto, and A. Triulzi, eds. *Remapping Ethiopia: Socialism and After*. London: James Currey, 259–275.

James, W., 2002b. Lifelines: Exchange marriage among the Gumuz. In: D.L. Donham and W. James, eds. *The Southern Marches of Imperial Ethiopia*. London: James Currey, 119–147.

Jepson, N., 2020. *In China's Wake: How the Commodity Boom Transformed Development Strategies in the Global South*. New York: Columbia University Press.

Jeuland, M. and Whittington, D., 2014. Water resources planning under climate change: Assessing the robustness of real options for the Blue Nile. *Water Resources Research*, 50 (3), 2086–2107.

JICA, 1977. *Feasibility Report on Power Development at Lake Tana Region*. Tokyo: Japan International Cooperation Agency.

JICA, 2018. *Preparatory Survey on Addis Ababa Transmission and Distribution System Rehabilitation and Upgrading Project: Final Report*. Tokyo: Japan International Cooperation Agency (JICA).

Johnson, C.A., 1982. *MITI and the Japanese Miracle: The Growth of Industrial Policy, 1925–1975*. Stanford, CA: Stanford University Press.

Johnson, K., 2018. Egypt–Sudan spat muddies prospects for deal on big Nile dam. *Foreign Policy*.

Johnson, M.S., Matthews, E., Bastviken, D., Deemer, B., Du, J., and Genovese, V., 2021. Spatiotemporal methane emission from global reservoirs. *Journal of Geophysical Research: Biogeosciences*, 126 (8), e2021JG006305.

Kassa, G., 1997. A note on the Finaa (Fimaa) institution among the pastoral afar of the Middle Awash Valley, North Eastern Ethiopia. *Journal of Ethiopian Studies*, 30 (2), 1–26.

Katzenstein, P.J., 2005. *A World of Regions: Asia and Europe in the American Imperium*. Ithaca, NY: Cornell University Press.

Keck, M.E. and Sikkink, K., 1998. *Activists beyond Borders: Advocacy Networks in International Politics*. Ithaca, NY: Cornell University Press.

Kefale, A. and Gebresenbet, F., 2014. The expansion of the sugar industry in the southern pastoral lowlands. In: D. Rahmato, M. Ayenew, A. Kefale, and B. Haberman, eds. *Reflections on Development in Ethiopia*. Addis Ababa: Forum for Social Studies, 247–268.

Kelsey, N. and Zysman, J., 2013. The green spiral. In: J. Zysman and M. Huberty, eds. *Can Green Sustain Growth? From the Religion to the Reality of Sustainable Prosperity*. Stanford, CA: Stanford University Press, 79–88.

Khagram, S., 2018. *Dams and Development: Transnational Struggles for Water and Power*. Ithaca, NY: Cornell University Press.

Khan, M.H., 2018. Power, pacts and political settlements: A reply to Tim Kelsall. *African Affairs*, 117 (469): 670–694.

Kibaroglu, A., 2017. State-of-the-art review of transboundary water governance in the Euphrates–Tigris river basin. *International Journal of Water Resources Development*, 35 (1): 1–26.

Kibaroglu, A. and Scheumann, W., 2011. Euphrates-Tigris rivers system: Political rapprochement and transboundary water cooperation. In: A. Kramer, A. Kibaroglu, and W. Scheumann, eds. *Turkey's Water Policy: National Frameworks and International Cooperation*. Berlin: Springer, 277–299.

Kloos, H., 1982. Development, drought, and famine in the Awash Valley of Ethiopia. *African Studies Review*, 25 (4), 21–48.

Kohli, A., 2004. *State-Directed Development: Political Power and Industrialization in the Global Periphery*. Cambridge: Cambridge University Press.

Kraak, E.P., 2012. Dams of Damocles: Between Rivers, States, and Geopolitics. PhD thesis. University of Oxford, Oxford.

Krueger, A.O., 1990. Government failures in development. *Journal of Economic Perspectives*, 4 (3), 9–23.

Kumar, S., 2015. India's development cooperation with Ethiopia in sugar production: An assessment. *RIS Discussion Paper*, 198.

Kuriakose, J., Anderson, K., Darko, D., Obuobie, E., Larkin, A., and Addo, S., 2022. Implications of large hydro dams for decarbonising Ghana's energy consistent with Paris climate objectives. *Energy for Sustainable Development*, 71, 433–446.

Lampton, D.M., Ho, S., and Kuik, C.-C., 2020. *Rivers of Iron: Railroads and Chinese Power in Southeast Asia*. Berkeley, CA: University of California Press.

Last, G.G., 1958. The power resources of Ethiopia. *The Ethiopian Observer*, 2 (11), 221–228.

Lavers, T., 2012a. Patterns of agrarian transformation in Ethiopia: State-mediated commercialisation and the 'land grab'. *The Journal of Peasant Studies*, 39 (3–4), 795–822.

Lavers, T., 2012b. 'Land grab' as development strategy? The political economy of agricultural investment in Ethiopia. *The Journal of Peasant Studies*, 39 (1), 105–132.

Lavers, T., 2016. Agricultural investment in Ethiopia: Undermining national sovereignty or tool for state building? *Development and Change*, 47 (5), 1078–1101.

Lavers, T., 2018. Responding to land-based conflict in Ethiopia: The land rights of ethnic minorities under federalism. *African Affairs*, 117 (468), 462–484.

Lavers, T., 2023. *Ethiopia's 'Developmental State': Political Order and Distributive Crisis*. Cambridge: Cambridge University Press.

Lavers, T. and Dye, B., 2019. Theorising the political economy of dams: Towards a research agenda. *FutureDAMS Working Paper*, 1.

Le Gouriellec, S., 2018. Regional power and contested hierarchy: Ethiopia, an 'imperfect hegemon' in the Horn of Africa. *International Affairs*, 94 (5), 1059–1075.

Lee, A. and Usman, Z., 2018. Taking stock of the political economy of power sector reforms in developing countries: A literature review. *Policy Research Working Paper Series*, 8518.

Lefort, R., 2012. Free market economy, 'developmental state' and party-state hegemony in Ethiopia: The case of the 'model farmers'. *The Journal of Modern African Studies*, 50 (04), 681–706.

Lefort, R., 2013. The theory and practice of Meles Zenawi: A response to Alex de Waal. *African Affairs*, 112 (448), 460–470.

Lefort, R., 2016. Unrest in Ethiopia: The ultimate warning shot? [online]. openDemocracy. Available from: www.opendemocracy.net/ren-lefort/unrest-in-ethiopia-ultimate-warning-shot [Accessed 4 February 2016].

Lefort, R., 2017. 'Ethnic clashes' in Ethiopia: Setting the record straight [online]. openDemocracy. Available from: www.opendemocracy.net/ren-lefort/ethnic-clashes-in-ethiopia-setting-record-straight [Accessed 4 March 2018].

Lehner, B. and Grill, C., 2013. Global river hydrography and network routing: Baseline data and new approaches to study the world's large river systems. *Hydrological Processes*, 27 (15), 2171–2186.

Lenin, V., 1920. Report on the Work of the Council of People's Commissars [online]. Seventeen Moments in Soviet History. Available from: http://soviethistory.msu.edu/1921-2/electrification-campaign/communism-is-soviet-power-electrification-of-the-whole-country [Accessed 9 June 2020].

Lin Yifu, J., ed., 2013. *The Industrial Policy Revolution I: The Role of Government beyond Ideology*. Basingstoke: Palgrave Macmillan.

Liu, Z., Schindler, S., and Liu, W., 2020. Demystifying Chinese overseas investment in infrastructure: Port development, the Belt and Road Initiative and regional development. *Journal of Transport Geography*, 87, 102812.

Maasho, A., 2010. Ethiopia outsources telecom management to France Telecom [online]. *Reuters*. Available from: www.reuters.com/article/ozabs-ethiopia-telecoms-20101203-idAFJOE6B207720101203 [Accessed 3 March 2023].

MacLean, L.M., Gore, C., Brass, J., and Baldwin, E., 2016. Expectations of power: The politics of state-building and access to electricity provision in Ghana and Uganda. *Journal of African Political Economy & Development*, 1, 103–134.

MacLean, L.M., Bob-Milliar, G.M., Baldwin, E., and Dickey, E., 2016. The construction of citizenship and the public provision of electricity during the 2014 World Cup in Ghana. *The Journal of Modern African Studies*, 54 (4), 555–590.

Mada Masr, 2020. Sources: US-proposed GERD deal sets Ethiopia water release at 37 bcm, major disputes remain [online]. Mada Masr. Available from: www.madamasr.com/en/2020/02/17/feature/politics/sources-us-proposed-gerd-deal-sets-ethiopia-water-release-at-37-bcm-major-disputes-remain [Accessed 8 May 2023].

Magome, M., 2020. Ethiopia PM asks South Africa leader to help in dam dispute [online]. *AP*. Available from: https://apnews.com/article/68d9e2a87fcced5bedefa0ceac01c5b8#:~:text=JOHANNESBURG%20(AP)%20—%20Ethiopia%27s%20prime,be%20Africa%27s%20largest%20hydraulic%20dam [Accessed 8 May 2023].

Malm, A., 2016. *Fossil Capital: The Rise of Steam Power and the Roots of Global Warming*. London: Verso Books.

Mamdani, M., 1996. *Citizen and Subject: Contemporary Africa and the Legacy of Late Colonialism*. Princeton, NJ: Princeton University Press.

Manek, N., 2021. Containing the volatile Sudan–Ethiopia border dispute. *International Crisis Group Briefing Paper*, 173.

Mann, M., 1986. *The Sources of Social Power: Volume 1, A History of Power from the Beginning to AD 1760*. Cambridge: Cambridge University Press.

Manyazewal, M., 2019. Financing Ethiopia's development. In: F. Cheru, C. Cramer, and A. Oqubay, eds. *The Oxford Handbook of the Ethiopian Economy*. Oxford: Oxford University Press, 175–190.

Markakis, J., 2011. *Ethiopia: The Last Two Frontiers*. Oxford: James Currey.

Markkanen, S., Braeckman, J.P., and Souvannaseng, P., 2020. Mapping the evolving complexity of large hydropower project finance in low and lower-middle income countries. *Green Finance*, 2 (2), 151–172.

Martin, T.D., 2001. *The Affirmative Action Empire: Nations and Nationalism in the Soviet Union, 1923–1939*. Ithaca, NY: Cornell University Press.

Maru, M.T., 2020. The emergence of another African conflict: Egypt, Ethiopia and geopolitics of the Renaissance Dam [online]. *Al-Jazeera*. Available from: https://studies.aljazeera.net/en/reports/emergence-another-african-conflict-egypt-ethiopia-and-geopolitics-renaissance-dam [Accessed 5 May 2023].

Mascagni, G., 2016. A fiscal history of Ethiopia: Taxation and aid dependence 1960–2010. *ICTD Working Paper*, 49.

McCann, J., 1981. Ethiopia, Britain, and negotiations for the Lake Tana Dam, 1922–1935. *The International Journal of African Historical Studies*, 14 (4), 667–699.

McCartney, M.P., Shiferaw, A., and Seleshi, Y., 2009. Estimating environmental flow requirements downstream of the Chara Chara weir on the Blue Nile River. *Hydrological Processes*, 23 (26), 3751–3758.

McCool, D., 1994. *Command of the Waters: Iron Triangles, Federal Water Development, and Indian Water*. Tucson, AZ: University of Arizona Press.

McCully, P., 1996. *Silenced Rivers: The Ecology and Politics of Large Dams*. London: Bloomsbury Academic.

McDonald, K., Bosshard, P., and Brewer, N., 2009. Exporting dams: China's hydropower industry goes global. *Journal of Environmental Management*, 90, S294–S302.

McDubus, C., 2016. Grand Ethiopian Renaissance Dam (GERD) could generate over 6,000MW: Study. *Africa-OnTheRise*.

Melese, A.T., 2017. Ethiopian-owned firms in the floriculture global value chain: With what capabilities? *CAE Working Paper*, 2.

Menga, F., 2017. Hydropolis: Reinterpreting the polis in water politics. *Political Geography*, 60, 100–109.

Mengistu, M.G., Simane, B., Eshete, G., and Workneh, T.S., 2015. A review on biogas technology and its contributions to sustainable rural livelihood in Ethiopia. *Renewable and Sustainable Energy Reviews*, 48, 306–316.

Meseret, E., 2020. Ethiopia skips latest US talks with Egypt over dam dispute [online]. *AP*. Available from: https://apnews.com/article/4a79f6abe0fb65668c6e67cfb831c89f [Accessed 5 May 2023].

Midttun, A., 1988. The negotiated political economy of a heavy industrial sector: The Norwegian hydropower complex in the 1970s and 1980s. *Scandinavian Political Studies*, 11 (2), 115–144.

Miescher, S.F., 2014. 'Nkrumah's baby': The Akosombo Dam and the dream of development in Ghana, 1952–1966. *Water History*, 6 (4), 341–366.

Miescher, S.F., 2022. *A Dam for Africa: Akosombo Stories from Ghana*. Bloomington, IN: Indiana University Press.

Migdal, J.S., 1988. *Strong Societies and Weak States: State–Society Relations and State Capabilities in the Third World*. Princeton, NJ: Princeton University Press.

Mihretu, M. and Llobet, G., 2017. *Looking beyond the Horizon: A Case Study of PVH's Commitment to Ethiopia's Hawassa Industrial Park*. Washington, DC: World Bank.

Milkias, P., 2003. Ethiopia, the TPLF, and the roots of the 2001 political tremor. *Northeast African Studies*, 10 (2), 13–66.

Mitchell, T., 1995. The object of development: America's Egypt. In: J. Crush, ed. *Power of Development*. London: Routledge, 129–157.

Mitchell, T., 2002. *Rule of Experts: Egypt, Techno-Politics, Modernity*. Berkeley, CA: University of California Press.

Mitchell, T., 2013. *Carbon Democracy: Political Power in the Age of Oil*. London: Verso.

Mkandawire, T., 2001. Thinking about developmental states in Africa. *Cambridge Journal of Economics*, 25 (3), 289–314.

Mkandawire, T., 2010. How the new poverty agenda neglected social and employment policies in Africa. *Journal of Human Development and Capabilities*, 11 (1), 37–55.

Moe, E., 2015. *Renewable Energy Transformation or Fossil Fuel Backlash: Vested Interests in the Political Economy*. Basingstoke: Palgrave Macmillan.

MoF, 2021. About PPP [online]. *Ministry of Finance*. Available from: www.mofed.gov.et/en/programmes-projects/ppp [Accessed 24 March 2021].

MoFA, 2008. *Draft Policy Statement for the Sustainable Development of Pastoral and Agro Pastoral Areas of Ethiopia*. Addis Ababa: Ministry of Federal Affairs.

MoFED, 2002. *Ethiopia: Sustainable Development and Poverty Reduction Program*. Addis Ababa: Ministry of Finance and Economic Development (MoFED), Federal Democratic Republic of Ethiopia.

MoFED, 2003. *Rural Development Policy and Strategies*. Addis Ababa: Ministry of Finance and Economic Development (MoFED).

MoFED, 2005. *Ethiopia: Building on Progress. A Plan for Accelerated and Sustained Development to End Poverty (PASDEP)*. Addis Ababa: Ministry of Finance and Economic Development (MoFED), Federal Democratic Republic of Ethiopia.

MoFED, 2010. *Growth and Transformation Plan (GTP)*. Addis Ababa: Ministry of Finance and Economic Development (MoFED), Federal Democratic Republic of Ethiopia.

Mohammed, A., 2018. Reform then competition is needed to realize MetEC's engineering potential. *Ethiopia Observer*.

Mohan, G., 2013. Beyond the enclave: Towards a critical political economy of China and Africa. *Development and Change*, 44 (6), 1255–1272.

Mohan, G. and Tan-Mullins, M., 2019. The geopolitics of South–South infrastructure development: Chinese-financed energy projects in the global South. *Urban Studies*, 56 (7), 1368–1385.

MoI, 2002a. *Industry Development Strategy of Ethiopia*. Addis Ababa: Ministry of Industry (MoI).

MoI, 2002b. *Foreign Affairs and National Security Policy and Strategy.* Addis Ababa: Ministry of Information.

MOIPAD, 2001. *Rural Development Policies, Strategies and Instruments.* Addis Ababa: Ministry of Information, Press and Audio-Visual Department.

Mold, A., 2012. Will it all end in tears? Infrastructure spending and African development in historical perspective. *Journal of International Development*, 24 (2), 237–254.

Molle, F., Mollinga, P.P., and Wester, P., 2009. Hydraulic bureaucracies and the hydraulic mission: Flows of water, flows of power. *Water Alternatives*, 2 (3), 328–349.

Moller, L.C., 2015. *Ethiopia's Great Run: The Growth Acceleration and How to Pace It.* Washington, DC: World Bank.

Moller, L.C., 2017. Explaining Ethiopia's growth acceleration: The role of infrastructure and macroeconomic policy. *World Development*, 96, 198–215.

Mondal, Md.A.H., Bryan, E., Ringler, C., and Rosegrant, M., 2017. Ethiopian power sector development: Renewable based universal electricity access and export strategies. *Renewable and Sustainable Energy Reviews*, 75, 11–20.

Monodanga, D., 2022. Some say the White Nile is flowing too slowly. Not everyone agrees. *The Continent*, 99.

MoPED, 1993. *An Economic Development Strategy for Ethiopia (A Comprehensive Guidance and a Development Strategy for the Future).* Addis Ababa: Ministry of Planning and Economic Development (MoPED).

Mosley, J., 2021. *Turkey and the Gulf States in the Horn of Africa: Fluctuating Dynamics of Engagement, Investment and Influence.* London: Rift Valley Institute.

Mosley, J. and Watson, E.E., 2016. Frontier transformations: Development visions, spaces and processes in Northern Kenya and Southern Ethiopia. *Journal of Eastern African Studies*, 10 (3), 452–475.

MoWE, 2011. *Alternatives to the Mandaya Project: Cascading Options Memo.* Addis Ababa: Ministry of Water and Energy.

MoWIE, 2017. *Light to All: National Electrification Program Implementation Road Map and Financing Prospectus.* Addis Ababa: Ministry of Water, Irrigation and Energy.

MoWIE, 2019. *National Electrification Program 2.0: Integrated Planning for Universal Access 'Lighting to All'.* Addis Ababa: Ministry of Water, Irrigation and Energy.

MoWR, 1998. *Tekeze River Basin Integrated Development Master Plan Project.* Addis Ababa: Ministry of Water Resources, Federal Democratic Republic of Ethiopia.

MoWR, 1999. *Abbay River Basin Integrated Development Master Plan Project.* Addis Ababa: Ministry of Water Resources, Federal Democratic Republic of Ethiopia.

MoWR, 2006. *Karadobi Multipurpose Project Pre-Feasibility Study: Final Report: Vol. 1 Main Report.* Addis Ababa: Ministry of Water Resources.

MoWR, 2007. *Beko-Abo Multipurpose Project Reconnaissance Study Report.* Addis Ababa: Ministry of Water Resources.

MoWR, 2013. *Beko-Abo Multipurpose Project: Pre-Feasibility Study Final Report: Volume 1 Main Report.* Addis Ababa: Ministry of Water Resources.

Müller-Mahn, D. and Gebreyes, M., 2019. Controversial connections: The water–energy–food nexus in the Blue Nile basin of Ethiopia. *Land*, 8 (9), 135.

Mursi Online, 2011. Speech by Meles Zenawi during the 13th Annual Pastoralists' Day Celebrations, Jinka, South Omo, 25 January.

Nazret, 2018. Ethiopia cancels turbine contract on Nile dam in reform push. Nazret.com.

NBE, 2015. *National Bank of Ethiopia: Annual Report 2014/15.* Addis Ababa: National Bank of Ethiopia.

NBI, 2010. *Agreement on the Nile River Basin Cooperative Framework.* Entebbe: Nile Basin Initiative.

NBI ENTRO, 2008. *Eastern Nile Power Trade Program Study.* Addis Ababa: Nile Basin Initiative, Eastern Nile Technical Regional Office.

Negash, T. and Tronvoll, K., 2000. *Brothers at War: Making Sense of the Eritrean-Ethiopian War.* Oxford: James Currey.

Newell, P., 2021. *Power Shift: The Global Political Economy of Energy Transitions*. Cambridge: Cambridge University Press.

Newell, P. and Phillips, J., 2016. Neoliberal energy transitions in the South: Kenyan experiences. *Geoforum*, 74, 39–48.

Nicol, A., 2000. Contested Margins: Water Resources, Decentralisation and the State in the Awash Valley, Ethiopia, 1985–88. PhD thesis. School of Oriental and African Studies, London.

Nicol, A. and Cascão, A.E., 2011. Against the flow: New power dynamics and upstream mobilisation in the Nile basin. *Review of African Political Economy*, 38 (128), 317–325.

NPC, 2016. *Growth and Transformation Plan II (GTP II)*. Addis Ababa: National Planning Commission (NPC), Federal Democratic Republic of Ethiopia.

Nugent, P., 2018. Africa's re-enchantment with big infrastructure: White elephants dancing in virtuous circles? In: J. Schubert, U. Engel, and E. Macamo, eds. *Extractive Industries and Changing State Dynamics in Africa*. London: Routledge, 22–40.

Nyssen, J., 2023. Ethiopia: Tigray War [online]. Ethiopia: Tigray War. Available from: https://ethiopiatigraywar.com/incidents.php [Accessed 11 July 2023].

Office of the Prime Minister, 1993. *National Population Policy of Ethiopia*. Addis Ababa: Office of the Prime Minister.

Ohlendorf, N., Jakob, M., and Steckel, J.C., 2022. The political economy of coal phase-out: Exploring the actors, objectives, and contextual factors shaping policies in eight major coal countries. *Energy Research & Social Science*, 90, 102590.

Oqubay, A., 2015. *Made in Africa: Industrial Policy in Ethiopia*. Oxford: Oxford University Press.

Oqubay, A. and Kefale, D.M., 2020. A strategic approach to industrial hubs: Learnings in Ethiopia. In: A. Oqubay and J.Y. Lin, eds. *The Oxford Handbook of Industrial Hubs and Economic Development*. Oxford: Oxford University Press, 877–913.

Orlowska, I., 2013. Forging a nation: The Ethiopian millennium celebration and the multiethnic state. *Nations and Nationalism*, 19 (2), 296–316.

Oya, C. and Schaefer, F., 2021. The politics of labour relations in global production networks: Collective action, industrial parks, and local conflict in the Ethiopian apparel sector. *World Development*, 146, 105564.

Padam, G., Rysankova, D., Portale, E., Bonsuk Koo, B., Keller, S., and Fleurantin, G., 2018. *Ethiopia beyond Connections: Energy Access Diagnostic Report Based on the Multi-Tier Framework*. Washington, DC: World Bank.

Parsons Brinckerhoff, 2014. *Ethiopian Power System Expansion Master Plan Study: Final Report*. Addis Ababa: Ethiopian Electric Power (EEP).

Patman, R.G., 2009. *The Soviet Union in the Horn of Africa: The Diplomacy of Intervention and Disengagement*. Cambridge: Cambridge University Press.

Pedersen, R.H. and Andersen, O.W., 2023. A contested agenda: Energy transitions in lower-income African countries. *Energy Policy*, 175: 113496.

Pegels, A., 2014. *Green Industrial Policy in Emerging Countries*. London: Routledge.

Pietrangeli, A. and Pallavicini, I., 2007. Hydroelectric cascade plants in the Omo Basin in Ethiopia. Presented at the ICOLD 75th Annual Meeting Saint Petersburg, Russia, 24–29 June.

Pilling, D., 2020. US ready to back Ethiopian reform with $5bn investment [online]. *Financial Times*. Available from: www.ft.com/content/b0c2963c-5e1a-11ea-8033-fa40a0d65a98 [Accessed 24 March 2021].

Plaut, M. and Vaughan, S., 2023. *Understanding Ethiopia's Tigray War*. London: Hurst & Company.

Plummer Braeckman, J. and Markkanen, S., 2021. Perceptions of risk in relation to large hydropower projects: a finance perspective. *FutureDAMS Working Paper*, 12.

Pontecorvo, L., 1938. *Engineering problems in Colonial Territories*. Rome: SA Tipografia Castaldi.

Power, M., Newell, P., Baker, L., Bulkeley, H., Kirshner, J., and Smith, A., 2016. The political economy of energy transitions in Mozambique and South Africa: The role of the Rising Powers. *Energy Research & Social Science*, 17, 10–19.

Power Technology, 2021. Gilgel Gibe III hydroelectric power project [online]. Available from: www.power-technology.com/projects/gilgel-gibe-iii-hydroelectric-power-project [Accessed 14 August 2023].

Puddu, L., 2012. Extraversion and development in northwestern Ethiopia: The case of the Humera Agricultural Project, 1967–1975. Presented at the 'Poverty and Empowerment in Africa' conference, 30 March to 1 April, University of Texas at Austin.

Puddu, L., 2017. Border diplomacy and state-building in north-western Ethiopia, c. 1965–1977. *Journal of Eastern African Studies*, 11 (2), 230–248.

Puddu, L., 2021. A contested financial frontier: Banking and empire building in Eritrea, 1952–1972. *Africa: Journal of the International African Institute*, 91 (5), 852–873.

Putnam, R.D., 1988. Diplomacy and domestic politics: The logic of two-level games. *International Organization*, 42 (3), 427–460.

Rahmato, D., 1984. *Agrarian Reform in Ethiopia*. Uppsala: Nordic Africa Institute.

Reisner, M., 1993. *Cadillac Desert*. Revised and updated ed. New York: Penguin Books.

Rettberg, S., 2010. Contested narratives of pastoral vulnerability and risk in Ethiopia's Afar region. *Pastoralism*, 1 (2), 248–273.

Reuters, 2018. Egypt, Ethiopia agree to settle differences over Nile mega-dam [online]. *Reuters*. Available from: www.reuters.com/article/us-egypt-ethiopia-idUSKBN1J60YL#:~:text=The%20two%20sides%20agreed%20to,Egypt%27s%20share%20of%20the%20Nile [Accessed 5 May 2023].

Reuters, 2019. Ethiopia charges former head of state electricity firm, others with corruption. *Reuters*, 27 December.

Richard Woodroofe and Associates, 1996. *Omo-Gibe River Basin Integrated Development Master Plan Study*. Addis Ababa: Ministry of Water Resources, Federal Democratic Republic of Ethiopia.

Rosenstein-Rodan, P.N., 1943. Problems of industrialisation of eastern and south-eastern Europe. *The Economic Journal*, 53 (210/211), 202–211.

Rostow, W.W., 1960. *The Stages of Economic Growth: A Non-Communist Manifesto*. Cambridge: Cambridge University Press.

Rowell, A., 2017. *Green Backlash: Global Subversion of the Environment Movement*. London: Routledge.

Roy, A., 1999. *The Cost of Living*. London: HarperCollins UK.

Rueschemeyer, D., 2005. Building states—inherently a long-term process? An argument from theory. In: M. Lange and D. Rueschemeyer, eds. *States and Development: Historical Antecedents of Stagnation and Advance*. Basingstoke: Palgrave Macmillan, 143–164.

RVI, 2023. *Resistance in the Peripheries: Civil War and Fragile Peace in Sudan and Ethiopia's Borderlands*. Nairobi: Rift Valley Institute.

Sadoff, C.W. and Grey, D., 2002. Beyond the river: The benefits of cooperation on international rivers. *Water Policy*, 4 (5), 389–403.

Salem, M., 2010. Egyptians discuss response to Ethiopian dam [online]. *Egypt Independent*. Available from: www.egyptindependent.com/egyptians-discuss-response-ethiopian-dam [Accessed 12 March 2021].

Salini Impregilo, 2015. Africa's giants [online]. Available from: https://library.webuildgroup.com/en/pubblications/africas-giants/intro.html [Accessed 20 June 2023].

Salini Impregilo, 2016a. 110 years of future [online]. Available from: https://library.webuildgroup.com/en/pubblications/110-years-of-future/intro.html# [Accessed 20 June 2023].

Salini Impregilo, 2016b. *Beyond: Delivering the Future for the Past 110 Years*. Rome: Salini Impregilo.

Salini Impregilo, 2018. The water tower of Africa [online]. Available from: www.webuildgroup.com/en/media/photogallery/the-water-tower-of-africa [Accessed 20 June 2023].

Sallam, H., 2022. *Classless Politics: Islamist Movements, the Left, and Authoritarian Legacies in Egypt*. New York: Columbia University Press.

Salman, S.M.A., 2009. *The World Bank Policy for Projects on International Waterways: An Historical and Legal Analysis*. Washington, DC: World Bank.

Salman, S.M.A., 2016. The Grand Ethiopian Renaissance Dam: The road to the declaration of principles and the Khartoum document. *Water International*, 41 (4), 512–527.

Sayigh, Y., 2022. Retain, restructure, or divest? Policy options for Egypt's military economy. *Carnegie Middle East Centre Working Paper*.

Schaefer, C., 2012. Rentier capitalism: Cash, credit and urban development in Addis Ababa, 1905–1936. *Journal of Ethiopian Studies*, 45, 53–72.

Schindler, S. and Kanai, J.M., 2021. Getting the territory right: Infrastructure-led development and the re-emergence of spatial planning strategies. *Regional Studies*, 55 (1), 40–51.

Schindler, S., DiCarlo, J., and Paudel, D., 2022. The new cold war and the rise of the 21st-century infrastructure state. *Transactions of the Institute of British Geographers*, 47 (2), 331–346.

Schmitz, H., Johnson, O., and Altenburg, T., 2015. Rent management: The heart of green industrial policy. *New Political Economy*, 20 (6), 812–831.

Schulz, C. and Adams, W.M., 2019. Debating dams: The World Commission on Dams 20 years on. *WIREs Water*, 6 (5), e1396.

Scoones, I., Leach, M., and Newell, P., 2015. The politics of green transformations. In: I. Scoones, M. Leach, and P. Newell, eds. *The Politics of Green Transformations*. London: Routledge, 1–24.

Scott, J.C., 1998. *Seeing Like a State: How Certain Schemes to Improve the Human Condition Have Failed*. London: Yale University Press.

Scudder, T., 2005. *The Future of Large Dams: Dealing with Social, Environmental, Institutional and Political Costs*. London: Routledge.

Scudder, T., 2012. Resettlement outcomes of large dams. In: C. Tortajada, D. Altinbilek, and A.K. Biswas, eds. *Impacts of Large Dams: A Global Assessment*. Berlin: Springer, 37–67.

Scudder, T., 2019. *Large Dams: Long Term Impacts on Riverine Communities and Free Flowing Rivers*. Singapore: Springer.

Selassie, H., 1958. Speech by Haile Selassie on the laying of the foundation stone for the Koka Dam hydroelectric project.

Selassie, H., 2011. *Selected Speeches of His Imperial Majesty Haile Selassie I*. Brooklyn, NY: Lion of Judah Society Publishers.

Siciliano, G. and Urban, F., 2017. China's hydropower development in Africa and Asia: Implications for resource access and development. In: G. Siciliano and F. Urban, eds. *Chinese Hydropower Development in Africa and Asia: Challenges and Opportunities for Sustainable Global Dam-Building*. London: Routledge, 1–13.

Simon, B., 2011. *A Tale of Two Elections: A National Endeavour to Put a Stop to an Avalanche* (in Amharic: *Ye-hulet Merchawoch Weg: Nadan Yegeta Hagerawi Rucha*). Addis Ababa: Mega Printing.

Sims, D., 2015. *Egypt's Desert Dreams: Development or Disaster?* Cairo: The American University in Cairo Press.

Skocpol, T., 1979. *States and Social Revolutions: A Comparative Analysis of France, Russia and China*. Cambridge: Cambridge University Press.

Slater, D., 2010. *Ordering Power: Contentious Politics and Authoritarian Leviathans in Southeast Asia*. Cambridge: Cambridge University Press.

Sneddon, C., 2015. *Concrete Revolution: Large Dams, Cold War Geopolitics, and the US Bureau of Reclamation*. Chicago, IL: University of Chicago Press.

SOGREAH, 2010. *Ethiopia Gibe III Hydropower Project: Independent Review and Studies Regarding the Environmental & Social Impact Assessments for the Gibe III Hydropower Project*. Final report. Echirolles, France: SOGREAH.

Soliman, A.H., El Zawahry, A., and Bekhit, H., 2019. GERD failure analysis and the impacts on downstream countries. In: A.M. Negm and S. Abdel-Fattah, eds. *Grand Ethiopian Renaissance Dam versus Aswan High Dam: A View from Egypt*. New York: Springer, 149–171.

Stack, L., 2013. With cameras rolling, Egyptian politicians threaten Ethiopia over dam [online]. Available from: https://archive.nytimes.com/thelede.blogs.nytimes.com/2013/06/

06/with-cameras-rolling-egyptian-politicians-threaten-ethiopia-over-dam [Accessed 7 July 2023].
Stevenson, E.G.J., 2018. Plantation development in the Turkana basin: The making of a new desert? *Land*, 7 (1), 16.
Stiglitz, J., 2003. *Globalization and Its Discontents*. New York: Penguin.
Studio Pietrangeli, 1989. *Beles 1515 Power Plant Pre-Feasibility Study*. Volume 1 Main Report. Rome: Studio Pietrangeli.
Studio Pietrangeli, 1990. *Tana Beles Project: Part 2*. Addis Ababa: Ministry of Construction, People's Democratic Republic of Ethiopia.
Studio Pietrangeli, 2023a. Description for Legadadi Dam (Ethiopia) [online]. Available from: www.pietrangeli.com/legadadi-buttress-gravity-dam-ethiopia-africa#:~:text=The%20purpose%20of%20the%20reservoir,increasing%20demand%20for%20potable%20water.&text=The%20released%20water%20passes%20through,%27000%20m3%2Fday [Accessed 22 June 2023].
Studio Pietrangeli, 2023b. Description for Gibe V multi-purpose project (Ethiopia) [online]. Available from: www.pietrangeli.com/gibe-v-rcc-gravity-dam-ethiopia-africa [Accessed 20 June 2023].
Sudan Tribune, 2022. Ethiopia, Egypt, Sudan hold secret talks on GERD dispute in UAE [online]. *Sudan Tribune*. Available from: https://sudantribune.com/article256582 [Accessed 21 April 2023].
Swain, A., 1997. Ethiopia, the Sudan, and Egypt: The Nile River dispute. *The Journal of Modern African Studies*, 35 (4), 675–694.
Swain, A., 2011. Challenges for water sharing in the Nile basin: Changing geo-politics and changing climate. *Hydrological Sciences Journal*, 56 (4), 687–702.
Swyngedouw, E., 2007. Technonatural revolutions: The scalar politics of Franco's hydro-social dream for Spain, 1939–1975. *Transactions of the Institute of British Geographers*, 32 (1), 9–28.
Swyngedouw, E., 2015. *Liquid Power: Contested Hydro-Modernities in Twentieth-Century Spain*. Cambridge, MA: MIT Press.
Tabikha, K., 2023. African Union urged to step in and settle Egypt-Ethiopia dam dispute [online]. *NMENA*. Available from: www.thenationalnews.com/mena/egypt/2023/03/09/african-union-urged-to-step-in-and-settle-egypt-ethiopia-dam-dispute [Accessed 21 April 2023].
Tadesse, F., 2019. Ethiopia to downsize GERD's installed capacity. *Addis Fortune*.
Tadesse, F., 2021. Council establishes corp. to absorb residual debts [online]. *Addis Fortune*. Available from: https://addisfortune.news/council-establishes-corp-to-absorb-residual-debts [Accessed 24 March 2021].
Tadesse, F., 2022. Ethiopia starts exporting electricity to neighboring Kenya [online]. *Bloomberg*. Available from: www.bloomberg.com/news/articles/2022-11-17/ethiopia-starts-exporting-electricity-to-neighboring-kenya?leadSource=uverify%20wall [Accessed 14 February 2023].
Tadesse, M. and Young, J., 2003. TPLF: Reform or decline? *Review of African Political Economy*, 30 (97), 389–403.
Takouleu, J.M., 2018. Burundi CMC and Orascom to build two 49.5 MW hydroelectric power plants [online]. Afrik21. Available from: www.afrik21.africa/en/burundi-cmc-and-orascom-to-build-two-49-5-mw-hydroelectric-power-plants [Accessed 8 May 2023].
Tareke, G., 1991. *Ethiopia: Power and Protest—Peasant Revolts in the Twentieth Century*. Cambridge: Cambridge University Press.
Tareke, G., 2009. *The Ethiopian Revolution: War in the Horn of Africa*. New Haven, CT: Yale University Press.
Tawfik, R., 2015. Revisiting hydro-hegemony from a benefit-sharing perspective: The case of the Grand Ethiopian Renaissance Dam. *DIE Discussion Paper*, 5.
Tawfik, R., 2016a. The Grand Ethiopian Renaissance Dam: A benefit-sharing project in the eastern Nile? *Water International*, 41 (4), 574–592.
Tawfik, R., 2016b. Reconsidering counter-hegemonic dam projects: The case of the Grand Ethiopian Renaissance Dam. *Water Policy*, wp2016162.

Tawfik, R., 2016c. Changing hydropolitical relations in the Nile basin: A protracted transition. *The International Spectator*, 51 (3), 67–81.
Tawfik, R., 2019. Beyond the river: Elite perceptions and regional cooperation in the eastern Nile basin. *Water Alternatives*, 12 (2), 655–675.
Tawfik, R., 2023. Regional mediation in African transboundary rivers conflicts: Assessing the African Union's role in the Renaissance Dam negotiations. *International Negotiation*, 1 (aop), 1–30.
Tazebaw, T., 2021. Amhara nationalism: The empire strikes back. *African Affairs*, 120 (479), 297–313.
Tekalign, Y., 2019. Regional security dilemma for Ethiopia's quest for access to the sea. *African Security Review*, 28 (3–4), 189–206.
Tekle, A., 1989. The determinants of the foreign policy of revolutionary Ethiopia. *The Journal of Modern African Studies*, 27 (3), 479–502.
Tekle, T.-A., 2012. Sudan's Bashir supports Ethiopia's Nile dam project—Sudan Tribune: Plural news and views on Sudan [online]. *Sudan Tribune*. Available from: https://sudantribune.com/spip.php?article41839 [Accessed 27 August 2020].
Teklemariam, M. and Beyene, K., 2005. Geothermal exploration and development in Ethiopia. *Proceedings of the World Geothermal Congress, Antalya, Turkey, 24–29 April 2005*. Antalya, Turkey.
Tendler, J., 1968. *Electric Power in Brazil: Entrepreneurship in the Public Sector*. Cambridge, MA: Harvard University Press.
Terrefe, B., 2020. Urban layers of political rupture: The 'new' politics of Addis Ababa's megaprojects. *Journal of Eastern African Studies*, 14 (3), 375–395.
Terrefe, B., 2022. Infrastructures of Renaissance: Tangible discourses in the EPRDF's Ethiopia. *Critical African Studies*, 14 (3), 250–273.
Teshome, K., 2018. GERD music album launched [online]. *InfoNile*. Available from: https://infonile.org/en/2018/05/11-58-billion-birr-collected-for-gerd [Accessed 7 July 2023].
TGE, 1994a. *An Economic Development Strategy for Ethiopia*. Addis Ababa: Transitional Government of Ethiopia.
TGE, 1994b. *National Energy Policy*. Addis Ababa: Transitional Government of Ethiopia.
The Indian Ocean Newsletter, 2009a. Diplomatic conflict over water. *The Indian Ocean Newsletter*, 7 February.
The Indian Ocean Newsletter, 2009b. ADB examines Kenyan request against Gibe III—Ethiopia. *The Indian Ocean Newsletter*, 27 March.
The New Arab, 2023. Egypt may withdraw from stalled UAE-based Nile Dam talks with Ethiopia over 'lack of progress' [online]. *The New Arab*. Available from: www.newarab.com/news/egypt-may-withdraw-uae-based-nile-talks-ethiopia [Accessed 8 May 2023].
The Oakland Institute, 2011. *Understanding Land Investment Deals in Africa. Country Report: Ethiopia*. Oakland, CA: The Oakland Institute.
The Reporter, 2022. Second turbine of GERD begins operation as third filling nears completion [online]. *The Reporter*. Available from: www.thereporterethiopia.com/25662 [Accessed 8 May 2023].
Thomson, M., 2005. Nile restrictions anger Ethiopia [online]. *BBC News*. Available from: http://news.bbc.co.uk/1/hi/world/africa/4232107.stm [Accessed 1 September 2020].
Tilly, C., 1992. *Coercion, Capital, and European States, AD 990–1992*. Cambridge, MA: Blackwell Publishers.
Tischler, J., 2013. *Light and Power for a Multiracial Nation: The Kariba Dam Scheme in the Central African Federation*. New York: Springer.
TPLF, 1983. *People's Democratic Programme of the Tigray People's Liberation Front (TPLF)*. TPLF.
Tronvoll, K., 2009. Ambiguous elections: The influence of non-electoral politics in Ethiopian democratisation. *The Journal of Modern African Studies*, 47 (3), 449–474.
Tronvoll, K., 2011. The Ethiopian 2010 federal and regional elections: Re-establishing the one-party state. *African Affairs*, 110 (438), 121–136.

Tsafos, N. and Carey, L., 2020. *Success Story #3: Attracting Foreign Capital in the Power Sector.* Washington, DC: Center for Strategic and International Studies (CSIS).

Tsikata, D.A., 2006. *Living in the Shadow of Ghana's Dams: Long Term Responses of Downstream and Lakeside Akosombo and Kpong Communities.* Leiden: Brill.

Tunnelbuilder, 2008. The Gilgel Gibe hydropower project in Ethiopia [online]. Available from: https://tunnelbuilder.com/News/The-Gilgel-Gibe-Hydropower-Project-in-Ethiopia.aspx [Accessed 20 June 2023].

Turton, D., 2011. Wilderness, wasteland or home? Three ways of imagining the Lower Omo Valley. *Journal of Eastern African Studies*, 5 (1), 158–176.

Turton, D., 2021. 'Breaking every rule in the book': The story of river basin development in Ethiopia's Omo Valley. In: E.C. Gabbert, F. Gebresenbet, J.G. Galaty, and G. Schlee, eds. *Lands of the Future: Anthropological Perspectives on Pastoralism, Land Deals and Tropes of Modernity in Eastern Africa.* New York: Berghahn Books, 231–248.

Tyce, M., 2021. *Energy Transitions, Green Transformations and the Insights of Different Research Traditions: Can Political Settlements Analysis Provide an Integrative Framework?* Manchester: Mimeo.

UNDP, 2018. *Understanding African Experiences in Formulating and Implementing Plans for Emergence: Growing Manufacturing Industry in Ethiopia.* Addis Ababa: United Nations Development Programme (UNDP).

United Arab Republic and Sudan, 1959. *Agreement between the Republic of the Sudan and the United Arab Republic for the Full Utilization of the Nile Waters.* Signed at Cairo on 8 November 1959.

Unruh, G.C., 2000. Understanding carbon lock-in. *Energy Policy*, 28 (12), 817–830.

Unruh, G.C., 2002. Escaping carbon lock-in. *Energy Policy*, 30 (4), 317–325.

USAID, 2019. *Grid Management Support Program: System Integration Study, (GMSP-SIS) Power Africa.* Washington, DC: USAID.

USAID and PowerAfrica, 2018. *Grid Management Support Program Systems Integration Study, (GMSP-SIS) Draft.* Addis Ababa: USAID/PowerAfrica.

USBR, 1964. *Land and Water Resources of the Blue Nile Basin: Ethiopia. Volume I.* Washington, DC: United States Department of the Interior, Bureau of Reclamation.

US Securities and Exchange Commission, 2016. SEC: Ethiopia's electric utility sold unregistered bonds in U.S. [online]. Available from: www.sec.gov/news/press-release/2016-113 [Accessed 7 July 2023].

van der Zwaan, B., Boccalon, A., and Dalla Longa, F., 2018. Prospects for hydropower in Ethiopia: An energy–water nexus analysis. *Energy Strategy Reviews*, 19, 19–30.

Vaughan, S., 2003. Ethnicity and Power in Ethiopia. PhD thesis. University of Edinburgh, Edinburgh.

Vaughan, S., 2011. Revolutionary democratic state-building: Party, state and people in the EPRDF's Ethiopia. *Journal of Eastern African Studies*, 5 (4), 619–640.

Vaughan, S. and Gebremichael, M., 2011. Rethinking business and politics in Ethiopia: The role of EFFORT, the Endowment Fund for the Rehabilitation of Tigray. *Africa Power and Politics Research Report*, 2.

Vaughan, S. and Gebremichael, M., 2020. Resettlement of Gumuz communities around Ethiopia's Blue Nile dam. *FutureDAMS Working Paper*, 10.

Vaughan, S. and Tronvoll, K., 2003. *The Culture of Power in Contemporary Ethiopian Political Life.* Stockholm: Swedish International Development Cooperation Agency.

Verbong, G. and Geels, F., 2007. The ongoing energy transition: Lessons from a socio-technical, multi-level analysis of the Dutch electricity system (1960–2004). *Energy Policy*, 35 (2), 1025–1037.

Verhoeven, H., 2013. The politics of African energy development: Ethiopia's hydro-agricultural state-building strategy and clashing paradigms of water security. *Philosophical Transactions of the Royal Society A: Mathematical, Physical and Engineering Sciences*, 371 (2002), 20120411.

Verhoeven, H., 2015. *Water, Civilisation and Power in Sudan: The Political Economy of Military-Islamist State Building.* Cambridge: Cambridge University Press.

Verhoeven, H., 2018. The Gulf and the Horn: Changing geographies of security interdependence and competing visions of regional order. *Civil Wars*, 20 (3), 333–357.

Verhoeven, H., 2021. The Grand Ethiopian Renaissance Dam: Africa's water tower, environmental justice and infrastructural power. *Daedalus*, 150 (4), 159–180.

Verhoeven, H. and Sennesael, F., 2022. *Energy and Water for Sovereignty: South Sudan's Regional Diplomacy and the Geopolitics of the Nile Basin*. New York: Columbia Center on Global Energy Policy.

Verhoeven, H. and Woldemariam, M., 2022. Who lost Ethiopia? The unmaking of an African anchor state and U.S. foreign policy. *Contemporary Security Policy*, 43 (4), 622–650.

Victor, D.G. and Heller, T.C., eds., 2007. *The Political Economy of Power Sector Reform: The Experiences of Five Major Developing Countries*. Cambridge: Cambridge University Press.

Vu, T., 2010. *Paths to Development in Asia: South Korea, Vietnam, China, and Indonesia*. Cambridge: Cambridge University Press.

Wade, R., 1990. *Governing the Market: Economic Theory and the Role of Government in East Asian Industrialization*. Princeton, NJ: Princeton University Press.

Wade, R.H., 2001. Capital and revenge: The IMF and Ethiopia. *Challenge*, 44 (5), 67–75.

Waldner, D., 1999. *State Building and Late Development*. Ithaca, NY: Cornell University Press.

Walsh, D. and Marks, S., 2020. Ethiopia escalates fight against its powerful Tigray region [online]. *New York Times*. Available from: www.nytimes.com/2020/11/05/world/africa/ethiopia-war-tigray.html [Accessed 2 May 2023].

WAPCOS, 1990. *Preliminary Water Resource Development Master Plan for Ethiopia. Vol. II Main Report*. Addis Ababa: Water and Power Consultancy Services (WAPCOS).

Warner, J. and Zawahri, N., 2012. Hegemony and asymmetry: Multiple-chessboard games on transboundary rivers. *International Environmental Agreements*, 12, 215–229.

Waterbury, J., 1979. *Hydropolitics of the Nile Valley*. Syracuse, NY: Syracuse University Press.

Waterbury, J., 1983. *The Egypt of Nasser and Sadat: The Political Economy of Two Regimes*. Princeton, NJ: Princeton University Press.

Waterbury, J., 2002. *The Nile Basin: National Determinants of Collective Action*. New Haven, CT: Yale University Press.

Waterbury, J. and Whittington, D., 1998. Playing chicken on the Nile? The implications of microdam development in the Ethiopian highlands and Egypt's New Valley Project. *Natural Resources Forum*, 22 (3), 155–163.

WeBuild, 2023. Using media channels to create an open, transparent dialogue [online]. Available from: www.webuildgroup.com/en/media [Accessed 20 June 2023].

Weis, T., 2015. Vanguard Capitalism: Party, State, and Market in the EPRDF's Ethiopia. PhD thesis. University of Oxford, Oxford.

Wester, P., Mollard, E., Silva-Ochoa, P., and Vargas-Velázquez, S., 2009. From half-full to half-empty: The hydraulic mission and water overexploitation in the Lerma-Chapala Basin, Mexico. *River Basin Trajectories: Societies, Environments and Development*, 8, 75.

Wheeler, K.G., Jeuland, M., Hall, J.W., Zagona, E., and Whittington, D., 2020. Understanding and managing new risks on the Nile with the Grand Ethiopian Renaissance Dam. *Nature Communications*, 11 (1), 5222.

Wheeler, K.G., Hall, J.W., Abdo, G.M., Dadson, S.J., Kasprzyk, J.R., Smith, R., and Zagona, E.A., 2018. Exploring cooperative transboundary river management strategies for the eastern Nile basin. *Water Resources Research*, 54 (11), 9224–9254.

Wheeler, K.G., Basheer, M., Mekonnen, Z.T., Eltoum, S.O., Mersha, A., Abdo, G.M., Zagona, E.A., Hall, J.W., and Dadson, S.J., 2016. Cooperative filling approaches for the Grand Ethiopian Renaissance Dam. *Water International*, 41 (4), 611–634.

Wheeler, K.G., Jeuland, M., Strzepek, K., Hall, J., Zagona, E.A., Abdo, G., Basson, T., Blackmore, D., Block, P., and Whittington, D., 2022. Comment on 'Egypt's water budget deficit and suggested mitigation policies for the Grand Ethiopian Renaissance Dam filling scenarios'. *Environmental Research Letters*, 17 (8): 088003.

Whitfield, L., ed., 2009. *The Politics of Aid: African Strategies for Dealing with Donors*. Oxford: Oxford University Press.

Whitfield, L. and Maile, F., 2021. Ethiopia's apparel export industry, the Tigray conflict, and US preferential market access [online]. *CBDS*. Available from: www.cbds.center/post/ethiopia-s-apparel-export-industry-the-tigray-conflict-and-us-preferential-market-access [Accessed 15 March 2022].
Whitfield, L. and Staritz, C., 2021. The learning trap in late industrialisation: Local firms and capability building in Ethiopia's apparel export industry. *The Journal of Development Studies*, 57 (6), 980–1000.
Whitfield, L., Therkildsen, O., Buur, L., and Kjær, A.M., 2015. *The Politics of African Industrial Policy: A Comparative Perspective*. Cambridge: Cambridge University Press.
Whittington, D., 2016. Why technical discussions are needed for the Grand Ethiopian Renaissance Dam [online]. *The Conversation*. Available from: https://theconversation.com/why-technical-discussions-are-needed-for-the-grand-ethiopian-renaissance-dam-60004 [Accessed 3 December 2021].
Whittington, D., Waterbury, J., and Jeuland, M., 2014. The Grand Renaissance Dam and prospects for cooperation on the eastern Nile. *Water Policy*, 16 (4), 595–608.
Williamson, J., 1990. What Washington means by policy reform. In: J. Williamson, ed. *Latin American Adjustment: How Much Has Happened?* Washington, DC: Institute for International Economics, 7–20.
Wittfogel, K.A., 1957. Oriental Despotism: A Comparative Study of Total Power. New Haven, CT: Yale University Press.
Woldegebrael, E.H., 2018. The materialization of 'developmental state' in Ethiopia: Insights from the Gibe III hydroelectric development project regime, Omo Valley. *L'Espace Politique. Revue en ligne de géographie politique et de géopolitique*, 35 (2018-2).
Woldegebrael, E.H., 2019. The Politics and Materiality of a Developmental State in the EPRDF's Ethiopia: A View from the Gibe III Hydropower Development Project. PhD thesis. l'Université Paris Nanterre, Paris.
Woldemariam, M., 2018. *Insurgent Fragmentation in the Horn of Africa: Rebellion and Its Discontents*. Cambridge: Cambridge University Press.
Wolde-Selassie, A., 2009. Social impact of resettlement in Beles Valley. In: A. Pankhurst and F. Piguet, eds. *Moving People in Ethiopia: Development, Displacement and the State*. Oxford: James Currey, 130–138.
Wondimu, S., 2023. The Politics of Urban Industrialization: Integrating the Urban–Industrial Nexus in Ethiopia's Disintegrating Ethno-Federal Party-State. PhD thesis. University of Sheffield, Sheffield.
Workneh, Y.A., 2021. The terms of debate on the existence of Amhara ethnicity with a focus on the emerging Amhara ethno-nationalism. *African Identities* 21(4): 786–804.
World Bank, 1976. *Project Performance Audit Report on Ethiopia: FInchaa Hydroelectric Project*. Washington, DC: World Bank.
World Bank, 1993. *The World Bank's Role in the Electric Power Sector: Policies for Effective Institutional, Regulatory, and Financial Reform*. Washington, DC: World Bank.
World Bank, 1996. *Ethiopia Energy Assessment*. Washington, DC: World Bank.
World Bank, 1997. *Project Appraisal Document: Federal Democratic Republic of Ethiopia Energy II Project*. Washington, DC: World Bank.
World Bank, 2005a. *Project Information Document: Ethiopia Electricity Access Expansion*. Washington, DC: World Bank.
World Bank, 2005b. *Project Appraisal Document on a Proposed Global Environmental Facility Trust Fund Grant in the Amount of US4.93 Million to the Federal Democratic Republic of Ethiopia for an Energy Access Project*. Washington, DC: World Bank.
World Bank, 2006a. *Ethiopia: Managing Water Resources to Maximize Sustainable Growth*. Washington, DC: World Bank.
World Bank, 2006b. *Implementation Completion Report (IDA-30190 PPFI-P9880) on a Credit in the Amount of US$200 Million to the Federal Democratic Republic of Ethiopia for an Energy II Project*. Washington, DC: World Bank.

World Bank, 2006c. *Project Appraisal Document on a Proposed Credit in the Amount of SDR 92.8 Million (US$133.4 Million Equivalent) to the Federal Democratic Republic of Ethiopia for an Electricity Access (Rural) Expansion Project*. Washington, DC: World Bank.

World Bank, 2007a. *Project Appraisal Document on a Proposed Credit in the Amount of SDR 86.0 Million (US$130 Million Equivalent) to the Federal Democratic Republic of Ethiopia for a Second Electricity Access Rural Expansion Project*. Washington, DC: World Bank.

World Bank, 2007b. *Project Appraisal Document on a Proposed Credit in the Amount of SDR 26.44 Million (US$41.05 Million Equivalent) to the Federal Democratic Republic of Ethiopia for an Ethiopia/Nile Basin Initiative Power Export Project: Ethiopia-Sudan Interconnector*. Washington, DC: World Bank.

World Bank, 2009a. Directions in hydropower: Scaling up for development. *Water Working Notes*, 21.

World Bank, 2009b. *Project Information Document (PID), Concept Stage: Eastern Nile First Joint Multipurpose Program Identification (JMP1 ID)*. Washington, DC: World Bank.

World Bank, 2012a. *Inclusive Green Growth: The Pathway to Sustainable Development*. Washington, DC: World Bank.

World Bank, 2012b. *Project Appraisal Document on Proposed Credits in the Amount of SDR 156.8 Million (US$243 Million Equivalent) to the Federal Democratic Republic of Ethiopia and in the Amount of SDR 284.5 Million (US$441 Million Equivalent) to the Republic of Kenya for the Eastern Electricity Highway Project (APL 1)*. Washington, DC: World Bank.

World Bank, 2013. *Implementation Completion and Results Report (IDA-4200) on a Credit in the Amount of SDR 92.80 Million (US$ 133.4 Million Equivalent) to the Federal Democratic Republic of Ethiopia for an Electricity Access (Rural) Expansion Project*. Washington, DC: World Bank.

World Bank, 2014. *Building Integrated Markets within the East African Community: EAC Opportunities in Public–Private Partnership Approaches to the Region's Infrastructure Needs*. Washington, DC: World Bank.

World Bank, 2015. *Ethiopia Poverty Assessment 2014*. Washington, DC: World Bank.

World Bank, 2017. *Moving Further on Civil Service Reforms in Ethiopia: Findings and Implications from a Civil Service Survey and Qualitative Analysis, Synthesis Report*. Addis Ababa: World Bank.

World Bank, 2018a. *Program Appraisal Document on a Proposed Regular Credit in the Amount of SDR 176.9 Million (US$250 Million Equivalent) and a Proposed Scale-Up Facility Credit in the Amount of US$125 million to the Federal Democratic Republic of Ethiopia for the Ethiopia Electrification Program*. Washington, DC: World Bank.

World Bank, 2018b. *Program Document on a Proposed Credit to the Federal Democratic Republic of Ethiopia for the Ethiopia Growth and Competitiveness Programmatic Development Policy Financing*. Washington, DC: World Bank.

World Bank, 2019a. Ethiopia's energy sector transformation. *ESMAP Impact*, 18. https://documents1.worldbank.org/curated/en/249971573762529445/pdf/Ethiopias-Energy-Sector-Transformation.pdf.

World Bank, 2019b. *Project Appraisal Document on a Proposed Credit to the Federal Democratic Republic of Ethiopia for the Renewable Energy Guarantees Program: Phase I*. Washington, DC: World Bank.

World Bank, 2020. *Restructuring Paper on a Proposed Project Restructuring of the Eastern Electricity Highway Project under the First Phase of the Eastern Africa Power Integration Program*. Washington, DC: World Bank.

World Commission on Dams, 2000. *Dams and Development: A New Framework for Decision-Making*. London: Earthscan.

World Economic Forum, 2012. Meles Zenawi: Accelerating infrastructure investments—Africa 2012 [online]. YouTube. Available from: www.youtube.com/watch?v=_mkHjtpGPaY [Accessed 11 June 2021].

Worster, D., 1985. *Rivers of Empire: Water, Aridity and the Growth of the American West*. New York: Pantheon Books.

Wubneh, M., 2015. This land is my land: The Ethio-Sudan boundary and the need to rectify arbitrary colonial boundaries. *Journal of Contemporary African Studies*, 33 (4), 441–466.

Yewondwossen, M., 2022. Aysha Wind Farm to enter the national grid [online]. *Capital Newspaper*. Available from: www.capitalethiopia.com/2022/02/28/aysha-wind-farm-to-enter-the-national-grid [Accessed 13 March 2023].

Yihdego, Z., Rieu-Clarke, A., and Cascão, A.E., 2017. *The Grand Ethiopian Renaissance Dam and the Nile Basin: Implications for Transboundary Water Cooperation*. London: Routledge.

Young, J., 1997. *Peasant Revolution in Ethiopia: The Tigray People's Liberation Front, 1975–1991*. Cambridge: Cambridge University Press.

Young, J., 1999. Along Ethiopia's western frontier: Gambella and Benishangul in transition. *The Journal of Modern African Studies*, 37 (02), 321–346.

Young, K.E. and Khan, T., 2022. Extended states: The politics and purpose of United Arab Emirates economic statecraft in the Horn of Africa. In: R. Mason and S. Mabon, eds. *The Gulf States and the Horn of Africa: Interests, Influence and Instability*. Manchester: Manchester University Press, 99–126.

YouTube, 2011. PM Meles Zenawi on the Ethiopian Renaissance Dam [online]. Available from: www.youtube.com/watch?v=e-Wz6y6jLXY&list=PLMtUFV4uLAyTI37nKmZugb2qYLVxfc0w_&index=137.

YouTube, 2013. Meles explaining what the Egyptians could do? [Renaissance Dam] [online]. Available from: www.youtube.com/watch?v=ILWYNjR4-TQ [Accessed 10 July 2023].

YouTube, 2017. In Amhara region 197 Projects are out of Operations due to shortage of electric power [online]. Available from: www.youtube.com/watch?v=NL9idn_VIQ8 [Accessed 11 July 2023].

YouTube, 2018. Andafta exclusive interview with Bereket Simon [online]. Available from: www.youtube.com/watch?v=sTFam8zZ_DA [Accessed 10 November 2021].

YouTube, 2019. PM Abiy Ahmed speech at the Peace Conference in Millennium Hall Ethiopia [online]. Available from: www.youtube.com/watch?v=qhgAJkYEpDE [Accessed 24 March 2021].

YouTube, 2022. 'God gave Ethiopia a special gift ... water!': Pietro Salini, CEO & founder of WeBuild [online]. Available from: www.youtube.com/watch?v=pYnt_TwntoU [Accessed 20 June 2023].

Zarfl, C., Lumsdon, A.E., Berlekamp, J., Tydecks, L., and Tockner, K., 2015. A global boom in hydropower dam construction. *Aquatic Sciences*, 77 (1), 161–170.

Zeitoun, M. and Warner, J., 2006. Hydro-hegemony: A framework for analysis of trans-boundary water conflicts. *Water Policy*, 8 (5), 435–460.

Zeleke, E.C., 2019. *Ethiopia in Theory: Revolution and Knowledge Production, 1964–2016*. Leiden: Brill.

Zenawi, M., 2006a. Speech by HE Meles Zenawi, prime minister of the Federal Democratic Republic of Ethiopia for the Africa Task Force, Brooks World Poverty Institute, Manchester University, UK, 3–4 August [online]. Available from: www.ethioembassy.org.uk/Archive/Prime%20Minister%20Meles%20Africa%20Task%20Force%20speech.htm [Accessed 24 July 2011].

Zenawi, M., 2006b. *African Development: Dead Ends and New Beginnings*. Mimeo.

Zenawi, M., 2009. Statement by HE Meles Zenaoui, prime minister of the Federal Democratic Republic of Ethiopia on behalf of the African Group, Copenhagen, Denmark, 16 December. Presented at the United Nations Climate Change Conference, Copenhagen.

Zenawi, M., 2011a. What does the green economy have to do with us (Africans)? [online]. UNEP. Available from: www.unep.org/environmentalgovernance/PerspectivesonRIO20/HEMrMelesZenawi/tabid/55724/Default.aspx [Accessed 17 April 2015].

Zenawi, M., 2011b. The speech delivered by H.E. Prime Minister Meles Zenawi to mark the official commencement of the Millennium Dam project [online]. *Horn Affairs*. Available from: https://hornaffairs.com/2011/04/02/ethiopia-great-dam-on-nile-launched [Accessed 25 August 2020].

Zenawi, M., 2012. States and markets: Neo-liberal limitations and the case for a developmental state. In: A. Noman, K. Botchwey, H. Stein, and J.E. Stiglitz, eds. *Good Growth and Governance in Africa: Rethinking Development Strategies.* Oxford: Oxford University Press, 140–174.

Zewde, B., 1991. *A History of Modern Ethiopia, 1855–1974.* London: James Currey.

Zewde, B., 2008a. Environment and capital: Notes for a history of the Wonji-Shoa sugar estate (1951–1974). In: B. Zewde, ed. *Society, State and History: Selected Essays.* Addis Ababa: Addis Ababa University Press, 120–146.

Zewde, B., 2008b. An overview and assessment of Gambella trade (1904–1935). In: B. Zewde, ed. *Society, State and History: Selected Essays.* Addis Ababa: Addis Ababa University Press, 147–166.

Zhang, C. and Heller, T.C., 2007. Reform of the Chinese electric power market: Economics and institutions. In: D.G. Victor and T.C. Heller, eds. *The Political Economy of Power Sector Reform: The Experiences of Five Major Developing Countries.* Cambridge: Cambridge University Press, 76–108.

Zhang, Y.-F., Parker, D., and Kirkpatrick, C., 2008. Electricity sector reform in developing countries: An econometric assessment of the effects of privatization, competition and regulation. *Journal of Regulatory Economics,* 33 (2), 159–178.

Index

For the benefit of digital users, indexed terms that span two pages (e.g., 52–53) may, on occasion, appear on only one of those pages.

Tables and figures are indicated by an italic *t* or *f* following the paragraph number.